Federal Government Reorganization

A Policy *and* Management Perspective

Edited by

Beryl A. Radin, PhD
American University

Joshua M. Chanin, JD, MPA
American University

JONES AND BARTLETT PUBLISHERS
Sudbury, Massachusetts
BOSTON TORONTO LONDON SINGAPORE

World Headquarters
Jones and Bartlett Publishers
40 Tall Pine Drive
Sudbury, MA 01776
978-443-5000
info@jbpub.com
www.jbpub.com

Jones and Bartlett Publishers Canada
6339 Ormindale Way
Mississauga, Ontario L5V 1J2
Canada

Jones and Bartlett Publishers International
Barb House, Barb Mews
London W6 7PA
United Kingdom

Jones and Bartlett's books and products are available through most bookstores and online booksellers. To contact Jones and Bartlett Publishers directly, call 800-832-0034, fax 978-443-8000, or visit our website www.jbpub.com.

Substantial discounts on bulk quantities of Jones and Bartlett's publications are available to corporations, professional associations, and other qualified organizations. For details and specific discount information, contact the special sales department at Jones and Bartlett via the above contact information or send an email to specialsales@jbpub.com.

Production Credits
Acquisitions Editor: Jeremy Spiegel
Editorial Assistant: Maro Asadoorian
Production Director: Amy Rose
Production Assistant: Julia Waugaman
Associate Marketing Manager: Lisa Gordon
Manufacturing and Inventory Control Supervisor: Amy Bacus
Cover Design: Brian Moore
Cover Image: © AbleStock
Composition: SNP Best-set Typesetter, Ltd.
Printing and Binding: Malloy Incorporated
Cover Printing: Malloy Incorporated

Library of Congress Cataloging-in-Publication Data
Radin, Beryl.
Federal government reorganization : a policy and management perspective / by Beryl A. Radin and Joshua M. Chanin.—1st ed.
p. cm.
Includes bibliographical references and index.
ISBN-13: 978-0-7637-5560-7
ISBN-10: 0-7637-5560-5
1. Federal government–United States. 2. Administrative agencies–United States. 3. United States–Politics and government–2001- I. Chanin, Joshua M. II. Title.
JK421.R33 2008
352.3′670973–dc22

2008035264

6048

Printed in the United States of America
12 11 10 09 08 10 9 8 7 6 5 4 3 2 1

CONTENTS

ACKNOWLEDGMENTS

This project started with our preparation for a graduate class entitled "Reorganization Policy and Management Perspectives," which took place in the Department of Public Administration and Policy at American University. The discussion that took place during the class helped us to clarify our views on this topic. We dedicate the book to the class members.

ABOUT THE EDITORS

Beryl A. Radin is a Scholar in Residence in the School of Public Affairs at American University. An elected member of the National Academy of Public Administration, she has written a number of books and articles on public management issues (including works on reorganization, performance management, and policy analysis). She was the Managing Editor of the *Journal of Public Administration Research and Theory* and served as a staff member in several federal government agencies.

Joshua M. Chanin is a PhD candidate in Public Administration and Justice, Law, and Society in the School of Public Affairs at American University in Washington, DC. His research interests include the application of constitutional law in public administration and policy, the implementation of public law, and bureaucratic behavior. He holds a JD-MPA from Indiana University–Bloomington.

CHAPTER 1

Introduction

Most 20th century presidents have made government reorganization a part of their search for executive control. Some have highlighted these issues more than others. Each chief executive seems to come into office with political energy, but after the campaign concludes, the president begins to focus on the process of governance. Presidents, like other chief executives, are attracted to reorganization for a range of reasons, and it seems that at particular periods in history, reorganization and tinkering with the structure of organizations become ends in themselves. During these periods, the advocates of organizational change have little difficulty convincing others that the link between the change in structure and other effects is obvious and easy to defend. At other times, however, the reorganization attempts seem merely to be shifting of boxes, and those observing or affected by the changes are cynical about their outcomes. These proposed changes can be defended for a range of reasons; some are recommendations that flow from management principles, whereas others are tied to specific policy outcomes that are desired.

Some of the most sophisticated treatments of reorganization issues are found in sources that are familiar for other reasons. Several political scientists have turned to the Bible—specifically the Book of Exodus—as a political document that deals with classic problems of leadership and revolution.[1] Those who have a fascination with organization structure can also return to this source to be reminded of the inevitability of the unresolved debate about the "proper" form of organizing relationships between diverse groups. The words are not found in the original text, but it is difficult to avoid using terms such as specialization, stratification, centralization, decentralization, autonomy, and control to describe the organizational response by Moses to the first years of the Exodus and then, after finding the Golden Calf after his 40 days on the mountaintop, asserting new forms of control on the people of Israel.

It is not surprising then that the quest of organizational structure is both universal and ubiquitous. As many have searched for the perfectibility of human conditions in other areas, so too has the field of public administration searched for the perfect organizational structure. The scientific management movement—the attempt to find the "one best way to manage"—can be viewed as the expression of the search for organizational truth and tranquility—the Promised Land of public administrators. Other types of proposals also show the tendency of some administrative reformers to proceed as if one single solution was appropriate to very diverse problems.

When one looks at the definition of administrative reorganization in *The Public Administration Dictionary*, it appears that the public administration field has equated reorganization with great efficiency. According to the dictionary, "By-products of administrative reorganization include greater economy, increased productivity, and clearer lines of authority and responsibility. Typically, reorganization plans are aimed at (1) eliminating waste and duplication of services by integrating agencies that carry on the same or similar functions; (2) reducing the number of agencies reporting to a chief administrator by consolidating many diverse units into fewer larger units; (3) providing staff and auxiliary services to help the chief administrator with authority and responsibility so that decisions can be made more effectively and accountability can be assigned for each such action; (4) eliminating elective positions and multiheaded boards that engage in routine administrative functions but are not extensively involved in policy making; (5) encouraging long- and short-range planning services to help decision makers; and (6) providing for continuing review of personnel, management, and budget procedures."[2] Furthermore, again according to the dictionary, reorganizations "have resulted in strengthening the role of chief executives and chief administrators, including presidents, governors, mayors, and city and county managers."[3]

From the middle l970s to the early 1980s, organizational structure was a frequent topic in many elements of the U.S. public administration community. During those years, it would have been quite unusual to attend a meeting of administrators, pick up an academic or practitioner journal in the field, or meet with representatives of interest groups without discussing the pros and cons of changing the way that programs were organized and administered. Since the 1980s, however, there has been less interest in reorganization issues. It is not clear why this has occurred. It may be because the issues that are on the agenda are so complex that structural approaches do not appear to be appropriate. Instead, there has been a focus on functions and other management approaches (such as collaboration, coordination, and networks), as well as attention to the substantive policy impacts of management decisions.

Despite its classic presence in the public management field, there is currently no textbook available that deals with the importance of organization and reorganization in the contemporary structure of the American government. The lack of attention to this subject is particularly problematic given the focus on the creation of the Department of Homeland Security (DHS) following the 9/11 disaster. Those who were charged with the creation of DHS had little information to use that might be drawn from experience involving the creation of other federal cabinet departments.

This book seeks to fill that vacuum by creating a reader that focuses in two ways on the literature that is available. First, it deals with the decision to change structural arrangements within the bureaucracy and explores the multitude of reasons why reorganization and changing the structure of government continue to be considered. This will be done by including a range of conceptual readings that allows a reader to understand the multiple and often conflicting goals involved in changing organizational structure. Second, it explores the consequences of reorganization activity by focusing on the results of a number of reorganizations at the federal level. These include examples involving the DHS, the Department of Defense (DoD), and the Department of Education (ED) and efforts to create a Department of Food Safety. These examples illustrate the different lenses that can be used to approach reorganization issues, particularly the differences between management and policy approaches.

WHY DO WE FOCUS ON REORGANIZATION?

The arguments for employing a reorganization strategy come from a diverse set of sources. Some emerge from the management literature in which proponents believe that there are general rules that should be applied across the board to address shared problems found in most (if not all) organizations. (As is illustrated by the Public Administration Dictionary, these rules often link reorganization to increased efficiency.) Others emerge from specific programs, policies, and problems that must be addressed and often seek to improve effectiveness as well as equity along with increased efficiency. Although these arguments can be discussed as separate explanations, in reality, many of these reasons are interrelated. Indeed, it is probably the convergence of these different reasons that explains the power and perceived saliency of the reorganization movement at particular points in time.

- Surrogate for policy change
- Public demand for change
- Imprinting of new actors
- Subordinating to private sector values
- Diffused innovation
- Improving policy technology
- Drive for stability and conflict avoidance

REORGANIZATION AS A SURROGATE FOR POLICY CHANGE

Reorganization often takes place during middle stages of the policy implementation process—that is, at a time when the first blush of implementation is completed and it becomes obvious that the expectations and goals associated with the policy adoption are not easily achieved. There are several options available to the major actors involved at this point in the policy process. They can identify the aspects of the policy that are causing the implementation problems and propose that these substantive problems with the policy be modified through formal decision processes. They can, as an alternative strategy, simply decide to live with the limitations of the implementation and scale back their expectations of what can be done about the policy intervention.

Reorganization efforts, however, offer themselves as a third alternative path. The major policy actors may decide that they do not want to take either of the other two approaches. They do not want to accept the limitations of the implementation passively, but at the same time, they recognize that they may not have political support to change the substance of the policy formally or, alternatively, they do not have a clear enough idea of what that substantive change should be to offer specific suggestions for change. Modifying the organization structure offers another way out. It provides a way of making change and taking formal action, but it does so under the guise of a procedural and organizational change rather than a substantive policy intervention. Although many of these changes have moved toward centralization, they tend to move in a cyclical direction. If the policy under consideration has emphasized decentralization in the past, then the proposal for change will likely move toward centralization. Conversely, if the past policy has been centralized, then it is quite likely that the reorganization will move toward fragmentation and diffusion. As surrogates for policy change, these efforts often are the organizational precursors of the ways that the substance of future policies will be conceptualized and organized.

REORGANIZATION AS A RESPONSE TO PUBLIC DEMANDS FOR CHANGE

Many reorganization efforts are a response to public expectations that something within the policy sector will be changed. Reorganization efforts that attempt to meet a public demand for action require policy actors to make a move that will be visible and will give those concerned about the issue a sense that action is being taken to address the problem at hand. When reorganization is used as the vehicle to satisfy these demands, the action taken to create or reform an organizational unit is highly symbolic and often appears to be a magical incantation or prayer offered by the responsible parties. Frequently, this motivation is used in response to a crisis situation, and changing the structure of the organizational unit responsible for meeting the crisis is a way of buying time. Within that time, policy actors may find a way of addressing the issue in substantive rather than procedural terms or—as is often more likely—use the delay as a way of dissipating interest about the policy question as new problems push away that initial concern. The type of reorganization that is undertaken to deal with demands for change can move in both centralized and decentralized directions. If the policy actors want to indicate that those at the top are taking responsibility for the problem, they might move the formal responsibility for the issue to the top of the organization. Often, however, the best way of indicating attention to an issue is to create a specialized organizational unit to deal with it; this may have the effect of moving the organization toward fragmentation.

REORGANIZATION THAT IMPRINTS THE AGENDA OF NEW ACTORS

Most of the reorganizations that have taken place at all levels of government are coincident in time with the advent of new political leadership. These actors know what many public administrators forget: reorganizations and shifts in organizational structures are political choices, not a mechanistic shifting of boxes. At the same time, the decision process around changes in structure is often less politically open and volatile than other forms of decision making. When a new political leader wants to exert authority and put his or her imprint on public functions, reorganization is an appealing form of change.

The reorganizations that have taken place to satisfy this set of concerns tend to move toward centralization of functions. The new leaders come in at the top of organizations and want to indicate to the outside world that they have control over their "kingdoms." At the same time, a centralizing organizational change has the effect of forcing the individuals within the organization to look upward and respond to the values and demands of the new leadership. In some cases, however, new actors have come into power and have used fragmentation as a way to "end run" existing operations. This has tended to occur in situations where centralization patterns were already in place.

REORGANIZATION BASED ON PRIVATE SECTOR VALUES

Arguments that emphasize increased efficiency (e.g., assertions of reduced costs and more expeditious action) are the most common positions taken to justify administrative reorganization. More frequently, these arguments are based on the need for reorganization because of overlap and duplication of functions, which result in complex and slow decisions procedures that, in turn, produce costly and inadequate services. Indeed, when individuals from the private sector are brought into public agencies, they are often appalled by the chaos that they see around them. Many of them do not understand that this "chaos" is the result of political bargains and decisions.

Although few advocates of services want to allege that their positions are intrinsically inefficient, the value of efficiency in the public sector has never been an easy attribute to define. The conflict between efficiency, effectiveness, and equity is well known. Despite attempts to rationalize the basis for tradeoffs between these values, the balance between them appears to be a temporal and idiosyncratic calculation for specific decision settings.

There are times when policy actors (both elected and appointed) place a stronger value on efficiency than on either effectiveness or equity, however. This seems to occur at periods in history when the private sector is viewed as the model for public sector activity and public officials want to become more like private sector corporate managers. During these periods, reorganization becomes a vehicle for diminishing the difference between the public and private arenas. Until recently, the private sector model was an automatic consolidation and centralization prescription. It was often accompanied by an increase in generalist staff functions and an emphasis on processes such as budgeting and financial improvement, data processing, and management analysis. With the interest in another approach (detailed in the volume *In Search of Excellence*),[4] an alternative private sector model was advanced that emphasized decentralization and the delegation of authority and responsibility to subunits within a larger organization.

Many reorganization efforts have emphasized the traditional efficiency-private sector model. Most of them have taken place in a political climate that devalues the equity and effectiveness goals and, instead, perceives that programs are expensive, inefficiently operated, and less than effective in addressing the problems of their client populations. Arguments for umbrella agencies–megadepartments–have often been coached in the language of efficiency. Although there is dispute about the real impact of such agencies in terms of cost and time savings, these arguments appear to be salient to political actors, who diminish the importance of equity and effectiveness goals.

REORGANIZATION AS A FORM OF DIFFUSED INNOVATION

A number of writers have described the interest in reorganization efforts as a form of innovation that diffuses among governmental units. The diffusion can take place in several forms of intergovernmental contact; that is, it appears to indicate that state activity is influenced by and influences federal activity and that states are dramatically impacted by what other states are doing. The research that has been conducted on this subject has indicated that this form of emulation is a common factor in stimulating organizational changes.[5]

Our knowledge of both the formal and informal contacts between governments indicates that it is not difficult to show how information about a new practice is transmitted across state boundary lines. Individuals who are engaged in similar kinds of activities find themselves attending the same meetings, reading the same journals, and attempting to solve similar problems. In our technologically sophisticated world, an effort that receives positive media coverage in one setting is likely to be viewed as worthy of emulation in another.

One could, of course, view the concept of diffused innovation as simply a fancy term for describing "trendiness." When one state tries something new, there is a tendency for other states (or other organizations or jurisdictions) to attempt to find a way to replicate it. This is particularly true if the original jurisdiction is viewed as a trend setter in other areas and their peers want to join them to be viewed as one of the front runners.

REORGANIZATION AS A WAY OF IMPROVING THE POLICY TECHNOLOGY

A number of reorganizations can be seen as evidence of that aesthetic maxim, "Form follows function." That is, changes in organization structure occur because of shifts in the policy itself. These shifts can be made in a formal fashion or through new ways of conceptualizing the ways in which the policy is implemented; they can be seen as new ways of organizing the policy technology.

This form of reorganization is driven by the substance of the policy itself. Unlike many of the other reasons for reorganization, the advocates of this approach begin with the demands of the policy and argue for organizational forms that make the policy implementation work most effectively. This approach is very often the way that client advocates think about organization; they begin with this question: How can the structure of the organization be used to assist in the effective delivery of services? This approach emphasizes the functional demands of the literal task at hand rather than imperatives that might flow from organizational or political perspectives. Depending on the perceived tasks, the prescription for change might move in either centralized or decentralized directions.

REORGANIZATION AS A DRIVE FOR STABILITY AND CONFLICT AVOIDANCE

Interest in reorganization appears to occur during periods when political leaders (and others) perceive that the public sector contains elements that are out of control. During these times, policy issues are often unsettled, with diverse sets of actors and forces demanding conflicting agendas and employing incompatible strategies. For those who value stability, times like this appear to hinge on anarchy and evoke serious concern about the future.

The type of organizational change that is characterized by these elements moves toward consolidation and leads one to work within the framework of existing organizational values, norms, and attitudes "to resolve demands for change regardless of source (and hence to resolve the conflict that inevitably is associated with the forces of change)."[6] Furthermore, "the basic component of consolidation is a strong commitment toward moderation, compromise, negotiation, and accommodation."[7]

If we see reorganization as a response to a basic need to take control, then one can see why it is a favorite technique in a number of fields where the pace of change is rapid, making policy actors feel as if they were continually reacting to externally imposed changes. Reorganization attempts to provide these actors with the sense of asserting some control, moving from a reactive to a proactive posture.

CENTRALIZATION VERSUS DECENTRALIZATION

As this discussion has indicated, the reasons for interest in reorganization lead an organizational designer in very different structural directions. Some of the reasons push either exclusively or predominantly toward a centralized structure; conversely, some of the reasons appear to emphasize a decentralized structural approach. It is often difficult, however, to attain clarity about the terms centralization and decentralization. One person's centralization is another's decentralization.

THE ORGANIZATION OF THIS BOOK

This volume was actually stimulated by the events of September 11, 2001. The disasters of that day instigated the most vigorous reorganization of the U.S. government since the aftermath of World War II. In response to weaknesses in its law enforcement, intelligence, and immigration infrastructures, among other areas exploited by the attackers, President George W. Bush began an effort to reshape the executive branch. The most public of his moves was the creation of the DHS, a cabinet-level agency charged with managing and coordinating all homeland security efforts. Was structural reorganization—something at which Bush balked initially, favoring instead the creation of an Office of Homeland Security within the Executive Office of the President—the most effective means of preventing a second attack? Did Bush have considerations in mind other than domestic security when he finally acquiesced to the demands of Congress, the press, and the public for a lead agency? In what ways does the administrative structure of homeland security efforts shape the government's ability to ensure the safety of Americans? What are the costs of such a design? For instance, to what extent was the Hurricane Katrina debacle a product of DHS's organizational design and operational method?

These questions, when considered in the context of homeland security and other policy areas, and with respect to reorganization in general, challenge the reader to engage with the major issues raised by administrative reorganization. Furthermore, the excerpts that follow are a way to revisit the issue as a proxy for many of the most important debates in public administration, public policy, and political science.

The book is divided into two parts, a structure reflective of the natural distinction between a management-based approach to reorganization and one that emphasizes reorganization as a solution to policy problems. The selections that have been chosen are meant to be illustrative of the span of public administration, public management, and public policy literatures that deal with this issue. The excerpts highlight the historical approach to the issue. They tend not to be current pieces, in part because there has been less interest in the structural strategy as a general strategy or approach to change.

The material in Part I of this volume addresses the classic structural management approach to executive branch reorganization and presents perspectives drawn from a more general view of the subject. Part I is also organized around four distinct sets of materials. The discussion begins with a series of primary source documents intended to introduce not only prominent reorganization efforts, but also the view of executive branch organization and operation that has come to define the traditional approach to the matter. Based largely on the thinking of progressive era scholars and the popularity of private sector managerial principles at the time, this philosophy drove both administrative scholarship and early reorganization efforts. Reorganization was a means to increased efficiency and economy and an indispensable step on the "one best way" to structure bureaucratic operation.

The works presented in Part II are organized around four specific reorganization efforts, each illustrative of the unique aspects of reorganization motivated by policy goals. The first set of literature discusses the DHS, followed by sections on the Department of Defense, the Department of Education, and the recent effort to create a Department of Food Safety. These materials focus on the decision to reorganize, the process of change and adjustment, and the policy effects flowing from each of these reorganization efforts. Several of the examples illustrate interest in other management strategies (such as collaboration and networks) rather than structural change.

The book concludes with a checklist for reorganization analysis that should be useful to individuals who are either evaluating a reorganization effort or attempting to determine whether a reorganization is likely to achieve what its proponents believe will occur.

NOTES FOR CHAPTER 1

1. See, for example, Aaron Wildavsky, 1984, *The Nursing Father: Moses As a Political Leader*, Tuscaloosa, AL: University of Alabama Press.
2. Ralph C. Chandler and Jack C. Plano, 1986, *The Public Administration Dictionary*, New York: Macmillan Publishing Company, p. 147.
3. Ibid.
4. Thomas J. Peters and Robert H. Waterman, Jr., 1982, *In Search of Excellence: Lessons from America's Best Run Companies*, New York: Harper and Row.
5. James L. Garnett and Charles H. Levine, "State Executive Branch Reorganization," *Administration and Society*, Vol. 12, No. 3, Nov. 1980.
6. Louis C. Gawthrop, *Bureaucratic Behavior in the Executive Branch*, New York: The Free Press, 1969, p. 181.
7. Ibid.

PART I

Reorganization in the Public Administration Literature

Issues related to organizational structure have been a part of the basic lexicon of the public administration field since its earliest days. Indeed, the classic detailing of administrative functions (POSTCORB) assumes that what is called "organizing" is an essential part of the administrative tool kit. Despite the experience of a number of practitioners and analyses by some public administration scholars, "organizing" has often been treated as a technical and neutral approach to administration. This approach tends to emphasize strategies that support a logical arrangement of organizational components; among the strategies are efforts that support a leader's span of control, increase coordination, and lead to greater efficiency.

This section of the book provides a reader with a range of perspectives that can be found in the public administration literature that both accept and challenge that classic approach. The diversity of perspectives that is included in the volume indicates that the field has long lived with a tension around this topic. Rhetorical support for reorganization has not always produced what its proponents imagined, but there has been a tendency for advocates of structural changes to continue to argue for those changes.

The four chapters in Part I explore four different aspects of this topic: issues related to authority, experience around diverse agendas, attempts to broaden the conceptual framework involving the topic, and lessons that emerged from attempts to make organizational structure changes.

The materials in Chapter 2, "Authority," focus on the question of how and with what procedural device could the president legally reorganize the bureaucracy? This topic highlights the issue of executive authority and the use of commissions (independent or otherwise) as a vehicle for obtaining such authority. These excerpts also document the evolution in philosophy that characterizes the dominant approach to reorganization. What began in the early 20th century as a right of passage for most incoming presidents has become a much more complicated and politically risky process and, as a result, much less common. For some, administrative reorganization is motivated not by the inevitability of orthodox administrative theory and a president's natural drive to dominate the bureaucracy but instead by a more selective and careful analysis and the need for a specific brand of policy solution.

The excerpts in Chapter 3, "Agendas," document different perspectives about the nature of reorganization itself and the goals of the efforts. In the 1960s and 1970s, administrative scholars began to emphasize the complexity of reorganization and the value of understanding the political nature of its pursuit. A president who ignored the role of Congress, interest groups, and the public in the process was likely to confront a difficult reorganization process and a high possibility of failure. This work also moved beyond process and motivation to a documentation of the wide-ranging effects of a reorganization effort. Creating, relocating, or eliminating an agency shifts access to resources and decision-making authority and changes the shape of political relationship and policy strategies throughout the bureaucracy.

Chapter 4, "Broadening the Framework," presents an expanded view of the traditional framework for understanding reorganization. A deeper understanding and a newfound willingness to admit to the intricacy of these issues appear to have generated a skeptical mainstream view of reorganization. How could a president conquer a hostile political environment and comprehend the maze of causes and effects well enough to undertake reorganization in a responsible and useful manner? The excerpts presented in this chapter indicate an attempt by students of reorganization to shift the paradigm of analysis. Whether focusing on a higher level of analysis or framing reorganization in different theoretical terms altogether, these selections manage to avoid the pervasive "all-or-nothing" logic that typically plagues critical evaluation of bureaucratic reorganization.

Chapter 5, "Lessons," includes several pieces that bring together these diverse interpretive frameworks and disparate angles from which to observe reorganization by presenting a set of "lessons learned." Some of these lessons are presented in the form of evaluations of specific reorganization efforts. Others provide detailed accounts of those issues frequently overlooked by reorganizers, including plan implementation and the effects of reorganization felt by subfederal governments. The materials in this final chapter of Part I describe reorganization from a practical, concrete standpoint and enhance understanding of federal executive reorganization.

CHAPTER 2

Authority

INTRODUCTION

Unlike the authority of a top official in the private sector, the President of the United States cannot embark on major reorganizations alone but must have both the necessary legal authority to reorganize, as well as political support for this action. Consistent with principles outlined in Articles I and II of the U.S. Constitution, executive branch authority to operate policy-making administrative agencies is not an inherent power. The president's ability to control (and thus to reorganize) is shared with the legislative branch, and in many cases, it is limited only to that which is delegated to the president by Congress.

Given these constitutional strictures, executive reorganization may not occur, no matter how popular politically or how potentially effective administratively, without the involvement, either formal or informal, of Congress. Historically, legal authority has existed in three forms. The first form—major reorganizations—includes those that involve the creation, elimination, or significant alteration of a cabinet agency and must be completed by formal statute. The Homeland Security Act of 2002, which created the Department of Homeland Security, is the most recent example. The second form is designed to facilitate noncabinet level reorganization. For this form, Congress has periodically employed a legislative device known as Reorganization Plan Authority. These temporary grants of authority typically require the president to present a reorganization plan to Congress within a very specific timeframe and allow Congress a right to reject any plan that does not meet predetermined requirements. Reorganization conducted by executive order—the third form of authority—may be reversed by subsequent presidents and stopped by a hostile Congress. President Nixon's establishment of the Environmental Protection Agency in 1973 is a good example of the small-scale executive branch reorganizations that emerged from executive order authority.

Regardless of which of the three techniques is employed, the pursuit of reorganization authority is an intensely political matter, inevitably involving a negotiation between the executive and the legislative branches over control of the bureaucracy. Each of the two branches has significant interest in these debates. A formal change in bureaucratic structure has the potential to modify preexisting Congressional committee fiefdoms and to redistribute resources in a way that significantly alters existing power bases. Similarly, although presidents may attempt to accomplish specific tactical and political goals without congressional participation, the president will face other problems involving budgets and other policy or program issues.

It is not rare for a president to try to gain reorganization authority from a hesitant or reluctant Congress. Various strategies and political and rhetorical devices have been employed in this pursuit. The appointment of a commission is among the common approaches. Presidents have used commissions to support what is viewed as an independent, objective perspective on the relative benefits of reorganization. Similarly, commissions have been used to justify or legitimize a preexisting position.

The goal of this chapter is to introduce to the reader the broad set of issues involved in a president's effort to reorganize the federal bureaucracy. The pieces were selected to represent a diverse historical context and to highlight the views of a range of political and administrative participants. The excerpts that are included in this chapter highlight a number of important issues: the separation of powers struggle between the executive and legislative branches, the pursuit of orthodox administrative goals and expanded executive control through structural change, the role of commissions in that process, and the inherent difficulty of negotiating a major reorganization and others.

The chapter's first piece, an excerpt from the report produced by the President's Committee on Administrative Management (referred to commonly as the Brownlow Committee), was delivered to President Roosevelt in 1937. Composed of three of the era's most prominent public administration scholars (Louis Brownlow, Charles Merriam, and Luther Gulick), the committee was created to prescribe solutions to what had become a highly disorganized and supremely dysfunctional bureaucracy. As the committee saw it, the situation demanded wholesale structural reorganization to deliver the necessary corrective increases in executive authority and streamlined, hierarchical accountability. The report famously argues the need for "12 great departments" to house and organize preexisting government programs.

Despite the knowledge that Congress would have to approve the committee's recommendations before they became law, the report seldom, if ever, mentioned the legislative branch. Roosevelt saw strong, unilateral leadership as the only pertinent response to the country's severe economic and political turmoil and used the report as a tool of battle for control of the bureaucracy, rather than as an offer to negotiation with Congress. As a result, Congress quickly rejected legislation articulating most of the Committee's recommendations. By 1939, after successful resolution of Roosevelt's court packing scandal and further negotiation on reorganization, Congress passed the Reorganization Act, which, among other things, created the Executive Office of the President and enabled future presidents to employ reorganization plan authority.

The second piece, an excerpt from the first Hoover Commission report, exemplifies a more conciliatory approach to bureaucratic reform. In 1949, President Truman appointed former president Herbert Hoover to chair a committee with the ostensible charge of reducing the size of the bloated post-World War II bureaucracy. Perhaps reflective of the relationship between the executive and the Congress and out of respect for the value of congressional committee proprieties, the Hoover Commission did not recommend widespread agency or program elimination. Instead, the commission outlined a plan for agency reorganization in order to eliminate "the wastes of overlapping and duplication" and to increase presidential control of agency leadership and policy. The commission relied on technocratic solutions such as "performance budgeting" and personnel system decentralization in order to facilitate its recommendations. The vast majority of the Hoover Commission recommendations were approved by Congress, one of the most significant of which led to the creation of the Department of Health, Education, and Welfare in 1953.

Twenty-two years after the first Hoover Commission delivered its report to President Truman, President Nixon submitted his plan for executive branch reorganization to Congress. This is the third document presented in this chapter. Although he created the Ash Council to help articulate his vision, Nixon's reorganization effort was largely a product of his own understanding of executive authority and his frustration at the complexity of his relationships with both Congress and a powerful set of interest groups. To effect these changes, Nixon submitted legislation proposing the creation of four megadepartments, each containing programs and agencies categorized by their major substantive purpose. Because of the hyperaggressive nature of his plan and the divisive strategy Nixon pursued in obtaining congressional authority, the proposed reorganization was dead on arrival. It is difficult to make such drastic changes even when using the highest degree of finesse with Congress; it is nearly impossible to do so using the combative style Nixon made famous.

The fourth document, President Carter's "Department of Energy Message to the Congress Transmitting Proposed Legislation," highlights the similarities between Carter and Nixon's management goals and the dissimilarities in their chosen approach to obtaining authority. Carter campaigned for president in 1976 on a platform of change; reorganization of the bureaucracy was one of his signatures as governor of Georgia and remained important in his quest for the White House. Rather than focus on wholesale changes, however, Carter moved much more incrementally and attempted to balance a reform agenda with the development of a cordial relationship with Congress. In 1978, Congress granted Carter limited reorganization plan authority, which he used to create the Department of Energy. Carter's success in establishing a cabinet-level Department of Education (discussed at length in Part II) is another noteworthy accomplishment. Carter's focus shifted from Nixon's management-driven rhetoric to a policy-based approach.

The chapter's fifth piece, an excerpt from the *9/11 Commission Report*, discusses six problems befalling the intelligence community and presents a series of concrete recommendations. The piece is significant for a number of reasons. First, the excerpt discusses incredibly high-profile subject matter and does so in a way that illustrates the independent commission model. Second, the report offers a multifaceted response to a well-known policy problem, bringing together both management and policy solutions. Third, the excerpt highlights the complex, multijurisdictional context within which policy problems must be addressed. In this setting, structural reorganization is only one of many possible tools for reform.

The next document, an excerpt from the Report of the National Commission on the Public Service (the Volcker Commission, named for its Chairman, former Chairman of the Federal Reserve, Paul Volcker), reflects the startling decline of management-centered reform proposals. The Volcker Commission report was published in 2003 but did not engender much attention from the George W. Bush administration. Created shortly after the inception of the Department of Homeland Security, the report did not seem to be able to generate conversation or attention. The report is also instructive for its approach and chosen content. The report's recommendations are constructed on managerial observations and tend to reflect many of the structurally driven orthodox administrative principles of the past.

The chapter's final piece is a timeline excerpted from Brian Balogh, Joanna Grislinger, and Philip Zelikow's "Making Democracy Work: A Brief History of Twentieth Century Executive Reorganization." The timeline charts every major executive reorganization action taken in the 20th century and shows each alongside corresponding reorganization studies, commissions, and proposals. It provides the reader with examples both of the persistent use of reorganization over time and the difficulty with which reorganization efforts are approved and implemented. The timeline also brings into sharp relief the complex and interwoven relationship between Congress and the president, as well as the shift from unilateral, management-driven reorganizations to the more selective, policy-based efforts that prevail today.

President's Committee on Administrative Management, *Administrative Management in the Government of the United States, January 8, 1937* (Washington DC: U.S. Government Printing Office, 1937).

ADMINISTRATION REORGANIZATION OF THE GOVERNMENT OF THE UNITED STATES

The primary purpose of a rational reorganization of the administrative agencies of the Executive Branch of the Government is to reduce to a manageable compass the number of agencies reporting to the President.

The Constitution of the United States sets up no administrative organization for the Government. The whole matter of executive power is dealt with in a few brief phrases. First in importance is: "The executive Power shall be vested in a President of the United States of America." Reference is also made to the Army and Navy, of which the President is named "Commander in Chief," and, indirectly to the "executive Departments"; and there is laid on the President alone the duty to "take Care that the Laws be faithfully executed." In these few words, supplemented by those defining the scope of the Legislative and the Judicial Branches, there is set forth the constitutional principle of the separation of powers, which places in the President, and in the President alone, the whole executive power of the Government of the United States.

The administrative organization of the Government to carry out "the executive Power" thus rests upon statute law, and upon departmental arrangements made under the authority of law. The history of these laws and arrangements is a reflection of our national problems and development. At the beginning, in 1789, there were but four departments: State, War, Treasury, and the Attorney General. The General Post Office was permanently established in 1794, and 4 years later, the Navy Department was created. Thus, by 1800 there were six departments, all of them directly under the President in accordance with the constitutional principle of the separation of powers.

For the next 50 years there was no change. Then came the creation of the Department of the Interior in 1849, of Agriculture in 1889, and of Commerce and Labor in 1903, from which the Department of Labor was separated in 1913.

Two new kinds of governmental agencies made their appearance in the generation after the Civil War. They were, first, executive agencies under the President but not connected with any department, such as the Civil Service Commission (1883); and, second, independent regulatory agencies, such as the Interstate Commerce Commission (1887), which were neither placed under the President nor connected with any department. Many additional agencies of these types appeared in subsequent years.

During the World War a large number of new agencies were established. These were chiefly councils, boards, commissions, administrations, and governmental corporations, and though not legally connected with the regular departments, they were definitely within the Executive Branch and under the President. In this period the innovation was the governmental corporation, which was found useful particularly in dealing with financial operations. Most of these agencies were abolished, or consolidated with the departments, in the years following the war.

During the recent depression similar need for emergency action has resulted again in the establishment of a large number of new agencies. These include administrations, boards, commissions, committees, governmental corporations, and authorities. The novel elements in this period are the extended use of the corporate form and the introduction of the "authority." Most of these agencies have been placed in the Executive Branch and under the President, but in the main they have not been connected by law with the regular departments.

As a result of this long development, there are now in the Government of the United States over 100 separately organized establishments and agencies presumably reporting to the President. Among them are the 10 regular executive departments and the many boards, commissions, administrations, authorities, corporations, and agencies which are under the President but not in a department. There are also a dozen agencies which are totally independent—a new and headless "fourth branch" of the Government.

THE EXECUTIVE BRANCH TODAY

The Executive Branch of the Government of the United States has thus grown up without plan or design like the barns, shacks, silos, tool sheds, and garages of an old farm. To look at it now, no one would ever recognize the structure which the founding fathers erected a century and a half ago to be the Government of the United States. A careful examination of the Government shows the following facts:

1. The structure of the Government throws an impossible task upon the Chief Executive. No President can possibly give adequate supervision to the multitude of agencies which have been set up to carry on the work of the Government, nor can he coordinate their activities and policies.
2. The normal managerial agencies designed to assist the Executive in thinking, planning, and managing, which one would expect to find in any large-scale organization, are either undeveloped or lacking.
3. The constitutional principle of the separation of powers and the responsibility of the President for "the executive Power" is impaired through the multiplicity and confusion of agencies which render effective action impossible.
4. Without plan or intent, there has grown up a headless "fourth branch" of the Government, responsible to no one, and impossible of coordination with the general policies and work of the Government as determined by the people through their duly elected representatives.

5. For purposes of management, boards and commissions have turned out to be failures. Their mechanism is inevitably slow, cumbersome, wasteful, and ineffective, and does not lend itself readily to cooperation with other agencies. Even strong men on boards find that their individual opinions are watered down in reaching board decisions. When freed from the work of management, boards are, however, extremely useful and necessary for consultation, discussion, and advice; for representation of diverse views and citizen opinion; for quasi-judicial action; and as a repository of corporate powers.
6. The conspicuously well-managed administrative units in the Government are almost without exception headed by single administrators.
7. Owing to the multiplicity of agencies and the lack of administrative management there is waste, overlapping, and duplication, which may be eliminated through coordination, consolidation, and proper managerial control.

These are the major features which stand out clearly in any examination of the structure of the Executive Branch of the Government.

There flow from these factors many obscure difficulties and problems. Among these is the time and energy which have been wasted for many years because of departmental jealousies and jurisdictional disputes among the department heads and bureau chiefs as to who should control particular activities. The people of the country have held the President responsible for failing to settle these internal quarrels, whereas in fact, because the President's authority is not commensurate with his responsibility, often he has been unable to compose the differences short of the summary dismissal of one of his Cabinet Members. The departments themselves and groups of citizens interested in particular activities often seek to settle such disputes by direct appeals to the Congress, there again only to find the same or almost the same differences represented, in the jurisdictional jealousies of congressional committees. . . .

The safeguarding of the citizen from narrow minded and dictatorial bureaucratic interference and control is one of the primary obligations of democratic government. It can be accomplished only by so centralizing the determination of administrative policy that there is a clear line of conduct laid down for all officialdom to follow and then by so decentralizing the actual administrative operation that the Government servant remains himself one of the people in touch with the people and does not degenerate into an isolated and arrogant bureaucrat.

These difficulties and defects in the organization of the Executive Branch have been clearly recognized for a generation and have been growing steadily worse decade by decade. The structure as it now stands is inefficient; it is a poor instrument for rendering public service; and it thwarts democratic control. With such a planless organization, good management is almost impossible—a fact of great importance in the modern world in which nothing can continue without good management, not even democracy.

PLAN OF REORGANIZATION

To meet these conditions and make and keep the Government thoroughly up-to-date, we make four principal recommendations, as follows:

1. Provide for 12 major executive departments, by the addition to the existing 10 of a Department of Social Welfare and a Department of Public Works.
2. Require and authorize the President to determine the appropriate assignment to the 12 executive departments of all operating administrative agencies and fix upon the Executive continuing responsibility and power for the maintenance of the effective division of duties among the departments.
3. Equip the President with the essential modern arms of management in budgeting, efficiency research, personnel, and planning.
4. Revive and extend the principle of Executive accountability to the Congress through the development of an effective independent audit and report on fiscal transactions and through the simplification of the confusing structure of the Government.

It is the purpose of these recommendations to make effective management possible by restoring the President to his proper place as Chief Executive and giving him both a governmental structure that can be managed and modern managerial agencies, and by restoring to the Congress effective legislative control over the Executive. One element of this program, that dealing with managerial agencies, has been discussed above. As a part of other phases of this program, many minor changes will be required. These are discussed in the following pages in connection with a fuller statement of our principal recommendations concerning departmental reorganization.

TWELVE MAJOR DEPARTMENTS

Any large industrial or commercial enterprise with plants, stores, or services scattered over a continent would, for the sake of good management, organize the business on the basis of the separate services, plants, or areas. Each one of these divisions would then have a manager, and there would be over all a president or general manager who would direct the whole enterprise, working through 8 to 10 executive assistants in accordance with the policies determined by the stockholders and the board of directors. This is in general what we propose for the Government of the United States, making allowance for the differences in method and purpose of the Government as a servant of the Nation.

No man can manage, coordinate, or control more than 100 separate agencies, particularly when in some of them responsibility to the Chief Executive is not definitely placed. The number of immediate subordinates with whom an executive can deal effectively is limited. Just as the hand can cover but a few keys on the piano, so there is for management a limited span of control. In the Army this has been said to be 3 subordinates; in business it has frequently been set at 5 or 6; and some students of government have placed the limit at 10 or 12. Obviously the number is not the same for all work or for all men, nor can it be determined mathematically. But one thing is clear: It should be the smallest possible number without bringing together in any department activities which are unrelated or in conflict with each other.

It is thus necessary to determine what are the new major fields of activity of the National Government and to make a place for them. These are disclosed in the multitude of new agencies and laws of the past 25 years. As we view them they seem to fall in five great categories: Public welfare, public works, public lending, conservation, and business controls. These are the great thrusts which have come to the surface in the last generation, not only in this country, but in all countries, though in different ways. Certain phases of these activities may not be permanent, but the major purposes are apparently here to stay, and deserve appropriate departmental homes.

An examination of the existing executive departments shows that there is no adequate place in the present structure for two of these new developments: Public welfare and public works. We therefore recommend that new departments be set up by law to cover these two fields, and that there be assigned to these departments by the President not only the appropriate new activities in these fields but also the old activities closely related thereto. The remainder of the new activities, which have to do with lending, regulating, and conservation, may be assigned to existing departments without altering their fundamental purposes.

In the case of conservation, however, it would seem desirable to establish a Department of Conservation, which would take-over most of the activities of the present Department of Interior. The name "conservation" should be among the departmental titles because it represents a major purpose of our Government today. We therefore recommend that the name of the Department of the Interior be changed to Department of Conservation.

In accordance with these recommendations, the operating divisions of the Executive Branch of the Federal Government would be as follows:

Department of State
Department of the Treasury
Department of War
Department of Justice
Post Office Department
Department of the Navy
Department of Conservation
Department of Agriculture
Department of Commerce
Department of Labor
Department of Social Welfare
Department of Public Works

The establishment of these 12 great departments directly responsible in administration to the Chief Executive in place of the present multitude of independent, and at times conflicting departments, boards, commissions, administrations, authorities, corporations, committees, and agencies will make possible the more simple, more effective, more efficient, more economical, and more democratically controlled management of public affairs.

The Hoover Commission Report on Organization of the Executive Branch of Government (New York: McGraw-Hill Book Co., 1949).

In this part of its report, the Commission on Organization of the Executive Branch of the Government deals with the essentials of effective organization of the executive branch. Without these essentials, all other steps to improve organization and management are doomed to failure.

The President, and under him his chief lieutenants, the department heads, must be held responsible and accountable to the people and the Congress for the conduct of the executive branch.

Responsibility and accountability are impossible without authority—the power to direct. The exercise of authority is impossible without a clear line of command from the top to the bottom, and a return line of responsibility and accountability from the bottom to the top.

The wise exercise of authority is impossible without the aids which staff institutions can provide to assemble facts and recommendations upon which judgment may be made and to supervise and report upon the execution of decisions.

Definite authority at the top, a clear line of authority from top to bottom, and adequate staff aids to the exercise of authority do not exist. Authority is diffused, lines of authority are confused, staff services are insufficient. Consequently, responsibility and accountability are impaired.

To remedy this situation is the first and essential step in the search for efficiency and economy in the executive branch of the Federal Government.

The critical state of world affairs requires the Government of the United States to speak and act with unity of purpose, firmness, and restraint in dealing with other nations. It must act decisively to preserve its human and material resources. It must develop strong machinery for the national defense, while seeking to construct an enduring world peace. It cannot perform these tasks if its organization for development and execution of policy is confused and disorderly, or if the Chief Executive is handicapped in providing firm direction to the departments and agencies.

If disorder in the administrative machinery makes the executive branch of the Government work at cross purposes within itself, the Nation as a whole must suffer. It must suffer—if its several programs conflict with each other and executive authority becomes confused—from waste in the expenditure of public funds, and from the lack of national unity that results from useless friction.

An energetic and unified executive is not a threat to free and responsible government, as Alexander Hamilton pointed out in "The Federalist" (No. 70). He declared that the ingredients of "safety in the republican sense" are "fast, a due dependence on the people; secondly, a due responsibility." Strength and unity in an executive make clear who is responsible for faults in administration and thus enable the legislature better to enforce accountability to the people.

FINDINGS

The commission has found that violation of these principles results from the conditions stated in the following findings.

First Finding

The executive branch is not organized into a workable number of major departments and agencies which the President can effectively direct, but is cut up into a large number of agencies, which divide responsibility and which are too great in number for effective direction from the top.

Second Finding

The President and the heads of departments lack the tools to frame programs and policies and to supervise their execution. No executive, public or private, can manage a large and complex establishment without staff assistance. Staff agencies must keep the President informed on the way in which the various departmental programs are related to each other, assist in defining specific programs pursuant to the instructions of the Congress, and help him supervise the execution of these programs.

Third Finding

The Federal Government has not taken aggressive steps to build a corps of administrators of the highest level of ability with an interest in the program of the Government as a whole.

Fourth Finding

Many of the statutes and regulations that control the administrative practices and procedures of the Government are unduly detailed and rigid.

Fifth Finding

Likewise, the budgetary processes of the Government needs improvement, in order to express the objectives of the Government in terms of the work to be done rather than in mere classifications of expenditures.

Sixth Finding

The accounting methods in the executive branch require standardization and simplification and accounting activities require decentralization if they are to become effective tools of management and if great expense and waste are to be eliminated.

Seventh Finding

General administrative services for various operating agencies—such as purchasing of supplies, maintenance of records, and the operation of public buildings are poorly organized or coordinated.

SUMMARY

Any systematic effort to improve the organization and administration of the Government, therefore, must:

1. Create a more orderly grouping of the functions of Government into major departments and agencies under the President.
2. Establish a clear line of control from the President to these department and agency heads and from them to their subordinates with correlative responsibility from these officials to the President, cutting through the barriers which have in many cases made bureaus and agencies partially independent of the Chief Executive.
3. Give the President and each department head strong staff services which should exist only to make executive work more effective, and which the President or department head should be free to organize at his discretion.
4. Develop a much greater number of capable administrators in the public service, and prepare them for promotion to any bureau or department in the Government where their services may be most effectively used.
5. Enforce the accountability of administrators by a much broader pattern of controls, so that the statutes and regulations which govern administrative practices will encourage, rather than destroy, initiative and enterprise.
6. Permit the operating departments and agencies to administer for themselves a larger share of the routine administrative services, under strict supervision and in conformity with high standards. Only by taking these steps can the operations of the executive branch be managed effectively, responsibly, and economically.

EXECUTIVE AUTHORITY AND ACCOUNTABILITY

It was a frequent finding of our various task forces that the President and his department heads do not have authority commensurate with the responsibility they must assume. In many instances authority is either lacking or is so diffused that it is almost impossible to hold anyone completely accountable for a particular program or operation. This tendency is dangerous and can, if extended far enough, lead to irresponsible government.

At the present time the President lacks authority to organize the agencies of the executive branch for the most effective discharge of his executive duties. While powers to reorganize have been granted to Presidents in the past, they have been intermittent and subject to many limitations and exclusions, thus seriously diminishing their effectiveness. . . .

In another area—fiscal management—no one in the executive branch has authority to set up a central accounting system. Such an instrument is absolutely essential to management and fiscal control. The influence of the Comptroller General—an agent of the Congress—in the determination of executive expenditures also seriously impairs the authority and discretion of the President and his department heads.

Still another basic weakness is to be found in the outmoded appropriation system which concentrates on detailed listings of positions and materials rather than on well-defined functional programs. This prevents the wisest expenditure of public monies; and often diffuses the spending power among so many organization units that it becomes impossible to hold any one person or unit accountable for accomplishing program objectives.

Finally, the enormous amount of detailed substantive legislation is still another feature of present practices which is not conducive to the most effective administration of the public business. There are, for example, 199 statutes affecting personnel management alone in the Department of Agriculture. Disposition of surplus property is governed by over 369 separate laws. The Bureau of Indian Affairs is required to administer over 5,000 statutes and 370 treaties; and the laws which govern the operations of the Reclamation Bureau run to no less than 803 pages.

It is not any one of these factors alone but, like the Lilliputian threads that bound Gulliver, it is the total complex of these restrictions—lack of organization authority; grants of independent executive powers to subordinate officials; restrictive controls over personnel; divided controls over accounting and preaudit of expenditures; diffusion of the spending power of appropriations; overly detailed legislation—that weakens the powers of management in the executive branch and makes it difficult if not impossible to fix responsibility.

Solution

The solution to this problem will require some fundamental and far-reaching changes in present legislative and administrative practices. The Commission's recommendations to the Congress are covered in detail in a number of its previous reports and need not be repeated at length here. However, the reforms required must provide that sufficient authority be delegated to the President and to his department heads to permit them to carry out responsibilities that have been assigned to them by the Constitution and the Congress.

The department heads must be free, with presidential approval, to reorganize their departments in the ways that, in their judgment, best suit the requirements of efficiency and economy. This means that the internal organization structure of executive agencies should not be prescribed by legislation.

The related practice of determining the precise functions and membership of coordinating and advisory bodies by statute should be discontinued in favor of more general enabling legislation which would provide a flexible framework within which the President can act.

Detailed legislation, including rigid itemized appropriation language which unnecessarily limits executive discretion and initiative, should also be avoided.

In the further interest of responsible management, independent grants of executive authority not subject to the control of the Chief Executive should not be made to department heads and subordinate officials.

The purely executive functions of quasi-legislative and quasi-judicial agencies, too, should be brought within the regular executive departments, thus placing these responsibilities within the ambit of executive control.

Likewise, departmental authority over personnel management must be strengthened by permitting those charged with management responsibilities to exercise more discretion in such phases of personnel administration as recruiting, selection, promotions, pay administration, and dismissals.

Finally, the President must have more authority to determine the kind of fiscal reporting he needs to obtain reliable information and to maintain sound fiscal controls.

These changes are the first steps necessary to achieve not only increased efficiency and economy in the Government, but also a greater measure of accountability of the executive branch to Congress.

SHARPENING THE TOOLS OF MANAGEMENT

Beyond the need for greater executive authority and discretion, the President and top officials in the executive branch require more adequate tools in the areas of fiscal management, personnel, supply, and housekeeping services, if the public business is to be conducted efficiently and economically.

PERSONNEL

Probably no problem in the management of the Government is more important than that of obtaining a capable and conscientious body of public servants. Unfortunately, personnel practices in the Federal Government give little room for optimism that these needs are being met.

The Civil Service Commission has not been organized to develop as a really effective staff arm of the President. Planning and administration of the personnel program have not kept pace with the tremendous expansion of employment in the Government.

The centralization of personnel transactions in the Civil Service Commission and in the departmental personnel offices has resulted in unjustifiable delays in handling personnel problems.

Recruitment machinery has been slow, impersonal, and cumbersome. Many personnel procedures are unnecessarily complicated, and the rigidity of certain of them does not permit the necessary latitude of judgment and discretion that operating officials need to do the most effective management job.

Insufficient attention has been given to such positive aspects of sound personnel management as developing better supervisor-employee relations, training, promotion, and incentives for superior performance. In short, the system is not constituted so as to attract and retain sufficient qualified people for the Government's tasks.

These criticisms should not be construed, however, as a reflection on the vast majority of our Federal employees, who are conscientious, hardworking, and devoted, but rather upon a system which has not fully kept pace with the needs of the Federal Government.

Solution

In our report on personnel management we make several recommendations to improve the quality of personnel administration in the Government. We recommend that the personnel system be decentralized so that the operating agencies of the Government will perform the day-to-day tasks of recruitment, selection, position classification, and other aspects of personnel management, under standards to be approved and enforced by the Civil Service Commission.

This will free the Commission from the details of centralized control of personnel operations and transactions, and permit its chairman to concentrate on planning and personnel standards, and on assisting the President and his department heads in developing sound and active personnel management programs. The chairman of the Civil Service Commission not only should serve as the President's principal staff advisor on civil service problems, but also should direct the Commission's operations.

On the agency level the personnel function should be represented in top management. The departments themselves, in recruiting employees, should use more active and attractive methods; and apply selection methods which will both give their supervisors wider latitude of judgment and insure that appointments are being made on a merit, and not only a political, basis.

To improve employee performance, line supervisors should play a greater role in the selection, advancement, and removal of employees. Forms and procedures in personnel processes should be simplified. Increased emphasis should be given to such matters as employee participation in management problems, in-service training, promotions, and the human relations aspect of management.

Salaries, pitifully low in the higher levels . . . must be substantially increased to attract and retain employees with first-rate abilities. This need was emphasized again and again by almost all of our task forces: by our task forces on personnel, on supply, on medical services, on budgeting and accounting, by our management engineering consultants, and by many other experts working in the various fields of our work.

Finally, all positions in the service with the exception of top level policy jobs should be filled by merit system methods.

All these improvements are necessary if we are to achieve a higher degree of competency, efficiency, and accountability in the Federal service.

THE WASTES OF OVERLAPPING AND DUPLICATION

There is probably no place in the Government where waste is more conspicuous than in the overlapping services of the Government. Many of these duplicating and competing services have stubbornly survived through repeated exposures and attempts at reorganization. Our reports and those of the task forces give numerous examples of overlapping and duplication throughout the Government. Here, for the purpose of highlighting the problem and pointing the way toward its solution, we shall briefly cite only three. [The three, dealing with water resource development, land and forestry management, and hospital construction are omitted herein.]

Solution

In several of our reports we recommend putting an end to such wasteful competition by consolidating these overlapping services. We also propose bringing the major construction activities together in one agency.

In addition to this, a Board of Impartial Review of all major public works is required in the President's Office to insure that projects planned are feasible, are supported by adequate basic data, and not in conflict with other works projects, and are being completed with utmost efficiency.

Moreover, to avoid other overlapping and duplication, as for example in the field of statistics, we recommend that the President's authority and staff of the Office of the Budget be strengthened. Likewise, to coordinate the various scientific research programs we recommend the creation of a National Science Foundation.

Finally, in order to provide the President with the necessary information and control of all executive programs we recommend that a position of Staff Secretary be created to keep him informed on current programs. The President will thus be able to achieve better coordination of executive activities.

These basic changes in organization supplemented by additional coordinating and planning devices are vital to the elimination and prevention of tremendous wastes in money and manpower in the Government.

DECENTRALIZATION UNDER CENTRALIZED CONTROL

As a general rule, economy can be achieved in administration by centralizing services common to all agencies. There is a limit, however, in the size and complexity of Government beyond which it is no longer feasible to furnish services centrally without creating serious bottlenecks, delays, and confusion. As a result the services become more costly and less efficient than if performed by the agencies themselves.

This point has long been reached in the operations of the Federal Government. It is no longer conceivable that personnel transactions for 2 million employees could be processed centrally, or that 3 million purchase orders for $6 billion worth of goods could be handled on a central basis. Yet in the fields of personnel, budgeting, and supply our task forces have found overcentralized operations which are resulting in inefficient and expensive management....

REORGANIZATION BY MAJOR PURPOSE

Improvements in such areas as authority, management tools, coordination, planning, procedures, and decentralization are not sufficient in themselves to bring about the maximum degree of efficiency in the options of the Government. The organizational structure of the executive branch must also undergo radical revision. Similarly, the departments and agencies themselves must be reorganized.

There are at present too many separate agencies to permit adequate attention and direction from the President. Many closely related functions also are so scattered that in certain fields such as labor, transportation, or medical services no one is charged with considering the problem as a whole.

Furthermore, many agencies contain functions which are totally unrelated to each other, if not inconsistent; creating a lack of central purpose and greatly increasing the problems of internal coordination.

Several areas of conflict, duplication and overlapping, at least partially due to faulty organization, have been cited.

In our previous reports we have made numerous recommendations designed to improve the organization structure of the executive branch, as well as the internal structure of the various departments and agencies.... Our studies have shown conclusively that the areas presenting the greatest problems of duplication and coordination are those in which services of a similar nature are located in different agencies in the executive branch. This dispersion of related locations has led to interagency rivalries and conflicts which have been extremely wasteful and costly.

Solution

In recommending reorganization changes it has been our constant objective to achieve the greatest possible degree of unity in the departmental structure. We have been mindful, too, of the excessive burden on the President of having so many agencies report to him. In our first report we recommend as a desirable goal, the reduction of the total number of agencies reporting to the President to about one-third of their present number. While it has not been entirely possible to reach this objective, we have, nevertheless, made recommendations which will reduce the total number of agencies so reporting, to what, in our judgment, is the smallest number feasible if a maximum unity of purpose in each department is also to be achieved.

To strengthen the organization of the principal central staff services we have recommended a consolidation of the functions of supply, records management, and buildings management in an Office of General Services.

To restore the Treasury Department to its historic role in fiscal matters and to remove from it options which are unrelated to its major purpose, we have recommended that the

Bureau of Narcotics, the Coast Guard, and the Bureau of Federal Supply be transferred to other departments and that the Treasury become the focal point for the proposed central accounting system.

To integrate the scattered transportation functions of the executive branch, we have recommended combining within a single transportation service in the Department of Commerce such related functions as those of the Maritime Commission relating to the construction, operation, charter and sale of ships, the Coast Guard, the National Advisory Committee for Aeronautics, the Public Roads Administration, the Office of Defense Transportation, and certain transportation safety functions of the Civil Aeronautics Board and Interstate Commerce Commission.

To remove the major areas of overlapping and duplication, we have recommended that the functions of flood control and river and harbor improvement work of the Army Corps of Engineers be consolidated with the Reclamation Service within the Department of the Interior. Similarly, we have recommended that the Bureau of Land Management in Interior be consolidated with the Forest Service in Agriculture.

Finally, in the field of labor we have recommended that several important labor and manpower functions such as the Bureau of Employees Compensation, and Selective Service System be transferred to the Department of Labor.

These are typical examples of reorganization proposals that we have made to achieve greater over-all efficiency and improved coordination in the executive branch by grouping services and activities according to major purpose.

President Richard M. Nixon, *Special Message to the Congress on Executive Branch Reorganization*, March 25, 1971.

The last two years have been a time of renewed interest in the question of how government is organized. The Congress has instituted a number of reforms in its own procedures and is considering others. Judicial reform–at all levels of government–has also become a matter of intense concern. The relationship between various levels of government has attracted increased attention–and so, of course, has the subject of executive reform.

This administration, with the counsel and the cooperation of the Congress, has taken a number of steps to reorganize the executive branch of the Federal Government. We have set up a new Domestic Council and a new Office of Management and Budget in the Executive Office of the President. We have created a new Environmental Protection Agency and a new United States Postal Service. We have worked to rationalize the internal structure of Federal departments and agencies.

All of these and other changes have been important, but none has been comprehensive. And now we face a fundamental choice. We can continue to tinker with the machinery and to make constructive changes here and there–each of them bringing some marginal improvement in the Government's capacities. Or we can step back, take a careful look, and then make a concerted and sustained effort to reorganize the executive branch according to a coherent, comprehensive view of what the Federal Government of this Nation ought to look like in the last third of the twentieth century. . . .

THE FRAGMENTATION OF FEDERAL RESPONSIBILITY

As we reflect on organizational problems in the Federal Government today, one seems to stand out above all others: the fact that the capacity to do things–the power to achieve goals and to solve problems–is exceedingly fragmented and broadly scattered throughout the Federal establishment. In addressing almost any of the great challenges of our time, the Federal Government finds itself speaking through a wide variety of offices and bureaus, departments and agencies. Often these units trip over one another as they move to meet a common problem. Sometimes they step on one another's toes. Frequently, they behave like a series of fragmented fiefdoms–unable to focus Federal resources or energies in a way which produces any concentrated impact. Consider these facts:

Nine different Federal departments and twenty independent agencies are now involved in education matters. Seven departments and eight independent agencies are involved in health. In many major cities, there are at least twenty or thirty separate manpower programs, funded by a variety of Federal offices. Three departments help develop our water resources and four agencies in two departments are involved in the management of public lands. Federal recreation areas are administered by six different agencies in three departments of the government. Seven agencies provide assistance for water and sewer systems. Six departments of the government collect similar economic information—often from the same sources—and at least seven departments are concerned with international trade. While we cannot eliminate all of this diffusion, we can do a great deal to bring similar functions under common commands.

It is important that we move boldly to consolidate the major activities of the Government. The programmatic jumble has already reached the point where it is virtually impossible to obtain an accurate count of just how many Federal grant programs exist. Some estimates go as high as 1,500. Despite impressive attempts by individual legislators and by the Office of Economic Opportunity, there is still no agreement on a comprehensive list. Again and again I hear of local officials who are unable to determine how many Federal programs serve their areas or how much Federal money is coming into their communities. One reason is that the assistance comes from such wide variety of Federal sources.

THE CONSEQUENCES OF SCATTERED RESPONSIBILITY

What are the consequences of this scattering of Federal responsibility? There are many.

In the first place, the diffusion of responsibility makes it extremely difficult to launch a coordinated attack on complex problems. It is as if the various units of an attacking army were operating under a variety of highly independent commands. When one part of the answer to a problem lies in one department and other parts lie in other departments, it is often impossible to bring the various parts together in a unified campaign to achieve a common goal.

Even our basic analysis of public needs often suffers from a piecemeal approach. Problems are defined so that they will fit within established jurisdictions and bureaucratic conventions. And the results of government action are typically measured by the degree of activity within each program rather than by the overall impact of related activities on the outside world.

The role of a given department in the policy making process can be fundamentally compromised by the way its mission is defined. The narrower the mission, the more likely it is that the department will see itself as an advocate within the administration for a special point of view. When any department or agency begins to represent a parochial interest, then its advice and support inevitably become less useful to the man who must serve all of the people as their President.

Even when departments make a concerted effort to broaden their perspectives, they often find it impossible to develop a comprehensive strategy for meeting public needs. Not even the best planners can set intelligent spending priorities, for example, unless they have an opportunity to consider the full array of alternative expenditures. But if one part of the problem is studied in one department and another part of the problem is studied elsewhere, who decides which element is more important? If one office considers one set of solutions and a separate agency investigates another set of solutions, who can compare the results? Too often, no official below the very highest levels of the Government has access to enough information to make such comparisons wisely. The result is that the

Government often fails to make a rational distribution of its resources among a number of program alternatives.

Divided responsibility can also mean that some problems slip between the cracks and disappear from the Government's view. Everybody's business becomes nobody's business and embarrassing gaps appear which no agency attempts to fill. At other times, various Federal authorities act as rivals, competing with one another for the same piece of "turf."

Sometimes one agency will actually duplicate the work of another; for instance, the same locality may receive two or more grants for the same project. On other occasions, Federal offices will actually find themselves working at cross purposes with one another; one agency will try to preserve a swamp, for example, while another is seeking to drain it. In an effort to minimize such problems, government officials must spend enormous amounts of time and energy negotiating with one another that should be directed toward meeting people's needs. And even when they are able to work out their differences, officials often reach compromise solutions which merely represent the lowest common denominator of their original positions. Bold and original ideas are thus sacrificed in the quest for intergovernmental harmony.

Scattered responsibility also contributes to the over-centralization of public decision making. Because competing offices are often in different chains of command, it is frequently impossible for them to resolve their differences except by referring them to higher authorities, a process which can mean interminable delays. In an attempt to provide a means for resolving such differences and for providing needed coordination, an entire new layer of bureaucracy has emerged at the interagency level. Last year, the Office of Management and Budget counted some 850 interagency committees. Even so, there are still many occasions when only the White House itself can resolve such inter-jurisdictional disputes. Too many questions thus surface at the Presidential level that should be resolved at levels of Government closer to the scene of the action.

Inefficient organization at the Federal level also undermines the effectiveness of State and local governments. Mayors and Governors waste countless hours and dollars touching base with a variety of Federal offices—each with its own separate procedures and its own separate policies. Some local officials are so perplexed by the vast array of Federal programs in a given problem area that they miss out on the very ones that would be most helpful to them. Many State and local governments find they must hire expensive specialists to guide them through the jungles of the Federal bureaucracy.

If it is confusing for lower levels of government to deal with this maze of Federal offices, that challenge can be even more bewildering for individual citizens. Whether it is a doctor seeking aid for a new health center, a businessman trying to get advice about selling in foreign markets, or a welfare recipient going from one office to another in order to take full advantage of Federal services, the people whom the Government is supposed to be serving are often forced to weave their way through a perplexing obstacle course as a condition of receiving help.

ORGANIZING AROUND GOALS

As we look at the present organization of the Federal Government, we find that many of the existing units deal with methods and subjects rather than with purposes and goals. If we have a question about labor we go to the Labor Department and if we have a business problem we go to the Commerce Department. If we are interested in housing we go to one department and if we are interested in highways we go to another.

The problem is that as our society has become more complex, we often find ourselves using a variety of means to achieve a single set of goals. We are interested, for example, in economic development–which requires new markets, more productive workers and better transportation systems. But which department do we go to for that? And what if we want to build a new city, with sufficient public facilities, adequate housing, and decent recreation areas–which department do we petition then?

We sometimes seem to have forgotten that government is not in business to deal with subjects on a chart but to achieve real objectives for real human beings. These objectives will never be fully achieved unless we change our old ways of thinking. It is not enough merely to reshuffle departments for the sake of reshuffling them. We must rebuild the executive branch according to a new understanding of how government can best be organized to perform effectively.

The key to that new understanding is the concept that the executive branch of the government should be organized around basic goals. Instead of grouping activities by narrow subjects or by limited constituencies, we should organize them around the great purposes of government in modern society. For only when a department is set up to achieve a given set of purposes, can we effectively hold that department accountable for achieving them. Only when the responsibility for realizing basic objectives is clearly focused in a specific governmental unit, can we reasonably hope that those objectives will be realized.

When government is organized by goals, then we can fairly expect that it will pay more attention to results and less attention to procedures. Then the success of government will at last be clearly linked to the things that happen in society rather than the things that happen in government.

Under the proposals which I am submitting, those in the Federal Government who deal with common or closely related problems would work together in the same organizational framework. Each department would be given a mission broad enough so that it could set comprehensive policy directions and resolve internally the policy conflicts which are most likely to arise. The responsibilities of each department would be defined in a way that minimizes parochialism and enables the President and the Congress to hold specific officials responsible for the achievement of specific goals.

These same organizational principles would also be applied to the internal organization of each department. Similar functions would be grouped together within each new entity, making it still easier to delegate authority to lower levels and further enhancing the accountability of subordinate officials. In addition, the proposals I submit today include a number of improvements in the management of Federal programs, so that we can take full advantage of the opportunities afforded us by organizational restructuring.

The administration is today transmitting to the Congress four bills which, if enacted, would replace seven of the present executive departments and several other agencies with four new departments: the Department of Natural Resources, the Department of Community Development, the Department of Human Resources and the Department of Economic Affairs. A special report and summary–which explain my recommendations in greater detail have also been prepared for each of the proposed new departments.

President Jimmy Carter, *Department of Energy Message to the Congress Transmitting Proposed Legislation*, March 1, 1977.

To the Congress of the United States:

I hereby transmit to the Congress proposed legislation which will create a new Cabinet Department of Energy.

This legislation is a major step in my Administration's program for a comprehensive reorganization of the Executive Branch.

Nowhere is the need for reorganization and consolidation greater than in energy policy. All but two of the Executive Branch's Cabinet departments now have some responsibility for energy policy, but no agency, anywhere in the Federal government, has the broad authority needed to deal with our energy problems in a comprehensive way.

The legislation I am submitting today will bring immediate order to this fragmented system:

- It will abolish the Federal Energy Administration, the Energy Research and Development Administration, and the Federal Power Commission, thereby eliminating three agencies whose missions overlap and sometimes conflict, and whose specialized perspectives have impeded progress toward a unified energy policy.
- It will allow us, for the first time, to match our research and development program to our overall energy policies and needs. This is particularly important if we are to make use of renewable energy sources such as solar power.
- It will enable us to move more quickly toward effective energy conservation by combining conservation programs which are now split between FEA and ERDA. And, to make certain that we will see results, the legislation creates an Assistant Secretary for Conservation, who will be personally responsible for seeing that the conservation program is carried out.
- It will place under one roof the powers to regulate fuels and fuel distribution systems, powers which are now shared by the FEA and the FPC along with the Securities and Exchange Commission and the Interstate Commerce Commission. An institutional structure built on the premise that fossil fuels are abundant and cheap no longer serves well in an era of fuel scarcity.

As this winter has shown us, uncoordinated regulatory policies can have serious impacts on our economic and social well-being. This reorganization can help us bring currently fragmented policies into a structure capable of both developing and implementing an overall national energy plan. At the same time, we must guard the quasi-judicial aspects of the regulatory process against improper influence. The legislation meets this concern by establishing a Board of Hearings and Appeals within the Department which is free from the control of the Secretary of Energy.

In addition to abolishing the FEA, ERDA, and the FPC, the legislation submitted today will transfer into the new Department several significant energy-related authorities and programs which now belong to other departments. These include the building thermal efficiency standards from Housing and Urban Development, the voluntary industrial compliance program from Commerce, and the Navy petroleum and oil shale reserves from Defense. The legislation provides for consultation between the Energy Department and the Department of Transportation on auto fuel efficiency standards, and establishes a role for the Energy Secretary in the REA loan program at Agriculture.

Where it is appropriate, these departments will still carry out the program, but the new Energy Department will give them the policy guidance needed to bring unity and rational order to our energy program.

Finally, this legislation transfers certain parts of the Interior Department—those concerning fuels data collection .and analysis, and coal mine research and development—into the new Department. Coal mine health and safety research will not be transferred. This will leave the Department of Interior still in charge of leasing energy resources under Federal control. We are leaving those functions in Interior because we believe that the responsibility for multiple-use of public lands, and for their environmental protection, belongs in one department—Interior—that can reflect a broad spectrum of concern. The Energy Department, however, will set long-term production goals and will have policy control over economic aspects of the leases. This will help us foster competition within the energy industries and encourage production of leased resources as expeditiously as possible.

This reorganization will also bring together our energy data gathering and analysis capabilities. More than twenty executive departments and agencies now operate more than 250 energy data programs. The FEA, ERDA, FPC and the Interior Department's Bureau of Mines together have more than 100 such programs. This fragmentation is not only uneconomic and frustrating: it can also have serious consequences. We have seen in recent weeks that, under our present system, we have no single source of information about where natural gas shortages were greatest and where supplies were still available to help make up those shortages. Consolidating these major data programs in an Energy Information Administration within the new department will now give us the ability to compile information which is complete, accurate and believable.

There are many things this legislation does not try to do.

I believe that health, safety and environmental regulation relating to energy—unlike economic regulation—should not be brought into the new Energy Department. Because public concerns about the safety of nuclear power are so serious, we must have a strong, independent voice to ensure that safety does not yield to energy supply pressures. Therefore, the Nuclear Regulatory Commission will remain as an independent body. For similar reasons, the Environmental Protection Agency should remain independent to voice environmental concern.

Even with a new Department of Energy, problems of interdepartmental coordination will remain, since virtually all government activity affects energy to some extent. Establishing this department, however, will give us one government body with sufficient scope and authority to do the massive job that remains to be done. Thus this legislation will abolish the Energy Resources Council. I intend to establish by Executive Order a non-statutory interdepartmental coordinating body, with the Secretary of Energy as its chairman to manage government-wide concerns involving energy.

This legislation contains no new substantive authorities. Instead, by eliminating three agencies and uniting a variety of existing energy authorities, the legislation I am submitting today will help reorganize the Executive Branch in a rational, orderly way. It is long overdue. I hope to work with the Congress to achieve our initial goal of a realistic and effective energy policy.

JIMMY CARTER
The White House
March 1, 1977

The 9/11 Commission Report: Final Report of the National Commission on Terrorist Attacks Upon the United States (New York: W.W. Norton, 2004).

THE NEED FOR A CHANGE

During the Cold War, intelligence agencies did not depend on seamless integration to track and count the thousands of military targets—such as tanks and missiles—fielded by the Soviet Union and other adversary states. Each agency concentrated on its specialized mission, acquiring its own information and then sharing it via formal, finished reports. The Department of Defense had given birth to and dominated the main agencies for technical collection of intelligence. Resources were shifted at an incremental pace, coping with challenges that arose over years, even decades. . . .

BOX 2-1 Members of the U.S. Intelligence Community

Office of the Director of Central Intelligence, which includes the Office of the Deputy Director of Central Intelligence for Community Management, the Community Management Staff, the Terrorism Threat Integration Center, the National Intelligence Council, and other community offices.

The Central Intelligence Agency (CIA), which performs human source collection, all-source analysis, and advanced science and technology.

National Intelligence Agencies

- National Security Agency (NSA), which performs signals collection and analysis
- National Geospatial-Intelligence Agency (NGA), which performs imagery collection and analysis National Reconnaissance Office (NRO), which develops, acquires, and launches space systems for intelligence collection
- Other national reconnaissance programs

Departmental Intelligence Agencies

- Defense Intelligence Agency (DIA) of the Department of Defense
- Intelligence entities of the Army, Navy, Air Force, and Marines
- Bureau of Intelligence and Research (INR) of the Department of State
- Office of Terrorism and Finance Intelligence of the Department of Treasury
- Office of Intelligence and the Counterterrorism and Counterintelligence Divisions of the Federal Bureau of Investigation of the Department of Justice
- Office of Intelligence of the Department of Energy
- Directorate of Information Analysis and Infrastructure Protection (IAIP) and Directorate of Coast Guard Intelligence of the Department of Homeland Security

The need to restructure the intelligence community grows out of six problems that have become apparent before and after 9/11:

- *Structural barriers to performing joint intelligence work.* National intelligence is still organized around the collection disciplines of the home agencies, not the joint mission. The importance of integrated, all-source analysis cannot be overstated. Without it, it is not possible to "connect the dots." No one component holds all the relevant information.

  By contrast, in organizing national defense, the Goldwater-Nichols legislation of 1986 created joint commands for operations in the field, the Unified Command Plan. The services—the Army, Navy, Air Force, and Marine Corps—organize, train, and equip their people and units to perform their missions. Then they assign personnel and units to the joint combatant commander, like the commanding general of the Central Command (CENTCOM). The Goldwater-Nichols Act required officers to serve tours outside their service in order to win promotion. The culture of the Defense Department was transformed, its collective mind-set moved from service-specific to "joint," and its operations became more integrated.[1]
- *Lack of common standards and practices across the foreign-domestic divide.* The leadership of the intelligence community should be able to pool information gathered overseas with information gathered in the United States, holding the work—wherever it is done—to a common standard of quality in how it is collected, processed (e.g., translated), reported, shared, and analyzed. A common set of personnel standards for intelligence can create a group of professionals better able to operate in joint activities, transcending their own service-specific mind-sets.
- *Divided management of national intelligence capabilities.* While the CIA was once "central" to our national intelligence capabilities, following the end of the Cold it has been less able to influence the use of the nation's imagery and signals intelligence capabilities in three national agencies housed within the Department of Defense: the National Security Agency, the National Geospatial-Intelligence Agency, and the National Reconnaissance Office. One of the lessons learned from the 1991 Gulf War was the value of national intelligence systems (satellites in particular) in precision warfare. Since that war, the department has appropriately drawn these agencies into its trans-formation of the military. Helping to orchestrate this transformation is the under secretary of defense for intelligence, a position established by Congress after 9/11. An unintended consequence of these developments has been the far greater demand made by Defense on technical systems, leaving the DCI less able to influence how these technical resources are allocated and used.
- *Weak capacity to set priorities and move resources.* The agencies are mainly organized around what they collect or the way they collect it. But the priorities for collection are national. As the DCI makes hard choices about moving resources, he or she must have the power to reach across agencies and reallocate effort.
- *Too many jobs.* The DCI now has at least three jobs. He is expected to run a particular agency, the CIA. He is expected to manage the loose confederation of agencies that is the intelligence community. He is expected to be the analyst in chief for the government, sifting evidence and directly briefing the President as his principal

intelligence adviser. No recent DCI has been able to do all three effectively. Usually what loses out is management of the intelligence community, a difficult task even in the best case because the DCI's current authorities are weak. With so much to do, the DCI often has not used even the authority he has. . . .

Recommendation: The current position of Director of Central Intelligence should be replaced by a National Intelligence Director with two main areas of responsibility: (1) to oversee national intelligence centers on specific subjects of interest across the U.S. government and (2) to manage the national intelligence program and oversee the agencies that contribute to it.

First, the National Intelligence Director should oversee *national intelligence centers* to provide all-source analysis and plan intelligence operations for the whole government on major problems.

- One such problem is counterterrorism. In this case, we believe that the center should be the intelligence entity (formerly TTIC) inside the National Counterterrorism Center we have proposed. It would sit there alongside the operations management unit we described earlier, with both making up the NCTC, in the Executive Office of the President. Other national intelligence centers—for instance, on counterproliferation, crime and narcotics, and China—would be housed in whatever department or agency is best suited for them.
- The National Intelligence Director would retain the present DCI's role as the principal intelligence adviser to the president. We hope the president will come to look directly to the directors of the national intelligence centers to provide all-source analysis in their areas of responsibility, balancing the advice of these intelligence chiefs against the contrasting viewpoints that may be offered by department heads at State, Defense, Homeland Security, Justice, and other agencies.

Second, the National Intelligence Director should manage the national intelligence program and oversee the component agencies of the intelligence community. . . .[2]

The National Intelligence Director should participate in an NSC executive committee that can resolve differences in priorities among the agencies and bring the major disputes to the president for decision. The National Intelligence Director should be located in the Executive Office of the President. This official, who would be confirmed by the Senate and would testify before Congress, would have a relatively small staff of several hundred people, taking the place of the existing community management offices housed at the CIA.

In managing the whole community, the National Intelligence Director is still providing a service function. With the partial exception of his or her responsibilities for overseeing the NCTC, the National Intelligence Director should support the consumers of national intelligence—the president and policymaking advisers such as the secretaries of state, defense, and homeland security and the attorney general.

We are wary of too easily equating government management problems with those of the private sector. But we have noticed that some very large private firms rely on a powerful CEO who has significant control over how money is spent and can hire or fire leaders of the major divisions, assisted by a relatively modest staff, while leaving responsibility for execution in the operating divisions.

There are disadvantages to separating the position of National Intelligence Director will not head a major agency of his or her own and may have a weaker base of support. But we believe that these disadvantages are outweighed by several other considerations:

- The National Intelligence Director must be able to directly oversee intelligence collection inside the United States. Yet law and custom has counseled against giving such a plain domestic role to the head of the CIA.
- The CIA will be one among several claimants for funds in setting national priorities. The National Intelligence Director should not be both one of the advocates and the judge of them all.
- Covert operations tend to be highly tactical, requiring close attention. The National Intelligence Director should rely on the relevant joint mission center to oversee these details, helping to coordinate closely with the White House. The CIA will be able to concentrate on building the capabilities to carry out such operations and on providing the personnel who will be directing and executing such operations in the field.
- Rebuilding the analytic and human intelligence collection capabilities of the CIA should be a full-time effort, and the director of the CIA should focus on extending its comparative advantages.

Urgent Business for America: Revitalizing the Federal Government for the 21st Century, Report of the National Commission on the Public Service (The Volcker Commission Report), January 2003.

. . . In this technological age, the government's widening span of interests inevitably leads to complications as organizations need to coordinate policy implementation. But as things stand, it takes too long to get even the clearest policies implemented. There are too many decision makers, too much central clearance, too many bases to touch, and too many overseers with conflicting agendas. Leadership responsibilities often fall into the awkward gap between inexperienced political appointees and unsupported career managers. Accountability is hard to discern and harder still to enforce. Policy change has become so difficult that federal employees themselves often come to share the cynicism about government that afflicts many of our citizens.

The system has evolved not by plan or considered analysis but by accretion over time, politically inspired tinkering, and neglect. Over time the "civil service system" was perceived as a barrier to effective government performance. Few leaders in Washington, even those who understood the importance of revitalizing the public service, were willing to expend the political capital deemed necessary to do so. And government reorganization has come to be viewed as a task so daunting, requiring such extensive and excruciating political negotiations, that it takes a national emergency to bring it about.

Without government reorganization, it will be very difficult to revitalize the public service. The fact of the matter is that we need both government reorganization and revitalization of the public service. Without structure and organization, no political leaders or body of public servants will be able to do the kind of job the citizens want and demand.

Recognition that there is much wrong with the current organization and management of the public service is widespread today. It stimulated the creation of this National Commission on the Public Service, and it has inspired our determined effort to call upon expert testimony and analysis to address what lies at the core of the current problems. We believe that the proposals in this report, when implemented, will make a significant difference in the quality of government performance.

The need to improve performance is urgent and compelling. The peace dividend many Americans expected from the end of the Cold War has quickly vanished in the face of new and sinister threats to our national security. The economic boom of the 1990s has ended, and Americans look to their government for fiscal and regulatory policies to cope with harsh new economic realities. The looming baby boomer retirement bulge will put greater pressure than ever before on government human services programs. Across the full range of government activities, new demands are accelerating, and the pace of change is quickening. At the same time, the federal government has had difficulty in adapting to the knowledge-based economy and taking advantage of the significant advances in technology.

The federal government is neither organized nor staffed nor adequately prepared to meet the demands of the 21st century. It was in recognition of that fact that the President found it necessary last year to propose the most sweeping change in the organization of the federal government in decades by creating the new Department of Homeland Security. But that imperfect reorganization covers only part of the government. With every passing day, the gap between expectations and responsive capacity is growing. If we do not make the necessary changes now, when our needs are clear, we will be forced to cope with the consequences later in crisis after crisis.

In this report, we have not shied away from proposing radical change. Our analysis and recommendations may discomfort parts of our audience. We accept that inevitability for a simple but important reason: the current organization of the federal government and the operation of public programs are not good enough. They are not good enough for the American people, not good enough to meet the extraordinary challenges of the century just beginning, and not good enough for the hundreds of thousands of talented federal workers who hate the constraints that keep them from serving their country with the full measure of their talents and energy. We must do better, much better, and soon.

The Organization of the Government: Fundamental reorganization of the federal government is urgently needed to improve its capacity for coherent design and efficient implementation of public policy.

The structure of the federal government is outmoded. Some programs no longer have viable missions. More often, too many agencies share responsibilities that could profitably be combined. Decision-making is too often entangled in knots of conflict, clearance, coordination, and delay. The necessity for coordination and consultation cannot be permitted to overwhelm and needlessly delay decision-making.

The simple reality is that federal public servants are constrained by their organizational environment. Changes in federal personnel systems will have limited impact if they are not accompanied by significant change in the operating structure of the executive branch. This is why we begin our recommendations with an emphasis on issues of organization.

Every agency has—or should have—a clear mission with structures and processes that follow from their particular responsibilities. With rare exception, agencies with related mandates should fit together in a broad organizational scheme that permits and encourages constructive interaction rather than battles over turf. Federal departments should be reorganized to bring together agencies that contribute to a broad mission in a manner responsible to direction from elected leaders and their appointees, and subject to careful oversight by Congress but sufficiently independent in administration to achieve their missions.

Recommendation 1: The federal government should be reorganized into a limited number of mission-related executive departments.

As the debate about homeland security illustrated, large-scale reorganization of the federal government is no easy task. In some ways, the barriers to success are compounded by a piecemeal approach. Consequently, we urge a broader, more comprehensive vision, recognizing that implementation will take considerable determination and time. The basic point is that a significant change in structure is essential for the responsive and efficient implementation of public policy that the new century demands.

Our goal is enhanced mission coherence and role clarification. Federal agencies that share closely related missions should be administered by the same organizational entity. A few large departments in which those agencies are grouped together should enhance their employees' sense of purpose and loyalty, provide opportunities for advancement and job mobility, and encourage interagency cooperation. It is a much more sensible approach to government organization than the current pattern in which agencies with similar responsibilities have been scattered throughout the government.

The reorganization that we recommend here will require significant improvements in the quality of top executives, in the management of operating units, and in the ability of agencies to meet their unique staffing needs. There must also be clearer definition of the distinct roles of federal employees. Those charged with policy decisions should be political appointees, most of whom would work in the central offices of the large departments. Under the secretary would be deputy, under, and assistant secretaries to manage the budget and policy development. Although we contemplate that these appointees would oversee the individual operating agencies within their departments, operational responsibility would be delegated to the operating agencies. This would promote the dual advantages of mission cohesion and of smaller operating units. . . .

> Recommendation 2: **The operating agencies in these new executive departments should be run by managers chosen for their operational skills and given the authority to develop management and personnel systems appropriate to their missions.**

Subject to clear objectives and performance criteria, these agencies should be given substantial flexibility in the choice of subordinate organizational structure and personnel systems. Employees government wide should continue to have the basic employment guarantees of merit hiring, nondiscrimination, and protection from arbitrary or political personnel actions. These grants of authority would be defined by the President and subject to oversight by the Office of Management and Budget and the Office of Personnel Management, as well as Congress. The Office of Personnel Management, the management side of OMB, and human resources and management specialists government wide have been subjected to personnel reductions in recent years. The added responsibilities recommended here will require a strengthening of these capabilities.

Many agencies currently have executives who serve in the role of chief management or operating officer, either by administrative appointment or by statute. The new Department of Homeland Security will have a presidentially appointed, Senate confirmed, Undersecretary for Management. There is considerable support for the view that such an officer can provide important management focus, particularly where the leadership of the agency is focused on policy development and implementation. We recommend that the decision as to whether such a position should exist be considered on an agency-by-agency basis, at smaller as well as larger agencies.

Of particular importance is that managers, whether political or career, have the appropriate experience, training, and skills to manage effectively. This should be a priority for the President in identifying executives for appointment and a matter for congressional inquiry during the confirmation process. Finally, we recommend that Congress pay particular attention to the management implications of any legislation it considers.

Recommendation 3: The President should be given expedited authority to recommend structural reorganization of federal agencies and departments.

We recommend a qualified restoration of the President's authority to reorganize departments and agencies as the most efficient way to ensure that the operations of the federal government keep pace with the demands placed upon it. We suggest as a model the executive reorganization authority that began with the Reorganization Act of 1932 (5 USC 901 et seq.) and continued with its successor statutes through the middle decades of the 20th century.

We would assign the initiating role to the President. He would propose structural reorganizations or new management approaches that would contribute to the accomplishment of agency missions. In general, these proposals would take into account recommendations from the departments and agencies, from the President's policy and management advisers, and from Congress and its committees.

To take effect, these proposals would have to be approved by Congress. But such reorganization proposals would have two characteristics intended to ensure both their coherence and a timely congressional response. Specifically, we suggest that each proposal:

- Not be subject to amendment,
- Be given an up-or-down vote within 45 legislative days of submission.

With these characteristics, Congress could reject a reorganization proposal through a majority vote against approval in either chamber.

Recommendation 4: The House and Senate should realign their committee oversight to match the mission-driven reorganization of the executive branch.

Operating agencies desperately need the support of an active Congress if they are to perform effectively. At the same time, broad grants of administrative flexibility demand effective congressional oversight, transparency, and clear reporting relationships, which in turn require that congressional committees and subcommittees organize themselves around the same central missions as the departments of the executive branch.

A mismatch of missions reduces Congress's ability to provide broad effective oversight and can lead instead to micromanagement of those aspects of agency activities that happen to be most visible.

At critical junctures in its past—in 1911, in 1946, and in 1973—Congress has reorganized its committee jurisdictions to reflect changes in the country and in the executive branch. As the executive branch evolves in the new century, the organization of Congress must evolve as well.

Brian Balogh, Joanna Grislinger, and Philip Zelikow, *Making Democracy Work: A Brief History of Twentieth Century Executive Reorganization* (Charlottesville, VA: Miller Center of Public Affairs, 2002).

Milestones in Twentieth-Century EXECUTIVE REORGANIZATION

	ACTIONS	STUDIES/COMMISSIONS/PROPOSALS
2002		President Bush proposes Department of Homeland Security
1995	ICC Terminated	
1993	Government Performance and Results Act	President Clinton forms National Performance Review. Issues report From Red Tape to Results: Creating a Government that Works Better and Costs Less; recommendations include: • closing field offices of the Department of Agriculture [implemented 1994] • simplifying federal purchasing procedures [implemented 1994]
1989	Department of Veterans Affairs becomes cabinet department; created from Veterans Administration	
1986	Goldwater-Nichols Department of Defense Reorganization Act • reorganizes Department of Defense	

Year	ACTIONS	STUDIES/COMMISSIONS/PROPOSALS
1985	Civil Aeronautics Board is eliminated Balanced Budget and Emergency Deficit Control Act (Gramm/Rudman/Hollings)	
1984		Grace Commission (established by President Reagan in 1982) issues President's Private Sector Survey on Cost Control: A Report to the President (2 vols.); also published as J. Peter Grace, War on Waste: President's Private Sector Survey on Cost Control (New York: Macmillan, 1984).
1980	Paperwork Reduction Act: establishes Office of Information and Regulatory Affairs	
1979	Department of Education created [absorbed education functions from Department of Health, Education and Welfare] Department of Health and Human Services created [absorbed non-education functions from Department of Health, Education and Welfare] Office of Personnel Management formed from Civil Service Commission	
1978	Federal Emergency Management Agency established by combining Office of Civil Defense with related functions in other agencies Civil Service Reform Act Ethics in Government Act	
1977	Department of Energy created [containing agencies/functions of Energy Research and Development Administration, Nuclear Regulatory Commission, Federal Energy Administration functions moved to or absorbed by Department of Energy, Economic Regulatory Administration]	Carter establishes Presidential Reorganization Project within the Office of Management and Budget; recommendations include: • creating Department of Energy [established 1977] • creating Department of Education [established 1979] • creating Department of Natural Resources [not implemented]

Year	ACTIONS	STUDIES/COMMISSIONS/PROPOSALS
1976	Government in the Sunshine Act	
1974	Freedom of Information Act Amendments passed; Privacy Act passed	
1972	Consumer Product Safety Commission established	
1970	Environmental Protection Agency created Occupational Safety and Health Administration created [Department of Labor] Domestic Council and Office of Management and Budget [previously Bureau of the Budget] established in the Executive Office via reorganization plan Federal Pay Comparability Act	
1969		Nixon creates Advisory Council on Government Organization [Ash Council]; Ash Council produces several memos between 1969–1971; recommendations include: • reorganizing Executive Office to create a Domestic Policy Council and to create Office of Management and Budget from Bureau of the Budget [Nixon implemented through a reorganization plan in 1970] • reorganizing current executive branch environmental functions [Environmental Protection Agency created by reorganization plan in 1970] • abolishing Departments of Agriculture; Interior; Commerce; Health, Education and Welfare; Housing and Urban Development; Labor; and Transportation, and transfer functions of those departments, and related independent agencies, into 4 new 'super-departments' of Natural Resources, Economic Affairs, Human Resources, and Community Development [not implemented] • creating new staff officers for program administration and coordination [not implemented]

Year	ACTIONS	STUDIES/COMMISSIONS/PROPOSALS
1967		Heineman Task Force submits reports to Johnson; recommendations include: • reorganization of executive branch into new, larger 'super departments' including departments of Social Services, National Resources, Economic Affairs, Science and Environmental Preservation, Department of Foreign Affairs, and Department of National Security Affairs [none of these changes implemented] • expanding the Executive Office and the president's staff, to include new offices of program coordination and program development [not implemented]
1966	Department of Transportation is created [includes Federal Highway Administration, Federal Railroad Administration, Federal Aviation Administration, National Transportation Safety Board, St. Lawrence Seaway Development Corporation, United States Coast Guard] <u>Freedom of Information Act</u>	President Johnson forms his second Task Force on Government Organization, chaired by Ben Heineman [Heineman Task Force]
1965	Department of Housing and Urban Development is established Equal Employment Opportunity Commission created	
1964		President Johnson forms Task Force on Government Reorganization [Price Task Force] recommendations include: • creating new executive departments regarding Housing and Community Development [Department of Housing and Urban Development established in 1965], Transportation [established in 1966], Education [created by Carter in 1977], Economic Development [not implemented] and Natural Resources [not implemented]
1962		President Kennedy proposes the Department of Housing and Urban Development in a reorganization plan; House rejects. [eventually implemented in 1965]

Year	ACTIONS	STUDIES/COMMISSIONS/PROPOSALS
1961		President's Advisory Committee on Government Organization [PACGO] makes recommendations to Eisenhower, • including reorganizing the executive branch by creating new, larger departments (i.e. departments of Natural Resources and Transportation) and merging related functions therein; Eisenhower does not propose reorganization; [Department of Transportation created by Johnson in 1966]
1959		Congress establishes the Advisory Commission on Intergovernmental Relations
1958		PACGO submits Defense Department reorganization bill to President Eisenhower, giving Secretary of Defense a unified staff and more authority to manage the different service branches; Congress passes bill
1957		Congress appoints U.S. Joint Federal-State Action Committee; releases report 1960
1956	Government Budget and Accounting Procedure Act	
1955		Second Hoover Commission releases report; recommendations include: • creation of a Senior Civil Service [not implemented]

Year	ACTIONS	STUDIES/COMMISSIONS/PROPOSALS
1953	Department of Health, Education and Welfare created by Eisenhower through a reorganization plan [incorporates functions of Federal Security Agency]	President Eisenhower gives his Special Advisory Committee official status; it becomes the President's Advisory Committee on Government Organization [PACGO] Congress forms Commission on the Organization of the Executive Branch [Second Hoover Commission] Eisenhower forms Rockefeller Committee on DoD Organization; Committee issues Report of the Rockefeller Committee on Department of Defense Organization; recommendations include: • consolidating functions of the Munitions Board, the Research and Development Board, and the Defense Supply Management Agency in the Secretary of Defense [implemented in 1953 via reorganization act] • creating 6 additional Assistant Secretaries and a general counsel; increasing authority of chair of Joint Chiefs of Staff [implemented in 1953 via reorganization act] Congress forms Commission on Intergovernmental Relations, chaired by Meyer Kestnbaum, directed at issues of federalism; issued report in 1955; few changes made
1952		President Eisenhower creates Special Advisory Committee on Government Organization
1950	Budget and Accounting Procedures Act	

1949

ACTIONS

Reorganization Act passed, giving Truman authority to initiate reorganization plans

National Security Council and National Security Resources Board moved into Executive Office of the President under a reorganization plan

General Services Administration established [consolidating functions previously in Bureau of Federal Supply, Office of Contract Settlement, Federal Works Agency, Public Buildings Administration, National Archives, War Assets Administration]

Congress passes National Security Act of 1949
- creating Department of Defense from National Military Establishment [executive departments of Army, Navy, Air Force become military, not executive, departments]

Congress passes Reorganization of the Department of State Act
- State Department reorganized

Classification Act

STUDIES/COMMISSIONS/PROPOSALS

Hoover Commission (I) sends reports to Congress; recommendations include:
- increasing the president's staff and strengthening the Executive Office and Bureau of the Budget regarding administrative management [Truman implemented through reorganization plan]
- increasing authority of department heads over internal department organization [department head of Civil Service Commission strengthened through a 1949 reorganization plan]
- forming Department of Social Service and Education [Department of Health, Education and Welfare created by Eisenhower in 1953]
- centralizing purchasing, records management, and management of public buildings [General Services Administration established in 1949]
- increasing unification of military establishment, reorganizing National Security Council [Hoover Commission supported the amendments to the 1947 National Security Act that became the 1949 National Security Act]
- restructuring the Department of Agriculture, Interior and Commerce and reorganizing the functions therein [not implemented]
- reorganizing State Department [implemented]
- centralizing authority over accounting in the Treasury Department [not implemented]

1947

ACTIONS

Congress passes National Security Act of 1947, taking steps to unify military services

- National Military Establishment created [Department of War and Department of the Navy moved within NME; Department of Air Force established within NME]
- National Security Council created
- National Security Resources Board created
- Munitions Board created
- Research and Development Board created
- Central Intelligence Agency established [under National Security Council]

STUDIES/COMMISSIONS/PROPOSALS

Congress forms Commission on Organization of the Executive Branch of the Government [Hoover Commission], a bipartisan commission to examine reorganization

ACTIONS		STUDIES/COMMISSIONS/PROPOSALS
1946	Atomic Energy Commission established as an independent regulatory commission Congress passes Administrative Procedure Act, unifying procedure in administrative agencies	
1945	National Intelligence Authority established [precursor to Central Intelligence Agency] Federal Employees Pay Act	
1942	Office of Strategic Services established [precursor to National Intelligence Authority] War Production Board [until 1945] [WPB took over Advisory Commission to the Council of National Defense, Council of National Defense, National Defense Advisory Commission, and Office of Production Management, each 1940–41]	

1939	Congress passes Reorganization Act giving President Roosevelt reorganization authority over the executive branch and authorizing six executive assistants
	
	Under Reorganization Act, Roosevelt submits a reorganization plan creating the Executive Office of the President, and moving into it the Bureau of the Budget [from the Department of Treasury] and National Resources Planning Board
	• Federal Works Agency established by Roosevelt through a reorganization plan [until 1949] [under WPA] [recommended by Brownlow Commission?]
	• Federal Loan Agency established by Roosevelt through a reorganization plan
	• Federal Security Agency established by Roosevelt through a reorganization plan
	  • Social Security Board moved to Federal Security Agency
	  • United States Public Health Service moved to Federal Security Agency [from Treasury]
	  • Office of Education moved to Federal Security Agency [from Interior]	

	ACTIONS	STUDIES/COMMISSIONS/PROPOSALS
1938		Roosevelt's executive and judicial reorganization bills defeated in Senate
1937		Brookings Institution issues its report, Investigation of Executive Agencies of the Government. Report to the Select Committee to Investigate Agencies of the Federal Government to Congress Roosevelt submits executive reorganization plan, based on Brownlow Commission Report, to Congress Roosevelt submits judicial reorganization plan to Congress
1936	Senate and House formed Select Committees on Reorganization and began study of reorganization with the Brookings Institution in order to reduce costs and overlapping	President Roosevelt forms the President's Committee on Administrative Management, led by Louis Brownlow [Brownlow Committee] to study management of government major recommendations include: • expanding the White House staff, providing 6 executive assistants to the president [implemented by Congress in 1939 Reorganization Act] • creating an Executive Office of the President, to include responsibility for planning, budgeting and civil service through the Civil Service Administration, Bureau of the Budget, and National Resources Planning Board [Executive Office containing Bureau of Budget and National Resources Planning Board created by Roosevelt under his authority under the 1939 Reorganization Act] • strengthening the personnel system in the executive branch by expanding civil service "upward, outward, and downward" • reorganizing administrative agencies by bringing them under one of 12 major departments: State, Treasury, War, Justice, Post Office, Navy, Conservation, Agriculture, Commerce, Labor, Social Welfare [Federal Security Agency created by Roosevelt in 1939], Public Works [Federal Works Administration established by Roosevelt in 1939]

Year	ACTIONS	STUDIES/COMMISSIONS/PROPOSALS
1936		• increasing president's fiscal management power by giving him authority over expenditures, and providing Congress with a post-audit • strengthening managerial agencies especially dealing with budget, efficiency and planning and personnel
1935	Federal Bureau of Investigation [previously Bureau of Investigation] established National Labor Relations Board established	
1934	Federal Bureau of Investigation [previously Bureau of Investigation] established National Labor Relations Board established Federal Communications Commission established [previously Federal Radio Commission]	
1932	Congress passes Economy Act, granting President Hoover the first peacetime statutory reorganization authority to submit reorganization plans to Congress subject to a legislative veto	Hoover submits 11 reorganization plans to Congress; Congress rejects all proposals
1930	Veterans Administration created as independent agency • replaced earlier temporary units of Veterans' Bureau (1921–30), Bureau of Pensions (1833–1930), National Home for Disabled Volunteer Soldiers, Bureau of War Risk Insurance (1914–21) [elevated to cabinet status 1989]	
1927	Federal Radio Commission established	

Year	ACTIONS	STUDIES/COMMISSIONS/PROPOSALS
1924		Joint Committee on Reorganization issues report; among recommendations: • recommends moving the newly created Bureau of the Budget out of the Treasury Department and under the direct control of the president [eventually occurs 1939] • recommends moving the GAO to Treasury [not implemented] • recommends creation of a department of defense [eventually established 1949], a department of education and welfare [eventually established 1953], and an expanded commerce department
1921	Budget and Accounting Act passed by Congress • creates General Accounting Office as a legislative agency, and the Bureau of the Budget [later Office of Management and Budget] as an executive agency in the Department of Treasury	
1920	Federal Power Commission established	Congress forms Joint Committee on Reorganization
1918	Congress passes Overman Act, providing president reorganization authority for war-related matters	
1914	Federal Trade Commission created as an independent regulatory commission	
1913	Department of Commerce and Department of Labor created	

Year	ACTIONS	STUDIES/COMMISSIONS/PROPOSALS
1911		President Taft's inquiry into Re-Efficiency and Economy (established 1910) becomes Commission on Economy and Efficiency [Taft Commission] [report 1912] among Commission's recommendations: • proposal of an executive office of the president containing a Bureau of Central Administrative Control, a Central Division of Budgeting within the Bureau of Central Administrative Planning, and a reorganized Civil Service Commission [the Executive Office of the President would be created in 1939] [the Bureau of the Budget created in 1921 in Department of Treasury; moved to Executive Office of the President in 1939]
1908	Bureau of Investigation formed [becomes Federal Bureau of Investigation in 1935]	
1906	Bureau of Immigration and Naturalization created Department of Agriculture created	
1905		President Theodore Roosevelt establishes Commission on Department Methods, chaired by Charles Keep [Keep Commission]; commission lasts until 1909; among Keep Commission recommendations: • proposed a General Supply Committee to centralize government purchasing [was established as General Services Administration in 1949] • proposed an interdepartmental Statistics Committee [established by Roosevelt through executive order]
1903	Antitrust Division created in Department of Justice Department of Commerce and Labor established	

SOURCES: Paul C. Light, *The Tides of Reform: Making Government Work, 1945–1995* (New Haven: Yale University Press, 1997); Donald Whitnah, ed. *Government Agencies* (Westport, Conn.: Greenwood Press, 1983); Ronald Penoyer, *Directory of Federal Agencies*, 2nd Ed. (Center for the Study of American Business, 1980).

NOTES FOR CHAPTER 2

1. For the Goldwater-Nichols Act, see Pub. L. No. 99-433, 100 Stat. 992 (1986). For a general discussion of the Act, see Gordon Lederman, *Reorganizing the Joint Chiefs of Staff: The Goldwater-Nichols Act of 1986* (Westport, CT: Greenwood, 1999); James Locher, 2003, *Victory on the Patomac: The Goldwater-Nichols Act Unifies the Pentagon*, (College Station, TX: Texas A&M Univ. Press).
2. The new program would replace the existing National Foreign Intelligence Program.

CHAPTER 3

Agendas

INTRODUCTION

For much of the 20th century, presidents saw bureaucratic reorganization as a means to a very specific set of management ends. Early reorganization efforts, including those of Roosevelt, Truman, and Nixon, were driven by orthodox administrative principles developed during the Progressive Era. Seeking increased administrative efficiency and enhanced accountability, presidents attempted to group agencies and programs by content areas. Executive control of the bureaucracy was pursued through structural hierarchies and streamlined administrative processes. Efficiency and economy—key private sector values—also figured prominently in motivating early reorganization efforts.

As important as the management reform effort was to the process of governing, the impact of these traditional management principles was not limited to pursuit of technical goals. In an era dominated by an economic depression, two world wars, and rapid administrative growth, reorganization also was seen as a vehicle for managing political and social crises.

Although some reorganization efforts did generate key structural and managerial advancements, several fell short of the goals articulated by experts and blue ribbon commission members and failed to achieve the wholesale change sought by sitting presidents. The limited success of such aggressive reorganization efforts contributed to a fundamental shift in official approaches to reorganization, as well as to a change in the tone and content of academic literature on the subject.

For several reasons, the orthodoxy of Brownlow, Gulick, and Goodnow was slowly replaced by an orthodoxy of skepticism. Many reorganization efforts did not achieve their promise of fiscal savings or streamlined executive authority. Despite organizational attempts to slow the government's expansion, the bureaucracy continued to grow in size and complexity. Grouping agencies by major interest was similarly troublesome; identifying a singular purpose within large, multifaceted agencies was nearly impossible because of the complexity. Administrative agencies operated multiple programs, served numerous constituencies, and were accountable to multiple congressional committees. Issue networks and decentralization seemed to be a better way of dealing with the policy making and management reality rather than did top-down structures. As a direct result, scholars began to see the limits of structural reorganization and questioned its effectiveness as a way of dealing with administrative ailments. Academic analysis of reorganization attempts began to be more nuanced. By the mid 1970s, the traditional management-driven approach had lost its intellectual cache. Reflective of these changes, Jimmy Carter was the first to rely on a more diverse reorganization strategy, mixing management, policy, and political justifications for change. Carter's multifaceted approach seemed to be a more convincing and more effective path to reform, and it represented the replacement of the single-minded reorganization effort with a more targeted, politically astute strategy.

The articles in this chapter mark the transition away from the orthodox principles of Roosevelt, Truman, and Nixon and highlight the scholarly search for a new pattern of rules and considerations common to executive branch reorganization. This pursuit began by acknowledging the relationship between the President and Congress and thus between politics and administration. As such, they questioned the politics–administration dichotomy.

The authors included in this chapter are some of the most influential voices in the fields of public administration and organizational behavior. Their writing and public service greatly influenced mainstream scholarly opinion on the subject and helped to shape reorganization efforts throughout the 1960s, 1970s, and 1980s. The material in this chapter highlights problems raised when presidents attempt to reorganize without any acknowledgment of or attention to the role of Congress or of political negotiation. The material also emphasizes a president's inability to correct bureaucratic pathologies through structural adjustment alone. As a whole, the chapter reflects an intellectual effort to move beyond traditional notions of federal executive reorganization.

The chapter's first piece, an excerpt from Harvey C. Mansfield's article "Federal Executive Reorganization: Thirty Years of Experience," presents a very practical analysis of executive reorganization. His decidedly tactical perspective on the subject provides a deeper understanding of past presidential motives and the insight that reorganizations may have a negative side.

Herbert Kaufman's article "Reflections on Administrative Reorganization" makes a case for understanding reorganization as a political operation. He concludes that if properly conceptualized, reorganization efforts may yield profound benefits in terms of influence, policy, and communication.

Rufus Miles arrives at a similar understanding of the issue. In his piece "Considerations for a President Bent on Reorganization," Miles presents 13 specific criteria intended to inform reorganization efforts. His insights are at once practical and mindful of the theoretical and contextual complexities of a federal reorganization.

In his piece "Government Reorganization and Public Purpose," Caspar Weinberger echoes the orthodox administrative principles that motivated Nixon's quest for instituting a reorganization that featured four major departments. He argues that by strengthening the executive branch through centralized bureaucratic structures and by circumventing the inefficient congressional committee system, with its close ties to powerful special interests, administrative policy will become more effective. Weinberger is very clearly a strong advocate of unilateral executive reorganization; his view perpetuates the notion that a direct link exists between a change in organization structure and enhanced operational effects.

In the chapter's final work, Peter Szanton addresses six factors with the potential to motivate a reorganization effort. In an excerpt titled "So You Want to Reorganize the Government?" drawn from his own edited volume, *Federal Reorganization*, Szanton hopes to illuminate the decision to reorganize by addressing the management objectives, political considerations, policy-based effects, and tactical prescriptions that must characterize a successful effort.

Harvey C. Mansfield, "Federal Executive Reorganization: Thirty Years of Experience," *Public Administration Review*, Vol. 29, No. 4. (July–August, 1969), pp. 332–345.

Reorganizations have political objects and objections, and so, notoriously, involve conflicts of purpose and contests of strength, unless the parties concerned share a common political indoctrination. I will argue accordingly that the principal gains in this field have been in the development of problem-solving institutions and in the climate of opinion surrounding their operation. Their limitations are important to understand, too, particularly in efforts to cope with the cumulative complexities of major domestic programs of recent years. The difficulties inherent in the volatile dynamics of executive-congressional relations and in the intractable dilemmas of federalism keep reappearing.

OBJECTIVES AND STANDARDS

Any reorganization contemplates change of some sort in an ongoing activity, and with it, ordinarily, some transfer of control. To secure a desired change it may be enough to issue an order or make a persuasive suggestion: to display a carrot or stick to the people already in place. A common alternative is to put someone else in charge, in the expectation that he will make or procure the wished-for change by measures formal or informal, very likely including steps to replace subordinates, to reorganize activities, and to secure additional legislative authority. . . . Reorganization, as the term is used here, presumes that these remedies may accompany or follow, but are not available or will not suffice to start the process of change. Instead, it decrees a change in organizational structure or jurisdiction as a beginning, and counts on this (and the shadow its prospect casts ahead) to alter the function in the desired direction or manner—whether correctly or not, we need not stop here to inquire: risks and uncertainties attend all courses of action.

Reorganization may take place at any hierarchical level in the Executive Branch, and may be wide or narrow in scope. Lesser instances are an almost daily occurrence somewhere. I will be concerned here only with those that for one reason or another involved some overt action by the President.

The motives animating a reorganization are likely to be complex; whether transparent or obscure. They differ for various participants, and so it makes a difference whose influence on the process is felt. A sharp shift in the direction of policy is a common object, often coupled with an implicit instruction to the agency to pay more heed to one and less to another element of its clientele. . . . A belief that more satisfactory results will flow from bringing previously unconnected units directly under a common head or—the reverse—from separating a unit hitherto attached, is another. Concepts of major purpose, common skill, or common clientele to be served are often invoked to justify such a belief. An upgrading or downgrading of status and priority for a program, for an agency, or for its head, is a third frequent motive, often related to expansion or shrinkage in the volume, cost, or controversial content of activities. . . .

An accommodation of the personal preferences of a valued official explains a good many more failures to transfer. A recognition of the potentialities of technological innovation, such as justified separate agencies for aviation, atomic energy, and space exploration—or, more prosaically, made current central accounting and disbursing in the Treasury feasible for the first time in the 1930s—furnishes a fifth sort of motive. A need to reconcile some conflicts below the presidential level by the erection of an intermediate supervisory office . . . is a sixth. An internal rearrangement calculated to emphasize different occupational talents and new career patterns, such as has transformed the General Accounting Office in the past 20 years, is a seventh, or perhaps a special case of the first.

These examples illustrate positive uses of reorganization. It has negative or defensive uses as well. One way of stopping an activity you dislike is to abolish the agency engaged in it, as the House Appropriations Committee did with Roosevelt's National Resources Planning Board in the Executive Office in 1943. A slightly less drastic alternative is to deliver the offender over to its natural enemies by consolidating it under the jurisdiction of a more powerful agency that is hostile or indifferent. Defensively, a means of countering adverse outside criticism of an agency is to blur the target by a reorganization made with little or no expectation of material changes in performance. Alternatively, a beleaguered agency may find shelter by being placed in the protective custody of a friendly office that is potent enough to ward off attack.

The variety of motives potentially in play, and in controversy, leads reformers as well as other politicians to reach for consensus-building goals, for labels for reorganization objectives that all must applaud. The first comprehensive study of organization and methods in the Executive Branch, launched by Senator Cockrell (D–Missouri) midway in the first Cleveland Administration, by vote of a Republican-controlled Senate, gave currency to the oldest and hardiest perennial among such phrases, "economy and efficiency."[1] President Taft's Commission on Economy and Efficiency popularized another, the elimination of "overlapping and duplication." But by 1937 these terms had become shibboleths for those whose interest in reorganization was limited to the reduction of governmental outlays for purposes they did not care about. The Brownlow Committee's report, greatly to its credit, disclaimed any specific promise of savings to be gained from the adoption of its recommendations, and asserted simply that (p. 3), "The efficiency of government rests upon two factors: the consent of the governed and good management." The report also achieved a minor triumph of political rhetoric by inventing the neutral term "administrative management"—still ambiguous, but less pretentious, less vulnerable—to describe its subject matter.

PURPOSES

After 30 years and despite PPBS, it seems fair to say that we are further than ever from a set of measurable and mutually compatible criteria for reorganization. For example, when

President Johnson in his annual message in January 1967 proposed, out of a blue sky, to merge the Departments of Commerce and Labor, his startled listeners were at no loss for principles to invoke, but no one offered a scientific demonstration pro or con.[2] The Reorganization Act of 1949 (section 2) currently lists six purposes, one or more of which the President must formally find will be served by any plan he proposes under the Act:

1. To promote the better execution of the laws, the more effective management of the executive branch of the Government and of its agencies and functions, and the expeditious administration of the public business;
2. To reduce expenditures and promote economy, to the fullest extent consistent with the efficient operation of the Government;
3. To increase the efficiency of the operations of the Government to the fullest extent practicable;
4. To group, coordinate, and consolidate agencies and functions of the Government, as nearly as may be, according to major purposes;
5. To reduce the number of agencies by consolidating those having similar functions under a single head, and to abolish such agencies or functions thereof as may not be necessary for the efficient conduct of the Government; and
6. To eliminate overlapping and duplication of effort.

This listing suffices to save the Act from the charge of unconstitutional delegation. It is vague enough to cover a good many ulterior motives. It does not tell a reorganizer where to begin or how to proceed. Clauses two through six codify the orthodox goals. Clause one gives the President his elbow room. While case studies have shown that the functional tendencies of various types of reorganizing moves can often be predicted with some confidence, the criteria remain subjective and the confidence is that of the skilled practitioner or veteran observer, and not the result of proof.

PROCESSES

It matters a good deal in the outcome how and from whom a reorganization move gets its start, what staff work goes into it, and what procedural gauntlet it must run before it takes effect. The Brownlow Committee of three, already knowledgeable in the subject matter, having no obvious partisan label, and accustomed to deal with political executives of both parties, was favored by three circumstances: its diagnosis and remedies, although published, coincided with the President's ardent views; the President, at the time of its report, was fresh from an overwhelming electoral victory; and the Committee took the existing levels of substantive government services and activities as given. Its trouble came, notwithstanding the election returns, in the subsequent effort to secure enabling legislation in the wake of the Supreme Court fight. The first Hoover Commission, larger, balanced in membership and bipartisan in sponsorship, but with no such singleness of purpose or outlook, drew strength from its chairman's dedication and from the cordiality that developed between him and President Truman. It was saved from grief by its tardy decision in the summer of 1948, against the predilections of its chairman and some of its conservative sponsors, to rule out proposals for retrenchment as a means of "economizing" and, like the Brownlow Committee, to accept existing service levels. The bipartisan coalition that necessitated this operating rule in 1948 and supported the passage of the Reorganization Act of 1949 was not needed in 1953. The second Hoover Commission accordingly indulged Mr. Hoover's preference for mingling reorganization with retrenchment; and, the climate having changed by the time they were made, this Commission's recommendations got nowhere.

From this succession we may tentatively conclude that while a reorganization may come as an incident of material policy change in a specific field, professional reorganizers are well advised to profess neutrality as to substantive goals and insist on the time-honored distinction between administration and policy.

We may also wonder whether a President is soon likely to resort again to a public body making a public report and having a jurisdiction as broad as the Executive Branch, as a source of reorganization proposals.[3] Even before the second Hoover Commission got under way, President Eisenhower was relying on an informal President's Advisory Committee on Government Organization, headed by Nelson A. Rockefeller; a continuation of the Temple University operation established during the 1952 Campaign.[4] President Kennedy relied mainly on informal advisers; and when he departed from this course to call publicly on James M. Landis for a report and recommendations relating to the independent regulatory commissions, the result was more grief than help. President Johnson kept entirely to informal advice. His most comprehensive effort—partly abortive because of his decision not to seek reelection in 1968—was the establishment in 1966 of an altogether unpublicized President's Task Force on Government Organization, headed by a private citizen, Ben W. Heineman, and comprised of other knowledgeable private consultants, some ex-officials lately in high places, and the then Budget Director and Secretary of Defense. With the help of Dean Don K. Price, he had used this technique before on a lesser scale in 1964. The Johnson Administration in four years accomplished more reorganization business than had been transacted in the two previous decades. Given the supporting staff resources now available in or to the Executive Office, and the supply of unofficial consultative talent among experienced former political executives, in academic quarters, and elsewhere, the advantages of confidentiality in getting advice and preparing reorganization proposals appear overwhelming, from the President's viewpoint. The appointment of a mixed public commission is likely to be read as a sign of weakness or irresolution on his part.

CONGRESSIONAL DISPOSITIONS

A reorganization takes effect legally by getting the consent of Congress in any of three ways: by statutory delegation, by express statutory action, or by reorganization plan. The first is available if the organic act establishing an agency gives its head (or his superior) the authority, expressly or by implication, to delegate functions and rearrange structures within that agency. An implication so drawn may be ratified by recognition in subsequent appropriations acts; the congressional consent, that is, may in practice come from the Appropriations Committee rather than the legislative committee having jurisdiction. The statutes and committees vary a great deal in the degree of delegation they permit in this respect. The 1967 Budget Bureau reorganization was of this sort; and the category is numerous—at subordinate levels and for internal reorganizations confined to a single agency or portion thereof, this must be the common method. By interagency agreement, reciprocal minor adjustments in the structure and functions of two or more agencies are also conceivable. But a broad delegation of reorganizing authority, extending beyond the jurisdiction of a single department, has been given the President on only three occasions of extreme emergency, and for limited periods: by the Overman Act of 1917, by the Economy Acts of March 3 and 20, 1933, and by the War Powers Act of December 1941. For most agencies, and for most of the time, some congressional committee has been in a position to enforce its interest in requiring an explicit expression of congressional approval.

The commonest form of reorganization on any substantial scale accordingly has been by statute, ad hoc. A count made in 1963 by the Legislative Reference Service for the House Government Operations Committee illustrates the various types of delegated authority and lists 157 statutory reorganizations effected during the period 1945–1962, as against 74 presidential reorganization plans submitted, of which 52 became law. These figures are unweighted; there were some elephants and some mice in both categories. The ratio, of more than two to one, was reduced by the flurry of plans in 1950 to carry out Hoover Commission proposals; for the rest of the period it was considerably higher. The statutory reorganizations include most of the major actions: the Taft-Hartley Act, the creation of the Department of Defense and the so-called unification of the armed services, a succession of changes in the State Department and foreign aid agencies, the establishment of the General Services Administration and the Departments of Housing and Urban Development and of Transportation, for instance. These were all controversial measures in which the reorganization was incidental to important alterations in powers as well as politics. Reorganization plans, by contrast, may not legally expand or extend powers beyond those already conferred by statute.

Statutory reorganizations are open to amendment and share the characteristics and uncertainties of congressional legislation. They may be initiated outside the government and be thrust down the President's throat, like the Taft-Hartley Act. They may embody the wishes of an official guild or employees' union and elude Budget Bureau control, like the Foreign Service Act of 1946. They may stall for want of sustained support, like the Harding Administration's proposals in the 1920s. They may be stopped in deadlock, like most proposals for the District of Columbia government until 1967. One feature they have in common: being subject to the jurisdiction of the respective legislative committees en route to enactment, they maximize the influence of these committees on the outcome.

Reference

Harvey C. Mansfield, 1968, "Commissions, Government," in *International Encyclopedia of the Social Sciences*, Macmillan and The Free Press, New York.

Herbert Kaufman, "Reflections on Administrative Reorganization," in J.A. Pechman (Ed.), *Setting National Priorities: The* 1978 *Budget*, Washington, DC: The Brookings Institution (1977).

Obviously, no reorganization is inherently right or wrong. No given administrative pattern will invariably increase efficiency, effectiveness, or responsiveness. In particular circumstances, identical organizational arrangements may produce diametrically opposite effects while radically different arrangements may produce identical effects. *It All Depends,* declared Harvey Sherman in his book by that title.[5] One can hardly quarrel with that.

None of this means, however, that there is no point to reorganizing. On the contrary, the consequences of reorganization are frequently profound. But the profound, determinable consequences do not lie in the engineering realm of efficiency, simplicity, size, and cost of government. Rather, the real payoffs are measured in terms of influence, policy, and communication.

EFFECTS ON INFLUENCE

For example, reorganization redistributes influence. If the Arms Control and Disarmament Agency had been set up in the Department of Defense instead of as an independent unit, it seems likely that the advocates of arms limitations would have had less impact on policy than they did. Policy recommendations to the President and the Congress filtered through the armed services community would almost certainly have been unlike the proposals emerging from an agency with a different perspective on the world, a different mission, and a different set of priorities. Moreover, the conduct of negotiations over disarmament and arms limitations would probably not have been as vigorous, patient, or perseverant under exclusive Defense Department auspices.

Similarly, if environmental protection were scattered among environmental protection units in other agencies instead of being lodged in the Environmental Protection Agency, chances are the views of environmentalists would have been swamped by oil interests in the Federal Energy Administration, air and highway interests in the Department of Transportation, coal interests in the Department of the Interior, and so on. Within the policy-making councils of the government, the environmentalists' voices would have been muffled, if not silenced.

Consumer groups are demanding a separate consumer agency for the same reason. Consumer units dispersed among producer-oriented agencies, they are convinced, would not carry much weight; they want a body beholden to them in the top levels of the government. Not only would they expect to acquire strength directly; central agencies also serve as rallying points for previously dispersed pressure groups with overlapping interests.

People will argue over the effect of such differences in structure on efficiency, and over the danger of needless complexity, and will come to different conclusions according to the goals they favor. They will commonly agree, however, that different structures strengthen the hands of some officials and interest groups and reduce the ability of others to get what they want. The effects are not precisely measurable or completely predictable, but their general thrust is usually discernible.

EFFECTS ON POLICY

Who acquires power and who is deprived of power would be of interest only to the people involved were it not for the implications of such redistributions for governmental policy; what the government *does* is determined by the distribution of influence. For example, if an overarching energy agency is given access to the inner councils of government and power over sister agencies, energy conservation is likely to be stressed even if it slows economic growth, inhibits the rise in the standard of living or even reduces the level of convenience and comfort, and perhaps even increases unemployment. At the same time, intensified striving after increases in energy production might lead to relaxation of environmental safeguards and uncontrolled prices for energy producers that are passed on to consumers. If the energy agency's powers are split up, lodged in hostile parent organizations, placed at low administrative levels, and given scant authority, other values will probably take precedence over energy considerations, with the result that vulnerability to political pressures by oil producing countries, to severe trade imbalances, and to recurrent domestic shortages will increase steadily.

If preferred status is accorded those who believe the economic marketplace is the best promoter of the manifold interests in our society, government regulation of economic activity will be reduced while efforts to break up industry-dominating combinations and competition-suppressing agreements are emphasized. If stronger positions are given to those who believe there are benefits in large-scale operations, and that the way to protect the public interest is to control them rather than to try to dissolve them in a vain quest to preserve a market through government power, then more and more industries will be treated as public utilities and subjected to surveillance and regulation by specialized government agencies.

To take still another example, the Occupational Safety and Health Administration was placed in the Department of Labor and its regulations were addressed heavily to mechanical hazards and to worker comfort. Had it been put under the assistant secretary for health in the Department of Health, Education, and Welfare, there is reason to surmise that chemical and biological dangers to workers probably would have received higher priority in the regulations.

Organizational arrangements in government, in short, affect not only the leaders and members of the organizations established or moved or redesigned; they impinge on the lives of millions of other people in this generation and the future.

SIGNALS

Organizational arrangements are also a means of communicating the government's intentions. They signal people inside the government, people throughout the country, and, indeed, people and governments throughout the world what this government's emphases will be. Such signals often influence the behavior of those who receive them. All too often, they are misconstrued, so the architects of administration would be mistaken to let the symbolic considerations dominate their designs. At the same time, however, administrative designers would be remiss if they did not take into account the interpretations that may be placed on their handiwork. How well their designs work depends in part on the designers' success in selecting organizational patterns that evoke from everyone concerned the kind of behavior the patterns are meant to produce. The symbolic component is a useful and, indeed, a powerful tool.

Thus, a leader who transfers, combines, and splits organizations in government for engineering purposes will usually find that nobody can be sure whether any progress has been made toward those goals. All too often, the effects on efficiency, simplicity, and cost cannot be determined at all. When they can be assessed, what is successful by one standard may be a failure by another; what improves things in one way makes them worse in another. Real political capital is thus consumed in the pursuit of phantom goals. In contrast, a leader who shifts organizations around to confer power on selected people or remove it from others in order to mold government policies, and to impress on everyone what his or her values and priorities are, will more often be rewarded with a sense of having expended political resources for significant accomplishments. The calculus of reorganization is essentially the calculus of politics itself. . . .

NO MIRACLE CURES

Those, however, who cling to the belief that any combination of means will instantaneously transform the character, image, or performance of the executive branch, are doomed to disappointment.

The civilian work force of the government grew only modestly over two decades, while the budget as a whole was doubling in constant dollars (increasing fivefold in current dollars).[6] There is not much opportunity for cutbacks here, which is one reason why both the President and the secretary of Health, Education, and Welfare assured civil servants that reorganization would not mean loss of jobs for them. Perhaps the *rate* of growth of federal employment can be held down (though this rate depends on whether new federal initiatives are undertaken in the years ahead, which is a distinct possibility); even if the rate is limited, however, the effects will be felt in the remote rather than in the near future. In any case, the monetary savings through control of civilian personnel growth cannot be more than a small fraction of federal outlays, since all the compensation and benefits of the civilian work force come to under 11 percent of the total, so that marginal reductions in this area would hardly change the overall budget at all.

Reorganizers have also grown wary of claiming massive savings in operations for their reforms. For the most part, they assert that their changes will produce more output per dollar spent rather than the expenditure of fewer dollars; thus, even if the changes end up increasing total outlays, they contend that the total will be lower than it would have been without the reforms.[7] Whether or not such claims are eventually justified, the *immediate* effect on budgets is almost sure to be indiscernible. In this context, the recent statement by Secretary of Health, Education, and Welfare Califano that the reorganization of his department would yield savings of $2 billion in the first two years and at least $2 billion annually by 1981[8] is surprising. He placed particular emphasis on the elimination of fraud and abuse in various benefit programs, but it is not clear whether the costs of intensified enforcement have been included in his estimates. Furthermore, it is not self-evident how regrouping units in the departments, as opposed to changing procedures or adding auditors and investigators, will contribute to prevention of fraud and abuse.

In short, nobody should expect sudden, swift, dramatic diminishment in the size and cost of the executive branch of the federal government as a result of reorganization. Indeed, the upward trend will probably persist for a long time—possibly more gradually than might otherwise have been the case, but upwards all the same.

Even if anticipated structural revisions succeed, they will be slow in coming. The executive branch is very big, and the specific faults that need correcting keep changing. "Our confused and wasteful system that took so long to grow," President Carter told the American people in his first informal address to the nation, "will take a long time to change."[9] His staff member spearheading reorganization testified that it would be "a four-year effort at least."[10] The administration harbors no illusions about the length of the campaign on which it is embarked. The 1977–78 controversies over government organization are only the opening skirmishes in what promises to be a long, hard, and frequently futile endeavor.

Rufus E. Miles, Jr., "Considerations for a President Bent on Reorganization," *Public Administration Review*, Vol. 37, No. 2. (March–April, 1977), pp. 155–162.

President Carter spoke often during his campaign of his intention to reorganize the federal government. Previous Presidents, especially Lyndon Johnson and Richard Nixon, carried with them into the White House similar convictions that the effectiveness of the United States Government could be substantially improved through reorganization. Each appointed study commissions with sweeping mandates. Two such commissions were appointed by Johnson and one by Nixon; all recommended major regroupings of federal functions.[11] Yet most of such restructuring never occurred.

President Johnson was successful in 1965 and 1966 in gaining congressional approval of two new departments–Housing and Urban Development, and Transportation–but when he tried to combine the Departments of Commerce and Labor into a single department in 1967, it was a fiasco. Thereafter, he recommended no more consolidations to Congress. In 1971, President Nixon built his State of the Union message around sweeping reorganization proposals that would have created Departments of Community Development, Human Resources, Natural Resources, and Economic Affairs, replacing the Departments of Agriculture, Interior, Commerce, Labor, Housing and Urban Development, and Health, Education, and Welfare. These sweeping changes were also pigeon-holed by Congress. The natural inference was that it was much easier to gain congressional approval for the creation of new departments than for the consolidation and abolition of existing departments.

Since neither President succeeded in bringing about any of the major consolidations their advisers counseled, was it faulty advice, congressional obstinacy, or presidential ineptitude and lack of "follow-through" that blocked their purposes? Or was it that the President and his advisers look at the subject of organization in a very different way than does Congress? None of the three advisory commissions, it should be noted, had members with congressional experience. In any event, President Carter and his advisers would do well to ponder the lessons of this experience.

The principles of organization that should guide a President in considering how to structure the federal government differ in many respects from those that normally guide the head of a huge industrial corporation, and even in some respects from those that should guide governors of states. The organization of the federal government affects and reflects many of the purposes and values of the body politic and should be thought of as one of the dynamics that shapes the future of our national society. Organization is especially important at the federal level in expressing the nation's priorities, in allocating resources, in attracting its most competent leader-executives to key positions, and in accomplishing the purposes of the President, the Congress, and the body politic. It may be useful at the outset of a new administration to offer a number of criteria—not an exhaustive list—that the President and his advisers might do well to take into account in considering major reorganization proposals. Following are 13 such criteria.

1. Organization is an important expression of social values; are the values that deserve greatest emphasis at this stage of the nation's development given appropriate organizational recognition?

   The act of elevating the organizational status of a function, especially when it involves creating an organization that is directly answerable to the President, is, first and foremost, an expression of the importance that the President, the Congress, and the public attach to the purposes of that organization. . . . When the American people became deeply concerned in the late 1960s over the deterioration of the environment, two new agencies were created, both directly answerable to the President: the Council on Environmental Quality and the Environmental Protection Agency. When the energy crisis descended on the world, the Federal Energy Agency was created, again directly answerable to the President. *Each of these new agencies was created to reflect a new national priority.*

   Expression of national priority is the foremost purpose for creating a new Cabinet department or agency directly answerable to the President. It is the first criterion by which any major organizational proposal should be judged: Does the function to be elevated deserve a higher national priority than it has had, or, conversely, do functions that are to be submerged deserve relatively lower priority than they have had? Submergence may sometimes be a worthwhile price for improved coordination, but the costs need to be carefully weighed in relation to the benefits. . . .
2. Organizations should be placed in a favorable environment for the performance of their central missions.

   Accidents of history, or the vagaries of politics have resulted in placing various organizations in settings hostile to them, or where their major problems are not treated with suitable understanding and emphasis. One major purpose of government reorganization is to correct such conditions and place agencies where they can perform more effectively. . . .

   The fact that an agency is suitably placed in one decade may not mean that it is appropriately placed one or two decades later. Conditions can change rapidly, and when they do, organizational shifts may become logical and desirable. The water pollution control function that was vested in the Public Health Service in the 1950s and was elevated briefly to agency status within the Department of HEW in the mid-1960s was transferred in the late 1960s to the Interior Department, and was finally made a major component of the new Environmental Protection Agency when it was created at the beginning of the 1970s. Agencies should be placed in settings that are most conducive to the achievement of their central missions.
3. Organization affects the allocation of resources.

   Other factors equal, the higher the organizational level of any agency, the stronger the voice of its chief in advocating its cause and its fiscal needs in the highest councils of government. A third echelon official rarely can plead his case before the President, and does not often swing much weight with the Office of Management and Budget. The fact of being low in the hierarchy tends unconsciously to establish in the minds of those who make budget recommendations to the President an assumption that the function deserves a smaller share of the nation's fiscal resources than if it were organizationally directly answerable to the President.

Not only does the organizational *level* influence resource allocation, but so does organizational *placement.* The most conspicuous example of this is the effect of the "uncontrollable" parts of [an agency's] budget on the "controllable" parts. . . . When uncontrollable requirements are increasing so rapidly, the pressures are unavoidably great to hold down or cut back the controllable parts of the department's budget. Organizational setting and status inescapably affect budget allocations.

4. Organization by reasonably broad purpose serves the President best, not so narrow as to be overly responsive to specific clientele groups, nor so broad as to be unmanageable.

   The President and the public are usually best served when Cabinet officers are put in charge of organizations whose purposes are sufficiently broad so that they exceed the span of concern of any single clientele group. One of the functions of Cabinet officers should be to aid the President in his always difficult task of making all clientele groups understand that resources are limited, that not all programs can be of highest priority, or of equal priority, and that governance is the process of making hard choices in a manner that will enlist confidence in the fairness of the decision-making process and the decision makers themselves, even when the clienteles do not agree with the decisions. This role can be better performed when the portfolio of a Cabinet officer is broad enough to encompass a substantial range of programs and clientele groups, some of which are competing with one another for attention and resources.

   On the other hand, a President is poorly served when the portfolio of assignments to a Cabinet officer is so broad as to exceed the capacity of all but a Superman (or perhaps even him) to perform them effectively. If the scope of a Department is excessively broad, certain responsibilities that the President and the nation may wish to treat as being of first order of importance will inescapably slip to second or third order and effective leadership of these functions will then become virtually impossible. The advantage gained by he wishes to fend off as many officials as possible breadth of perspective is then more than offset by who might be classified as special pleaders, he is failure of effective performance. Emphasis should likely to prefer a small number of officials directly therefore be placed on a *reasonably* broad set of purposes and responsibilities, *not the broader the better.*

5. Wide span of control has significant in improving administration and reducing unnecessary layers of bureaucracy.

   While Presidents may prefer Cabinet departments that are few in number, broad in scope, and large in size, there are various advantages to having a dozen or more of lesser size and range. An organizational structure that is in the form of a steep pyramid, with narrow spans of control at each echelon, requires long lines of communication causing distortions of purpose, and it escalates administrative costs. It also increases problems of coordination. Anthony Downs in his *Inside Bureaucracy*[12] illuminates this point forcefully. His principles are worth quoting:

> The foregoing analysis underlies our statement of three principles of organizational control. The fist is the Law of Imperfect Control: *No one can fully control the behavior of a large organization.* The second is the Law of Diminishing Control: *The larger any organization becomes, the weaker is the control over its actions exercised by those at the top.* The third is the Law of Decreasing Coordination: *The larger any organization becomes, the poorer is the coordination among its actions.*

These principles argue for avoiding gigantic departments, unless there is an overriding reason for their existence. . . .

Span of control also has important political implications. Wide span of control satisfies many constituencies; narrow span of control satisfies few. Wide span of control puts more key program administrators organizationally close to the President, thus making the program constituencies feel that their cases are being heard and understood by the President. Depending on the President, this may or may not be an advantage. If he wishes to fend off as many officials as possible who might be classified as special pleaders, he is likely to prefer small number of officials directly answerable to him; if he can take the time and wants to hear what they have to say, he will enlarge the range of important membership in his official family. But from the standpoint of the Congress and its constituencies, there is no question but that wide span of control is preferable.

6. Organizational form and prestige are especially important at the federal level in attracting and retaining first-rate leader-managers.

   The principal attraction high government posts have to offer is the combination of prestige and power (opportunity to influence outcomes and be of service to the nation). Both prestige and power diminish rapidly as the number of echelons between the President and any official increases. Frustration sets in when opportunities to influence outcomes become disappointing. Since many are making a financial sacrifice to come to Washington, the psychic rewards must be substantial (or the appointees have independent means, or both) in order to keep them at their posts very long. . . . Because of these factors, it is in the President's interest and in the public interest to have a rather large number of Cabinet posts.

7. Balance is important in government organization: excessive concentration of important responsibilities in one agency diminishes the effective performance of most of them.

   Balance is an underrated criterion by which to judge the merit of organizational proposals. . . . [O]verconcentration [of resources and responsibilities] produces a situation in which some parts of the Secretary's responsibilities are bound to be given short shrift and conducted in a less than distinguished manner, to say the least. . . .

   Administering so huge an array of programs is also complicated by the nature of congressional relationships. The Congress would not tolerate a concentration of power in one substantive committee that would parallel the concentration of responsibilities vested in [one superdepartment]. Congress is much more mindful of the principle of balance and divides power and responsibility more evenly among its committees. Consequently, [an agency] must deal with many different committees, a fact that markedly complicates the congressional relationships [between Congress and the agency]. A coordinated approach to the manifold problems and programs of [the agency] is virtually impossible because of both volume and proliferation among congressional committees and subcommittees.

Finally, balance is important in dealing with the organized groups of society that have a strong interest in the outcomes of the various federal programs. The greater the number of groups, the less access they have to the Secretary. They must concentrate their communications and lobbying on lower level officials. And the greater the number of lower level officials with little or no access to the Secretary, the more unmanageable the Department becomes.

8. When purposes overlap, one must be designated as dominant; otherwise responsibility is unclear.

   No matter what principles of organization are followed, it is inevitable that programs and purposes will overlap. The concerns of the Department of State overlap with those of the Department of Defense. The concerns of the CIA overlap with both. . . . Similar overlaps occur throughout the government. Many are inevitable because purposes cannot be defined so as to put them in tight compartments.

   Whenever a program function cuts across two or more major purposes, it is necessary to decide, first, which purpose is dominant in order to decide where to put the unit, organizationally, and second, how to coordinate such cross-cutting functions. . . . The clarity with which the dominant purpose is identified and the function placed accordingly has much to do with the efficiency of governmental administration.

9. When purposes overlap, a system of coordination must be established.

   The most difficult task of public management is not deciding how the functions of government should be divided among organizational units, but how the functions can and should be effectively coordinated after they have been divided. All government is a complex set of matrices; if work is divided on one set of principles or axes, it must be coordinated on another. This is the basic reason for the classic organization by line and staff, a useful, almost indispensable method of coordination but not the full answer to the need for coordinating related functions.

10. Programs should be grouped on the basis of their affinity or the potential for cross-fertilization.

    The grouping of programs within an organization should depend, in part, on the importance of the actual and potential interrelationships between them. If there are or should be numerous such interrelationships, the argument for putting them together in the same department is strong. If a bureau has few important relationships within the setting where it currently is located, and if its relationships with bureaus that are currently located in another department are far more important, and should be developed and encouraged, then it is a good candidate for transfer.

11. Reorganizations have traumatic effects which should be carefully weighed.

    Reorganizations vary widely in the degree to which they disrupt the skein of human relationships that are the communications and nerve networks of every organization. Some reorganizations cause little or no disruption, while others are traumatic. The creation of the Department of Health, Education, and Welfare in 1953, out of what had previously been the Federal Security Agency, was one of the easiest reorganizations ever performed. Only the name was changed, the administrator was made a Cabinet Secretary, and three new positions were added. The cost, in administrative disruption, was close to zero. Other reorganizations have involved much reshuffling of people from one organizational and physical location to another, necessitating a whole new set of human relationships, superiors getting acquainted with new subordinates and vice versa, old habits and trusted communications patterns terminated and new ones initiated. . . .

    Traumatic reorganizations may be analogized to surgical operations. It is important that their purposes be carefully assessed and a thoughtful judgment reached that the wielding of the surgical knife is going to achieve a purpose that, after a period of recuperation, will be worth the trauma inflicted. And the surgical knife should not be wielded again and again before the healing process from earlier incisions has been completed. Yet this is what sometimes happens in government reorganizations. Agencies are kept in a constant state of disruption by having presidential appointees who may average two years of service, or less, conclude that the organizational structure left by their predecessors is not sound because the results being produced are not satisfactory. Hence, they feel they must reorganize. The problem may not be organizational at all, or not primarily organizational, and it may be partly a problem of too much reorganization. Repetitive reorganization without proper initial diagnosis is like repetitive surgery without proper diagnosis: obviously an unsound and unhealthy approach to the cure of the malady.

    It is essential, therefore, that the initial diagnosis of any malfunctioning be carefully made, that reorganizations be designed to achieve clearly defined purposes, and that they be no more disruptive than they need to be to accomplish their overriding purpose. In medicine this is known as minimal or conservative surgery.

12. Reorganizations that require congressional approval or acquiescence should be carefully weighed to make sure that they are worth the expenditure of political capital required and have a reasonable chance of approval.

    By no means the least of the criteria for judging the desirability of a reorganization proposal is the assessment of its political costs and its likelihood of approval by Congress. Congress and the President (and the President's advisers) have different perspectives on the subject of organization. Power is divided differently in Congress than it is in the Executive Branch, and reorganizations that would shift power from one committee to another, or that would demote, relatively speaking, an organizational unit in which powerful committee chairmen and members have a special interest run the hazard of being defeated, ignored, or amended in a manner that would seem unacceptable to the President. Even though the President presides over the Executive Branch, the Constitution gives Congress a significant role in the design of the executive structure. The President must respect the congressional role and the interests of Congress as he considers his own priorities in the matter of reorganization.

A few reorganizations may have low political costs. There are a number of such reorganization options open to the President. The more difficult problem arises when the political costs begin to rise because of the pressure groups that would be offended and the Congressmen and their staffs whose bailiwicks would be adversely affected. When the political costs are substantial, the President should be apprised of this fact in advance and, obviously, should not seek reorganizations that will be politically expensive unless he is prepared to spend a substantial amount of political capital in gaining their approval. Reorganization plans submitted and turned down or ignored (if they require affirmative legislation) are humiliating, the more so if the President's own party controls Congress. It is important, therefore, before drawing a trial balance on a series of models of reorganization to examine the positions that the key interest groups and congressmen (and staffs) are likely to take on the various models, and cast them into the balance in arriving at judgments as to both desirability and feasibility.

13. Economy as a ground for major reorganization is a will-o'-the-wisp.

Last and least important among the criteria for judging among reorganization models is the matter of whether dollar savings can be accomplished. It is extremely difficult to predict how much, if anything, can be saved by a major reorganization, and it is impossible to prove, after the fact, how much, if any, has been saved. The comparison that must be made in a continually shifting context is the amount that a new organizational pattern will cost compared to what would have been required under the former organization. Since it is never possible to know what costs would have been without the reorganization, such calculations are close to meaningless. The rationale that lies behind most reorganizations is that the new structure will increase the *effectiveness* of government, not reduce its costs.

Almost invariably, reorganizations that elevate the status of a subordinate organization to a higher level, especially those that create new Cabinet Departments or new agencies directly answerable to the President, result in larger staffs for the new Secretary or agency head, and those staffs are more highly paid than when the organization was at a lower level. Indeed, that is one of the purposes of such elevation. If a function needs stronger leadership, one important way in which such leadership can become effective is by creating higher and more prestigious positions and providing such leaders with the opportunity to surround themselves with first-rate staff. It would be a mistake to pretend or predict that these officials are going to be so competent, managerially speaking, that they will be able to reduce the costs of the subordinate units of the organization in sufficient degree to more than offset the added costs of the larger and higher paid staff at the top. It *could happen*; the likelihood is great that it will not. *The officials in such an organization have far greater interest in accomplishing more effectively the missions assigned to their agencies than they do in reducing the staff.*

Even more unlikely is that savings will be made by creating larger aggregations of agencies and putting a new superstructure over them. The additional layer is almost certain to cost more money. To the extent that savings are achievable in the federal government through improved management, they are likely to be made through changes in policies and procedures, not organization.

Thus, it would be a mistake to place the subject of economy high on a list of important criteria for judging the desirability of any proposed reorganization. It is, of course, necessary to consider estimated costs in relation to possible benefits, but these estimates should rarely, if ever, be a controlling consideration.

Obviously, almost no reorganization proposal is likely to rank high in respect to all of these criteria. Some of the criteria pull in opposite directions. But all deserve to be thought about as various reorganization plans are being considered.

Caspar W. Weinberger, "Government Reorganization and Public Purpose," *Publius*, Vol. 8, No. 2, Government Reorganization and the Federal System (Spring, 1978), pp. 39–48.

A . . . reorganization proposed in 1971 suggested that we eliminate and consolidate several existing federal executive departments, and consolidate most of their existing programs into four major departments. The 1971 Presidential reorganization proposal was based on the idea that "how the government is put together often determines how well the government can do its job." (Once it is determined what the government ought to do, there are numerous ways of structuring the machinery for carrying out those agreed-upon tasks.) The 1971 reorganization plan assumed that we would continue to do much that we were doing, but that there were far better ways or organizing the government to do it.

Thus, while recommending no major changes in the departments of State, Treasury, Defense and Justice, the plan envisioned the elimination of several existing departments and agencies, and the consolidation of their functions into four new departments: Community Development; Natural Resources, Human Resources; and Economic Affairs. These four would replace the departments of Agriculture;[13] Commerce; Labor; Health, Education and Welfare; Interior; Housing and Urban Development; and Transportation. The newly created departments would be large, of course, but fewer agencies and few officials would report to the President.

The main thesis of that reorganization proposal was that although we had good people and had spent much money, we had an ineffective government. This feeling was based largely on the frustrations of any President who feels, quite correctly, that he can pull a great many levers and push several buttons, but that very little may happen thereafter. The flow of power from the White House is frequently diffused and complex, and it is sometimes months, sometimes forever, before policy decisions made in the Congress or the White House are actually carried out. Most presidents have concluded, I think correctly, that this situation exists because there are too many semi-independent agencies; that there is no real chain of authority and responsibility from the President downward; that there is no real mechanism for assuring that once policy is decided, it is actually carried out; and that there is no mechanism for overseeing how policy is carried out. Most of these problems have come about because each problem, each activity or new program is treated typically as a separate matter unrelated to anything in the past or the future. As a result, the total structure grows and grows, without any particular plan or coordinated approach, into a jerry-

---

Source: Caspar W. Weinberger, "Government Reorganisation and Public Purpose," *Publius*, Spring 1978, Vol. 8, No. 2, pp. 39–48, by permission of Oxford University Press.

built apparatus that not only sprawls untidily on paper charts but also becomes difficult to operate, and far more difficult to control or to respond in a uniform, coordinated way.

The idea of comprehensive change, or even comprehensive examination of the entire problem of reorganization, generally has been repugnant to Congress, despite the substantial success of the two Hoover Commissions. They did examine the entire structure, did recommend thorough, comprehensive and structural changes, and lived to see many of them put into effect.

The results of the one-by-one approach of the Congress in addressing various problems are familiar but nonetheless dismaying. Nine federal departments and twenty independent agencies deal with educational matters. Seven departments and eight independent agencies administer various national health programs. Three departments help to develop water resources, and four agencies and two departments manage public lands. Seven agencies deal with water and sewer systems. Six departments collect similar economic information, often from the same source-usually the private sector.[14]

Besides being unresponsive to policy decisions of elected officials, the government has become so hydra-headed and disorganized that the people, whose government it is, cannot cope with it. Thus, to the individual citizen, the government is a large, impenetrable maze. Neither the President nor elected officials can find out who is responsible because innumerable agencies and individuals have created the bits and pieces. A recent example of the disorganization—and the uncertainty that once levers have been pulled something will happen—is the drought relief program that President Carter signed early in his administration. Six months later, it had not produced a single check for a single farmer in any drought-stricken region of the country.

The typical reorganization remedy is to group related functions under a single-headed agency that reports to someone in authority. That official in turn reports up the line until an elected or appointed policy-making official is found, to whom several managers report. The direct line of responsibility, the grouping of related functions, the assurance that not too many people will report to any one individual, and sufficient authority in each department or agency head to manage and run his own units consistent with the overall policy these are the basic hallmarks of good administration and good organization.

The private sector, if the subject is regulation, may think that it prefers a divided, weak, ineffective regulatory unit unable to carry out regulatory policies that may have been approved by the peoples' representatives or instituted by policy making officials.[15] But if another area of activity is involved—such as assistance from government to increase our foreign trade, or loans for small business, or construction of projects to develop our water resources in order to increase the irrigatable lands, or disaster relief, or any one of numerous other activities—then the private sector suffers the same frustrations and has the same interest in securing a sound, responsive, well-organized and effective government as do the Chief Executive and his immediate appointees.

A basic question remains—whether the activities of government are either necessary or desirable. When that question is answered by majority votes or other expressions of popular will, then the question recurs as to whether the government will be able to do those things effectively, or indeed at all. If a self-governing democracy is to mean anything, the public interest requires that organizational structure—or lack of it—not stand in the way of government implementation of such policy decisions. Good organization cannot assure good programmatic results. But had organization can prevent a government from acting and thus can frustrate the public will, and finally give credence to the belief that popular government cannot work.

With such a wide consensus that our present government organization urgently requires radical change, and with such general agreement that government is badly organized, why are we unable to do the things that the public has asked of its government? Why are we unable to do the things that popularly elected or appointed policymaking officials have agreed to do? And why have we still done so little to improve organization? The answers seem to lie in the ability of various organized, highly vocal groups—which know what they want from government and are totally uninterested in the operation or success or efficiency of government as a whole—to keep things as they are in their separate fields. Thus, a particular group will force through, for example, the Hill-Burton hospital program under which the federal government subsidizes and encourages construction of more hospital facilities.

For a time, such a program may be needed and funds may actually flow to a necessary purpose. Then, it becomes apparent that we have overdone it, that the Hill-Burton program begins to resemble the Sorcerer's Apprentice: more and more hospital beds are built, but the occupancy rate and the necessity for continuing Hill-Burton keep falling. The cost of construction and the cost of borrowing keep increasing, so that the more hospital facilities that are constructed, the higher the charges to pay for them; the higher the charges, the more difficulty other parts of government, such as Medicare, may have in meeting those charges. Thus, the government will contribute greatly to ever-increasing inflation of hospital costs.

Yet, any suggestion that the Hill-Burton program be terminated is met with fierce and determined opposition from various associations representing hospitals that have not yet built or sufficiently expanded or rebuilt; from the staff of the congressional committees which oversee the program and which fiercely resent any diminution in their authority; and from the permanent civil service groups which administer the program and which foresee only disaster if their programs are eliminated.[16]

Therefore, as a first step, real organization would require the elimination of unnecessary programs like Hill-Burton and the units that administer them. This step would automatically improve the organization of any department by reducing the span of control of the supervising officials and the waste and negative effects of spending more money on a non-existent need. But that same opposition is voiced when any reorganization or change in an existing program needed or otherwise—is proposed.

The unholy trinity of the lobbying groups, the congressional committee staffs who fear reduction of their authority, and the people whose career is to administer the program, thus far has been strong enough to defeat almost any more to improve, change, or eliminate existing programs. These groups have also been successful in preventing any meaningful reorganization of the structures by which existing programs are supposed to be carried out.[17]

People who think they benefit from existing programs have all their lines laid to individual congressional staff members or permanent Civil Service members who are able to tilt government action favorably in their direction; and with every instinct of self-preservation, they cry out against any proposed change. The reason for their success is simple: they have a definite, affirmative, specific program—to stay alive.

On the other hand, the opposition–i.e., those who want rational, coordinated, effective reorganization, which by definition requires major, radical programmatic changes–does not have any real political strength because it does not represent any groups whose battle cry is "survival." Nor does it enter the fray with anything like the fervor of those who make up the Iron Triangle, as Theodore White has called the advocates of the status quo. That, coupled with congressional fear of presidential or executive capability, thus far has defeated all recent attempts to reorganize the government.

This is not a partisan matter, nor is it really even a philosophic or ideological problem. Quite simply, it is a situation in which small, narrowly based groups who have what they want and are afraid of losing it, inevitably have proven stronger than large groups with more-or-less amorphous and less single-minded attitudes. Further, the situation simply underlines and reaffirms the old adage that "the man with the agenda can always carry the meeting."

Peter Szanton, "So You Want to Reorganize the Government?," in Peter Szanton, (Ed.), *Federal Reorganization: What Have We Learned?* Chatham, NJ: Chatham House (1981).

WHY REORGANIZE, AND WHY NOT?

The first rule of reorganization is to understand your purpose. Specifying a rationale is essential because some reasons may justify the effort; others do not.

Virtually all substantial reorganizations claim one or more of six objectives.[18] They seek to

1. *Shake up* an organization to demonstrate the decisiveness or managerial reach of a new executive or simply to place his (or her) mark upon it.
2. *Simplify or "streamline"* an organization (or the government as a whole.) This was the rationale for Jimmy Carter's promise, in the 1976 campaign, to reduce the number of federal agencies from 1900 to 200.
3. *Reduce costs* by minimizing overlap and duplication, achieving supposed economies of scale and efficiencies in management. This is the traditional rationale for reorganization and, at least until recently, the objective commanding greatest public and congressional support.
4. *Symbolize priorities* by giving them clear organizational embodiment. The belief that education was too important to bury in a huge department preoccupied with problems of health and welfare was the main rationale for the recent creation of the Department of Education.
5. *Improve program effectiveness* by bringing separate but logically related programs under more unified direction. This was the principal rationale for the creation of the departments of Defense and, more recently, Energy. It is also the reason for various systems of coordination among programs in separate departments or agencies.
6. *Improve policy integration* by placing competitive or conflicting interests within a single organization or subjecting them to processes of coordination. The brief and entirely unavailing attempt of President Johnson to merge the Departments of Labor and Commerce had this purpose.

These objectives partially overlap, and in most reorganizations, more than one objective is sought. The creation of the Energy Department, for example, might have been justified in

---

Source: Peter Szanton, "So You Want to Reorganize the Government?," in Peter Szanton, (Ed.), *Federal Reorganization: What Have We Learned?* Chatham, NJ: Chatham House (1981).

part on each ground. But one or two objectives are usually dominant, and clarity as to which these are is essential to any judgment as to whether the effort is likely to prove worthwhile. The six objectives form a rough hierarchy. The earlier are trivial or quixotic; the later difficult but substantial. The break-even point comes directly in the middle. Depending on the degree of difficulty to be expected, objectives 4–6 may justify reorganization; objectives 1–3 almost invariably do not. Why not?

SHAKING THINGS UP

It is understandable and legitimate for an incoming executive to want to place his mark on his own office and perhaps on other units that directly support it. Then let him import a few trusted assistants and rearrange staff assignments as he likes. Neither is hard. Imposing substantial change on line operations—bureaus staffed with career officials and responsible for operating programs—will prove vastly more difficult. If the reasons for attempting it are powerful and the means well-chosen, the attempt may be justified. But simply establishing "who's boss" is a flagrantly insufficient rationale. And the outcome of so motivated a "reform" is likely to prove embarrassing. Bureaucracies do not regard line reorganization as a rubdown, stimulating and pleasant. To them it is surgery, involving anxiety before the event, trauma in the course of it, a lengthy convalescence afterward, and considerable uncertainty about outcome. The patient's capacity to resist the procedure, moreover, is impressive. Bureaucracies may stop a proposed reorganization by inducing interest-group or congressional outcries, or by discovering legal or administrative barriers. And what they cannot stop they can delay. All career bureaucrats have seen wave on wave of senior executives come and go. The average tenure of cabinet officers is less than two years, and of assistant secretaries less than a year and a half.[19] And the initial priorities of senior officials are even less durable. So strategies of bureaucratic delay generally succeed.

SIMPLIFYING GOVERNMENT

The problem here is not that the goal is attainable only at excessive cost; this goal is an illusion. We are long past the point at which the federal government can be simple or readily understandable. Its jobs are too numerous, too large, too complex, and too inconsistent. It now undertakes not only the irreducible jobs of government—maintaining order, dispensing justice, conducting relations with other states, defending the nation from external threat—it now undertakes to ensure stable prices, full employment, environmental quality, equal opportunity, favorable trade balances, consumer protection, safety in the workplace, and so on. No government seeking ends as large, diffuse, and interconnected as those can be simple.

CUTTING COSTS

Here is a worthy and sometimes attainable objective that reorganization is too blunt and clumsy an instrument to achieve. . . . Substantial savings may be possible when programs are eliminated, but the President's reorganization powers are usually limited to expressly preclude that result. At most, therefore, reorganization can reduce overhead or administrative costs, where potential savings are quite limited. Total personnel costs are just over 10 percent of the federal budget (and declining), and administrative costs are typically a small fraction of these. . . . [A] recent study of $50 billion worth of federal programs concluded that 10 percent of total administrative expenses might be saved through reorganization—a sum amounting to 4/100ths of 1 percent of the total program costs.

So none of these first three objectives of reorganization are serious. The costs of attempting any of them will greatly outweigh likely gains. And some costs may be unexpected. An important source of internal controversy in the first years of the Carter administration, for example, was the tension between the President's commitment to reorganization and his view of it as a means of streamlining the government. From the perspective of most of his senior aides, "streamlining" not only failed to advance any substantive policy goal but competed with policy objectives for the President's time and political capital. So the President's predilections to reorganize were steadily resisted by the officials closest to him, especially his domestic policy adviser and Vice-president Mondale. The result was that although great effort and substantial time were expended at high levels in the planning of ambitious change, the only substantial reorganizations proposed by the Carter administration were those made unavoidable by either explicit campaign commitments or powerful congressional pressure.[20] Even when the reorganizers sought to advance major administration policy goals—in the attempt, for example, to help make good on the President's promise of a new urban policy by consolidating urban development programs in a Department of Community and Economic Development—their political isolation denied them a timely hearing for the proposal.

Objectives 4–6—symbolizing new priorities, improving the effectiveness of related programs through unified direction, and better integrating policy by placing conflicting interests under the same oversight—are different matters; substantial and potentially attainable ends that may well justify reorganization.

USEFUL SYMBOLISM

Creating a prominent new organization may meet an important political need. The creation of the Department of Health, Education, and Welfare (HEW) in 1953 powerfully symbolized the acceptance of federal responsibility for minimum standards of social welfare; it was accordingly treated by the press as a major event, though its substance amounted to little more than the application of new names and ranks to old programs. Similarly, the Department of Housing and Urban Development (HUD) expressed the 1960's recognition of a special federal responsibility for cities and the urban poor; and the Department of Energy embodies the priority now attached to reliable fuel supplies. As these examples suggest, symbolizing a national concern is far easier than relieving it. Still, institutionalizing a priority gives it visible expression, places it permanently on the national agenda, and creates an assured source of advocacy for efforts to deal with it.

PROGRAM EFFECTIVENESS

Similarly, improving the effectiveness of government is a substantial purpose, and placing related programs under some form of common direction is a potentially powerful way of achieving it. It is well to emphasize the potential. Organizations create distinctive cultures. Organizations with long histories or important missions or records of great accomplishment generate independent cultures with distinctive values, practices, and traditions. They prove highly resistant to change. Thus, after more than three decades of subordination to a common superior, the three military departments still equip, train, and deploy themselves on only partially consistent assumptions as to the nation's most pressing military needs. Still, the existence of a Department of Defense, headed by a single Secretary, has clearly produced a better integrated and more effective set of military forces than would have been possible otherwise.

THE INTEGRATION OF POLICY

Finally, reorganization can help integrate policy. Arrangements that with conflicting interests to a common superior and thus force (or at least facilitate) comparisons and tradeoffs among them serve perhaps the highest purpose of government—that of mediating and resolving disputes among antagonistic interests.

It is a function more than ordinarily important now. This is a period in which two powerful trends have conjoined. The federal government has undertaken an enormous range of large, numerous, interconnected, and partly contradictory responsibilities. The maintenance of minimum levels of coherence and consistency in federal actions is therefore inherently difficult. At the same time, each of the central political institutions that historically have mediated between contending interests and imposed a measure of discipline on our pluralistic politics has weakened. Political parties, congressional leadership, and the Presidency have all diminished in influence as tolerance for authority generally has decreased and the power special interests and the intensity of single-issue politics has grown. At bottom, of course, these trends produce a problem not of organizational but of politics. However structured, staffed, or budgeted, institutions cannot wield a power that political forces deny them. But institutions may be well or poorly designed to exercise whatever potential they have. The central institutions of government, especially the cabinet departments and the Executive Office of the President, may therefore either partially offset or further magnify the effects of these trends.

It will prove especially important that their effects be offset if national politics in the next decade is dominated by issues like energy policy, whose resolution requires distributing not benefits but costs. No political system readily accepts costs. A system where authority is very widely diffused may reject them entirely. Faced with the problem of allocating costs, the tendency of a system of diffused authority is toward paralysis. Energy again illustrates the point.

So for those concerned about the effectiveness of the American government in the last decades of the twentieth century, an overriding talk is to reconstruct those institutions that tend to resolve disputes rather than create them, that represent common interests rather than special ones, that look to the longer term rather than the pressures of the moment. The job is to strengthen those institutions individually and rebuild the linkages among them—linkages like those that previously tied the majority party, congressional leadership, and the Presidency.

NOTES FOR CHAPTER 3

1. Oscar Kraines, 1966, *Congress and the Challenge of Big Government*, Harvard University Press, Cambridge, MA.
2. See Theodore J. Lowi, July–August 1967, "Why Merge Commerce and Labor?" *Challenge*, pp. 12–15.
3. I have touched on some of the general considerations in the article on "Commissions, Government," 1968, in the *International Encyclopedia of the Social Sciences*, Macmillan and The Free Press, New York. Senator Abraham Ribicoff (D–Connecticut), heading the Government Operations Subcommittee on Executive Reorganization, held hearings and got through the Senate in July 1968 a bill, S. 3640, to establish a Hoover-type commission to review the organization and management of the Executive Branch. It had the blessings of Marion Folsom and the Committee for Economic Development and of the president-elect of the American Society for Public Administration, among others; and the opposition, as untimely, of the Budget Bureau; it was sidetracked in the House. A highlight in the testimony, *Hearings, Modernizing the Federal Government*, January 31, 1968, 90th Congress, Second Session, p. 226, is a commentary from Luther Gulick tracing the periodic need for reorganization to "*inertia . . . empire-building . . .* and the inevitable tendency to build *new structures on the foundation of temporary political slogans . . .*" and advocating an "outside" commission as capable of criticizing arrangements the President is inhibited from attacking directly because of personnel commitments to incumbents in positions close to him.
4. See *The Temple University Survey of Federal Reorganization*, 1953, Robert L. Johnson, Director (2 vols.), Philadelphia.
5. Harvey Sherman *It All Depends: A Pragmatic Approach to Organization*, 1966, University of Alabama Press, especially chapter 2. See also Seidman, *Politics, Position, and Power: The Dynamics of Federal Organization*, New York: Oxford University Press. Peri E. Arnold, May–June 1974, "Reorganization and Politics: A Reflection on the Adequacy of Administrative Theory," *Public Administration Review*, vol. 34, pp. 205–211; and Herbert A. Simon, Donald W. Smithburg, and Victor A. Thompson, 1950, *Public Administration*, New York: Knopf, chapter 7.
6. From 1956 to 1976, civilian employment in the federal government, including postal workers, went from 2.4 million to 2.8 million, an increase of 17%. In the same interval, total federal outlays rose from $70.5 billion to $366.5 billion in current dollars and from $133.0 billion to $264.4 billion in constant (fiscal year 1972) dollars.
7. See, for example, Harry S. Truman's classic statement accompanying Reorganization Plan Number 5, 1950 (March 13, 1950): "The taking effect of the reorganizations included in this plan may not in itself result in substantial immediate savings. However, many benefits in improved operations are probable during the next years which will result in a reduction in expenditures as compared with those that would be otherwise necessary. An itemization of these reductions in advance of actual experience under this plan is not practicable." Similarly, Franklin D. Roosevelt remarked that the transfer of agencies would not save much money. "It is awfully erroneous," he said, "to assume that it is in the reorganization of Departments and Bureaus that you save money;" Richard Polenberg, 1966, *Reorganizing Roosevelt's Government: The Controversy over Executive Reorganization, 1936–1939*, Cambridge, MA: Harvard University Press, p. 8.
8. U.S. Department of Health, Education, and Welfare, HEW *News*, March 8, 1977, p. 2.
9. "The President's Address to the Nation," February 7, 1977, in *Weekly Compilation of Presidential Documents*, vol. 13, p. 141.
10. David S. Broder, *Washington Post*, March 12, 1977.
11. The two Johnson Task Forces were headed by Don K. Price (report submitted in November 1964 and declassified by the Lyndon Baines Johnson Library in 1976) and by Ben W. Heineman (report submitted in sections during 1967 and declassified by the Lyndon B. Johnson Library in 1976). The Nixon task force, chaired by Roy Ash, reported in 1970 (its full report has not

yet been made public, but its basic recommendations were converted into a broad set of reorganization proposals made by President Nixon in 1971). For a full explication of the Nixon proposals, 1971, see *Papers Relating to the President's Departmental Reorganization Program*, U.S. Government Printing Office, Washington, DC. A revised version of this document was also issued in 1972.

12. See Anthony Downs, 1967, *Inside Bureaucracy*, the Rand Corporation, Little Brown and Co., Boston, p. 271.
13. In the initial plan. Later, the usual predictable pressures from various farm lobbies saved, once again, the ponderous Department of Agriculture from any suggestion of change.
14. Papers relating to the President's Departmental Reorganization Program, p. 6, Office of Management and Budget, February 1972.
15. An American Bar Association Commission strongly urged that a weak, ineffective Federal Trade Commission be reorganized and strengthened in 1969.
16. See generally, Wilson and Rachal, Winter 1977, "Can the Government Regulate Itself," *The Public Interest*, 13.
17. See, for example, Davidson, "Reorganization Guidelines," *Washington Post*, January 23, 1977.
18. It should be acknowledged that reasons never claimed also produce reorganizations or affect those undertaken on other grounds. The standings of key subordinates are probably the most powerful such reasons. President Johnson sought to make the Under Secretary of State for Economic Affairs simultaneously a Special Assistant to the President and tried to graft part of the Federal Aviation Administration onto the Defense Department. The first intention is explicable only in the light of Johnson's personal relationship with Thomas Mann and the second reflected his desire to have Robert McNamara run the SST project. Similarly, President Nixon's awarding of the National Oceanic and Atmospheric Administration to the Department of Commerce rather than the logically appropriate Department of the Interior reflected his deep hostility to Interior Secretary Hickel.
19. Our government is truly remarkable in this and at a considerable disadvantage because of it. Secretaries of State tend to remain in place far longer than most cabinet officers, but Alexander Haig will be the eighth Secretary of State with whom Andrei Gromyko has dealt as Soviet Foreign Minister.
20. In the first category were the modest reduction in size of the Executive Office of the President, the creation of new cabinet departments of Energy and Education, and the redistribution of responsibility for enforcement of equal rights in employment. In the second were the creation of the Federal Emergency Management Agency and the International Development Cooperation Administration, the loosening of ACTION'S control over the Peace Corps, and the revision of responsibilities for foreign trade. The only exception to the rule was service reform, where organizational change was an unavoidable result of policy change.

    Meanwhile, much came to nothing. In particular, the extensive, president-commissioned explorations of possible cabinet department of Natural Resources, of Community and Economic Development, of Trade, Technology, Industry, and of Food and Nutrition were abandoned when no EOP champions could be found for them, and an ambitious set of organizational questions put by the President to the Department of Defense was studied slowly unto death by the department and then silently interred.

CHAPTER 4

Broadening the Framework

INTRODUCTION

The first set of materials in this volume introduced administrative reorganization in terms of a very specific set of orthodox, management-based prescriptions, each pursued in the context of a the politics–administrative dichotomy. The next set of excerpts exemplified the critical search for a set of generalizeable prescriptions that attempt to explain the managerial and political realities overlooked by the traditional view. Scholars of the 1970s and 1980s examined the relatively high number of reorganization efforts of the period and began to describe a more complex picture of things.

A significant set of voices in the scholarly community began to frame the reorganization issue in new ways. Some saw reorganization as a political strategy that could respond to public demands for change without making substantive policy change. Some recognized that reorganization offers an opportunity for new actors to imprint their own agendas. In an era when private sector norms became an increasing basis for federal government change, reformers could draw on reorganization efforts by the private sector. Others saw reorganization as a tool of policy implementation, and still others thought the reorganization could be a way to avoid conflict, achieve stability, and regain control.

A range of questions emerged from these new frames. Some dealt with issues that had not been viewed as associated with reorganization (e.g., issues of federalism and policy devolution). Analysts began to consider whether reorganization decisions had an impact on centralization or decentralization of authority and policy-making capacity.

This type of paradigm shift—away from defining reorganization as a function of the politics–administration dichotomy and toward a view of reorganization as a means to understanding broader historical, legal, and political trends—is the focus of this chapter's material. The articles included in this chapter include voices in the field that broaden the conceptual and analytical framework typically used to examine federal reorganization.

Peri Arnold's piece, "Reorganization and Politics: A Reflection on the Adequacy of Administrative Theory," focuses on the historical inadequacies of orthodox theory. To that end, Arnold finds fault both with the ignorance of early thought and with modern mainstream criticism, which tends to couch its prescriptions in terms that do nothing but perpetuate the politics–administration dichotomy in other disguised forms.

The next excerpt is drawn from James G. March and Johan P. Olsen's piece, "Organizing Political Life: What Reorganization Tells Us about Government." The authors use the framework of rhetoric to conceptualize the familiar administrative and political aspects of reorganization and introduce the discussion of reorganization their classic metaphor for the policy process: the garbage can. March and Olsen argue that administrative reorganizations are like garbage cans in that they contain choice opportunities, problems, and solutions. The application of this framework injects at least three fresh insights into the conversation. First, that persistent attention to the reorganization from political actors is paramount to short-run success of the effort. Second, an understanding of the causal links between problems and solutions is critical to the long-run prosperity of any administrative change. Third, improved governance is tied to the existence of a symbiotic relationship between administrative and political rhetorics and existing social and institutional value structures.

In "Operationalizing the Constitution Via Administrative Reorganization," James L. Garnett argues that in addition to specific management and policy effects of reorganization, the process of bureaucratic reorganization has served to maintain the legitimacy and livelihood of the American constitutional democracy. More specifically, Garnett argues that reorganizing during the 20th century involved questions related to the separation of powers as well as a means of reducing the friction and ambiguity created by shared powers. Garnett's perspective is unique in that his is the only framework that couches the value of bureaucratic reorganization not in policy or management terms, but in terms of constitutional values.

The final piece, an excerpt from Harold Seidman's classic volume *Politics, Position, and Power*, offers another analytical framework for understanding bureaucratic reform and reorganization. Seidman argues that the key to improved governance lies in political choices that lead to clear administrative goals, not in specific organizational structures or management techniques. In making this case, Seidman discusses a popular alternative to structural reorganization: enhanced coordination between agencies and legislative committees. He concludes that the quest for the perfect coordination technique, like the search for the one best organizational structure before it, is destined for failure. Magic solutions do not exist, and relying on them exclusively to solve administrative problems places the policy and the policymaker at further risk.

Peri E. Arnold, May–June, 1974, "Reorganization and Politics: A Reflection on the Adequacy of Administrative Theory," *Public Administration Review*, Vol. 34, No. 3, pp. 205–211.

The history of the study of administration exhibits a tension between administration and politics. In earlier years public administrationists operated as if politics might, like the bump in the night, simply disappear. But we can no longer avoid politics. When we speak of administration, politics stares us in the face.

The origins of the study of administration lie in a victorious reform movement. Civil service reform sought to drive venality from politics. It aimed at the transformation of politics. The means for this transformation were merit employment and administrative order. As a tactic, the reform movement separated administration from politics. The new study of administration reified that distinction. Woodrow Wilson announced the credo of the new study. Administration "was a part of political life only as the methods of the countinghouse are a part of the life of society; only as machinery is part of the manufactured product."[1] It followed, of course, that the machinery should run efficiently.

Efficiency became our goal and touchstone. Early public administrationists adopted the values of their cousins in the growing administrative sciences. But the student of business administration knows that the businessman needs a concept of efficiency. The businessman has a vital interest in profits and organizational vitality, and possesses a balance sheet as a measure. But the public administrationist cannot make that assumption about the political decision maker. Here is the root of public administration's problem with politics. The politician deals in power not profits. His interests lie in serving his constituency. Will the interests of the politician coincide with prerequisites for organizational order and efficiency?

Our best attempt at an answer can be seen in public administration's treatment of the presidency. The President's Committee on Administrative Management (Brownlow Committee) offered the first whole formulation of an answer. The President's political efficacy lies in his ability to manage the Executive Branch. Herbert Emmerich succinctly stated this doctrine:[2]

> Executive organization, which in my view was exemplified in the reports of the Brownlow Committee and of the first Hoover commission, concerns those elements of structure, personnel, budgetary and other systems of a government which produce an energetic and viable administrative management, capable of responding to the needs and the will of the country and its citizens.

But in a system of checks and balances the president is not the only significant political decision maker. How does this doctrine deal with the 535 politicians on the other end of

Pennsylvania Avenue? Why should these politicians be guided by the prescriptions of the public administrationist? Congress necessarily becomes the enemy of good administration. It is characterized by uncertainty and undercuts order. But of course the Brownlow formulation has not really worked for the President. Presidents do not succeed by alienating Congress. This is demonstrated by programs designed to achieve coordination and increased control through reorganization of the Executive Branch.[3] Presidents from 1921 on have increased their capacity for management. But their record at large-scale administrative reorganizations is bleak. The proposals of the Brownlow Committee, the first and second Hoover Commissions, President Johnson's proposal to merge Commerce and Labor, and President Nixon's plan to reorganize most of the departments were, by and large, stillborn.

This is bad news for public administrationists. Specialists in public administration were the first social scientists to have regular access at high levels of the Executive Branch. For example, President Taft's Commission on Economy and Efficiency was chaired by Frederick A. Cleveland and included Frank J. Goodnow and W.F. Willoughby. Have we provided 60 years of bad advice? On the contrary, public administrationists have probably given better advice than anybody should have expected. The good advice we gave resulted from the insight, experience, and skill of individual scholars. But as a field we flew by the seat of our pants. We should hold our field in the kind of awe we reserve for pilots who manage safe landings at the wrong airport. We also flew with bad maps.

The history of our attempts at administrative reorganization, and the administrative theories behind these attempts, suggest the failure of our maps. Some reform proposals have been successful, but many more have not. Our failures are rooted in the inutility of our theories. Explanations of both the successes and failures of administrative reorganization require a move beyond traditional and existing theory in public administration.

The manifold problems in our theory, and thus our study and practice, can best be seen in a case which allows us to confront them in a specific and delimited setting. The fundamental logic of administrative reorganization has been the tenets of administrative orthodoxy. The propositions that administrative organization should be structured by like functions and purpose, that overlapping functions should be minimized, and that control should be unified, lie within every proposal for reorganization. . . .

Public administration, particularly in its more orthodox and management oriented forms, assumes an undemonstrable organizational integrity for government. Herbert Hoover assumed that the great executive departments are functional divisions of the responsibilities of government. The agencies are conceived as logical parts of the whole. With that concept as a foundation, reorganization doctrine is spun, relying on the political decision maker's capacity and desire for instituting reform.

But agencies exist in separate and distinct galaxies. Each administrative agency works and survives within a close-knit fabric of power relations and supports. They serve, promote, and regulate valued goods within society. Over time the relations between the agency and the constituency benefiting from its functions grow into an umbilical cord, nourishing the constituency and sustaining the agency.[4]

Herbert Hoover and his administrative doctrine failed to see the disunity of government. His own experience as an administrator demonstrates how wide of the mark he was. Yet recent proposals for administrative reorganization demonstrate that orthodox doctrines are very much alive.

As the fate of President Nixon's proposals for reorganization demonstrate, we have learned little about the relationship between politics and administration since the 1920s. Certainly, no sophisticated public administrationist deems it necessary to talk about the politics–administration dichotomy. That, after all, is old hat. But public administration has developed, in both theory and practice, as if that dichotomy was still its fundamental canon. It is ironic that this period between early 1920 and the 1970s represents an era of incredible growth in the size of the federal bureaucracy and is framed by attempts to bring about the same kind of reorganization in the federal departments, for the same reasons and ending in the same failure. Where is the positive impact of theory in public administration?

The pluralist–representative perspective seems, on its face, to provide a meaningful response to our problem. Virtually all the current textbooks have borrowed this approach to explain the politics of bureaucracy. This reflects the intellectual power of all those from Appleby, Long, and Waldo to Seidman who argued that we must come to understand administration by looking at its relation to a political environment. But therein lies the weakness of this perspective. The pluralist representative approach could never produce alternative theory because it smuggled in the politics administration dichotomy. We were asked to study the political environment of administration. The logical separation remains. Where, beyond case studies, has this led?

On the other hand, we have the development of the new science of administration. Its leading spokesman demanded that we leave behind the homilies and posturing of earlier years. But "behavioral" public administration also carried with it the seed of orthodoxy. The science-manque of the 1920s was built upon faith in efficiency. When Herbert Simon set out to demolish the old public administration he failed to see past "the principles." He was perfectly willing to accept the traditional concept of the study of administration. He simply desired to erect a scientific discipline over that concept. Simon stated:[5]

> In the design of administrative organizations, as in their operations, over-all efficiency must be the guiding criterion. Mutually incompatible advantages must be balanced against each other, just as an architect weighs the advantages of additional closet space against the advantages of a larger living room.

Simon accepted the purposes and aims of "the principles" at the same time he found them illogical and unscientific. Public administration was on the right road. It simply needed science. But the study of public administration was not on the right road. There was a significant part of the essence of administration in the public sector that our field of study refused to address. Politics remained peripheral to administration, simply "the environment."

Herein is the fundamental weakness of theory in public administration. The utility of a theory must be judged by how much that theory explains. Our middle-range theories have failed because they draw the universe of administration too exclusively. Politics remain external to administration. Politics remained the uncertain force that tore apart the order and logic of administrative theory. The persona of this drama is the politician. At best we could teach him the virtue of administrative order. At worst we simply shrug our shoulders and remind ourselves that the study of administration begins with the recognition of the cupidity of the politician.

Our present task is to redraw our theoretical universe. We will not understand public administration until we understand administration as a political process. This is not a call to study the political environment of administration. We must begin with the proposition that the administrative acts of government are policy outputs. That, like all policy outputs, they involve processes that distribute costs and benefits. Moreover it seems reasonable to suggest that, like all policy outputs, these may be categorized into different analytic groups, each group correlating with different political processes and outcomes.[6]

For example, is the failure of some reorganization attempts and the success of others a function of their differences as policy and the differing political processes they engender? On the very limited basis of our view of Hoover's reorganization attempts in the 1920s we can see the promise of this kind of analysis. Hoover's successes and failures are inexplicable from the perspective of traditional administrative theory. A pluralist representative perspective takes us towards some understanding of the case but fails to provide a useful theoretical framework with which to replicate explanation and attempt prediction. A policy analysis of administration holds that promise.

Today public administration is enmeshed in a useful debate about its strengths, failures, and future.[7] The administrative mechanism of government is itself enmeshed in a battle over the access of new groups and the question of elite control. Whether it be the administration of local schools, federal funds for law enforcement, or the administration of national defense agencies, the "business-like" aspects of government have been transformed into political questions in a way which would have been inexplicable to the young Wilson or Herbert Hoover. Too often, these phenomena have been inexplicable to those of us who currently make a living studying public administration. Our maps are wrong and our theory weak. We have just begun to reach for new intellectual tools.

James G. March, Johan P. Olson, June 1983, "Organizing Political Life: What Reorganization Tells Us About Government," *The American Political Science Review*, Vol. 77, No. 2, pp. 281–296.

REORGANIZATION RHETORIC

The history of administrative reorganization in the twentieth century is a history of rhetoric. Efforts at reorganization in the United States have produced a litany for conventional discourse. Two orthodox rhetorics infuse the speaking and writing of persons involved in reorganization as well as students of it. The first is that of orthodox administrative theory. This rhetoric speaks of the design of administrative structures and procedures to facilitate the efficiency and effectiveness of bureaucratic hierarchies. Mainly prescriptive in its orientation, administrative orthodoxy has been linked to religious and moral movements,[8] and is deeply ingrained in American culture.[9]

The rhetoric of administration proclaims that explicit, comprehensive planning of administrative structures is possible and necessary, that piecemeal change creates chaos. Since Theodore Roosevelt claimed in 1907 that the executive branch had grown up entirely without plan,[10] it has become a standard cliche to see the bureaucracy as having grown, "like Topsy," in a haphazard fashion without unity of purpose. As new tasks and constituencies have been identified, office has been piled upon office, with little attention to fitting new structures into old ones and resultant administrative confusion.[11] Thus, it is argued that conventional processes of change in bureaucracies are too decentralized to be effective, that there is a need to consider the entire organization of the administrative branch of government at one time and to eliminate "antiquated machinery" through comprehensive reorganization.[12]

Administrative orthodoxy emphasizes economy and control. It speaks of offices that could be abolished, salaries that could be reduced, positions that could be eliminated, and expenses that could be curtailed.[13] It calls for strong managerial leadership, clear lines of authority and responsibility, manageable spans of control, meritocratic personnel procedures, and the utilization of modern techniques for management. It sees administration as the neutral instrument of public policies, and reorganization as a way of making that

Source: From "Organizing Political Life: What Reorganization Tells Us About Government," by James G. March and Johan P. Olsen in American Political Science Review. Vol 77, No. 2. June 1983, pp. 281–296.

instrument more efficient and effective through the application of some simple principles of organizing. Failures of reorganization are interpreted as being the result of the way parochial or special interests overcome efforts to implement administrative policies in the public interest.[14]

Administrative rhetoric is the official language of laws governing reorganizations, many public statements about it, and the obligatory terminology of reports. Although for many years most analyses of governmental expenditures have indicated that reorganizations cannot result in major savings,[15] the rituals of reorganization seem to require symbols of economy and efficiency to be used.[16] Franklin Roosevelt argued that "we have to get over the notion that the purpose of reorganization is economy,"[17] but in public he often paid tribute to the same notion. And since 1949, the reorganization statute has specified explicitly that reorganizations should be presented and justified in terms of their contribution: "(1) to promote the better execution of the laws, the more effective management of the executive branch and of its agencies and functions, and the expeditious administration of the public business; (2) to reduce expenditures and promote economy to the fullest extent consistent with the efficient operation of the Government; (3) to increase the efficiency of the operations of the Government to the fullest extent practicable; (4) to group, coordinate, and consolidate agencies and functions of the Government, as nearly as may be, according to major purposes; (5) to reduce the number of agencies by consolidating those having similar functions under a single head, and to abolish such agencies or *advisory* functions thereof as may not be necessary for the efficient conduct of the Government; and (6) to eliminate overlapping and duplication of effort."

The language could have been taken from any of a number of early pioneers in administrative theory. Similar terminology fills discussions of organization wherever bureaucracies are found in business firms, armies, hospitals, and schools. And it persists. When President Carter proposed that the Reorganization Act of 1949 be amended to eliminate the requirement for detailed savings estimates and to substitute information on improvements in service, Congress defended the faith and retained the requirement that the President estimate any reduction or increase in expenditures, itemized as far as practical.[18]

The second rhetoric of reorganization is the rhetoric of realpolitik. It is equally conventional. It speaks of reorganization, like organization, in terms of a political struggle among contending interests. Fundamental political interests, within the bureaucracy and outside, seek access, representation, control, and policy benefits. Organizational forms reflect victorious interests and establish a mechanism for future dominance.[19] Conflicts and inconsistencies found in statutes, authorizations, and contradictory legislative mandates cannot be coordinated through reorganization. Congress, bureaucrats, and organized interests in society are linked in ways substantially less hierarchical than is assumed in orthodox administrative theory. Within such a breviary, the ideal of a neatly effective administrative structure is a dangerous illusion. Because the design of an administrative structure is an important political issue, to be effective the reorganization process must reflect the heterogeneous milieu and the values, beliefs, and interests present in ordinary legislative processes.[20]

The rhetoric of realpolitik is an empirical and prescriptive counterpoint to an orthodox administrative perspective. To the emphasis on managerial control, it juxtaposes an emphasis on political control. It argues that a single individual has neither the cognitive capacity, nor the time and energy, nor the moral and representational standing assumed by the managerial perspective. The dangers of a too powerful executive are real; good government cannot be reduced to good administration; and congressional and interest group parity or dominance in administrative affairs is a precondition for a good political system.[21] In the realpolitik story, the formal administrative hierarchy is a minor part of the structure of proper administrative control. Agencies are established as responses to group demands, or they subsequently develop a close following in society. If they do not, they do not last long.[22] Thus, administrators have several competing loyalties, constituencies, and bosses.

This second orthodoxy pictures policies, organizational structures, and day-to-day organizational actions as formed through a political struggle in which the president is only one of the actors. Other main participants include congressional committees and subcommittees, administrative agencies and bureaus, and organized interests in societies—often cooperating in "iron triangles." Reorganization efforts that ignore such networks of power and interests will fail or be inconsequential. Indeed, it would appear that the real interests of political actors will find expression proportionate to their power, regardless of administrative arrangements.[23] For example, in a case study of federal employment security policy, Rourke observed that power over policy continued to rest with a coalition of state agencies and employer groups even after a reorganization that moved this activity into the Department of Labor.[24]

Realpolitik rhetoric is conventional for commentaries on administrative organization; the litany of interests, politics, conflict, bargaining, and power is as stylized as the litany of coordination, chains of command, authority, and responsibility. Although it is largely rejected as an official basis for reorganization,[25] it is sometimes argued that awareness of realpolitik makes it possible to accomplish some limited modifications of the administrative structure.[26] The political process does not respond to "true power" instantaneously, automatically, or precisely. As a result, policy environments may be changed; new groups may be given access; program emphases may be modified incrementally.[27]

Realpolitik rhetoric, in fact, appears to be as sacred and as well known as the rhetoric of administration. Far from being concealed in the activities of governance, including the activities of bureaucratic agencies, realpolitik is confirmed by the language and performances of political actors and their observers. We would require an assumption of uncommon ignorance on the part of political participants to imagine that they do not know the gospel of political realism. Moreover, it would be an assumption easily refuted. The events of governance are routinely explained by reference to a political metaphor; bureaucrats routinely speak of their "constituencies"; and newspaper reports routinely use concepts of power, interest, and conflict as the fundamental basis for interpreting the events of government. If, as seems to be suggested in some discussions of symbols in politics, the political nature of bureaucratic life is a secret from the participants in the process, it is certainly a widely shared one. Most knowledgeable administrators and other political actors as well as students of administration and organization know both rhetorics and recite one or the other when appropriate. These rhetorics jointly help to define the basic frame of reference for public discussion and action, a set of understandings within which incremental changes can occur.[28]

A compelling feature of the history of administrative reorganization is the way in which these two rhetorics have persisted throughout the twentieth century. It is not the case that an older (administrative) orthodoxy has gradually been replaced by a newer (realpolitik) orthodoxy.[29] Some of the earliest comments on reorganization were comments on power, interests, and the interplay among self-interested actors,[30] and some of the most recent pronouncements on reorganization and organizational design have made it possible to describe the past few years as a high water mark for administrative rhetoric.[31] The canons of administrative thought and the canons of political realism are interdependent elements of contemporary faith, and both secure expression in reorganization.

THE TERMS OF POLITICAL TRADE

Neither presidents nor congresses succeed often in major reorganization projects. What is proposed is regularly defeated or abandoned. Presidents, in particular, go through a cycle of enthusiasm and disappointment. Most commonly (Franklin Roosevelt and Richard Nixon are partial counterexamples), they start reorganization studies at the beginning of their terms, but by the time the studies are completed, they seem to have concluded that reorganization either will not solve their administrative problems or will not be worth the political costs.[32] Many observers of the early days of a presidency, including some presidents, comment on the innocence, ignorance, and naiveté of new presidents about reorganization.[33] Presidents report that they miscalculated the difficulties of achieving substantial reform in the national government. Truman said he knew it would be difficult, but still he was surprised. "To talk about it and to do it are two different things."[34] Yet reorganization efforts, ad hoc committees, and commissions are undertaken again and again.

Although there are occasional political confrontations over reorganization, as when more than 100 Democratic congressmen deserted a Democratic president (Franklin Roosevelt) to defeat the 1938 Executive Reorganization Bill despite an overwhelming Democratic majority in the House of Representatives.[35] Pitched battles have usually been avoided by conventional political bargaining among the parties involved, and most plans for major reorganizations fail to survive normal political trading. Presidents are reluctant to use the reorganization authority they have in the face of opposition.[36] They are often unwilling to submit reorganization plans that are controversial or that they think will not pass.[37]

The inclination of presidents to retreat from reorganization proposals when faced with opposition is illustrated by studies of Presidents Wilson,[38] Johnson,[39] Nixon,[40] and Carter.[41] Even President Truman, one of the most successful reorganizers, hesitated when confronted with conflicts within the executive branch and with Congress. When he finally acted, he submitted mild, relatively uncontroversial proposals.[42] Hess observed that presidents complain about the ill-fitting shape of government, but generally see attempts at serious restructuring as no-win propositions.[43] Neither the voters nor the annals of history seem likely to reward them for such efforts.

In general, the historical pattern of political bargaining over administrative organization indicates that the structure of the bureaucracy is less important politically to the president than it is to many legislators. Particularly in times of war or during periods of active social reform, presidents tend to give priority to substantive problems, especially those with an apparent deadline.[44] For example, Franklin Roosevelt, who agreed with the Brownlow Committee[45] that most of the 100 agencies outside the executive departments ought to be included in those departments, nevertheless created numerous new agencies on an ad hoc basis to solve immediate problems.[46]

Most recent presidents have apparently considered reorganization an important part of their personal agendas, even a duty, but they have not considered it important enough to make significant political trades involving substantive legislative projects. For the most part, the political trading goes the other way. Presidents give up reorganization projects in order to secure legislative support for other things, and legislators give up opposition on other things in order to block administrative change. The somewhat paradoxical observation that presidents are more interested in legislation and Congress more interested in administration was made as early as 1910 by Senator Jonathan Dolliver in opposing the creation of the Taft Commission,[47] and the political bargains struck between presidents and congresses subsequently seem generally susceptible to such an interpretation.

Reorganization threatens prime perquisites of legislative office—access to bureaucratic operations and the linkages between agencies and committees. The internal structure of an agency and its location in the departmental structure of the government are perceived by congressmen as affecting legislative influence and control and thus the capability of furthering political careers through constituency services.[48] As a result, presidential proposals for reorganization have the consequence of providing a convenient trading chip in bargaining with Congress. Although explicit presidential cleverness cannot be excluded, it seems unlikely that reorganization efforts are deliberate sacrificial lambs, the result of conscious attempts to provide trading resources. It seems more likely that the persistent presidential pattern of generating and then abandoning reorganization is likely to be more a personal than a political one; the political sacrifice of reorganization projects, although unplanned, becomes convenient as the political situation unfolds.

REORGANIZATION AS GARBAGE CANS

Although some features of political trading are fairly stable over the history we have examined, political bargaining over reorganization is sensitive to contextual fluctuations and to short-run changes in political attention. Reorganization is an ecology of games[49] in which attention is problematic. Access rules for participants and issues change over time in response to experience, conscious attempts to control reorganizations, and the cumulative twists of history, but the general absence of precise rules controlling access makes it likely that reorganizations will become garbage cans, highly contextual combinations of people, choice opportunities, problems, and solutions.[50] Thus, the course of events surrounding a reorganization seems to depend less on properties of the reorganization proposals or efforts than on the happenstance of short-run political attention, over which reorganization groups typically have little control.

On the one hand, reorganization efforts have difficulty in sustaining the attention of major political actors. Although administrative reorganizations involve committees or commissions that are expected to proceed in parallel with activities in the rest of the government, the necessity of securing attention from political actors in order to be effective drives reorganization into competition for scarce resources of attention.[51] Presidents, congressional leaders, major interest groups, and higher civil servants are typically too busy to be more than very occasional participants. As a result, reorganization efforts often operate in an attention vacuum with respect to those political figures who are likely to be most supportive, and improbable promises of economies are made in an effort to secure attention. . . . [52]

At the same time as presidents and other major political supporters for reorganization are hard-pressed to maintain attention on the issue, less central actors move to the forefront. Like discussions of institutional goals and long-term planning,[53] reorganizations attract numerous otherwise-unoccupied participants and unresolved issues. Any particular reorganization proposal or topic for discussion is an arena for debating a wide range of current concerns and ancient philosophies. Since there are few established rules of relevance and access, reorganizations tend to become collections of solutions looking for problems, ideologies looking for soapboxes, pet projects looking for supporters, and people looking for jobs, reputations, or entertainment. The linkages among these concerns seem to be testimony more to their simultaneity than to their content, and administrative reform becomes associated with issues, symbols, and projects that sometimes seem remote from the initial impetus behind the effort. . . . [54]

Although incremental and less visible changes not linked to a major reorganization effort often succeed,[55] comprehensive reorganization tends to consolidate an opposition,[56] provide an occasion for negative logrolling in Congress,[57] and an opportunity to deal a blow to presidential prestige.[58] Reorganizations also become vulnerable to the focused attention of significant actors. . . .

In such a context, it has been argued that inviting people into the process involves compromises on the changes to be proposed,[59] that extended participation delays the process, and that radical changes need to be made fairly quickly if they are to occur at all. Conversely, it has been proposed that reorganization efforts would be more successful if they involved a more explicitly participatory style.[60] Although the latter argument is drawn from research on participation that has received a good deal of attention in recent years, the empirical support is limited. . . . [61]

SHORT-RUN FAILURES AND LONG-RUN SUCCESSES

Bureaucratic reform seems to require long-run commitment, patience, and perseverance.[62] Despite the frequency and intensity of serious efforts, major reorganizations seem to have been largely unsuccessful. Most reorganizations produce some formal administrative change. Of 102 reorganization plans submitted to same groups that had seen the recommendations Congress between 1939 and 1970, only 22 were rejected,[63] and 72% of the proposals from the first Hoover Commission have been listed as implemented by the President on his own. Changes resulting from efforts at comprehensive reorganization seem small compared to changes produced by continuous, incremental change.[64] Frequently, organizational change seems to occur first, and formal reorganization later, rather than the other way around. As observed by Short,[65] a common pattern is that offices are initially created by a department head, later acquire implicit statutory recognition in an appropriation act or hearing, and only much later are formally recognized in substantive legislation.

In terms of their effects on administrative costs, size of staff, productivity, or spending, most major reorganization efforts have been described by outsiders, and frequently by participants, as substantial failures. Few efficiencies are achieved; little gain in responsiveness is recorded; control seems as elusive after the efforts as before. It is a record of "problems identified, but not solved, of promises made but not kept . . . the source of frustration and disillusionment."[66]

Any specific major reorganization project is likely to fail, but persistent repetition of similar ideas and similar arguments over a relatively long period of time appears to make some difference. Persistence both increases the likelihood that a proposal will be current at an opportune time and creates a diffuse climate of availability and legitimacy for it. Recommendations that produce a storm at one time are later accepted with little opposition.[67] For example, one year after the acrimonious defeat of his 1938 reorganization plan, Franklin Roosevelt was able to get the Reorganization Act of 1939 passed without serious controversy.[68] Different times, different meanings. The same groups that had seen the recommendations of the Brownlow committee and the 1938 plan as an aggrandizement of presidential power described the very similar suggestions in the 1945 reorganizations, and later proposed by the first Hoover Commission, in positive terms. Now, a strong, unified executive was considered to be essential to democratic institutions. Instead of talking about presidential dictatorship, the themes harked back to Hamilton's quest for leadership, and the Hoover proposals became a "monumental effort to bring order out of chaos."[69]

Reorganization can be viewed as a form of civic education.[70] Finer observed that although any reorganization effort is at the mercy of a hundred irrelevant political hazards and thus cannot be sure of practical results, one thing is in its power–it can educate the public and help to change the climate of opinion.[71] The President's Advisory Committee on Management also suggested that such "secondary consequences" as a general change in the climate of opinion could well turn out in the long run to be more consequential than the immediate recommendations,[72] and Herbert Hoover listed as one of the purposes of the Hoover Commission "to open the doors of understanding of the functions of government to our people at large. They are a lesson in civil government of significant educational value."[73]

Reorganization studies provide concepts and ideas; they keep theories and proposals alive. They create precedents. They develop a logic of argument that is carried over to subsequent reorganization efforts. They develop "solutions" waiting for "problems" and circumstances. They organize support and motivation for administrative change. Each of these occurs over relatively long time periods, and the relevant ideas evolve in a subtle way over a series of experiences. Successive reorganizations have enlarged the concept of reorganization itself well beyond its original connotation of changes in office procedures,[74] and have shifted the definition of the responsibility of the President in reorganization;[75] they have participated in elaborating the role of the President as manager. The possibility of reorganization stimulates self-inspection on the part of agencies and offices and sometimes fulfills the intentions of the reorganization without formal structural change.[76] Finally, an imitative burst of state reorganizations typically follows federal commissions.[77]

Because of these secondary returns to persistence, the achievement record of reorganization efforts seems more impressive in the long run than in the short run. Proposals for change that have been made in the context of reorganization committees frequently are implemented years later. To credit such implementation to the reorganization commission in which the proposal first appeared, or to the series of efforts through which it is repeated, would be an overstatement. The same political forces that place an issue on the agenda of a committee often keep it on the agendas of other groups. However, formal considerations of administrative reorganization are part of the broad educational process by which possible changes gain credence and support. That long-run educational process cannot easily be justified in terms of short-run observable effects. As a result, it depends heavily on the ways in which each new administration comes to see reform as feasible and desirable, despite the long history of disappointments with administrative reorganization. And it depends on the somewhat irrational and arbitrary commitments of professional students of administrative reform and the handful of political leaders for whom this is an enduring concern.

REORGANIZATION AND SOCIAL VALUES

For the most part, reorganizations have been proposed and understood in instrumental terms, as possible solutions to perceived problems.[78] Nevertheless, there are few attempts by the initiators of reorganizations to discover what really happened as a consequence of their efforts. Salamon argued that "serious empirical work on the real effects of reorganization is not only deficient, it is nonexistent. . . . Given the millions of dollars and thousands of person-years of effort that have gone into the generation of proposals for organizational change in the federal government over the past half century, this situation would be scandalous were it not so common."[79] Similar comments can be found in Brown,[80] Garnett,[81] Kaufman,[82] Miles,[83] and Mosher.[84] In those rare cases where information is available, it is not attended to reliably;[85] Seidman observed that one of his greatest frustrations as a reorganizer was that "we never had the time or staff to analyze the results of reorganization."[86] He reported that the White House typically lost interest in reorganization as soon as a decision was made.

One possible reason for the reluctance to evaluate results, of course, is an awareness that it is hard to cite much success in improving either efficiency or control through major reorganization. Although struggles over organization charts can be emotional,[87] most observers agree on the limited success of reorganization in achieving manifest instrumental goals. Since the two Hoover Commissions alone spent almost five million dollars (in direct costs) and generated about six million words of reports,[88] a formal cost/benefit analysis may not be appealing to someone who has faith in the importance of reorganization efforts.

Persistence in the face of apparent failure and indifference to careful evaluation of the consequences of action are, of course, often observed in human behavior—particularly in domains of strong beliefs and ambiguous experience. If a favorite social reform fails to achieve its promised success, we may conclude that the problem lies not in the reform, but in our failure to push it hard enough, far enough, or long enough. In such cases, it is not only that our interpretation of the outcomes of action are confounded by our ideologies, but also that our actions have symbolic meaning that is independent of their instrumental consequences. Action is an affirmation of belief and an assertion of virtue. Similarly, organization and reorganization are expressions of social values.[89] Organizations are cultural systems embedded in a wider culture, and reorganizations are symbolic and rhetorical events of some significance to that wider culture.[90]

Although personal or group influences make it difficult to secure agreement on the specifics of any reorganization, the idea of reorganization rarely produces dissent. Everyone is for it, in principle.[91] One of the major themes of White House mail after Truman became president was the need for reorganization and reform;[92] in Truman's 21-point address of September 1945, reorganization ranked tenth in public interest, a higher ranking than either the full employment bill, the regulation of prices and wages, the control of the atomic bomb, or the housing shortage.[93] Congress is more ready to approve the creation of new departments than the consolidation or elimination of them, but it is more ready to talk about simplification than growth.[94] Congressional actors protect their own committees; bureaucratic actors protect their own agencies; presidents protect their own pet projects; but all of them advocate the principles of simplification, reduction in government, and reorganization.[95] Observers report that reorganizers who want to succeed must exhibit substantive neutrality, claim a distinction between administration and policy,[96] and appear to eschew politics.[97] Similarly, although his Secretary of Health, Education, and Welfare planned the largest reorganization in the history of HEW under conditions of extreme secrecy and began to execute it during the 1978–1979 congressional recess, President Carter spoke of an open and participatory reorganization process.[98]

Reorganization sometimes appears to be a code word symbolizing a general frustration with bureaucracy and governmental intrusion in private lives.[99] When President Carter promised to "bring the horrible bureaucratic mess under control" and restore sound principles of organization and management,[100] he was reciting a traditional theme. The Brownlow Committee argued that "the safeguarding of the citizen from narrow minded and dictatorial bureaucratic interference and control is one of the primary obligations of democratic government" and that "the forward march of American democracy at this point in history depends more on effective management than upon any other single factor."[101] The argument was repeated by Truman,[102] and Nixon announced that restoring confidence in government "requires us to give more profound and more critical attention to the question of government organization than any single group of national leaders since the Constitutional Convention adjourned in Philadelphia in September 1787."[103]

More generally, efforts at comprehensive administrative reorganization, like other governmental programs, are symbols of the possibility of meaningful action. Confessions of impotence are not acceptable; leaders are expected to act,[104] and reorganizations provide an opportunity to symbolize action.[105] Presidents who promise reforms apparently do not suffer if they fail to implement them.[106] Announcing a major reorganization symbolizes the possibility of effective leadership, and the belief in that possibility may be of greater significance than the execution of it.[107] The most important things appear to be statements of intent, an assurance of proper values, and a willingness to try.[108]

It is tempting in looking at such disparities between action and words to see the actions as reflecting basic underlying forces, and the words as deceits.[109] Thus, Salamon argues that reorganization often becomes an alternative to action, a way to express concern about a program for which no resources are available.[110] And Seidman discusses reorganization as a tactic for creating an illusion of progress where none exists.[111] The history leaves no doubt that some consciousness of such tactics is present throughout the period we have been examining. Neither presidents nor other political actors are completely innocent. But such a view may be misleading. Any effective deceit is testimony to a belief deeply enough held to warrant the costs of hypocrisy. If we observe that everyone says the same thing while doing different things, we are observing something important about the political system, the beliefs on which it rests. Virtuous words sustain the meaning and importance of virtue, even among sinners. To view the symbols of politics as intentional efforts by sophisticated actors to deceive the innocent is likely to exaggerate the extent to which things as fundamental as optimism that mankind can direct and control its environment for the better[112] can be manipulated arbitrarily as a tactic. Leaders need reassurance, too. More generally, organization and reorganization, like much action, are tied to the discovery, clarification, and elaboration of meaning as well as to immediate action or decision making.[113] It is part of the process by which a society develops an understanding of what constitutes a good society without necessarily being able to achieve it, and how alternative institutions may be imagined to contribute to such a world.[114]

The preponderant evidence is that the symbols of administrative reform are important to politicians, not only as ways to fool the voters but also as reflections of their own beliefs. Incoming administrations, like their supporters, believe in the possibility of making a difference, and the recurrence of major reorganization efforts is tied to that belief. Since progress through intentional action is an enduring part of American secular religion, and since sacred beliefs must be exhibited by sacred institutions, the necessary logic of public life is efficacy. In the case of leaders, a belief in the efficacy of action is less difficult to sustain than it might be among others. Political success makes it relatively easy for political leaders to resolve the ambiguities of experience by an interpretation that confirms their own competence and sagacity. Winning an election is likely to lead them to believe in their skill, intelligence, political understanding, and hard work.[115] They are surrounded by evidence of their own capabilities for control, evidence that is partly a consequence of the staging and rhetoric of their activities. They sustain those beliefs through the acting out of decisiveness and decision. Efforts at administration reform, like other political efforts, express—and thereby confirm—a fundamental confidence in the possibility of directing and controlling human existence, or, more specifically, the government.

Such a perspective may provide an interpretation of the cultural ritual of reorganization and of the rhetorical duality of that ritual. The rhetoric of administration and the rhetoric of realpolitik are mutually supporting and are embedded in a culture in which each is important. The ritual of reorganization is a reminder of both sets of beliefs and testimony to their efficacy. On the one hand, a commitment to administrative purity is made tolerable by an appreciation of realpolitik, much as a commitment to personal purity is made tolerable by an appreciation of human weakness. At the same time, a commitment to a realpolitik rhetoric is made consistent with human hopes by a faith in the imaginability of improvement through human intelligence. It should not be surprising to find that both rhetorics survive and thrive, and that both find expression in the symbols of reorganization. The orthodoxy of administration is the voice of the prologue to comprehensive administrative reform; the orthodoxy of realpolitik is the voice of the epilogue; the myths of the first shade into the myths of the second over the course of a major effort at reorganization; and both sets of myths are needed for a normatively proper interpretation of the reorganization saga.

The simultaneous recitation of the stories of classical administration and the stories of political realism are a reflection of the duality of social beliefs, as are the uses of the sacred symbols of economy, efficiency, constituency pressure, and interest groups. Because immediate structural change may be of less consequence than the reinforcement of social beliefs and long-term educational effects, there is little interest in studies of the immediate results of reorganizations, and what people say and what they do are only loosely linked. Presidents make only modest use of the reorganization authority they have fought to achieve, at least in part because the symbolic value of the authority is more critical to them than its exercise. And presidents are more likely to be punished for not making promises of administrative reform than for not implementing them, because providing rhetorical support for the administrative and realpolitik orthodoxies is of greater significance for their roles as leaders of the public bureaucracy than is rearranging organizational structures.[116]

IMPLICATIONS FOR GOVERNANCE

Reorganization is a domain of rhetoric, trading, problematic attention, and symbolic action. It is described both as fundamental to governmental power[117] and as not worth the time and effort involved.[118] Its effects are uncertain; hopes for a firm theoretical basis for institutional design have been mostly unfulfilled;[119] and prescriptions tend to be contradictory.[120] No matter what principles of organization are followed, it seems to be inevitable that administrative problems will persist.[121] The balancing of leadership, expertise, and interest representation is delicate.[122] There is little agreement on criteria;[123] goals are discovered as well as implemented;[124] and post hoc revision of intentions and desires is common. A result is that few presidents have been comfortable with a role as overseer of the bureaucracy,[125] and comprehensive reorganization seems more valuable as a proposal than as a project. Although history shows long-run changes that may be partly attributable to the cumulative effect of major reorganization efforts, short-run achievements are meager. Powerful figures receive both easy victories and seemingly inexplicable defeats. Attempts to interpret reorganization through simple models of political competition tend to miss the mark.[126] An open structure makes attention critical, but hard to arrange arbitrarily. As participants move onto and off the stage, short-run outcomes are hard to predict or control. Woven around this experience are two conventional rhetorics, widely known and routinely recited, by which individuals talk about the problems of reorganization and interpret their experience with it. The rhetorics exhibit and reaffirm fundamental social values, particularly those associated with personal efficacy, with intention, interest, power, and rational choice.

These features of reorganization are not unique to that arena. They are cited frequently as general features of political life. As a result, it may be possible to extend some features of the interpretation we have made to a more general consideration of political institutions and processes, to the problems of governance. The history of reorganization leads us to some of the most honored of traditions of political thought: the role of intentions, reflection, and choice in the development of political institutions;[127] the importance of legitimacy and the relation between political drama and social values; and the contrast between the vision of coherence found in relatively macro theories of broad political and social trends and the vision of confusion often found in their micro political cousins.

We focus on three basic observations about governance, drawn from the history of major reorganization efforts in the United States. The first observation is that the short-run course of action in most political domains is heavily influenced by the problematics of attention, by the ways in which choice opportunities, problems, solutions, and participants are associated in terms of their simultaneous availability. The idea that attention is a prime scarce resource in governing is not a new one. In most cases, however, concerns about attention (or activation) arise as an annoying, but ultimately minor, constraint or complication within some more "basic" vision. The basic idea is that political processes and outcomes are determined by formal or legal rules, structures, power, or traditions, subject to attention constraints. Our observations suggest that perhaps we should shift the focus, that the core reality is the organization of attention, and that metaphors like the ecology of games or garbage-can decision processes capture a key essential of political events.[128]

The second observation is that the long-run development of political institutions is less a product of intentions, plans, and consistent decisions than incremental adaptation to changing problems with available solutions within gradually evolving structures of meaning. Sait argued that "the great monuments of human activity—such as the state itself or the common law—have taken shape like the coral islands, planlessly, by a series of minor adjustments that result from the more or less mechanical reaction of man to his environment."[129] The statistical properties of that long-run development may, in fact, be both predictable and, to some extent, controllable. Although it is difficult to guess when an opportunity to attach a favorite solution to some problem will arise, a solution that is persistently available is likely to find an occasion. The implication is not that governing is impossible. Rather, it is that governance becomes less a matter of engineering than of gardening;[130] less a matter of hunting than of gathering. "Consider a round, sloped multi-goal soccer field on which individuals play soccer. Many different people (but not everyone) can join the game (or leave it) at different times. Some people can throw balls into the game or remove them. Individuals while they are in the game try to kick whatever ball comes near them in the direction of goals they like and away from goals that they wish to avoid. The slope of the field produces a bias in how the balls fall and what goals are reached, but the course of a specific decision and the actual outcomes are not easily anticipated. After the fact, they may look rather obvious; and usually normatively reassuring."[131]

The third observation is that governance is an interpretation of life and an affirmation of legitimate values and institutions. In a society that emphasizes rationality, self-interest, and efficacy, politics honors administrative and realpolitik rhetoric. It provides symbolic and ritual confirmation of the possibility of meaningful individual and collective action. The argument is not that symbols are important to politics, although they certainly are. Rather, the argument is the reverse—that politics is important to symbols, that a primary contribution of politics to life is in the development of meaning. It is not necessary to decide here whether decision making and the allocation of resources or symbols and the construction of meaning are more fundamental. They are heavily intertwined, and discussions of primacy may obscure that fact. But it seems unlikely that a theory of governance can represent or improve the phenomena of governing without including the ways political institutions, rhetoric, and the rituals of decisions facilitate the maintenance and change of social values and the interpretation of human existence.

References

D. C. Argyrades, 1965, "Some aspects of civil service reorganization in Greece," *International Review of Administrative Sciences*, vol. 31, pp. 297–307.

C. L. Berg, 1975, "Lapse of reorganization authority," *Public Administration Review*, vol. 35, pp. 195–199.

R. A. Chapman and J. R. Greenaway, 1980, *The Dynamics of Administrative Reform*, Croom Helm, London.

Executive Office of the President (Nixon). Office of Management and Budget. Revised February 1972, *Papers relating to the President's departmental reorganization program: a reference compilation*, U.S. Government Printing Office, Washington, DC.

J. W. Fesler, 1975, "Public administration and the social sciences: 1946 to 1960," in F. C. Mosher (Ed.), *American Public Administration: Past, Present, Future*. University of Alabama Press, Tuscaloosa, AL.

A. Gorvine, 1966, "Administrative reform: function of political and economic change," in G. S. Birkhead (Ed.), *Administrative Problems in Pakistan*, Syracuse University Press, Syracuse University.

R. T. Groves, 1967, "Administrative reform and the politics of reform: the case of Venezuela," *Public Administration Review*, vol. 27, pp. 436–445.

D. H. Haider, 1979, "Presidential management initiatives: a Ford legacy to executive management improvement," *Public Administration Review*, vol. 39, pp. 248–259.

F. Heady, 1947, "A new approach to federal executive reorganization," *American Political Science Review*, vol. 41, pp. 1118–1126.

F. Heady, 1949, "The Reorganization Act of 1949," *Public Administration Review*, vol. 9, pp. 165–174.

B. D. Karl, 1963, *Executive Reorganization and Reform in the New Deal: The Genesis of Administrative Management, 1900–1939*. Harvard University Press, Cambridge, MA.

O. Kraines, 1958, *Congress and the Challenge of Big Government*. Bookman, New York.

J. G. March, 1981, "Footnotes to organizational change," *Administrative Science Quarterly*, vol. 17, pp. 563–577.

R. Mayntz and F. W. Scharpf, 1975, *Policy-Making in the German Federal Bureaucracy*. Elsevier, Amsterdam.

K. J. Meier, 1980, "Executive reorganization of government: impact on employment and expenditures," *American Journal of Political Science*, vol. 24, pp. 396–412.

D. R. Morgan and J. P. Pelissero, 1980, "Urban policy: does political structure matter?" *American Political Science Review*, vol. 74, pp. 999–1006.

F. C. Mosher, 1965, "Some notes on reorganizations in public agencies," in R. C. Martin (Ed.), *Public Administration and Democracy*. Syracuse University Press, Syracuse, NY.

President's Advisory Committee on Management, 1953, "Improvement of management in the federal government." 1952 Reprinted in *Public Administration Review*, vol. 13, pp. 38–49.

P. G. Roness, 1979, *Reorganisering Av Departementa, Eit Politisk Styringsmiddel?* Universitetsforlaget, Bergen.

G. B. Siegel and N. Kleber, 1965, "Formalism in Brazilian administrative reform," *International Review of Administrative Sciences*, vol. 31, pp. 175–184.

U.S. Commission on the Organization of the Executive Branch of the Government (Hoover Commission), 1971, *Hoover Commission Report on the organization of the executive branch of the government.* Reprint of the 1949 edition. Greenwood, Westport, CN.

G. A. Weber, 1919, *Organized Efforts for the Improvement of Methods of Administration in the United States.* D. Appleton, New York.

James L. Garnett, "Operationalizing the Constitution Via Administrative Reorganization: Oilcans, Trends, and Proverbs," *Public Administration Review*, Vol. 47, No. 1, The American Constitution and the Administrative State (January–February 1987), pp. 35–44.

Campaigns to reorganize administrative structures of federal, state, and local governments have been the battlegrounds over which much of American public administrative theory has been spawned, advocated, and criticized.[132] These reorganization battles over structure, power, process, and doctrine have often been so pitched that opponents or advocates of reorganization have accused the opposition of insanity, tyranny, godlessness, naiveté, backwardness, and questionable ancestry. Despite such controversy, government reorganizing has played a vital role in making the constitutional system work.

Administrative reorganizations have been characterized as *garbage cans,* "highly contextual combinations of people, choice opportunities, problems, and solution."[133] This essay views reorganizations as *oilcans,* lubricating constitutional machinery so it can function. More specifically, reorganizing has been an extraconstitutional means of reducing friction and conflict stemming from constitutional issues surrounding the proper balance and separation of powers.[134] Reorganizing within the existing constitutional framework to flesh out and operationalize it has dominated over efforts to overhaul the constitution itself into a parliamentary or other system.[135]

Instead of junking the 1787 model for a different constitutional system, Americans, using their spirit for tinkering and inventiveness, have relied on repairing and lubricating the old model to keep it running. Reorganizing to repair and improve the system of government has largely been an adaptive process combining *ideology* and *pragmatism* to meet changing needs. As with many machinery lubricants, reorganizations have rarely been neutral interventions but have often been terrifically heated while doing their job. Reorganizations typically create as well as reduce political and administrative friction. But reorganizing has also avoided tackling constitutional issues head-on, instead confronting issues of governance at a relatively less volatile and more manageable level.

This essay first addresses reorganization's facilitating, lubricating role, observing the different emphases and trends taken to keep constitutional machinery running to achieve system goals of *accountability* and *competence.* This essay concludes by examining some proverbs of reorganization and by drawing implications for future reorganization practice and research.

REORGANIZATION AS LUBRICANT FOR THE CONSTITUTIONAL SYSTEM

The U.S. Constitution is conspicuously mute about administrative structure. Article 1, Section 8 sets forth the powers of Congress, but the Constitution is conspicuously silent about how Congress or the President should exercise these powers. The Constitution makes no mention of "administration" or "management" and refers sparingly to "executing the laws." Article 2, Section 2 makes the President ". . . Commander in Chief of the Army and Navy of the United States, and of the militia of the several states. . . ," but no equally clear designation of the President as Commander in Chief of the Executive Branch exists. Article 2, Section 2 mentions "Heads" and "principal Officers" of "executive Departments." But the Constitution avoids specifying which executive departments should exist, how many are needed, and how these departments should be organized. The only mention of "organizing" appears in Article 1, Section 8, giving Congress power "to provide for organizing, arming, and disciplining the Militia. . . . " Here, "organizing" more accurately means "mobilizing" than "structuring." Because administrative organization gets no real attention in the Constitution, no express provision is made for reorganizing. By implication rather than through express provision, the U.S. Constitution allows structural and other changes through enacting laws or amending the Constitution itself.

The constitutional upper hand given Congress, fragmentation of powers, and the void about administrative organization and management have been criticized as weak foundations for achieving efficient administration.[136] The U.S. Constitution places more emphasis on governmental *accountability,* ability to control those in power and hold them responsible for their actions, than on *competence,* ability of government to do its business. The constitutional Framers were not necessarily against strong, efficient management, although suspicion of British executive excesses still ran strong. The role of administration was perceived differently at a time when members of Congress outnumbered the entire executive branch workforce in Washington.[137] Constitutional machinery was designed for its time, before the onslaught of modernizing and bureaucratizing forces. . . .

Much reorganizing during the twentieth century at all levels of government has been an attempt either to carry out the logic inherent in separation of powers or to reduce the friction and ambiguity created by it. Reorganizations have essentially served to lubricate and preserve constitutional machinery by emphasizing popular representation, neutral expertise, and executive leadership.[138] Each of these three thrusts has affected government's *accountability* and *competence. . . .*

Why have Americans relied on reorganizing the 1787 model rather than make fundamental constitutional changes? Reverence for the Constitution's sanctity has not prevented important amendments on other issues. Has difficulty amending the Constitution discouraged that option? Since no amendment to reorganize administration has been tried except for limiting presidents to two consecutive terms, the federal level offers little direct experience, although other amendments have faced tough hurdles. But at least 31 of the state reorganizations attempted since 1900 used constitutional amendment. The record shows that the all-or-nothing nature of constitutional revision makes it the riskier strategy. All three of the total reorganization defeats from 1947–1985 came via constitutional amendment.[139] Reorganizing by statute has dominated in the states, although reorganizations in the 1960s and 1970s utilized a greater range of legal mechanisms. Municipalities typically change structures via charter revision rather than ordinance, but like states have primarily kept the basic tripartite separation of powers system. For those states and localities which have revamped their structures via constitution or charter, the reorganization oilcan has served to lubricate administrative machinery between major overhauls of the same basic model.

Another explanation for foregoing profound constitutional change involves tactics. Some reformers felt they could repair constitutional inadequacies better through periodic, partial adjustments than by attempting to overhaul the entire system. For example, reformers advocating executive leadership calculated that strengthening the executive under the guise of more businesslike, more scientific administration deflected much opposition that would likely have arisen from a more threatening direct assault on the Constitution. In the words of Luther Gulick: "We could sell it [administration orthodoxy] . . . because both the conservatives and the liberals believed in science and believed in rationality. . . . We were not trying to develop a systematic, logical, comprehensive philosophy of the political or administrative system of our government."[140]

Gulick's admission provides another reason for relying on periodic lubrications and tuneups to modify government organization: reformulating a comprehensive administrative and political system is exceedingly difficult to conceptualize and an even harder object of consensus. Explaining another case of "nonconstitutional management of a constitutional problem," Edward Hamilton observes: ". . . a student of the Constitution might remind us, the straightforward remedy even the most seem obvious. The document contains an orderly procedure for amendment, or even for total revision. But few would maintain that the present strength of the political consensus is sufficiently impressive to warrant confidence that a wholesale revision would improvements than new defects."[141]

Thus, for reasons of legal and political tactics and a lack of consensus about what would replace the 1787 model, Americans have chosen to reorganize periodically, adapting governmental machinery to changing conditions and needs.

PROVERBS OF REORGANIZATION

Just as orthodox administrative theory produced what later critics termed the "proverbs of administration,"[142] some "proverbs of reorganization" have evolved. This bicentennial period is an appropriate occasion to reexamine these proverbs since they address key aspects of the relationship between the Constitution and administrative reorganization. The first two proverbs question how well the reorganization oilcan has served to improve government's competence. The third proverb emphasizes politics, power, and control-accountability issues. The fourth proverb stresses the role of administrative ideology in organizing and reorganizing government. As often happens, earlier principles or proverbs of reorganization have been "debunked" and replaced with newer conventional wisdoms. This section examines both the former and current proverbs.

REORGANIZATION AS ECONOMY

Former Proverb: Administrative reorganizations promote government economy. Current Proverb: Reorganizations fail to save governments money.

Economy has been a standard rationale for federal, state, and local reorganizations. Early, congressionally initiated efforts at federal reorganization, like the Cockrell Committee (1887–89) and Dockery-Cockrell Committee (1893–95), set the tone with a preoccupation on administrative detail and economy. Major federal reorganizations since then have generally paid lip service to the proverb of economy, but conventional wisdom about federal reorganization refutes these claims.[143] One analyst summarizes this conventional wisdom this way: "Of all the forms of reorganization . . . reorganization for efficiency and economy is clearly the most discredited."[144]

Measuring the economic effects of reorganization is difficult. Many factors affect government expenditures before, during, and after reorganization. Such historical factors as economic health, inflation, greater population, changes in a government's role, mandates from higher level governments, and higher demands on entitlement programs affect government spending regardless of reorganization. The difficulty of measuring savings, even those that actually exist, has reinforced the notion that no economies exist.

The conventional wisdom that reorganization produces little economy has also been fed by the types of reorganizations adopted. Most major federal, state, and local reorganizations have combined changing the organization chart *and* revising management procedures. Reorganizations in the first half of this century tended to emphasize changes in organization charts changes in grouping and reporting relationships. But more recent reorganizations emphasize revised management procedures. Reorganizations primarily geared to modernizing management procedures, privatizing service delivery, revamping priorities, or retrenching government may well reduce spending. Most reorganizations thus far studied have been growth-oriented in a generally expanding government sector. Reorganizations in the face of budget shortages, like the 1981 reorganization in Tennessee to cut transportation department costs, will likely do more than pay lip service to economy.

To summarize, savings via reorganization are likely to be modest rather than drastic,[145] long-term rather than short-term,[146] on a departmental or program level rather than systemwide,[147] result more from tangible workforce reductions and management systems improvements,[148] and be less likely to reduce the overall bottom line than to offset other expenses or be targeted for new priorities. Without more incisive analysis, existing conventional wisdom that reorganization in general is antithetical to economizing is just as untested and proverbial as blanket claims for economy.

REORGANIZATION AS MANAGEMENT REFORM

Former proverb: Reorganizing government to achieve the correct structure produces more effective and efficient administration.[149] Current proverb: Governmental structure has little influence on performance.

Classical reformers believed strongly that "correct" structures adhering to the canons of integration would produce good outcomes.[150] More recently President Nixon echoed this belief, "Just as inadequate organization can frustrate good men and women, so it can dissipate good money . . . the major cause of the ineffectiveness of government is not a matter of men or of money. It is principally a matter of machinery."[151] Belief that structure is central to administrative performance pervaded classical organization theory and also dominated federal, state, and local governments for the first half of the twentieth century.

Claims that reorganization produces government efficiency and effectiveness received heavy criticism from skeptics in the first decades of the twentieth century, yet remained largely unscathed. Rigorous intellectual criticism in the 1940s exposed the shaky premises underpinning administrative orthodoxy without stopping its use by government practitioners.[152] But findings of several policy scientists in the 1960s and 1970s that socioeconomic characteristics of a state or community explained policy outcomes better than any political or organizational "black box" deflated the importance of structure.[153] This emphasis on socioeconomic determinants exposed the proverb of structuralism and itself became a "new orthodoxy." But this attack on structural orthodoxy prompted a counterattack from other forces who criticized the atheoretical nature of this research, the bias of using expenditures to measure policy outcomes, and the paucity of administrative variables used.[154]

Despite criticism of determinants research, the idea that structure counts little remains conventional wisdom.[155] Instead of demonstrating the irrelevance of structure, critics turned the tables, challenging believers to prove that structure *does* make a difference. Some scholars have continued to suspect that structure matters more than the "new orthodoxy" admits. Also, public officials have continued to mouth the importance of structure before reorganizing. But without evidence that organizational structure indeed affects administrative and service performance, advocates of structural reorganization have "kept a low profile."

But evidence that structural arrangements do make a difference continues to be found in business and is reported again in government. In business, where effectiveness and efficiency are usually easier to measure, structure's contribution has been demonstrated better.[156] In addition, public sector research on service delivery in transportation,[157] sanitation,[158] and police[159] among others shows that organizational structure does effect service efficiency and effectiveness. Some of these researchers cautiously and rightfully call for further research on the relationship between structure and performance before making sweeping conclusions. Criteria for evaluating reorganizations need to be tailored to the specific situation and organization rather than relying on global measures, but the conventional wisdom that structure makes little or no difference to government performance needs reassessment.

REORGANIZATION AS POLITICS

Former Proverb: Reorganization is *a businesslike, scientific, apolitical process. Current Proverb: Reorganization is nothing more than the continuation of politics by other means.*

Some reformers who preached the canons of integration de-emphasized the role of politics in reorganizing. Since they viewed reorganizations as apolitical, businesslike applications of scientific principles, politics was considered irrelevant or a necessary evil which might undermine scientific principles.[160] After World War II, scholars brought politics back into the reorganization process or, more accurately, better articulated the politics always present.[161] Perhaps because politics was so obviously salient yet overlooked, analysts overcompensated with a new conventional wisdom that reorganization is virtually all politics. Lester Salamon articulates this thinking: "'War,' Karl von Clausewitz once wrote, 'is nothing more than the continuation of politics by other means.' The same, it can now safely be asserted, is also true of that peculiar form of warfare known as government reorganization."[162]

Few practitioners or observers would deny the presence and sometimes pervasiveness of politics in reorganizing. Even authorities associated with orthodoxy, like Gulick, appreciated reorganization's political nature. Yet reorganization is more than just politics, often embodying management science, cultural values, human psychology, and other elements.[163] Preoccupation with reorganization's political aspects is as great a proverb as neglecting or denying its political nature.

ROOSEVELT AND BROWNLOW AS ZENITH OF REORGANIZATION

Former Proverb: The reorganization movement reached its zenith with the Brownlow Committee and the federal Reorganization Act of 1939. Current Proverb: The FDR-Brownlow impact on governmental organization has been vastly inflated.

Efforts by President Franklin Roosevelt and his Committee on Administrative Management (Brownlow Committee) perhaps have received more scrutiny than any other reorganization. Some have hailed this effort as a watershed or high point in the reorganization movement.[164]

Skeptics emphasize the weak act itself. The Reorganization Act of 1939, which finally passed after backlash to Roosevelt's court-packing and other factors led to initial defeat in 1938, was a political document watered down by compromise. The compromise Act of 1939 omitted extending the Civil Service Merit system, modernizing accounting procedures, overhauling 100 independent agencies, authorities, boards, and commissions and consolidating them into existing and new cabinet departments, and other Brownlow recommendations. Conventional wisdom on the Reorganization Act of 1939 views it as a product of political compromise much in keeping with other reorganization efforts like those following the Taft Commission and Hoover Commissions which accomplished less than they set out to achieve.[165]

But Roosevelt, Brownlow, Merriam, and Gulick have had the last laugh. Though the 1939 Act accomplished little directly, President Roosevelt soon after used reorganization plans authorized by the Act to transfer budgeting, research, and planning capabilities to the Executive Office of the President. This strengthening of presidential managerial capacity laid groundwork for the extensive managerial control exercised by the Office of Management and Budget during President Reagan's administration.[166] In addition, the orthodox doctrine exemplified in the *Papers on the Science of Administration*, first assembled as staff working papers for the Brownlow Committee, still permeates government administration in the United States today.[167] Hierarchy, specialization, grouping by function, unity of command, and other orthodox precepts so shape organizational life despite their being debunked in academic circles that practitioners and scholars have difficulty thinking in different terms. Even when actions depart from orthodox theory, orthodoxy remains a frame of reference. The current proverb depreciating the result of Roosevelt's reorganizing efforts is just as much a proverb as the one sanctifying these efforts.

IMPLICATIONS

Barring crisis, Americans have repeatedly preferred to seek partial, satisfying solutions to governmental problems. This also holds for the underlying system of governance. Administrative reorganization has been one device for accomplishing what Don K. Price has termed "adjustment without amendment."[168] Given the lack of consensus about what fundamental constitutional amendments are necessary, reorganizations will continue to make needed and unneeded adjustments. Reorganizations will occur at all governmental levels, reflecting new or altered priorities,[169] power shifts,[170] changes in governmental role,[171] or need to modernize.[172]

As controversy over the proverbs shows, the record of reorganizing has rarely achieved the glowing promises claimed. Americans must not only become more realistic in their expectations for reorganizing—oilcans and tuneups can only accomplish so much. They must also become more selective and creative when reorganizing, or they will continue to misuse or underutilize this tool. Government's approach to organizing and reorganizing has predominantly emphasized *tradition* ("we have always organized this way") and *ideology* ("doctrine tells us to organize this way"). The prevailing mindset limits use of generic organization theory in government, including applying organizational design to create organizations for contingent tasks, technologies, employees, and conditions.[173]

A design dilemma must be faced in future organizing and reorganizing. Americans' allegiance to doctrine, whether embodied in popular representation, neutral expertise, or executive leadership, and their preference for ad hoc structural tinkering run against the concept of organizational design—intentionally tailoring structure to fit with political and management strategy, technology, and other factors. But some consider reorganizing more like gardening than engineering or architecture. "Like gardening, reorganization is not an act, but a process, a continuing job. And like gardening, reorganization is work whose benefits may largely accrue to one's successors."[174] Even if the organic view of reorganizing is more appropriate than the mechanistic, greater intentionality promises to yield more benefits to future successors. Gardens need not grow like topsy. Perhaps reorganizers should be emulating genetic engineering to produce new hybrids designed for special tasks and needs.

Also as the proverbs show, the subject of reorganization tends to produce more heat than light. Both former and current proverbs tend to the extremes toward particular perspectives. What is needed is more practice and research based on broader, more balanced views of reorganization, its limitations, and possibilities.

Reference

G. Ross Stephens, January 1973, "Monetary Savings from State Reorganization in Missouri or You'll Wonder Where the Money Went," *Midwest Review of Public Administration*, vol. 7, pp. 32–35.

Harold Seidman, 1998, *Politics, Positions and Power: The Dynamics of Federal Organization*, 5th Edition, Oxford University Press, New York.

In ancient times alchemists believed implicitly in the existence of a philosopher's stone, which would provide the key to the universe and, in effect, solve all of the problems of humankind. The quest for coordination is in many respects the twentieth-century equivalent of the medieval search for the philosopher's stone. If only we can find the right formula for coordination, we can reconcile the irreconcilable, harmonize competing and wholly divergent interests, overcome irrationalities in our government structures, and make hard policy choices to which no one will disagree.

When interagency committees such as the Economic Opportunity Council fail as coordinators, the fault is sought in the formula, not in deeper underlying causes. The council's inability to perform its statutory duties as coordinator of the federal government's antipoverty efforts was attributed to the fact that the law (1) placed coordinating responsibility on a body of peers who could not be expected voluntarily to relinquish decision-making control over planning for or operation of programs, and (2) designated the director of the Office of Economic Opportunity, then a non-Cabinet-level official, as chairman with coordinative authority over officials of greater status. The formula was changed to provide that the council have an independent chairman and staff, but with no better results. The original council at least met a few times; the restructured council was never convened at all. Again, revision of the formula was prescribed as the remedy. The comptroller general proposed that the council's functions be transferred to an Office of Community Resources in the Executive Office of the President, which would provide staff support for President Nixon's interdepartmental Urban Affairs Council.[175]

Whether we are dealing with poverty, science, telecommunications, AIDS, drugs, or international and national security programs, the search for a coordinating formula seems to follow almost a set pattern: (1) establishment of an interagency committee chaired by an agency head and with no staff or contributed staff; (2) designation of a "neutral" chair and provision for independent staff; and (3) transfer of coordinating functions to the White House or Executive Office of the President, establishment of a special presidential assistant, and reconstitution of the interagency committee as a presidential advisory council.

Defective machinery may contribute to the difficulties of coordinating multifaceted federal programs, which cut across traditional agency jurisdictions, but it is seldom, if ever, at the root of the problem. The power to coordinate does not normally carry with it the authority to issue binding orders. Executive orders customarily confer broad powers "to

---

Source: Harold Seidman, 1998, Politics, Positions and Power: The Dynamics of Federal Organization, 5th Edition, Oxford University Press, New York. By Permission of Oxford University Press, Inc.

facilitate and coordinate" federal programs and direct each department and agency to "cooperate" with the official designated as coordinator. However, buried in the boiler plate at the end of the order there is usually a section reading, "Nothing in this order shall be construed as subjecting any function vested by law in, or assigned pursuant to law to, any federal department or agency or head thereof to the authority of any other agency or officer or as abrogating or restricting any such function in any manner."[176]

Neither the president nor a coordinator appointed by him can perform the functions vested by law in the heads of departments and agencies. When conflicts result from clashes in statutory missions or differences in legislative mandates, they cannot be reconciled through the magic of coordination. Too often organic disease is mistakenly diagnosed as a simple case of inadequate coordination.

If agencies are to work together harmoniously, they must share at least some community of interests about basic goals. Without such a community of interests and compatible objectives, problems cannot be resolved by coordination. Senator Frank Moss ascribed the conflict between the National Park Service and the Army Corps of Engineers over the Florida Everglades to "uncoordinated activities." Park service officials complained that the engineers drained the Everglades National Park almost *dry* in their efforts to halt wetlands flooding and reclaim glade country for agriculture. The Army Corps Engineers argued that wetlands were "for the birds" and flood control for the people.[177] Coordinating devices may reveal or even exacerbate the conflict, but they cannot produce agreement among the agencies when a choice must be made as to whether a single piece of land should be drained for flood control and reclaimed for agriculture or maintained as wetlands to preserve unique and valuable forms of aquatic life.

Coordination is rarely neutral. To the extent that it results in mutual agreement or a decision on some policy, course of action, or inaction, it inevitably advances some interests at the expense of others or more than others. Coordination contains no more magic than the philosopher's stone. In does, however, contain a good deal of the substance with which alchemists were concerned: the proper placement and relationship of the elements to achieve a given result. Coordinators are seldom judged objectively or evaluated by realistic standards. Coordination may influence people, but it makes few friends. The tendency is to consider that coordination most effective which operates to one's own advantage. Few coordinating systems have worked as successfully as the Office of Management and Budget's procedures for clearing proposed legislation and reports on legislation and advising agencies as to the relationship of legislative proposals to "the administration's program," but the legislative clearance process is by no means universally admired. By doing its job well, OMB has gained few friends among members of Congress and interest groups whose pet bills have been held "not in accord with the administration's program."

The term *coordination* is used in laws and executive orders as if it had a precise, commonly understood meaning. Yet probably no word in our administrative terminology raises more difficult problems of definition. For James D. Mooney, coordination is no less than "the determining principle of organization, the form which contains all other principles, the beginning and the end of all organized effort."[178] Coordination is also defined as concerted action, animated by a common purpose, responding to recognized signals and using practiced skills. Coordination describes both a process—the act of coordinating—and a goal: the bringing together of diverse elements into a harmonious relationship in support of common objectives. The power to coordinate in and of itself confers no additional legal authority, but merely provides a license to seek harmonious action by whatever means may be available under existing authorities.

In current usage, coordination has come to be identified primarily with the formal processes by which we attempt to adjudicate disagreements among agencies. Mooney would regard the proliferation of coordinating mechanisms, such as interagency committees, as prima facie evidence of "lack of coordinated effort" resulting from inexact definitions of jobs and functions.[179] Coordinating machinery becomes necessary only when coordination cannot be achieved by sound organization, good management, and informal cooperation among agencies engaged in related and mutually supporting activities.

Formal coordinating processes are time-consuming and the results are generally inconclusive. True coordination sometimes may be obtained only by going outside the formal processes.

By overemphasizing coordinating machinery, we have created the false impression that most federal activities are uncoordinated. This is by no means the case. Without informal or so-called lateral coordination, which takes place at almost every stage in the development and execution of national programs and at every level within the federal structure, the government probably would grind to a halt. Skilled bureaucrats develop their own informational networks. Managers who are motivated by a desire to get something done find ways and means of bridging the jurisdictional gaps. Informal coordination is greatly facilitated when people share the same goals, operate from a common set of legal authorities and information assumptions, agree on standards, have compatible professional outlooks, and can help each other. Where these conditions exist, there is no need for the intervention of third parties to secure harmonious action.

Politicization of the senior career service inevitably disrupts the networks and impedes lateral coordination. It is argued by some that the networks are instruments of bureaucratic ideologies that must be controlled if an administration is to achieve its political objectives.[180]

Coordination does not necessarily require imposition of authority from the top. State and local governments have the crucial role in the process of administering and coordinating federal assistance programs. The functions of establishing state, regional, and local goals, developing comprehensive plans, and determining priorities among grant proposals in terms of these goals and financial restraints is a local responsibility. Effective performance of these functions by state and local governments can reduce or eliminate need for coordinating arrangements at the federal level.

Complete reliance on voluntary cooperation is not feasible, however, except in Utopia. The goals of our pluralistic society, as reflected in federal programs, are frequently contradictory. No matter how the government is organized, it is impossible to define jobs and design programs in such a way as to eliminate all overlaps and potential conflicts among agencies. Even when the will to cooperate is present, good intentions may be thwarted by the size of the federal establishment, the growing complexity and compartmentalized character of federal programs, differences among professional groups, and the absence of a clear sense of direction and coherence of policy either in the White House or in the Congress. We cannot produce harmony by synthetic substitutes when the essential ingredients are lacking within the governmental system. The much maligned interagency committees are the result, not the cause, of our inability to agree on coherent national objectives and to find a workable solution to our organizational dilemma.

Interagency committees are the crabgrass in the garden of government institutions. Nobody wants them, but everyone has them. Committees seem to thrive on scorn and ridicule and multiply so rapidly that attempts to weed them out appear futile. For every committee uprooted by Presidents Kennedy, Johnson, Carter's, and Clinton's much publicized "committee-killing" exercises, another has been born to take it place.

Interagency committees as a general institutional class have no admirers and few defenders. Former Secretary of Defense Robert Lovett ascribed the proliferation of interagency committees to the "foul-up factor," or the tendency of every agency with even the most peripheral interest to insist on getting into the act. According to Lovett, committees have now so blanketed the whole executive branch as to give it "an embalmed atmosphere."[181] From his observation, committees are composed of "some rather lonely, melancholy men who have been assigned a responsibility but haven't the authority to make decisions at their levels, and so they tend to seek their own kind. They thereupon coagulate into a sort of glutinous mass, and suddenly come out as a committee."[182] Lovett concluded that "two heads are not always better than one, particularly when they are growing on the same body."[183]

NOTES FOR CHAPTER 4

1. W. Wilson, December 1941, "The Study of Administration," *Political Science Quarterly*, vol. LVI, p. 485. This is a reprint of the original article of 1887.
2. H. Emmerich, 1971, *Federal Organization and Administrative Management*, University of Alabama Press, University, AL, p. 102.
3. Congressional reaction to the Brownlow Committee report serves as a good example of this point. For a detailed description of the congressional view of the report, see Richard Polenberg, 1966, *Reorganizing Roosevelt's Government*, Harvard University Press, Cambridge.
4. This point is, of course, made by those who write from a pluralist-representative perspective. A classic statement of this position may be seen in Norton Long, Autumn 1949, "Power and Administration," *Public Administration Review*, vol. *IX*, pp. 257–264. A recent work within this perspective is H. Seidman, 1970, *Politics, Position and Power*, Oxford University Press, New York.
5. H. Simon, 1965, *Administrative Behavior*, 2nd ed., The Free Press, New York.
6. The analytic possibilities of a typology of public policies are shown by Theodore J. Lowi, July 1964, "American Business, Public Policy, Case-Studies, and Political Science," *World Politics*, vol. XVI, pp. 677–715.
7. For examples of this agitation about the study of public administration, see Frank Marini (Ed.), 1971, *Toward a New Public Administration*, Chandler, Scranton, PA, and Dwight Waldo (Ed.), 1971, *Public Administration in a Time of Turbulence*, Chandler, Scranton, PA.
8. M. D. Cohen, 1977, "Religious revivalism and the administrative centralization movement." *Administration and Society*, vol. 9, 219–232; H. Emmerich, 1971, *Federal Organization and Administrative Management*, University of Alabama Press, University, AL; R. C. Moe, March 1978, *Executive Branch Reorganization: An Overview*, Senate Committee on Governmental Affairs. Committee Print.
9. D. Waldo, 1961, "Organization theory: an elephantine problem," *Public Administration Review*, vol. 21, 210–225.
10. H. Emmerich, 1971, *Federal Organization and Administrative Management.* University of Alabama Press, University, p. 39.
11. President's Committee on Administrative Management (Brownlow Commission), 1937, Report of the President's Committee: Administrative management in the government of the United States. U.S. Government Printing Office, Washington, DC, p. 29; W. B. Graves, 1949, "Reorganization of the executive branch of the government of the United States: a compilation of basic information and significant documents, 1912–1948." *Public Affairs Bulletin No.* 66. Library of Congress Legislative Reference Service, Washington, DC; The Commission on Organization of the Executive Branch of Government (first Hoover Commission), 1947–1949, chaired by Herbert Hoover; Joint Committee, U.S. Congress. House. Joint Committee on Reorganization of the Administrative Branch of the government, 1924, Report of the Joint Committee on Reorganization. 68th Congress, 1st session: Doc. no. 356. Government Printing Office, Washington, DC; Presidential Papers of President Nixon, 1972, p. 9; W. F. Willoughby, 1923, *The Reorganization of the Administrative Branch of the National Government*, Johns Hopkins Press, Baltimore, MD.
12. L. Gulick, 1937, "Science, values and public administration," in L. Gulick and L. F. Urwick (Eds.), *Papers on the Science of Administration*, Institute of Public Administration, New York; L. Meriam and L. F. Schmekebier, 1939, *Reorganization of the National Government: What Does It Involve?* Brookings, Washington, DC; W. F. Willoughby, 1923, *The Reorganization of the Administrative Branch of the National Government*, Johns Hopkins Press, Baltimore, MD.
13. L. D. White, 1958, *The Republican Era*, Macmillan, New York, p. 85.
14. President's Committee on Administrative Management (Brownlow Commission), 1937, Report of the President's Committee: Administrative management in the government of the United States. U.S. Government Printing Office, Washington, DC, pp. 3, 52; First Hoover Commission,

1949, p. viii; R. P. Nathan, 1975, *The Plot That Failed: Nixon and the Administrative Presidency*, Wiley, New York, pp. 115–116, 124; Nixon Papers, 1972, p. 20; E. S. Redford and M. Blisset, 1981, *Organizing the Executive Branch*, University of Chicago Press, Chicago; C. Roberts (Ed.), 1973, *Has the President Too Much Power?* Harper's Magazine Press, New York, p. 200; Reorganization Act of 1977; Statement by the President on signing S.262 into law, weekly compilation of Presidential documents, April 13, 1977, pp. 493–494; C. W. Weinberger, 1978, "Government reorganization and public purpose," *Publius*, vol. 8, pp. 39–48.

15. A. N. Holcombe, 1921, "Administrative reorganization in the federal government," *Annals of the American Academy of Political and Social Science*, vol. 95, 242–251; P. Hurt, 1932, "Who should reorganize the national administration?" *American Political Science Review*, vol. 26, pp. 1082–1098; L. Meriam and L. F. Schmekebier, 1975, *Reorganization of the National Government: What Does It Involve?* Brookings, Washington, DC; Donald K. Price, "1984 and beyond: social engineering or political values?" in Frederick C. Mosher (Ed.), *American Public Administration: Past, Present, Future*, University: University of Alabama Press, 1975.

16. C. Aikin and L. W. Koenig, 1949, "Introduction to Hoover Commission: a symposium," *American Political Science Review*, vol. 43, 933–940; J. P. Harris, 1937, "The progress of administrative reorganization in the seventy-fifth Congress," *American Political Science Review*, vol. 31, 862–870; W. E. Pemberton, 1979, *Bureaucratic Politics: Executive Reorganization During the Truman Administration*, University of Missouri Press, Columbia.

17. R. Polenberg, 1966, *Reorganizing Roosevelt's Government; The Controversy Over Executive Reorganization 1936–39*, Harvard University Press, Cambridge, MA, p. 8.

18. H. Seidman, 1980, *Politics, Position and Power: The Dynamics of Federal Organization*, 3rd ed, Oxford University Press, New York, p. 12.

19. E. S. Redford and M. Blisset, 1981, *Organizing the Executive Branch*, University of Chicago Press, Chicago. C. Roberts (Ed.), *Has the President Too Much Power?* Harper's Magazine Press, New York, p. 224.

20. P. E. Arnold, 1974, "Reorganization and politics: a reflection on the adequacy of administration theory," *Public Administration Review*, vol. 34, pp. 205–211; D. R. Beam, 1978, "Public administration is alive and well and living in the White House," *Public Administration Review*, vol. 38, pp. 72–77; W. Coy, 1946, "Basic problems, in Federal executive reorganization re-examined: a symposium," *American Political Science Review*, vol. 40, pp. 1124–1137; G. H. Durham, 1949, "An appraisal of the Hoover Commission approach to administrative reorganization in the national government," *Western Political Quarterly*, vol. 2, 615–623; J. W. Fesler, 1957, "Administrative literature and the second Hoover Commission reports," *American Political Science Review*, vol. 51, pp. 135–157; G. A. Graham, 1938, "Reorganization-a question of executive institutions," *American Political Science Review*, vol. 32, 708–718; J. P. Harris, 1937, "The progress of administrative reorganization in the seventy-fifth Congress," *American Political Science Review*, vol. 31, pp. 862–870; F. Heady, 1949, "The reports of the Hoover Commission," *Review of Politics*, vol. 11, pp. 355–378; E. P. Herring, 1934, "Social forces and the reorganization of the federal bureaucracy," *Southwestern Social Science Quarterly*, vol. 15, pp. 185–200; A. Leiserson, 1947, "Political limitations on executive reorganization," in *Federal Executive Reorganization Reexamined: A Symposium, II. American Political Science Review*, vol. 41, pp. 68–84; H. C. Mansfield, 1970, "Reorganizing the federal executive branch: limits of institutionalization," *Law and Contemporary Problems*, vol. 35, pp. 461–495; J. D. Millett, 1949, "Departmental management," *American Political Science Review*, vol. 43, pp. 959–966; R. C. Moe, March 1978, *Executive Branch Reorganization: An Overview*, Senate Committee on Governmental Affairs, Committee Print; R. G. Noll, 1971, *Reforming Regulation: An Evaluation of the Ash Council Proposals, A Staff Paper*, Brookings, Washington, DC; V. Ostrom, 1973, *The Intellectual Crisis in American Public Administration*, University of Alabama Press, Tuscaloosa, AL; E. S. Redford, 1950, "The value of the Hoover Commission reports to the educator," *American Political Science Review*, vol. 44, pp. 283–298; F. E. Rourke, 1957, "The politics of administrative organization: a case history," *Journal of Politics*, vol. 19, 461–478; L. M. Salamon,

1981a, "The goals of reorganization," *Administration and Society*, vol. 12, pp. 471–500; L. M. Salamon, 1981b, "The question of goals," in P. Szanton (Ed.), *Federal Reorganization: What Have We Learned?* Chatham, Chatham, NJ; S. Scher, 1962, "The politics of agency organization," *Western Political Quarterly*, vol. 15, pp. 328–344; A. Schick, 1975, "The trauma of politics: public administration in the sixties," in F. C. Mosher (Ed.), *American Public Administration: Past, Present, Future*. University of Alabama Press, Tuscaloosa, AL; H. Seidman, 1980, *Politics, Position and Power: The Dynamics of Federal Organization*, 3rd ed, Oxford University Press, New York.

21. P. E. Arnold and L. J. Roos, 1974, "Toward a theory of congressional-executive relations," *Review of Politics*, vol. 26, pp. 410–429; W. Coy, 1946, "Basic problems, in Federal executive reorganization re-examined: a symposium," *American Political Science Review*, vol. 40, pp. 1124–1137; M. E. Dimock, 1951, "The objectives of governmental reorganization," *Public Administration Review*, vol. 11, pp. 233–241; G. H. Durham, 1949, "An appraisal of the Hoover Commission approach to administrative reorganization in the national government," *Western Political Quarterly*, vol. 2, pp. 615–623; J. W. Fesler, 1957, "Administrative literature and the second Hoover Commission reports," *American Political Science Review*, vol. 51, pp. 135–157; H. Finer, 1949, "The Hoover Commission reports," *Political Science Quarterly*, vol. 64, Part I, pp. 405–419; Part II, pp. 579–595; S. Hess, 1976, *Organizing the Presidency*, Brookings, Washington, DC; C. S. Hyneman, 1939, "Administrative reorganization," *Journal of Politics*, vol. 1, pp. 62–75; C. S. Hyneman, 1950, *Bureaucracy in a Democracy*, Harper, New York; R. M. La Follette, Jr., 1947, "Systematizing congressional control," in *Federal Executive Reorganization Reexamined: A Symposium, II. American Political Science Review*, vol. 41, pp. 58–68; J. D. Millett and L. Rogers, 1941, "The legislative veto and the Reorganization Act of 1939," *Public Administration Review*, vol. I, pp. 176–189; F. C. Mosher, et al., 1974, *Watergate: Implications for Responsible Government*, Basic Books, New York; R. P. Nathan, 1975, *The Plot That Failed: Nixon and the Administrative Presidency*, Wiley, New York; R. P. Nathan, 1976, "The administrative presidency," *Public Interest*, vol. 44, pp. 40–54; C. Roberts (Ed.), 1973, *Has the President Too Much Power?* Harper's Magazine Press, New York; Reorganization Act of 1977; H. A. Simon, 1957, *Administrative Behavior: A Study of Decision-Making Processes in Administrative Organization*, Macmillan, New York; H. A. Simon, D. W. Smithburg, and V. A. Thompson, 1950, *Public Administration*, Alfred A. Knopf, New York; E. C. Woods, 1943, "A proposed reorganization of the executive branch of the federal government," *American Political Science Review*, vol. 37, pp. 476–490.

22. E. P. Herring, 1934, "Social forces and the reorganization of the federal bureaucracy," *Southwestern Social Science Quarterly*, vol. 15, pp. 185–200; J. D. Millett, 1949, "Departmental management," *American Political Science Review*, vol. 43, pp. 959–966.

23. W. Coy, 1946, "Basic problems, in Federal executive reorganization re-examined: a symposium," *American Political Science Review*, vol. 40, pp. 1124–1137; M. E. Dimock, 1951, "The objectives of governmental reorganization," *Public Administration Review*, vol. 11, pp. 233–241.

24. F. E. Rourke, 1957, "The politics of administrative organization: a case history," *Journal of Politics*, vol. 19, pp. 461–478.

25. R. C. Moe, March 1978, *Executive Branch Reorganization: An Overview*, Senate Committee on Governmental Affairs. Committee Print.

26. P. E. Arnold, 1974, "Reorganization and politics: a reflection on the adequacy of administration theory," *Public Administration Review*, vol. 34, pp. 205–211; R. P. Nathan, 1975, *The Plot That Failed: Nixon and the Administrative Presidency*, Wiley, New York; R. P. Nathan, 1976, "The administrative presidency," *Public Interest*, vol. 44, pp. 40–54; H. Seidman, 1980, *Politics, Position and Power: The Dynamics of Federal Organization*, 3rd ed, Oxford University Press, New York.

27. E. S. Redford and M. Blisset, 1981, *Organizing the Executive Branch*, University of Chicago Press, Chicago. C. Roberts (Ed.), 1973, *Has the President Too Much Power?* Harper's Magazine Press, New York; L. M. Salamon, 1981a, "The goals of reorganization," *Administration and*

Society, vol. 12, pp. 471–500; L. M. Salamon, 1981b, "The question of goals," in P. Szanton (Ed.), *Federal Reorganization: What Have We Learned?* Chatham, Chatham, NJ; H. Seidman, 1980, *Politics, Position and Power: The Dynamics of Federal Organization*, 3rd ed, Oxford University Press, New York.

28. C. Grafton, 1979, The reorganization of federal agencies. *Administration and Society*, vol. 10, pp. 437–464; H. C. Mansfield, 1969, "Federal executive reorganization: thirty years of experience," *Public Administration Review*, vol. 29, pp. 332–345; J. G. March, 1980, *How We Talk and How We Act: Administrative Theory and Administrative Life*, Seventh David D. Henry Lecture, Urbana, IL; J. G. March, 1981a, "Decisions in organizations and theories of choice," in A. H. Van de Ven and W. F. Joyce (Eds.), *Perspectives on Organization Design and Behavior*, Wiley, New York; J. G. March and J. P. Olsen, 1976, *Ambiguity and Choice in Organizations*, Universitetsforlaget, Bergen; F. C. Mosher (Ed.), 1967, *Government Reorganization: Cases and Commentary*, Bobbs-Merrill, Indianapolis, p. 497; M. Musicus, 1964, "Reappraising reorganization," *Public Administration Review*, vol. 24, pp. 107–112.
29. J. L. Garnett and C. H. Levine, 1980, "State executive branch reorganization: patterns and perspectives," *Administration and Society*, vol. 12, pp. 227–276.
30. F. W. Coker, 1922, "Dogmas of administrative reform as exemplified in the recent reorganization in Ohio," *American Political Science Review*, vol. 16, pp. 399–411; G. A. Graham, 1938, "Reorganization-a question of executive institutions," *American Political Science Review*, vol. 32, pp. 708–718; J. P. Harris, 1937, "The progress of administrative reorganization in the seventy-fifth Congress," *American Political Science Review*, vol. 31, pp. 862–870; E. P. Herring, 1934, "Social forces and the reorganization of the federal bureaucracy," *Southwestern Social Science Quarterly*, vol. 15, pp. 185–200; A. N. Holcombe, 1921, "Administrative reorganization in the federal government," *Annals of the American Academy of Political and Social Science*, vol. 95, pp. 242–251; C. S. Hyneman, 1939, "Administrative reorganization," *Journal of Politics*, vol. 1, pp. 62–75; W. F. Willoughby, 1923, *The Reorganization of the Administrative Branch of the National Government*, Johns Hopkins Press, Baltimore, MD.
31. D. R. Beam, 1978, "Public administration is alive and well and living in the White House," *Public Administration Review*, vol. 38, pp. 72–77; C. W. Weinberger, 1978, "Government reorganization and public purpose," *Publius*, vol. 8, pp. 39–48; H. J. Zoffer, 1976, "Introduction," in R. H. Kilman, L. R. Pondy, &and D. P. Slevin (Ed.), *The Management of Organizational Design*. North Holland, Amsterdam, p. xi.
32. R. G. Brown, 1979, *Reorganizing the National Health Service: A Case Study in Administrative Change*, Blackwell/Robertson, Oxford, p. 165; H. C. Mansfield, 1969, "Federal executive reorganization: thirty years of experience," *Public Administration Review*, vol. 29, p. 338; R. E. Miles, Jr., 1977, "Considerations for a president bent on reorganization," *Public Administration Review*, vol. 37, p. 155; M. Musicus, 1964, "Reappraising reorganization," *Public Administration Review*, vol. 24, pp. 107–112; W. E. Pemberton, 1979, *Bureaucratic Politics: Executive Reorganization During the Truman Administration*, University of Missouri Press, Columbia, p. 52; E. S. Redford and M. Blisset, 1981, *Organizing the Executive Branch*, University of Chicago Press, Chicago. C. Roberts (Ed.), 1973, *Has the President Too Much Power?* Harper's Magazine Press, New York; P. Szanton (Ed.), 1981, *Federal Reorganization: What Have We Learned?* Chatham, Chatham, NJ, p. 5.
33. J. A. Califano, Jr., 1981, *Governing America: An Insider's Report From the White House and the Cabinet*, Simon and Schuster, New York, p. 14; B. W. Heineman, Jr., and C. A. Hessler, 1980, *Memorandum for the President*, Random House, New York, p. 9; S. Hess, 1976, *Organizing the Presidency*, Brookings, Washington, DC, p. 33; R. C. Moe, March 1978, *Executive Branch Reorganization: An Overview*, Senate Committee on Governmental Affairs. Committee Print, pp. 60–61; R. P. Nathan, 1976, "The administrative presidency," *Public Interest*, vol. 44, pp. 40–54; W. E. Pemberton, 1979, *Bureaucratic Politics: Executive Reorganization During the Truman Administration*, University of Missouri Press, Columbia, MO; H. Seidman, 1980, *Politics, Position and Power: The Dynamics of Federal Organization*, 3rd ed, Oxford University Press, New York.

34. W. E. Pemberton, 1979, *Bureaucratic Politics: Executive Reorganization During the Truman Administration*, University of Missouri Press, Columbia, MO, pp. 47, 175.
35. R. Polenberg, 1966, *Reorganizing Roosevelt's Government; The Controversy Over Executive Reorganization 1936–39*, Harvard University Press, Cambridge, MA.
36. E. P. Herring, 1934, "Social forces and the reorganization of the federal bureaucracy," *Southwestern Social Science Quarterly*, vol. 15, pp. 185–200; P. Hurt, 1932, "Who should reorganize the national administration?" *American Political Science Review*, vol. 26, pp. 1082–1098; H. C. Mansfield, 1969, "Federal executive reorganization: thirty years of experience," *Public Administration Review*, vol. 29, pp. 332–345; R. Polenberg, 1966, *Reorganizing Roosevelt's Government: The Controversy Over Executive Reorganization 1936–39*, Harvard University Press, Cambridge, MA; E. S. Redford and M. Blisset, 1981, *Organizing the Executive Branch*, University of Chicago Press, Chicago. C. Roberts (Ed.), 1973, *Has the President Too Much Power?* Harper's Magazine Press, New York; Rogers, 1938; H. Seidman, 1980, *Politics, Position and Power: The Dynamics of Federal Organization*, 3rd ed, Oxford University Press, New York; H. Zink, 1950, "Government reform in the United States of America," *Political Quarterly*, vol. 21, pp. 69–79.
37. E. S. Redford and M. Blisset, 1981, *Organizing the Executive Branch*, University of Chicago Press, Chicago; C. Roberts (Ed.), 1973, *Has the President Too Much Power?* Harper's Magazine Press, New York; Harold Seidman, 1980, *Politics, Position and Power: The Dynamics of Federal Organization*, 3rd ed, Oxford University Press, New York, p. 106.
38. E. H. Hobbs, 1953, *Executive Reorganization in the National Government*, University of Mississippi Press, Oxford, p. 18.
39. E. S. Redford and M. Blisset, 1981, *Organizing the Executive Branch*, University of Chicago Press, Chicago. C. Roberts (Ed.), 1973, *Has the President Too Much Power?* Harper's Magazine Press, New York.
40. S. Leibfried, 1979, *The bureaucracy of the "statist reserve": the case of the U.S.A.*, Cornell University, Ithaca, NY, Western Societies Program: Occasional Papers No. 12; R. P. Nathan, 1975, *The Plot That Failed: Nixon and the Administrative Presidency*, Wiley, New York.
41. B. W. Heineman, Jr., and C. A. Hessler, 1980, *Memorandum for the President*, Random House, New York, p. 34.
42. W. E. Pemberton, 1979, *Bureaucratic Politics: Executive Reorganization During the Truman Administration*, University of Missouri Press, Columbia, MO, pp. 28, 154–157.
43. S. Hess, 1976, *Organizing the Presidency*, Brookings, Washington, DC, p. 19.
44. S. Hess, 1976, *Organizing the Presidency*. Brookings, Washington, DC; A. N. Holcombe, 1921, "Administrative reorganization in the federal government," *Annals of the American Academy of Political and Social Science*, vol. 95, 242–251, p. 249; R. E. Miles, Jr., 1977, "Considerations for a president bent on reorganization," *Public Administration Review*, vol. 37, pp. 155-162; E. Redford and M. Blisset, 1981, *Organizing the Executive Branch*, University of Chicago Press, Chicago. C. Roberts (Ed.), 1973, *Has the President Too Much Power?* Harper's Magazine Press, New York; E. C. Woods, 1943, A proposed reorganization of the executive branch of the federal government, *American Political Science Review*, vol. 37, pp. 476–490.
45. President's Committee on Administrative Management (Brownlow Commission), 1939, Report of the President's Committee: Administrative management in the government of the United States. Washington, D.C.: U.S. Government Printing Office, p. 29.
46. R. Polenberg, 1966, *Reorganizing Roosevelt's Government; The Controversy Over Executive Reorganization* 1936–39, Harvard University Press, Cambridge, MA; H. Zink, 1950, "Government reform in the United States of America," *Political Quarterly*, vol. 21, pp. 69–79.
47. H. C. Mansfield, 1970, "Reorganizing the federal executive branch: limits of institutionalization," *Law and Contemporary Problems*, vol. 35, pp. 461–495.
48. W. E. Pemberton, 1979, *Bureaucratic Politics: Executive Reorganization During the Truman Administration*. University of Missouri Press, Columbia, MO, p. 18; S. Scher, 1962, "The politics of agency organization," *Western Political Quarterly*, vol. 15, pp. 328–344.

49. N. Long, 1958, "The local community as an ecology of games," *American Journal of Sociology*, vol. 44, pp. 251–261.
50. M. D. Cohen, J. G. March, and J. P. Olsen, 1972, "A garbage can model of organizational choice," *Administrative Science Quarterly*, vol. 17, pp. 1–25; J. G. March and J. P. Olsen, 1976, *Ambiguity and Choice in Organizations*, Universitetsforlaget, Bergen, pp. 314–315.
51. R. G. Brown, 1979, *Reorganizing the National Health Service: A Case Study in Administrative Change*, Blackwell/Robertson, Oxford, p. 172.
52. C. Aikin and L. W. Koenig, 1949, "Introduction to Hoover Commission: a symposium," *American Political Science Review*, vol. 43, pp. 933–940; R. G. Brown, 1979, "Reorganizing the national health service: a case study in administrative change," Blackwell/Robertson, Oxford, p. 200; D. M. Fox (Ed.), 1974, "President Nixon's proposals for executive reorganization," *Public Administration Review*, vol. 34, 487–495.
53. M. D. Cohen and J. G. March, 1974, *Leadership and Ambiguity: The American College President*, McGraw-Hill, New York.
54. M. D. Cohen, J. G. March, and J. P. Olsen, 1973, "A garbage can model of organizational choice," *Administrative Science Quarterly*, vol. 17, pp. 1–25; J. G. March and J. P. Olsen, 1976, *Ambiguity and choice in organizations*, Universitetsforlaget, Bergen.
55. H. Emmerich, 1971, *Federal Organization and Administrative Management*, University of Alabama Press, University; E. S. Redford and M. Blisset, 1981, *Organizing the Executive Branch*, University of Chicago Press, Chicago. C. Roberts (Ed.), 1973, *Has the President Too Much Power?* Harper's Magazine Press, New York; H. Seidman, 1980, *Politics, Position and Power: The Dynamics of Federal Organization*, 3rd ed, Oxford University Press, New York; P. Szanton, (Ed.), 1981, *Federal Reorganization: What Have We Learned?* Chatham, Chatham, NJ, p. 120.
56. W. Coy, 1946, "Basic problems, in Federal executive reorganization re-examined: a symposium," *American Political Science Review*, vol. 40, pp. 1124–1137; J. P. Harris, 1937, "The progress of administrative reorganization in the seventy-fifth Congress," *American Political Science Review*, vol. 31, pp. 862–870; E. H. Hobbs, 1953, *Executive Reorganization in the National Government*, University of Mississippi Press, Oxford, p. 49; Herbert Kaufman, 1977, Reflections on administrative reorganization, in J. A. Pechman (Ed.), *Setting National Priorities: The 1978 Budget*, Brookings, p. 410, Washington, DC; B. Lance, 1977, Foreword in T. G. Fain (Ed.), *Federal Reorganization: The Executive Branch*, Bowker, New York, p. xi; R. Polenberg, 1966, *Reorganizing Roosevelt's Government; The Controversy Over Executive Reorganization* 1936–39, Harvard University Press, Cambridge, MA.
57. H. C. Mansfield, 1970, "Reorganizing the federal executive branch: limits of institutionalization." *Law and Contemporary Problems*, vol. 35, pp. 461–495.
58. L. Rogers, 1938, "Reorganization: post mortem notes," *Political Science Quarterly*, vol. 53, pp. 161–172.
59. H. Kaufman, 1971, *The Limits of Organizational Change*, University of Alabama Press, Tuscaloosa, AL, p. 76.
60. B. Lance, 1977, Foreword in T. G. Fain (Ed.), *Federal Reorganization: The Executive Branch*, Bowker, New York, p. x.
61. F. C. Mosher (Ed.), 1967, *Government Reorganization: Cases and Commentary*, Bobbs-Merrill, Indianapolis.
62. D. S. Brown, 1977, "Reforming the bureaucracy: some suggestions for the new president," *Public Administration Review*, vol. 37, p. 164; President's Committee on Administrative Management (Brownlow Commission), 1937, Report of the President's Committee: Administrative management in the government of the United States. U.S. Government Printing Office, Washington, DC, p. 18; F. Heady, 1949c, "The operation of a mixed commission," *American Political Science Review*, vol. 43, pp. 940–952.
63. Ronald C. Moe, March 1978, *Executive Branch Reorganization: An Overview*. Senate Committee on Governmental Affairs. Committee Print.

64. Peri E. Arnold, 1974, "Reorganization and politics: a reflection on the adequacy of administration theory," *Public Administration Review* vol. 34, No. 3 (May–June, 1974), pp. 205–211; James R. Dempsey, 1979, "Carter reorganization: a midterm appraisal," *Public Administration Review*, vol. 39, pp. 74–78; James Hart, 1948, *The American Presidency in Action*, Macmillan, New York; E. P. Herring, 1934, "Social forces and the reorganization of the federal bureaucracy," *Southwestern Social Science Quarterly*, vol. 15, pp. 185–200; E. H. Hobbs, 1953, *Executive Reorganization in the National Government*, University of Mississippi Press, Oxford; Harold Kaufman, 1971, *The Limits of Organizational Change*, University of Alabama Press, Tuscaloosa, AL; Herbert Kaufman, 1976, *Are Government Organizations Immortal?* Brookings, Washington, DC; Harvey C. Mansfield, 1969, "Federal executive reorganization: thirty years of experience," *Public Administration Review*, vol. 29, pp. 332–345; R. P. Nathan, 1976, "The administrative presidency," *Public Interest*, vol. 44, pp. 40–54; W. E. Pemberton, 1979, *Bureaucratic Politics: Executive Reorganization During the Truman Administration*, University of Missouri Press, Columbia, MO; Richard Polenberg, 1966, *Reorganizing Roosevelt's Government; The Controversy Over Executive Reorganization* 1936–39, Harvard University Press, Cambridge, MA; E. S. Redford and M. Blisset, 1981, *Organizing the Executive Branch*, University of Chicago Press, Chicago. C. Roberts (Ed.), 1973, *Has the President Too Much Power?* Harper's Magazine Press, New York; L. Sproull, S. Weiner, and D. Wolf, 1978, *Organizing an Anarchy*, University of Chicago Press, Chicago.
65. L. M. Short, 1923, *The development of national administrative organization in the United States*, Johns Hopkins Press, Baltimore, MD.
66. B. Lance, 1977, Foreword in T. G. Fain (Ed.), *Federal Reorganization: The Executive Branch*, Bowker, New York.
67. J. P. Harris, 1937, "The progress of administrative reorganization in the seventy-fifth Congress," *American Political Science Review*, vol. 31, pp. 862–870; P. Hurt, 1932, "Who should reorganize the national administration?" *American Political Science Review*, vol. 26, pp. 1082–1098; R. C. Moe, March 1978, *Executive Branch Reorganization: An Overview*. Senate Committee on Governmental Affairs. Committee Print; M. Musicus, 1964, "Reappraising reorganization," *Public Administration Review*, vol. 24, pp. 107–112; R. P. Nathan, 1975, *The Plot That Failed: Nixon and the Administrative Presidency*, Wiley, New York.
68. H. C. Mansfield, 1970, "Reorganizing the federal executive branch: limits of institutionalization," *Law and Contemporary Problems*, vol. 35, pp. 461–495.
69. H. Emmerich, 1971, *Federal Organization and Administrative Management*, University of Alabama Press, Tuscaloosa, AL, p. 87; James W. Fesler, 1957, Administrative literature and the second Hoover Commission reports, *American Political Science Review*, vol. 51, pp. 135–157; J. P. Harris, 1937, "The progress of administrative reorganization in the seventy-fifth Congress," *American Political Science Review*, vol. 31, pp. 862–870.
70. C. Aikin and L. W. Koenig, 1949, "Introduction to Hoover Commission: a symposium," *American Political Science Review*, vol. 43, pp. 933–940; Peri E. Arnold, 1976, "The first Hoover Commission and the managerial presidency," *Journal of Politics*, vol. 38, pp. 46–70; H. Emmerich, *Federal Organization and Administrative Management*, University of Alabama Press, Tuscaloosa, AL; Tyrus. G. Fain (Ed.), *Federal Reorganization: The Executive Branch*, Bowker, New York, p. xxi; Herman. Finer, 1949, "The Hoover Commission reports," *Political Science Quarterly*, vol. 64, Part I, pp. 405–419; Part II, pp. 579–595; Emmet. P. Herring, 1934, "Social forces and the reorganization of the federal bureaucracy," *Southwestern Social Science Quarterly*, vol. 15, pp. 185–200; Ferrel Heady, 1949a, "The reports of the Hoover Commission," *Review of Politics*, vol. 11, pp. 355–378; E. H. Hobbs, *Executive Reorganization in the National Government*, University of Mississippi Press, Oxford; H. C. Mansfield, 1969, "Federal executive reorganization: thirty years of experience," *Public Administration Review*, vol. 29, pp. 332–345; H. C. Mansfield, 1970, "Reorganizing the federal executive branch: limits of institutionalization," *Law and Contemporary Problems*, vol. 35, pp. 461–495; Ronald. C. Moe, March 1978, *Executive Branch Reorganization: An Overview*, Senate Committee on Governmental Affairs.

Committee Print, p. 16; M. Musicus, 1964, "Reappraising reorganization," *Public Administration Review*, vol. 24, pp. 107–112; R. Polenberg, 1966, *Reorganizing Roosevelt's Government; The Controversy Over Executive Reorganization* 1936–39, Harvard University Press, Cambridge, MA; E. S. Redford and M. Blisset, 1981, *Organizing the Executive Branch*, University of Chicago Press, Chicago; C. Roberts (Ed.), 1973, *Has the President Too Much Power?* Harper's Magazine Press, New York, pp. 203, 208, 214; Lloyd M. Short, 1947, "Adjusting the departmental system," in *Federal executive Reorganization Re-Examined: A Symposium, II. American Political Science Review*, vol. 41, pp. 48–58.

71. H. Finer, 1949, "The Hoover Commission reports," *Political Science Quarterly*, vol. 64, Part I, p. 407.

72. President's Committee on Administrative Management (Brownlow Commission). 1937. Report of the President's Committee: Administrative management in the government of the United States. U.S. Government Printing Office, Washington, DC.

73. N. MacNeil and H. W. Metz, 1956, *The Hoover Report 1953–1955: What It Means to You as a Citizen and Taxpayer*, Macmillan, New York, p. v.

74. L. D. White, 1958, *The Republican Era*, Macmillan, New York, p. 86.

75. H. Emmerich, 1971, *Federal Organization and Administrative Management*, University of Alabama Press, Tuscaloosa, AL; W. G. Harding, 1921, "Business in government and the problem of governmental reorganization for greater efficiency," *Academy of Political Science Proceedings*, vol. 9, pp. 430–431; O. Kraines, 1970, "The president versus Congress: the Keep Commission, 1905–1909, first comprehensive presidential inquiry into administration," *Western Political Science Quarterly*, vol. 23, pp. 5–54; Ronald C. Moe, March 1978, *Executive Branch Reorganization: An Overview*, Senate Committee on Governmental Affairs. Committee Print; E. S. Redford and M. Blisset, 1981, *Organizing the Executive Branch*, University of Chicago Press, Chicago; C. Roberts (Ed.), 1973, *Has the President Too Much Power?* Harper's Magazine Press, New York.

76. H. T. Pinkett, 1965, "The Keep Commission, 1905–1909: a Rooseveltian effort for administrative reform," *Journal of American History*, vol. 52, pp. 297–312.

77. J. Brademas, 1978, "Federal reorganization and its likely impact on state and local government," *Publius*, vol. 8, pp. 25–37; A. E. Buck, 1938, *The Reorganization of State Governments in the United States*, Columbia University Press, New York; Council of State Governments, 1950, *Reorganizing State Government*, Council of State Governments, Chicago; J. L. Garnett, 1980, *Reorganizing State Government: The Executive Branch*, Westview Press, Boulder, CO; James L. Garnett and Charles H. Levine, 1980, "State executive branch reorganization: patterns and perspectives," *Administration and Society*, vol. 12, pp. 227–276; Herbert Kaufman, 1963, *Politics and Policies in State and Local Governments*, Prentice- Hall, Inc., Englewood Cliffs, NJ.

78. F. C. Mosher (Ed.), 1967, *Government Reorganization: Cases and Commentary*, Bobbs-Merrill, Indianapolis; J. P. Olsen, 1976, "Reorganization as a garbage can," in James G. March and Johan P. Olsen (Eds.), *Ambiguity and Choice in Organizations*, Universitetsforlaget, Bergen.

79. L. M. Salamon, 1981b, "The question of goals," in Peter Szanton (Ed.), *Federal Reorganization: What Have We Learned?* Chatham, Chatham, NJ, p. 60.

80. R. G. Brown, 1979, *Reorganizing the National Health Service: A Case Study in Administrative Change*, Blackwell/Robertson, Oxford.

81. J. L. Garnett, 1980, *Reorganizing State Government: The Executive Branch*, Westview Press, Boulder.

82. H. Kaufman, 1977. "Reflections on administrative reorganization," in Joseph A. Pechman (Ed.), *Setting National Priorities: The 1978 Budget*, Brookings, Washington, DC.

83. R. E. Miles, Jr., 1977, "Considerations for a president bent on reorganization," *Public Administration Review*, vol. 37, pp. 155–162.

84. Mosher, 1967, *Government Reorganization: Cases and Commentary.*

85. F. Heady, 1949c, "The operation of a mixed commission," *American Political Science Review*, vol. 43, pp. 940–952; Richard Polenberg, 1966, *Reorganizing Roosevelt's Government; The Controversy Over Executive Reorganization* 1936–39, Harvard University Press, Cambridge, MA.
86. H. Seidman, 1974, "Remarks," in Douglas M. Fox (Ed.), President Nixon's proposals for executive reorganization, *Public Administration Review*, vol. 34, p. 489.
87. H. Emmerich, 1971, *Federal Organization and Administrative Management*, University of Alabama Press, Tuscaloosa, AL, pp. 129–130; L. Sproull, S. Weiner, and D. Wolf, 1978, *Organizing an Anarchy*, University of Chicago Press, Chicago, p. 160.
88. H. Emmerich, 1971, *Federal Organization and Administrative Management*, University of Alabama Press, Tuscaloosa, AL, p. 101.
89. R. E. Miles, Jr., 1977, "Considerations for a president bent on reorganization," *Public Administration Review*, vol. 37, pp. 155–162; H. Seidman, 1980, *Politics, Position and Power: The Dynamics of Federal Organization*, 3rd ed, Oxford University Press, New York.
90. J. W. Meyer and B. Rowan, 1977, "Institutionalized organizations: formal structure as myth and ceremony," *American Journal of Sociology*, vol. 83, pp. 340–363.
91. H. Seidman, 1980, *Politics, Position and Power: The Dynamics of Federal Organization*, 3rd ed, Oxford University Press, New York, p. 126.
92. P. E. Arnold, 1976, "The first Hoover Commission and the managerial presidency," *Journal of Politics*, vol. 38, p. 57.
93. W. E. Pemberton, 1979, *Bureaucratic Politics: Executive Reorganization During the Truman Administration*, University of Missouri Press, Columbia, MO, p. 30.
94. R. E. Miles, Jr., 1977, "Considerations for a president bent on reorganization," *Public Administration Review*, vol. 37, pp. 155–162.
95. H. Emmerich, 1971, *Federal Organization and Administrative Management*, University of Alabama Press, Tuscaloosa, AL, p. 129; J. P. Harris, 1937, "The progress of administrative reorganization in the seventy-fifth Congress," *American Political Science Review*, vol. 31, pp. 862–870; E. P. Herring, 1934, Social forces and the reorganization of the federal bureaucracy, *Southwestern Social Science Quarterly*, vol. 15, pp. 185–200; A. N. Holcombe, 1921, "Administrative reorganization in the federal government," *Annals of the American Academy of Political and Social Science*, vol. 95, pp. 242–251; Peyton Hurt, 1932, "Who should reorganize the national administration?" *American Political Science Review*, vol. 26, pp. 1082–1098; Richard Polenberg, 1966, *Reorganizing Roosevelt's Government; The Controversy Over Executive Reorganization* 1936–39. Harvard University Press, Cambridge, MA; H. Seidman, 1980, *Politics, Position and Power: The Dynamics of Federal Organization*, 3rd ed, Oxford University Press, New York.
96. H. C. Mansfield, 1969, "Federal executive reorganization: thirty years of experience," *Public Administration Review*, vol. 29, p. 335.
97. H. Seidman, 1980, *Politics, Position and Power: The Dynamics of Federal Organization*, 3rd ed, Oxford University Press, New York, p. 10–11.
98. J. A. Califano, Jr., 1981, *Governing America: An Insider's Report From the White House and the Cabinet*, Simon and Schuster, New York, pp. 42–45.
99. H. Seidman, 1980, *Politics, Position and Power: The Dynamics of Federal Organization*, 3rd ed, Oxford University Press, New York, p. 125.
100. R. C. Moe, March 1978, *Executive Branch Reorganization: An Overview*, Senate Committee on Governmental Affairs. Committee Print, p. 49; Harold Seidman, 1980, *Politics, Position and Power: The Dynamics of Federal Organization*, 3rd ed, Oxford University Press, New York.
101. President's Committee on Administrative Management (Brownlow Commission), 1937, Report of the President's Committee: Administrative management in the government of the United States. U.S. Government Printing Office, Washington, DC, pp. 33, 53.
102. W. E. Pemberton, 1979, *Bureaucratic Politics: Executive Reorganization During the Truman Administration*, University of Missouri Press, Columbia, MO, p. 3.

103. Nixon, "Papers . . . ," 1972, p. 4; reprinted in Nathan, 1975, pp. 134–135.

104. R. G. Brown, 1979, *Reorganizing the National Health Service: A Case Study in Administrative Change*, Blackwell/Robertson, Oxford; Frederick C. Mosher, (Ed.), 1965, *Government Reorganization: Cases and Commentary*, Bobbs-Merrill, Indianapolis; G. Vickers, 1965, *The Art of Judgment*, Basic Books, New York.

105. R. A. Dahl, 1980, "Introduction," in J. Hersey, *Aspects of the Presidency*, Ticknor and Fields, New York; N. Johnson, 1976, "Recent administrative reform in Britain," in A. F. Leemans (Ed.), 1976, *The Management of Change in Government*, Martinus Nijhoff, The Hague.

106. I. M. Destler, 1981, "Implementing reorganization," in P. Szanton (Ed.), *Federal Reorganization: What Have We Learned?* Chatham House, Chatham, NJ, p. 166.

107. T. G. Fain (Ed.), 1977, *Federal Reorganization: The Executive Branch*, Bowker, New York, p. xxiii; L. Sproull, S. Weiner, and D. Wolf, 1978, *Organizing an Anarchy*. University of Chicago Press, Chicago.

108. M. Edelman, 1964, *The Symbolic Uses of Politics*, University of Illinois Press, Urbana, IL, pp. 78–79.

109. C. Aikin and L. W. Koenig, 1949, "Introduction to Hoover Commission: a symposium," *American Political Science Review*, vol. 43, pp. 933–940; J. P. Harris, 1937, "The progress of administrative reorganization in the seventy-fifth Congress," *American Political Science Review*, vol. 31, pp. 862–870; W. E. Pemberton, 1979, *Bureaucratic Politics: Executive Reorganization During the Truman Administration*, University of Missouri Press, Columbia, MO, p. 15.

110. L. M. Salamon, 1981b, "The question of goals," in Peter Szanton (Ed.), *Federal Reorganization: What Have We Learned?* Chatham, Chatham, NJ, p. 76.

111. H. Seidman, 1980, *Politics, Position and Power: The Dynamics of Federal Organization*, 3rd ed, Oxford University Press, New York, pp. 115, 316.

112. F. C. Mosher (Ed.), 1975, *American Public Administration: Past, Present, Future*. University of Alabama Press, Tuscaloosa, AL, p. 4.

113. J. G. March and G. Sevon, 1983, "Gossip, information and decision making," in L. S. Sproull and P. D. Larkey (Eds.), *Advances in Information Processing in Organizations*, vol. 1, JAI, Greenwich, CT.

114. R. B. Hawkins, Jr., 1978, "Government reorganization: a federal interest," *Publius*, vol. 8, 3–12; James G. March and Johan P. Olsen, 1976, *Ambiguity and Choice in Organizations*, Universitetsforlaget, Bergen; S. Wolin, 1960, *Politics and Vision: Continuity and Innovation in Western Political Thought*, Little, Brown, Boston.

115. S. Hess, 1976, *Organizing the Presidency*, Brookings, Washington, DC, p. 18.

116. M. D. Cohen and J. G. March, 1974, *Leadership and Ambiguity: The American College President*, McGraw-Hill, New York; James G. March, 1980, *How We Talk and How We Act: Administrative Theory and Administrative Life*, Seventh David D. Henry Lecture, Urbana, IL; T. J. Peters, 1978, "Symbols, patterns and settings: an optimistic case for getting things done," *Organizational Dynamics*, vol. 7, pp. 3–23; J. Pfeffer, 1981, "Management as symbolic action: the creation and maintenance of organizational paradigms," in L. L. Cummings and B. M. Staw (Eds.), *Research in Organizational Behavior*, vol. 3, JAI, Greenwich, CT; L. R. Pondy, 1978, "Leadership is a language game," in M. W. McCall, Jr. and M. M. Lombardo (Eds.), *Leadership*, Duke University Press, Durham, NC; K. E. Weick, 1979, "Cognitive processes in organization," in B. M. Staw (Ed.), *Research in Organizational Behavior*, vol. 1, JAI, Greenwich, CT.

117. T. G. Fain (Ed.), 1977, *Federal Reorganization: The Executive Branch*, Bowker, New York, p. xxiii; Hawkins, 1978.

118. M. E. Dimock, 1951, "The objectives of governmental reorganization," *Public Administration Review*, vol. 11, pp. 233–241.

119. D. M. Fox (Ed.), 1974, "President Nixon's proposals for executive reorganization," *Public Administration Review*, vol. 34, pp. 487–495; Harold Seidman, 1974, "Remarks," in Douglas M. Fox

(Ed.), "President Nixon's proposals for executive reorganization," *Public Administration Review*, vol. 34, pp. 487–495; Harold Seidman, 1980, *Politics, Position and Power: The Dynamics of Federal Organization*, 3rd ed, Oxford University Press, New York; Peter Szanton (Ed.), 1981, *Federal Reorganization: What Have We Learned?* Chatham, Chatham, NJ.

120. H. Kaufman, 1977, "Reflections on administrative reorganization," in Joseph A. Pechman (Ed.), *Setting National Priorities: The 1978 Budget*, Brookings, Washington, DC; Herbert A. Simon, 1957, *Administrative Behavior: A Study of Decision-Making Processes in Administrative Organization*, Macmillan, New York.

121. J. G. March and H. A. Simon, 1977, *Organizations*, Wiley, New York; R. E. Miles, Jr., 1977, "Considerations for a president bent on reorganization," *Public Administration Review*, vol. 37, pp. 155–162.

122. H. Kaufman, 1956, "Emerging conflicts in the doctrine of American public administration," *American Political Science Review*, vol. 50, pp. 1057–1073; P. Laegereid and Johan P. Olsen, 1981, "The storting–a last stronghold of the political amateur," Unpublished manuscript, University of Bergen.

123. J. D. Millett, 1949, "Departmental management," *American Political Science Review*, vol. 43, pp. 959–966.

124. J. G. March and J. P. Olsen, 1976, *Ambiguity and Choice in Organizations*, Universitetsforlaget, Bergen.

125. R. A. Dahl, 1980, Introduction, in J. Jersey, *Aspects of the presidency*, Ticknor and Fields, New York, p. xvi; Ronald C. Moe, March 1978, *Executive Branch Reorganization: An Overview*, Senate Committee on Governmental Affairs. Committee Print, p. 60.

126. J. L. Garnett and C. H. Levine, 1980, "State executive branch reorganization: patterns and perspectives," *Administration and Society*, vol. 12, 227–276.

127. A. Hamilton, J. Jay, and J. Madison, 1964 ed., *The Federalist Papers*. Pocket Books, New York; J. S. Mill, 1861 (1962), *Considerations on Representative Government*, Gateway Editions, South Bend, IN; W. R. Scott, 1981, *Organizations: Rational, Natural, and Open Systems*, Prentice Hall, Englewood Cliffs, NJ.

128. J. W. Kingdon, 1983, *An Idea Whose Time Has Come: Agendas, Alternatives, and Public Policies*. Little, Brown, Boston; J. G. March and J. P. Olsen, 1976, *Ambiguity and Choice in Organizations*, Universitetsforlaget, Bergen, Chapter 3.

129. E. M. Sait, 1938, *Political Institutions-A Preface*. Appleton-Century-Crofts, New York, p. vi.

130. P. Szanton (Ed.), 1981, *Federal Reorganization: What Have We Learned?* Chatham, Chatham, NJ, p. 24.

131. J. G. March and P. Romelaer, 1976, "Position and presence in the drift of decisions," in James G. March and Johan P. Olsen (Eds.), *Ambiguity and Choice in Organizations*, Universitetsforlaget, Bergen, p. 276.

132. The flavor of this theory is captured in Charles S. Hyneman, 1939, "Administrative Reorganization: An Adventure into Science and Theology," *Journal of Politics*, vol. 1, pp. 62–75; Dwight Waldo, 1984, *The Administrative State: A Study of the Political Theory of Public Administration*, 2nd ed., Holmes and Meier Publishers, New York; James L. Garnett, 1980, *Reorganizing State Government: The Executive Branch*, Westview Press, Boulder, CO; Peri E. Arnold, 1986, *Making the Managerial Presidency: Comprehensive Reorganization Planning, 1905–1980*, Princeton University Press, Princeton.

133. J. G. March and J. P. Olson, June 1983, "Organizing Political Life: What Reorganization Tells Us About Government," *The American Political Science Review*, vol. 77, No. 2, pp. 281–296.

134. A similar thesis is taken by Peri E. Arnold, Summer 1981, "Executive Reorganization and the Origins of the Managerial Presidency," *Polity*, vol. 8, pp. 565–599.

135. See Waldo, The Administrative State, and Donald L. Robinson (Ed.), 1985, *Reforming American Government: The Bicentennial Papers of the Committee on the Constitutional System*, Westview Press, Boulder.
136. See Waldo, The Administrative State, and Arnold, Making the Managerial Presidency.
137. Arnold, Making the Managerial Presidency, p. 8.
138. This discussion inevitably draws from Herbert Kauffman, December 1956, "Emerging Conflicts in the Doctrines of American Public Administration," *American Political Science Review*, vol. 50, pp. 1057–1073.
139. Garnett, *Reorganizing State Government*, updated by author.
140. L. H. Gulick, interview with James L. Garnett, November 30, 1976.
141. E. K. Hamilton, 1980, "On Nonconstitutional Management of a Constitutional Problem," in Charles H. Levine (Ed.), *Managing Fiscal Stress: The Crisis in the Public Sector*, Chatham House, Chatham, NJ, p. 53.
142. H. A. Simon, Winter 1946, "The Proverbs of Administration," *Public Administration Review*, vol. 6, pp. 53–67.
143. The prevailing proverb is best expressed in Harold Seidman, 1970, *Politics, Position, and Power: The Dynamics of Federal Organization*, Oxford University Press, New York; Lester Salamon, 1981, "The Question of Goals," in Peter Szanton (Ed.), *Federal Reorganization: What Have We Learned?* Chatham House, Chatham, NJ.
144. Salamon, "The Question of Goals," p. 66.
145. J. Conant, January/February 1986, "Reorganization and the Bottom Line," *Public Administration Review*, vol. 46, pp. 48–56.
146. K. J. Meier 1980, "Executive Reorganization of Government: Impact on Employment and Expenditures," *American Journal of Political Science*, vol. 24, pp. 396–412, and Salamon, "The Question of Goals."
147. Conant, "Reorganization and the Bottom Line."
148. Conant, "Reorganization and the Bottom Line."
149. Even though many reorganization studies use the terms interchangeably, efficiency and effectiveness are different concepts. *Efficiency* is the ratio of service or product inputs to outputs. *Effectiveness* is the degree to which an agency or program achieves its objectives.
150. See, for example, J. M. Mathews, August 1922, "State Administrative Reorganization," *American Political Science Review*, vol. 16, pp. 387–398; Buck, *Reorganization of State Governments;* and Gulick, interview.
151. Nixon, "President's Message," p. 3.
152. H. A. Simon, Winter 1946, "The Proverbs of Administration," *Public Administration Review*, vol. 6, pp. 53–67; H. Simon, 1947, *Administrative Behavior: A Study of the Decision Making Processes in Administrative Organization*, Free Press, Macmillan, New York; and Waldo, *The Administrative State.*
153. See R. E. Dawson and J. A. Robinson, 1963, "Inter-party Competition, Economic Variables and Welfare Policies in the American States," *Journal of Politics*, vol. 25, pp. 265–289: Thomas R. Dye, 1966, *Politics, Economics, and the Public: Policy Outcomes in the American States*, Rand McNally, Chicago.
154. The most perceptive critiques of determinants research include Herbert Jacob and Michael Lipsky, 1968, "Outputs, Structure, and Power: An Assessment of Changes in the Study of State and Local Politics," *The Journal of Politics*, vol. 30, pp. 510–538; Phillip M. Gregg, Fall 1974, "Units and Levels of Analysis," *Publius*, vol. 4, pp. 59–86.
155. Leading the prevailing proverb that structure counts little and influencing many others through their significant work are: H. A. Simon, *Administrative Behavior*, J. G. March and H. A. Simon,

1958, *Organizations*, John Wiley and Sons, New York; H. Kaufman, 1977, "Reflections on Administrative Reorganization," in Joseph Pechman (Ed.), *Setting National Priorities: The 1978 Budget*, The Brookings Institution, Washington, DC).

156. Demonstrating the salience of structure for business performance are Joan Woodward, 1958, *Management and Technology*, Her Majesty's Stationery Office, London; Alfred D. Chandler, Jr., 1973, *Strategy and structure: Chapters in the History of the American Industrial Enterprise*, The MIT Press, Cambridge, MA; and James W. Frederickson, April 1986, "The Strategic Decision Process and Organizational Structure," *The Academy of Management Review*, vol. 11, p. 297.
157. J. L. Perry and T. T. Babitsky, January/February 1986, "Comparative Performance in Urban Bus Transit: Assessing Privatization Strategies," *Public Administration Review*, vol. 46, pp. 57–66.
158. J. M. Hartman, assisted by Linda M. Mitchell, 1984, "Sanitation," in Charles Brecher and Raymond D. Horton (Eds.), *Setting Municipal Priorities: American Cities and the New York Experience*. New York University Press, New York, pp. 415–445.
159. D. C. Smith, "Police," in Brecher and Horton, *Setting Municipal Priorities*, pp. 380–414.
160. See, for example, Buck, The Reorganization of State Governments, p. 28.
161. Many scholars stress the political nature of reorganization, especially Harold Seidman, *Politics, Position, and Power;* and Salamon, "A Question of Goals."
162. Salamon, "A Question of Goals," p. 58.
163. Cultural and communications aspects of reorganization have recently been explored by Steven Maynard-Moody, Donald D. Stull, and Jerry Mitchell, July/August, 1986, "Reorganization as Status Drama: Building, Maintaining, and Displacing Dominant Subcultures," *Public Administration Review*, vol. 46, pp. 301–310, 354.
164. See B. D. Karl, 1970, *Executive Reorganization and Reform in the New Deal*, Harvard University Press, Cambridge; and H. Emmerich, 1971, *Federal Organization and Administrative Management*, University of Alabama Press, Tuscaloosa, AL.
165. R. Polenberg, 1966, *Reorganizing Roosevelt's Government*, Harvard University Press, Cambridge; and H. C. Mansfield, "Federal Executive Reorganization: Thirty Years of Experience," July/August 1969, *Public Administration Review*, vol. 29, pp. 332–345.
166. "Budget Office Evolves Into Key Policy Maker," September 14, 1985, *Congressional Quarterly*, pp. 1809 and 1815.
167. L. H. Gulick and L. Urwick (eds.), 1937, *Papers on the Science of Administration*, Institute of Public Administration, New York.
168. D. K. Price, "Words of Caution About Structural Change," in Robinson, (ed.), *Reforming American Government*, Westview Press, Boulder, CO, 1985, p. 47.
169. R. E. Miles, Jr., March/April 1977, "Considerations for a President Bent on Reorganization," *Public Administration Review*, vol. 37, pp. 155–162.
170. Garnett, *Reorganizing State Government;* and Seidman and Gilmour, *Politics, Position, and Power.*
171. S. Beer, Fall 1973, "The Modernization of American Federalism," *Publius*, vol. 3, pp. 50–95.
172. F. C. Mosher, (ed.), 1967, *Governmental Reorganization: Cases and Commentary*, Bobbs-Merrill, Indianapolis.
173. B. Bozeman and M. Crow, 1986, "Organization Theory and State Government Structure: Are There Lessons Worth Learning?" *State Government*, vol. 58, pp. 144–151.
174. P. Szanton, 1981, "So You Want to Reorganize the Government?" in Peter Szanton (ed.), *Federal Reorganization: What Have We Learned?* Chatham House, Chatham, NJ, p. 24.
175. Comptroller General of the United States, March 18, 1969, *Review of Economic Opportunity Programs*, pp. 163–165.
176. See, for example, Section 4 of Executive Order No. i 1452, January 23, 1969, establishing the Council for Urban Affairs.

177. Senate Committee on Government Operations, October 17, 1967, Hearings on S.R. 886 to redesignate the Department of the Interior as a Department of Natural Resources, p. 16.
178. J. D. Mooney, 1937, "The Principles of Organization," in Luther Gulick and L. Urwick (eds.), *Papers on the Science of Administration*, Institute of Public Administration, p. 93.
179. Ibid.
180. S. M. Butler, Michael Sanera, and W. Bruce Weinrod, 1984, *Mandate for Leadership II*, The Heritage Foundation, p. 484.
181. Senate Committee on Government Operations, Subcommittee on National Policy Machinery, *Organizing for National Security, Hearing*, vol. 1, p. 15, 1961.
182. Ibid., p. 30.
183. Ibid., p. 15.

CHAPTER 5

Lessons

INTRODUCTION

To this point, the material presented in this book has framed reorganization almost entirely in theoretical terms. This is so even though a number of the excerpts have come from actual policy documents. This chapter broadens the traditional frameworks to include unique historical, legal, and analytical considerations.

Thus, the pieces in this chapter move beyond a theoretical understanding of reorganization and grapple with the more concrete and detailed side of the issue as well. Reorganizations do in fact involve the physical relocation of employees, reassignment of office space, and the mixing of bureaucratic cultures. How a proposed reorganization addresses these and other practical challenges often has more of an impact on the success of the effort than do those issues debated in theoretical pieces.

The excerpts included in this chapter were selected with the hope of introducing the reader to the practical side of executive reorganization. The chapter offers a diverse exposition on the various difficulties inherent in any reorganization process and presents a focus on day-to-day concerns that are not discussed by many scholars and high-level policy makers. Several of the included pieces may enable the reader to gain a fuller understanding of the reorganization process, from the early stages of initiation through implementation and evaluation.

Chapter 5 begins with an excerpt from "A Mini-Symposium: President Nixon's Proposals for Executive Reorganization," during which leading administrative scholars debated the merits of Nixon's plan to create four large departments built around the major functions of executive branch programs and agencies. In addition to their consideration of the important theoretical issues at play (orthodox administrative design principles, using structural means to facilitate political ends, and executive-legislative relations, among them), Douglas M. Fox, Harold Seidman, and Harvey Mansfield address practical concerns that other analyses tend to overlook.

The second piece in the chapter is John Brademas's "Federal Reorganization and its Likely Impacts on State and Local Government." Written while Brademas was a member of Congress during the Carter Administration, the excerpt discusses reorganization in the context of the American federal system, a reality frequently overlooked by scholars and policymakers alike. As is clear from many of the documents in Part I, most of the literature on reorganization is written from a Washington and executive branch perspective, with a focus on the issues most relevant to the president and his management agenda. Brademas offers a view of reorganization from his Congressional office and provides an understanding of the differences inherent in the goals and approaches taken by each branch.

John Dempsey's analysis of President Carter's reorganization effort further emphasizes the difficulty of formulating and implementing a broad-based reorganization effort. In "Carter Reorganization: A Midterm Appraisal," Dempsey highlights the problems created when proper attention is not paid to the role of Congress or to the intensely political nature of the pursuit. Dempsey asserts that unless Carter places more focus on these areas, much of his reorganization effort will continue to languish and ultimately fail to achieve significant structural change.

For I. M. Destler, implementation is the bottom line. In his piece "Implementing Reorganization," drawn from Szanton's edited text, *Federal Reorganization*, Destler makes his case by highlighting common pitfalls associated with implementing reorganization efforts. He also offers experienced and prudent ways to address mechanical issues related to action on law and regulations, budget, personnel, and space limitations, as well as the behavioral and cultural adjustments he deems so critical.

History also tells us that no president since Carter received temporary reorganization plan authority from Congress to reorganize the executive branch. Perhaps because of many of the arguments discussed by Louis Fisher and Ronald C. Moe in "Presidential Reorganization Authority: Is It Worth the Cost?" the authority granted to Carter in the Reorganization Act of 1977 has never been renewed. In any case, the authors conclude that the reorganization plan method too heavily favors the executive over Congress and that the traditional legislative means are a more effective way to ensure the effective, if slow and messy, political negotiation between branches over design and control of the bureaucracy.

Susan Gates's piece "Organizing for Reorganization" was originally printed in the RAND Corporation's publication, *High Performance Government: Structure, Leadership, Incentives*. It presents a fascinating proposal for the implementation of the Volcker Commission reorganization recommendations. Gates's model is built around the Base Realignment and Closure (BRAC) process, on which the Department of Defense and Congress rely to facilitate the closing of domestic military bases. Drawing from the BRAC's emphasis on wide political participation, Gates's implementation plan would demand input from members of both the executive and legislative branches, as well as the appointment of an independent blue ribbon commission. Furthermore, her plan would incorporate a Presidential "approval or rejection" requirement, a procedural device pivotal to BRAC's success. Gates's idea is a creative one and, despite its flaws, succeeds in focusing attention on the importance of implementation.

Douglas M. Fox, Alan L. Dean, Harold Seidman, Harvey Mansfield, James Fesler, and Robert Gilmour, "A Mini-Symposium: President Nixon's Proposals for Executive Reorganization," *Public Administration Review*, Vol. 34, No. 5. (September–October, 1974), pp. 487–495.

REMARKS BY DOUGLAS M. FOX

A few words about the Nixon proposals are in order. The President proposed to consolidate the Departments of Interior, Commerce, Labor, HUD, HEW, and Transportation, as well as some other functions of other departments, such as Agriculture, into four new departments: Community Development (DCD), Natural Resources (DNR), Human Resources (DHR), and Economic Affairs (DEA). The secretary would be given increased managerial authority and staff. Programs would be organized around functional goals of the agency rather than clientele, and decentralization granting much more authority to field offices would take place.

In my paper, I criticized the Nixon proposals on a number of counts, which Alan Dean rebuts in order in his opening remarks. I argued that the Nixon Administration relied too heavily on "tinkering with the machinery" as a cause for defects in programs, when it should instead look more closely at the programs and the individuals heading them. I also questioned the seeming ad hoc nature of a plan which the Administration sold as the embodiment of administrative science: why, for example, were the independent agencies left out of the plan? I asserted that the Administration had oversold its argument that reorganization would lead to less emphasis on agency clientele and more concern with functional policy organization, because clientele groups had sufficient informal political power to prevent this outcome. I stated that I felt cabinet secretaries would have too many other responsibilities to enable them to devote sufficient time to departmental management. I submitted that there might be a contradiction between the theme of increasing the secretary's authority and the theme of decentralizing authority to the field. Finally, I argued that special agencies designed to help have-not groups would be submerged with other agencies in the reorganization, thus reducing the access of the poor and underprivileged to government. . . .

REMARKS BY HAROLD SEIDMAN

What I have to say shouldn't be interpreted as a defense of the status quo. If you were to ask my opinion of whether the establishment of a DCD and DNR would make a difference, I would say "yes," but probably not much. One of the difficulties we have is that in dealing with reorganization matters we're sailing on an unknown sea. We're dealing here with mythology—we expect that reorganizations will produce miracles, as a matter of faith. We've had almost no systematic analysis to determine what in fact reorganizations achieve. This was one of my great frustrations when I was responsible for the President's reorganization program. We never had the time or staff to analyze the results of reorganizations. At the National Academy of Public Administration we did do three case studies of reorganizations to see what they accomplished in terms of the objective stated by the President. We found, interestingly enough, that once the reorganizations went through, there ceased to be any interest in the White House. If there had been some follow-up, the likelihood of achieving the President's objectives might have been enhanced. There were some changes in a direction totally different from that desired by the President.

I think we are overlooking several things. First, reorganization of the Executive Branch can't achieve very much unless there is a parallel reorganization of Congress. While this is not to argue that nothing should be done at the Executive Branch level, only limited results can be expected if no changes are made in Congress. In fact, some of the eccentricities you find in administrative structure are only mirror images of the congressional committee structure. It's no accident that we have four different water and sewer programs, because these come out of four separate committees of Congress. These are very important programs for a congressman's constituency, and a congressman wants to be sure that it will remain in an agency under the jurisdiction of his committee. As a result of this, in traffic safety, we got two agencies for the same program so that two committees would have a crack at the confirmation of the administrator. Although they compromised in conference to provide that one man could perform both jobs, it was agreed that he would have to be confirmed for two different positions. Questions concerning the impact of the President's reorganization proposals on committee jurisdictions were raised repeatedly during the House overview hearings. I think to be realistic we have to look at the system as a whole and not just part of the system.

Secondly, I think that we must recognize that the Executive Branch structure is a microcosm of our society, and reflects all of the tensions, differences, and interests that exist in a pluralistic society. To think that you can have a nice, neat, orderly Executive Branch structure when you don't have a nice, neat, orderly society is another illusion. The Executive Branch structure also reflects competition among groups for access and allocation of resources. I think you have to start looking at organization structure from the bottom up as well as from the top down; if you do this, you come out with somewhat different answers. The question of access is very important: How do you provide compensatory mechanisms within the system so that some of those who are less powerful will not be denied access or participation?

You have to look again—and this does not come out in the congressional hearings on the reorganization plan—at some of the policy implications of the proposals. There is very definitely an interrelationship between organization structure and policy. You do not reorganize merely to get a neater grouping of activities, but to get a different policy emphasis. If you put the highway program in the Department of Community Development, certainly the intention is to get a different kind of program than you have today. I think that it is important to tie it in with community planning, which would make it a different kind of program. To put Rural Electrification Administration in the Department of Community Development represents a policy judgment—that the two per cent subsidized loans now should be going not primarily for electrifying farms but for electrification of communities in rural areas. The relocation of REA represents a judgment as to what the program emphasis ought to be from now on. I don't think that this kind of problem is being sufficiently explored. . . .

REMARKS BY HARVEY MANSFIELD

. . . It is plain that the President's proposals put their faith in hierarchy. When you do that, you either ignore or attempt to suppress at least two and perhaps three other kinds of influence that one way or another will find some means of expression. One is clientele influences, already mentioned. Look at the recent seizure of the Bureau of Indian Affairs by Indians, which resulted in their getting amnesty, carting away files and documents, and being paid cash to leave town. If the BIA is moved to another department, will it make any difference in this regard?

To take another case, I read recently in the paper about contributions by dairy producers to re-election campaign funds and then what happened to the price of milk which is within the jurisdiction of the Department of Agriculture. So the adoption of a principle of hierarchy does not secure, although it may encourage guarantees of protection from clientele interests.

Another kind of thing, in conflict with the notion of hierarchy, doesn't get overt recognition in these proposals, although doubtless the people who made these proposals were not entirely innocent of an acquaintance with these other things. I refer not only to conflicts among clienteles of the same agency but also to incompatible activities addressed to the same clientele. That is to say, the Department of Agriculture may prefer producers against consumers when these interests are opposed. But there are also situations where an agency does different things to the same clientele and these different things contain elements of incompatibility. Take the Bureau of Mines, for instance. Among other things, it has to gather, collect, interpret, and compile the statistics that go into the Minerals Yearbook. For that, it needs the active cooperation of the mining companies. It can do that with one hand, but with the other hand it is supposed to come down with some stringent safety regulations to impose on the same companies. That kind of incompatibility of function, I suppose, is the justification for having a separate Environmental Protection Agency and the justification for a separately organized Consumer Protection Agency, FDA, FTC, or whatever. The fact that groups and the agencies they deal with are linked to a common subject matter underlines the force of Fesler's comment that it may be "areas of concern" rather than related or common goals and purposes which are the justification for making broad groupings for organizational purposes.

Another kind of incompatibility has to do with the links of policies to politics and consequently to the appropriate forms of administration. Some types of policies, which Ted Lowi calls distributive, involve the government in giving things away, and have consequently been determined by patronage politics. Correspondingly, such policies are likely to be administered by agencies congenially organized by and for patronage. Another type of policy is regulatory. It consists of giving people, not what the government has, but what benefits the government can confer on one group by imposing constraints on some other group. This is a quite different sort of policy, it produces a different sort of politics, and consequently a different sort of administrative agency, such as a regulatory commission. Finally, redistributive policies, which involve major shifts in allocations of wealth, provoke class politics that can't be contained within the sub-systems which commonly resolve regulatory issues. An agency that administers redistributive policies needs an organization insulated against parochial constituencies. These organizational differentiations may exist submerged in the internal workings of a large organization and be missed if you look only at its top. If you don't pay close attention to the internal arrangements when a reorganization proposal is made, you may get only a superficial and perhaps unrealistic view of its functional propensities.

A third ground for skepticism is that taking hierarchy as the main basis for organization assumes either explicitly or implicitly that it is the President who is entitled to determine the government's programs. In the days of the Brownlow Committee, this was orthodox doctrine. Today I suppose I would say that the President is entitled to try and make it so; but not entitled to expect that his claim will go uncontested. From the beginning of the Republic two contradictory doctrines have been invoked in conflicts, between the President and people working either with or through him on the one hand, and congressional committees on the other hand, as to who is entitled to give instructions to the several components of the Executive Branch. Congressional committees, especially the appropriations committees, sometimes take a very firm position on insisting that as far as instructions to agencies are concerned, their marching orders come from the committee and it is up to the committee, and not the President, to say how high they should jump.

Let me mention briefly two other points. There may have been internal staff work, but there hasn't been much outside discussion, it seems to me, of some of the dilemmas of decentralization. It may well be that coterminous boundaries for regions constitute an important problem of decentralization, but it appears that in at least some programs the overriding problem is getting a field organization in which an agency's headquarters can place confidence. Alan Dean said that you can't delegate what you don't have; you can't decentralize authority without having that authority to begin with. That seems to me only half true, in that sometimes you can have a sort of confederism that is described as delegation, but that allows no sufficient central authority or control over policy. So, regardless of what the field man is told, you're not in a position to issue instructions that will be observed, and in the same spirit. A recent example of that—since HUD has been brought into the discussion—seems to me the inability of the federal department in that field to find expert real estate people to work in some field offices, whose integrity and competence can be trusted. It is not only a matter of getting a policy set in Washington and getting funds for it. Decentralization requires more than simply getting field instructions worked out.

John Brademas, "Federal Reorganization and Its Likely Impact on State and Local Government," *Publius*, Vol. 8, No. 2, Government Reorganization and the Federal System (Spring, 1978), pp. 25–37.

GOVERNMENT REORGANIZATION AND THE FEDERAL SYSTEM

It will be my purpose here not so much to attempt to measure impacts of federal reorganization on state and local activities as to make some observations about reorganization which I hope will be helpful to anyone interested in the subject. To begin with, we must avoid the danger of considering too narrowly the effects of reorganization of the executive branch of the national government on state and local governments. Let us examine some of the factors that constitute the broader context within which we should consider the issue of reorganizing the executive branch.

1. The American Constitution and its political system are unique and complex. They are characterized by separated institutions sharing powers. Although responsive to different, if at times overlapping constituencies, the President, Congress and the courts all have real influence in the decision-making process. For example, reorganization focuses on decisions taken by the executive; the actions of Congress can produce policy despite and over executive branch objections. Congress itself has initiated reorganizations of the executive. In opposition to the views of the Nixon Administration, it was Congress that mandated by law the location of both the Rehabilitation Services Administration and the Administration on Aging in the Department of Health, Education and Welfare.
2. Our system of governing is made more complex by our decentralized political parties. Members of the House and Senate, like governors and mayors, are not beholden to the President or to a national party organization. Our national parties are not highly disciplined structures but loose coalitions linked by ties of history, ideology, self-interest and our electoral mechanism. American parties are not consistently effective instruments for setting national policies in clear directions.
3. A third element that enriches the complexity of our governing processes is our federal system. For the Founding Fathers, the federal system embraced a national government exercising a limited number of specific powers and state governments retaining all those powers not delegated to the national government. Our Constitution has proved flexible enough, however, to accommodate the changing needs

Source: John Brademas, "Federal Reorganization and its Likely Impact on State and Local Government," *Publius*, Spring 1978, Vol. 8, No. 2, pp. 25–37, by permission of Oxford University Press.

> of the nation so that now the national and state governments share many powers and are not two rigidly confined and exclusive spheres of authority. The late Morton Grodzins aptly characterized our federal system as a "marble cake": "Whenever you slice through it, you reveal an inseparable mixture of differently colored ingredients. There is no neat horizontal stratification. . . . So it is with federal, state and local responsibilities in the chaotic marble cake of American government."[1]

Reality is still more complex than Grodzin's analogy suggests. We do not enjoy today even the simplicity of a federal-state-local arrangement. There are school boards, metropolitan governments, regional compacts and a variety of other special authorities. And although powers may be clearly delineated in some activities—e.g., national defense at one end of the spectrum and fire protection at the other—the marbled layer cake metaphor is useful to describe the overlapping of authority in other areas like education, pollution control and economic development. So, separation of powers, decentralized parties, and a federal system in constant flux are fundamental to our consideration of the impact of reorganization of the federal executive on state and local governments.

Yet, federal executive reorganization is only one among many federal policies that affect what state and local governments do. Statutory formulas for distribution of federal grants, revenue sharing, and overall federal postures on urban, suburban and rural problems have a direct and significant impact on state and local governments. Moreover, many general policies of the federal government—policies adopted without specific state and local concerns in mind—can nonetheless powerfully influence state and local governments. Two instances of what I mean are the President's commitments to a balanced budget and to zero-based budgeting. Also, political developments on the national plane—such as change, after years of divided government, in the partisan pattern of control of the federal executive and legislative branches by the same party—obviously can have significant impact on the relationships between states and localities and the federal government.

Another set of significant factors is the entire range of non-governmental social, economic and human variables. Rates of inflation, the growth of GNP, the level of unemployment, the birth rate, the supply and price of OPEC oil—all are factors over which the federal government is not sovereign but which nonetheless profoundly affect the entire system. Finally, we cannot forget to take into account human behavior and personal idiosyncrasy. Members of the same cabinet in an administration committed to executive reorganization may seek to meet that commitment in radically different ways.

Thus, reorganization of the federal executive does not occur in isolation; it takes place in and through extraordinarily complex institutions and processes. Reorganization is only one among many policies that shape relations with states and localities; these relations, too, are significantly molded by factors outside or beyond the control of government. . . .

POLICY AND REORGANIZATION

The following are at least some of the questions that should be directed to every proposed reorganization:

1. What are the policies that will be affected by reorganization and how will they be affected? For example, will the plan likely result in more effective delivery of services to the clientele? Will money be saved without diminution of services? And where are the hard evidence and analysis to substantiate the change? No one can object to making the bureaucracy tidier or the life of administrators easier so long as reaching these goals does not subvert the purposes of the programs they administer.
2. What are the trade-offs in a proposed reorganization? For example, is location at a higher level in the bureaucracy to be the price for less adequate funding of the program?
3. Has the proposed reorganization been subjected to the consideration and questioning of Congress, state and local officials and others affected by the change? Or, despite the genuine merits of the reorganization, has consultation been so lacking or so cosmetic and has it aroused such suspicion and hostility that the plan has been crippled?

The kinds of questions I have been raising as a Member of Congress are the same kinds of questions that state and local officials should ask in assessing the impact on their activities of a proposed reorganization. Reorganization clearly will affect the capacity of state and local officials to get a hearing, to voice their concerns, to have access. Because funds will flow through the channels established by reorganization, these officials must ask if these channels will move the money in different directions important to states and localities.

The ways in which state and local governments organize themselves also can be significantly affected by changes in the organization of the federal executive. Usually, there will be a tendency to parallel the new federal organization in order to be able to take advantage of the federal programs effectively.

It should be noted that legislation following federal reorganization often provides incentives, or in some cases a mandate, for states and cities to develop organizational structures compatible with the federal organization and the policies it reflects. . . .

I have argued that reorganization usually involves substantive policy; for precisely this reason there can be no simple prescriptions for an appropriate organization. Decisions about reorganization often mean decisions about competing goods rather than about discovering the right answer. The preferred reorganization may therefore depend largely on one's judgment about preferred policy; and in turn that judgment, understandably, will be significantly affected by where one sits. A president, OMB director, cabinet secretary, senator or congressman, governor or state legislator, mayor or school board member are likely to perceive differently the policy impact of a particular reorganization. The answer to the question of whether any reorganization is good from a policy perspective is again: "It All Depends."

I hope that it is clear why I believe that the process of reorganizing the federal government would be improved greatly if it were to become more openly and explicitly political; not in a partisan sense but in the simple acknowledgment that organization involves policy. In evolving reorganization proposals, the federal executive must be open to the realization that reorganization means policy, and open therefore to honest, de facto consultation with Members of Congress, interested groups, state and local officials and others affected by the proposed change. Reorganizers should, therefore, abandon the view that, for example, Congressional concern with reorganization is tiresome meddling with matters that are none of Congress' business. Even as the federal executive must do much better in consulting Congress and the interest groups, reorganizers must be more sensitive to hearing the views of state and local officials. . . .

John R. Dempsey, "Carter Reorganization: A Midterm Appraisal," *Public Administration Review*, Vol. 39, No. 1. (January–February, 1979), pp. 74–78.

During the 1976 campaign, candidate Jimmy Carter promised, if elected, to reorganize the federal government. From the New Hampshire primary, where he told the voters, "don't vote for me unless you want to see the executive branch of government completely reorganized,"[2] right up until election eve, Carter hammered hard at the need for reorganization. Coupled as it was with a promise to institute more effective management practices in the federal government, it is likely that the reorganization theme appealed to many voters. It may well have been one of the factors that led to his election.

Reorganization on a major scale is never an easy task. Carter's reorganization efforts, if they are to be successful, will take at least one full term of office. Nonetheless, it is now possible–over two years since his election–to offer a reorganization "progress report," and an appraisal of the quality of the reorganization efforts that have been made to date.

The Carter reorganization effort has three major elements. Stated simply, these elements are, agency reorganization, conversion of federal executive budgeting to a zerobase format, and civil service reform.

Despite the fact that the President tends to view all of these elements as parts of a comprehensive reorganization "package," each of them deserves separate consideration.

AGENCY REORGANIZATION

During his campaign, Mr. Carter often described a "maze" of government agencies, frequently with overlapping jurisdictions, that needed to be reorganized to make the government more effective and more responsive to the needs of its citizens. The primary vehicle which President Carter created to deal with agency reorganization is the President's Reorganization Project (PRP), and its major tool is the Reorganization Act of 1977.

Created in the Office of Management and Budget (OMB) as a visible symbol of the President's commitment to reorganization, PRP is a hybrid organization composed of political appointees, OMB careerists, and personnel "detailed" to the project from the operating agencies. Under the general control of OMB's Executive Associate Director for Reorganization and Management, PRP is divided into five sections:

- Defense and International Affairs
- Human Resources
- Economic and Community Development
- Natural Resources
- General Government

Each of these divisions is broken down, in turn, into a number of study groups assigned to specific agencies, programs, or activities. It is the responsibility of these study groups to "reorganize the government" along more rational lines; eliminate duplication and overlap; consolidate functions where appropriate; and abolish any agencies or other organizations who lack a legitimate purpose. In carrying out its responsibilities, PRP has relied heavily on authority vested in the President by the Reorganization Act of April 6, 1977. Under the Act, Reorganization Plans are submitted to Congress by the President, and they become effective unless vetoed by either house of Congress within sixty days.

During the nearly two years of its existence, PRP has worked closely with the agencies, concerned interest groups, and interested members of the public, to develop programs and proposals for reorganizing the government. Where reorganization goals can not be met solely by Reorganization Plan, PRP has participated in drafting the legislation necessary to fill the gaps. The PRP has become, during the past year and a half, one of the most visible and active parts of the Carter administration.

Despite the flurry of activity, however, very little substantive reorganization has been accomplished. As this is written, only six Reorganization Plans have been submitted to the Congress. Though five of these plans have been approved and approval is likely for the sixth, their results can hardly be seen as major reorganization accomplishments.

The first approved plan reorganized the Executive Office of the President. The second combined the United States Information Agency with the State Department's Bureau of Educational and Cultural Affairs. The third plan consolidated a number of "equal employment" activities in the Equal Employment Opportunity Commission. These activities include ensuring equal employment opportunities for federal employees (previously the job of the U.S. Civil Service Commission), and enforcing the Equal Pay and Age Discrimination Acts (previously the responsibility of the Department of Labor). The fourth plan created the Federal Emergency Management Agency to improve the nation's system of emergency preparedness. The fifth plan replaced the Civil Service Commission with two new organizations—the Office of Personnel Management and the Merit Systems Protection Board. . . . The sixth plan, currently pending in Congress, clarifies the responsibilities of the Departments of Treasury and Labor for administering the Employee Retirement Income Security Act of 1974 (ERISA).

Beyond the submission of formal Reorganization Plans, PRP has been involved in other activities. PRP staff work contributed significantly to developing the Justice System Improvement Act of 1978. This act, if passed by the Congress, will reorganize the Law Enforcement Assistance Administration, and create a National Institute of Justice and a Bureau of Justice Statistics. PRP has also been heavily involved in plans to create a new Department of Education. In the near future, the President will send to Congress a PRP-developed plan to reorganize the federal government's system of legal representation.

While these approved and proposed changes are not insignificant, they are a long way from Jimmy Carter's New Hampshire promise to "completely reorganize" the federal government. The PRP may be a conscientious, hard-working group, but its results to date leave a great deal to be desired. There are probably several explanations.

One problem, of course, is the very difficult task involved. What was conceived as an exercise in management improvement has turned into a complex political struggle. This eventuality could have been predicted by anyone familiar with the political undergirdings of the federal bureaucracy—but it seems to have eluded the Carter planners who designed the reorganization project. Now—midway through President Carter's first term—an awareness of reorganization's political implications seems to be taking hold. At a recent meeting of the American Political Science Association, Harrison Wellford, the President's chief reorganization assistant, described reorganization as, ". . . an exercise in power, not in architecture."[3] Whether this awareness will lead to more successful reorganization initiatives in the future remains to be seen.

Further problems for agency reorganization have been caused by the jealousies and jurisdictional conflicts that characterize the congressional process. According to the procedures established by the Reorganization Act of 1977, all reorganization plans are handled by the Government Operations Committees in the House and Senate. The authorizing committees of the Congress, naturally enough, dislike seeing "their" agencies dismantled or reshaped by a process in which they have no direct involvement. As a result, powerful authorizing committee chairmen often wield unofficial "veto" power over reorganization plans, and the threat of those vetoes dissuades the administration from submitting reorganization plans without the chairmen's prior approval. While this practice tends to violate the spirit of the Reorganization Act of 1977, it nonetheless reflects the realities of the congressional process.

Finally, the shortcomings of the agency reorganization effort can be seen simply as microcosms of some of the larger problems that have plagued the Carter administration as a whole. Inadequate staff work, poor coordination and consultation with the Congress, and the tendency to seek "too much, too soon" have hurt the reorganization effort, just as they have hindered many other administration initiative. Further, the President's own reputation has not helped the effort. One of a President's biggest assets in dealing with official Washington is fear—fear that if his will is not obeyed, his wrath will be felt. Jimmy Carter is admired by very many people in Washington; he is feared by very few. During the past year and a half, agencies have concluded that failure to accede to presidential wishes does not spell the automatic disaster it might have during the Johnson and Nixon years. Accordingly they have been more adamant and outspoken about "protecting their turf." Agencies have (rather openly) sought and found allies in Congress to frustrate reorganization efforts that threaten their position in the federal hierarchy. The result has been to make the already difficult reorganization task even tougher.

I. M. Destler, "Implementing Reorganization," in Peter Szanton, (Ed.), *Federal Reorganization: What Have We Learned?* Chatham, NJ: Chatham House (1981).

For reorganization, as for any other change, implementation is the bottom line. Without it, the whole exercise is show and symbolism. Yet in real-life attempts at reorganization, serious concern with implementation is typically too little and too late. Enormous attention is devoted to analyzing and deciding what changes should be made. The problem of getting from here to there is addressed only belatedly. To paraphrase Erwin Hargrove, implementation often seems the "missing link" in reorganization.[4]

There are two broad ways of defining implementation. The first centers on the concrete steps required to make formal reorganization decisions effective and complete—drafting orders, getting needed legislative action, reallocating money and personnel slots, bringing on new staff, juggling office space. The second, more ambitious definition is linked to purpose; implementation here is tied to actual behavioral change, achieving the alterations in governmental process or outcome (e.g., efficiency, shifted priorities, improved coordination) that were the reorganization's goal. . . .

CONCRETE PROBLEMS

Implementation can be analyzed most directly in terms of the specific things that must be done to translate a general reorganization decision into an operating reality. Stephen K. Bailey wrote in 1968 that "the *essential* controls of an agency head over constituent units are three, and only three: 1) control of legislative proposals; 2) control of budgetary totals; 3) control of major personnel appointments and assignments."[5] Not surprisingly, these correspond closely to the major resources involved in implementing reorganization—with one addition, the allocation of office space.

Laws and Regulations

Once an executive opts for a particular reorganization, he must assure that his decision has the required legal standing. This will always require drafting and issuance of internal orders

---

within the agency affected. It will often require an executive order or equivalent presidential action document.[6] It will sometimes require changes in statute, achievable either through reorganization plan (if the Congress has extended this authority to the President, as it did for Carter in 1977–80) or through the normal legislative process. Use of the latter is required, under current law, if the proposal involves creation of a new executive department, abolishing an executive department or independent regulatory agency, or establishing or continuing agencies or functions beyond what current law authorizes.

In cases where the executive has some choice among these instruments, or in his relative reliance on them, the tradeoff is fairly straightforward. Changing a statute has the greatest visibility and credibility, and conveys the broadest legitimacy on reorganization. It also contributes to permanence. But it most restricts executive flexibility, inviting Congress to specify the details of administration. Internal memoranda have the opposite advantages and drawbacks. . . .

Public administration doctrine has long favored the more flexible instruments and less specificity in statutes in order to give Presidents and cabinet members greater leeway in running and restructuring their own domains. . . . For those seeking to carry out a particular organizational mandate, a statute or executive order is often important to their credibility. . . . In cases where particular sensitivity to Congress is required for an agency's functioning, statutory entrenchment may be a blessing. . . .

For any new agency performing functions specified in statute, one crucial implementation step is assuring that it has, on its first day of operation, all the legal authority for these functions and that the necessary internal orders exist for assigning these functions within the agency. . . .

Budgeting

When an agency, new or old, assumes a function elsewhere, it must get control of the funds necessary to do so. To this end, statutes typically authorize transfer of such "unexpended balances of appropriations, allocations and other funds employed" as the OMB director determines are linked to these functions. If the amounts involved do not follow automatically from the functions, such determinations are generally preceded by an adversary process, between the gaming and losing agency, brokered by the responsible OMB staff officer.

Budgetary changes can also help implement reorganization in other ways. If the goal is to reinforce an existing cabinet secretary vis-a-vis subordinate units, a budget planning process that sharpens tradeoffs at his level is a vital means. So it can be also, at least potentially, for a Secretary of State with an interdepartmental leadership mandate-hence proposals for a comprehensive foreign affairs budget or programming system. Conversely, if the aim is to give a subunit greater autonomy . . . budgetary tradeoffs and budget staffing need to be decentralized, to reinforce the subunit head. . . .

Implementation of a reorganization may also require changes in how OMB reviews an agency budget. Autonomy is advanced, for example, by giving a subunit a separate OMB ceiling for budget planning purposes.

Personnel

Perhaps most important, reorganizations are implemented through decisions about people—where they work, what they do. The most general personnel decisions, of course, involve establishing ranks and titles of officials created by the reorganization, providing personnel ceilings for new organizations, and adjusting them for old ones. Here also, "determination orders" by the OMB director are the established means of allocating and transferring positions. . . . Agencies will also seek maximum flexibility in using the positions they gain or retain—to limit, for example, the number of unwanted incumbents they must take along with the job slots.

Probably the most crucial implementing action involving personnel is the timely placement of persons committed to a reorganization in key leadership positions. . . . The prospect that a well-regarded individual will head a new organization can contribute to favorable congressional action. . . . Conversely, Congress may balk if members have reservations. . . .

[P]ractitioners of reorganization generally agree that the post most important to fill early, aside from that of head of a new agency, is that of chief administrative official. If this person is not in place to orchestrate slots, money, space, and management procedures when the major program subordinates are designed, they are likely to make separate uncoordinated decisions, which must be modified later, or to reach for control of particular matters in order to secure their own turf. For as one veteran implementer puts it, reorganization "sets loose strivings in people." It also sets loose fears that if they don't grab what is theirs today, it won't be there tomorrow. A strong, fair central administrator cannot eliminate such strivings, but he can arbitrate among the strivers and bring some order to their operating environment.

Even when a strongly motivated official is in charge, with a clear mandate, making the required internal personnel changes can be a time-consuming and painful process.

Space

. . . [W]hat makes any organization effective, most of all, is the combination of an important job to perform and the leverage to perform it. Nevertheless, it seems wrong to conclude that the immediate physical environment is unrelated to, or even inversely correlated with, a reorganization's chance of success. Office space is not always addressed in organizational analyses, but it has both operational and symbolic importance. . . . One obvious way to reinforce the officials upon whom a reorganization depends, therefore, is to give them office locations that will be read as signs of presidential or secretarial favor.

Another symbolic way that space can be used to strengthen an organization is to give a new or restructured agency an attractive central building of its own as soon as possible after its creation. . . . For delay tends to reinforce the impression that nothing has really changed, that the old ways of doing business are going continue.

And more than appearances are at stake, for location does, in fact, have a direct impact on how officials carry out their day-to-day work. "Nothing 'propinques' like propinquity," and even in the telephone age, the best way to build allegiance to new organizational units and their purposes is to bring people together physically, building up informal as well as formal contact. Conversely, if an aim of reorganization is to break up old working units, then physical separation is an important means to this end. And last but not least, consolidating the space of those in an organization likely to be dealing most regularly with one another brings obvious gains in efficiency reducing, for example, the time required for sheer physical movement of people and intragovernmental mail. . . .

Putting It All Together

In practice, action on law and regulations, budget, personnel, and space must proceed simultaneously. This typically involves three central federal agencies–the Office of Management and Budget, the General Services Administration, and the Office of Personnel Management–working together and with the specific agencies affected. Ideally, each of the three should maintain a substantial standing competence for implementing reorganization. In practice, this is hard to do because the workload is discontinuous–there are occasional major reorganizations, like energy, interspersed with many smaller ones, like trade. Thus, in practice, available central staff capacity (and experience with past reorganizations) is often less than needed when a major implementation effort is required.

There is also the prior or simultaneous need to maintain communication with the Congress, particularly the government operations committees, to assure that statutes are enacted in a form consistent with reorganization's purpose, and that there is a receptive voice when experience indicates that amendments are required.

IMPLEMENTATION AS BEHAVIORAL CHANGE

Thus far, this chapter has focused mainly on mechanics. But if reorganization is to be real, it must ultimately change the way people do public business. This means that the primary actors in the policy area affected–the bureaucrats, the client groups, and the congressional constituents–must shift to enduring new patterns of behavior. To all these groups, an effective implementation effort must therefore send a twofold signal: that what is happening is real change, with considerable force behind it; and that they can, in most cases, find ways to live with it, even benefit from it, if they cooperate. Without the first message, no one will have reason to depart from business as usual. Without the second, those affected may see resistance as their only option, whatever its risks. Eliciting such behavioral change is particularly complicated, of course, if the target is discretionary behavior of many officials dispersed through the organization.

Looked at this way, implementation becomes not a mechanical process of selecting the appropriate formal devices but a political/behavioral challenge. The starting point is recognition that, at least for large organizations and major programs, no executive can amass the political force necessary to impose enduring change; the resources available for resistance, and the sheer inertia, will simply be too great. But neither clienteles nor career bureaucracies are ever monolithic. Within them are interests that can serve the executive's purpose if he learns how to work with them, reinforce them, and influence them. And they have experience and skills he badly needs above all, knowledge of existing systems and how to make them work.

Thus conceived, real organizational change is a gradual process, just like any other serious policy enterprise, with the executive using his leverage to elicit not just compliance but support, systematically working with and rewarding those inside and outside groups whose purposes coincide with his own or can be brought to do so. Hugh Heclo and Arnold Kanter are among those whose writings suggest means of achieving this end-working for "conditionally cooperative behavior" rather than absolute loyalty; avoiding frontal challenges to the professional self-esteem of the dominant professional group-such as the McNamara regime mounted, intentionally or not, to the uniformed services. One can also look at promotion systems and ways of influencing what and who they reward. And one can cultivate external constituencies, seeking ways that their interests and needs can be reconciled with a new order. The prerequisite for doing these things is a willingness to grasp the organization in its own terms, to learn what moves bureaucrats within it and the external interests that press in on it, not in order to accept these things as they are but to explore the potential and limits of possible change.

WHY IMPLEMENTATION IS NEGLECTED

Treated as behavioral change, implementation is obviously difficult, and the reasons for its neglect become clearer. As long as reorganization staffs stick to designing proposals for change and maneuvering to get them to executives for decision, their job may not be easy, but at least they are working their own terrain. And as long as the executive sticks to decision making, he is staying on his. But when they move into the details of agency orders, budget processes, personnel allocations, even office space allocation, they enter an alien domain. They move from a process with one central decider–the executive–or one focused decision process–enactment of a law by Congress–to battling to influence hundreds and thousands of decisions made at lower bureaucratic levels, decisions that draw on information available mainly at these levels.

Thus neglect of implementation does not arise simply from intellectual error, though there is a recurrent tendency of executives and their staffs to exaggerate the impact of their formal actions on real-life organizational processes. There is a deeper cause: the detailed work of implementation brings them onto ground where their bargaining advantages are few and the capacity of others to neutralize their actions is very great. Thus in terms of maximizing their own interests, executives and their staffs would devote great energy to implementation only if there were commensurate rewards. If in fact there were a political equivalent of the economic marketplace, and implementation of wisely designed organizational reforms led more or less clearly or visibly to greater market rewards, then it would be worth the effort. But this is seldom the case.

Moreover, the main rewards may lie outside the executive's time. A serious focus on implementation or organizational change means, in most instances, a commitment to evolution, to building up new systems and new competences slowly even if surely. Yet the tenure of the typical political executive will not permit such a priority.

Rewards do come, however, from expressing visible dissatisfaction with current organization and taking sweeping if superficial visible action with respect to it. Candidate Carter apparently saw substantial political gains from a high-visibility commitment with very generalized goals making government more efficient and more compassionate. President Carter did not seem to have been damaged by the fact that his administration had not generated an exceptional amount of reorganization, much less by the fact that the jury is still out on whether his most visible new creations—the Departments of Energy and Education—are successful by any criterion other than symbolism and attractiveness to certain constituencies.

Such generalized stakes in the appearance of reorganization are hardly confined to Presidents. Three months after becoming Deputy Undersecretary of State for Administration, William B. Macomber launched his management "program for the seventies" with considerable public fanfare. Once his 13 task forces issued their reports, his staff gleaned from them 505 separate change proposals, and Macomber then issued a series of "Management Reform Bulletins" intended to publicize concrete progress in carrying them out. One intention may have been to maintain the momentum of reform, but the process degenerated into one where public relations took precedence over real achievement. Two hundred and fifty officials had served on the task forces, but in the implementation phase the same enormous range of problems were being tackled by only a handful of persons really committed to the program, most of them engaged part-time. They were almost inevitably driven to seek some degree of apparent compliance with as large a number of specific proposals as possible, and then to report this as success, which is exactly what they did. In the short run, this gave reformers their day in the sun, while also giving resisters and skeptics the assurance that little was really changing. Over time, of course, the credibility of the reform effort was substantially eroded, and the prospects for real system change were undercut. But the Deputy Undersecretary had already made his reputation as a reformer, and he was soon off to become Ambassador to Turkey.

Thus executives often get more rewards for appearing to reorganize than for actually doing so, or more from visible structural change than from reforms that actually achieve the specific reorganization goals. But even in the case of those who really want enduring change, there are barriers to giving implementation timely consideration.

Logically, attention to implementation should begin as soon as the general targets of likely reorganization are clear—people should be studying the real-life operating patterns of these agencies, discovering interests and sources of energy supporting change from within, assessing motivations of line officials and how they can work with or change these motivations, and building support for particular ideas before they are finally adopted. In pursuing this task, the general Carter administration priority to "bottom up" organizational studies has real merit. But moves that would prepare the way for prompt implementation—shifting personnel, canvassing office space, mobilizing congressional support—may be resisted for the simple reason that they tend to preempt the executive's decision, and to go beyond the mandate of the staffs or advisers working on reorganization. Lyndon Johnson explicitly told his reorganization task force that implementation was his job; they should concern themselves, in total confidentiality, with recommending what they thought was right. By contrast, one of the advantages of an ongoing reorganization staff like the

President's Reorganization Project is that it can continue working on issues after the decision is made, and can see them through. But three years is probably not long enough, particularly if the President's commitment to organization change is perceived to be declining in the latter part of this period.

When a reorganization program is more lightly staffed, or when change proponents seize a sudden opportunity to win formal adoption of a proposal, there may be no advance effort aimed at implementation at all. As William Backus has written, the idea of establishing "country directors" as senior officials within the regional bureaus had long been considered at the State Department. But the actual order came suddenly, when Undersecretary U. Alexis Johnson and Deputy Undersecretary William Crockett seized the occasion of the President's issuance of NSAM 341 (establishing the Senior Interdepartmental Group) to get Secretary Rusk to approve that same day a State Department order (Foreign Affairs Manual Circular 385) creating the country director positions. This haste meant, apparently, that the reform was denied the impetus it might have gained from inclusion in the presidential order to which it was logically related. (Country directors were to be interagency leaders at their level just as the Undersecretary and Assistant Secretaries were to be under NSAM 341.)

More important, haste contributed to the fact that "the geographic assistant secretaries, whose bureaus were to be reorganized by the CD change, had little input into the decision process. . . . Thus those most affected by the change and most directly in a position to influence its success, with the possible exception of the CDs themselves, had little personal stake in the idea, and in some cases actually opposed it."[7] In fact, the reform had only limited success in practice. But this episode is one example of a recurrent pattern. Reformers maneuver to get the top executive to order a formal change, since it is the most important single step in advancing their cause. The executive does so as a one-shot action, either assuming that it will be self-executing or, more likely, because he is willing to do this small bit for those who propose it. But he does not follow through, does not reinforce implementation with his own behavior, does not work with those directly affected. This was the pattern with Rusk on the country directors, and with President Johnson, for the most part, on the SIG. Soon the reform loses credibility.

There seem to be only two types of organizational reforms where considerable resistance to implementation is not built in. One is where the action required follows straightforwardly from an authoritative decision as in the Wriston case. Merger of the foreign and departmental services in State was highly controversial, but once the Secretary was ready to take it on, carrying it out required mainly central administrative persistence. And progress could be monitored by counting the number of department officials who became FSOs. The second is where the reorganization planners are themselves the implementers, as in the actions of successive administrations to reshape national security processes. In each case the national security assistant was responsible for recommending change to the President and carrying it through, whether it was Cutler under Eisenhower, Bundy under Kennedy, Kissinger under Nixon, or Brzezinski under Carter. And they were dealing with something they had considerable leverage over: how "presidential" national security issues would be staffed to provide a basis for presidential decisions. But while their formal (or, under Bundy, informal) systems operated more or less as designed, this did not make them identical to the Presidents' actual systems for making decisions. In fact, the greatest divergence came under the strongest national security adviser, Henry Kissinger, who in practice operated, with Nixon, a two-man, closed policy-making system on key issues, notwithstanding Nixon's declaration that his NSC system "insures that all agencies and departments receive a fair hearing before I make my decisions."

These two circumstances are not typical of reorganization. More often than not, its implementation requires discretionary decisions that cannot be controlled by executive decree (e.g., country directors behaving as leaders), decisions by those deep inside the agency whose processes are the target for change. And more often than not, the planners are not the implementers. In more normal circumstances, therefore, executives have to ask how constructive participation can be encouraged. How can senior career officials be brought to participate in shaping proposed changes so that they can share reform objectives and share responsibility and credit for their realization without the executive's very openness inviting excessive delay or sabotage? And students of the practice of reorganization must ask how executives and their staff analysts can develop a feel and a sympathy for the world of middle-level operations and shape reforms to relate to this world? How can executives be motivated to seek real change, over a sustained period? How can the rewards for superficial visible impact in one's own name be diminished, and the rewards for sticking with the job to accomplish something real be increased?

Such questions have no easy answers, if indeed they have answers at all. One necessary approach, also difficult to implement, must be to find ways to measure organizational change while it is taking place.

In a memo dated July 1971, an aide to Macomber expressed concern—well after his reform studies were completed and their implementation was under way—that "we have not yet established criteria for evaluation" of progress. This being the case, there was ultimately no way to distinguish paper compliance from real results. There was thus no way to reward systematically those bureaucrats who took the reform program seriously and worked for its fulfillment. Nor, absent such accepted measures, is the executive who opts for real organizational change likely to be recognized and rewarded either.

Louis Fisher and Ronald C. Moe, "Presidential Reorganization Authority: Is It Worth the Cost?," *Political Science Quarterly*, Vol. 96, No. 2. (Summer 1981), pp. 301–318.

The nation functioned reasonably well throughout most of its history without the reorganization plan authority. Indeed, through at least a third of its fifty year existence, the reorganization plan authority has been allowed to lapse without any evident threat to the polity. In short, the law is not a critical element in our system. This being the case, the burden of proof for its renewal rests with the proponents, who should be prepared to prove that the law meets a demonstrated need and that it does not engender significant unanticipated and undesirable side effects.

Our studies indicate that from the passage of the first reorganization act in 1932 to the present certain fundamental issues have resisted resolution. Key questions raised long ago and never satisfactorily answered are seldom addressed today. It is not even clear who benefits, if anyone, from this legislation. What is certain, however, is that the successive reorganization laws have tended to degrade the institutional relationship between the president and Congress.

"ECONOMY" IN GOVERNMENT

The issue of renewing the president's reorganization authority in 1981 needs some historical perspective.[8] The decision in 1932 to give the president authority to submit reorganization proposals did not emerge out of whole cloth. It was the logical outgrowth of two powerful concepts that enjoyed favor at the time—the notion that a theory of administration could be developed that was at once apolitical and scientific, and the idea that the president should actively "manage" the executive branch. Both strains of thought found expression in the broader movement to reorganize the executive branch.

"To Herbert Hoover," noted Herbert Emmerich, "belongs the undoubted credit for the invention and espousal of the important peacetime reorganization device—presidential initiative subject to the legislative veto."[9] This "invention" was not a pure creative act. Herbert Hoover, a product of the Progressive Era, believed in the tenets of Frederick W. Taylor's "Scientific Management" movement. Taylor wrote that there was One Best Way to manage a manufacturing activity. Although he was specifically concerned with managing the work process in the factory, he was convinced, as were his followers, that the principles of Scientific Management were applicable to public administration as well.[10]

Source: Louis Fisher and Ronald C. Moe, "Presidential Reorganization Authority: Is It Worth the Cost?," *Political Science Quarterly*, Vol. 96, No. 2. (Summer 1981), pp. 301–318. Used with permission from the Academy of Political Science.

Scientific Management was influential not so much because of its specialized procedures as the fundamental idea it fostered—namely, the infinite perfectibility of human institutions.[11] The public administration community was persuaded, as were most political reformers, that the proper vehicle to achieve this infinite perfectibility was the institutionalized presidency. In the 1920s the president gradually emerged as the dominant force in supervising the administrative agencies.[12] It was also during these years that Herbert Hoover became the most "prominent theoretician-practitioner in American public administration."[13]

Between 1949 and 1980, presidents submitted 103 reorganization plans to Congress, 83 of which became effective. Rarely, however, can reductions in expenditures be directly traced to these reorganization plans.[14] It appears, nonetheless, that the paucity of demonstrable savings has not substantially diminished the appeal of the economy premise for executive reorganizations.

In 1977, President Jimmy Carter requested that the itemized-savings requirement of the reorganization act be deleted; in its place the president offered to provide information on the improvements in management, efficiency, and delivery of federal services that his plan would produce. The Senate balked at this request and reinserted the old requirement that there be an itemized estimate of any reduction or increase in expenditures anticipated in the plan.[15] Furthermore, in 1980, at the request of the House Government Operations Committee, the president submitted a report on the "savings"—they were modest—that had resulted from his first nine reorganization plans.[16] Whatever else may have been accomplished by the reorganization plan process, the formal objective of substantially reducing government expenditures has not been achieved.

CONSTITUTIONAL EXPEDIENCY

The delegation of reorganization authority to the president has been accompanied by statutory standards that are vague, outmoded, and in some cases disingenuous. Ill-defined standards raise the question of an unconstitutional delegation of authority, while the legislative veto has been accommodated only with substantial discomfort and strained analyses.

Although Hoover was the first president to ask for reorganization authority, subject to a legislative veto, he was also the first to question the constitutionality of this disapproval procedure. Near the close of his term in 1933, Hoover vetoed a tax bill that contained a committee veto provision. To his veto message he attached an opinion by Attorney General William Mitchell, who said that the one house veto in the reorganization act "raises a grave question as to the validity" of the entire procedure.[17] Senator James F. Byrnes, member of the Appropriations Committee, successfully offered an amendment in 1933 to delete the legislative veto from the reorganization authority after concluding that the attorney general was "probably correct."[18]

In recent years, presidents have been placed in an uncomfortable position. They have opposed all legislative vetoes except the one in the reorganization act. Beginning in 1949, various high officials in the Justice Department developed arguments to justify this particular legislative veto while casting doubt on all others. In 1977, Attorney General Griffin Bell wrote to President Carter that the one-house veto attached to the reorganization authority is the only constitutionally valid legislative veto.[19] The checkered history of the reorganization statutes, and the evident difficulty of distinguishing those laws from others, has weakened any principled objection the president might have to the legislative veto. The position appears to be: it is acceptable when the president is advantaged, but unconstitutional when Congress is advantaged.

Time and mutual acceptance have not settled the constitutional issue involved in the reorganization acts. As recently as 1977, Congressman Jack Brooks introduced a bill calling for an affirmative vote by Congress, in the form of a joint resolution, to confirm a reorganization plan. Any other disapproval procedure, he said, would represent an unconstitutional delegation of power. When the House Government Operations Committee, chaired by Brooks, agreed to retain the one-house veto, he noted at the meeting of the full committee that the measure was "the best unconstitutional bill you could draw up."[20]

POLITICAL RATIONALE

While the statutory objective "economy and efficiency" has rarely been satisfied, and constitutional doubts remain, it is possible to argue that reorganization authority is worthwhile because it accomplishes important nonstatutory political objectives. . . .

The original reorganization plan procedure was largely supported on the ground that, in denying Congress (or the president) the right to amend plans once submitted, it prevented interest groups and agency leaders from blocking desirable, yet controversial, legislation. The Reorganization Act of 1977 permits the president to transmit amendments to a plan after it has been forwarded to Congress, thereby reintroducing this suspect element of politics into the reorganization process. Congress may now recommend amendments requested by interest groups, and the president may be obliged to submit them as a price for passage.

The amendment option itself is now one of the bargaining chips in the negotiations between Congress and the president. The amendment process reintroduces the possibility of interest-group and agency pressure upon Congress and dilutes the remaining justification for the reorganization plan authority. President Carter introduced ten reorganization plans, and in five instances he later submitted amendments. The 1977 provisions for presidential amendments to submitted reorganization plans blurs the distinction between the reorganization process and the regular legislative process. . . .

ENHANCING PRESIDENTIAL MANAGEMENT

The reorganization plan process is considered by many to be a useful tool for the president to use against the bureaucratic fiefdoms. He can redistribute influence in a policy field by restructuring organizations. Reorganization plans may be considered, in some instances, as presidentially imposed treaties upon bureaucratic combatants.

There is another side, however, to the reorganization plan process for the institutional presidency. If a president is going to ask that the reorganization authority be renewed, he must show that it is a delegation of authority that is needed and will be used. Historically, the pattern of reorganization plan use has been uneven and opportunistic. . . .

The benefits for the president, however, should be weighted against some of the costs. Concentration on process and procedures tends to obscure substantive issues and often results in pyrrhic victories for the president. Considerable resources in the OMB and the various departments and agencies are exhausted discussing and planning for reorganizations. Even the prospect of a reorganization, irrespective of whether it comes to fruition, causes much maneuvering and preparation within agencies. . . .

DEBASING THE PROCESS

We do not deny that a case can be marshalled for renewing the president's reorganization authority. The record shows that this authority has been used often and, in some instances, has achieved major results. Passage of reorganization authority can be a useful exercise in symbolic politics, sending a message to voters that both branches are committed to efficient government. Presidents may seek the authority to convince the bureaucracy that the White House is in charge, exerting control on the "subgovemments" in which agencies play a leading role. The reorganization process allows the president to skirt the political obstacles that exist in the regular legislative process. The argument will also be heard that it is unfair to deny future presidents a power that most presidents have had since the 1930s. The case for the plan method of reorganization has been succinctly argued by Harvey Mansfield.

The particular utility of the plan method is not to displace previous methods of securing a reorganization, but to capitalize the advantages of its unique characteristics. The statute is not to be had for the asking. Each President must negotiate for it anew. What he gets, that he could not otherwise secure, is an opportunity from time to time to present the Congress, the country, and the entrenched interests with a reorganization package of his own devising, as a fait accompli, barring a veto; and if a protest is raised, an opportunity to appeal directly to the full membership of either house for support in a floor vote within a stipulated time on the package as he put it together, bypassing both the leadership and the legislative committee seniors if they are unsympathetic. This is an opportunity our constitutional system otherwise seldom affords.[21]

We believe these virtues, however, are more than offset by several serious shortcomings. First, to our minds there is something unseemly, and ultimately self-defeating, about lauding a method that seeks to circumvent the constitutional process. When a method is employed to reach an objective that might not have gained the backing of a majority in each House, the system of lawmaking is, to some degree, debased. "Stealthiness" appears to be a virtue that is rewarded, at least in the short run.

Second, the reorganization plan method is premised on an essentially negative view of Congress that does not comport with the facts. It assumes that members of Congress are irresponsible and will not support sensible legislative proposals submitted by the executive branch. The record suggests, however, that Congress can, and does, act with dispatch on organizational matters. Moreover, instead of cultivating an atmosphere of trust and mutual respect, the process breeds cynicism and suspicion. The plan method is grounded in a similarly hostile attitude toward the bureaucracy. Once legislators and agency officials are stereotyped as untrustworthy, the attitude is corrosive. It is difficult to look upon them favorably for other decisions.

Third, the delegation of the reorganization power to the president is unnecessary and potentially counterproductive. Little of value has been accomplished by reorganization plan that could not have been done through the regular legislative process. The mere existence of the authority places pressure on presidents to use the process lest they appear frivolous for having requested the authority in the first instance. Presidential staffs engage in reorganization for the sake of reorganization. The process becomes the goal.

Given this environment and the time and resource constraints present in the institutional presidency and in Congress, it is not surprising that many plans exhibit inadequate preparation and technical knowledge. On Capitol Hill, a debate on substance is necessarily subordinated to the exigency of appearance. Members have little time to uncover inconsistencies, contradictions, or other defects that may be hidden within a reorganization plan. Furthermore, congressional ambivalence over the delegation of reorganization authority to the president has resulted in misunderstanding, confusion, and recrimination between the two branches. On the one hand, Congress gives the president authority to skirt the regular legislative process, yet when the president invokes the power, he risks being accused of violating the established system.

After each presidential "misuse," Congress responds by adding restrictions and exemptions, gradually circumscribing the power; today the reorganization act is but a shadow of the 1949 statute. The original design has been so diluted that recourse ought now to be had to the regular legislative process—a conclusion especially compelling in view of the 1977 change that allows presidents to submit amendments to their plans. Having introduced one more element of the legislative process, it is wise to take the next step and let the regular procedure prevail.

This is not to suggest that it is always inappropriate for Congress to delegate to the president certain powers to reorganize the executive branch. When the two Hoover Commissions submitted their reports, there was some justification for permitting a "fast track" legislative process. The individual plans were part of a systematic approach to reorganization. Also, during periods of national emergencies, it may be advisable to delegate to the president substantial reorganization authority, subject to a congressional veto. During normal periods, however, both branches are ill-served by the reorganization plan method. If a proposal is noncontroversial, the regular legislative process will do. If controversial, there is all the more reason to insist on full congressional review and affirmative action by both houses. Only the normal legislative process can properly address the emerging organizational issues of the 1980s.

Susan M. Gates, "Organizing for Reorganization," in Robert Klitgaard and Paul C. Light (Eds.), *High Performance Government: Structure, Leadership, Incentives*, Santa Monica, CA: RAND Corporation (2005).

FOUR TASKS OF GOVERNMENT REDESIGN

To restructure the government around core missions and to ensure that an effective structure is maintained, four key tasks must be performed:

1. Identify core missions
2. Divide current executive branch activities along mission lines
3. Make midcourse corrections
4. Maintain the mission-based structure over time

The final task, maintenance, includes activities such as dealing with boundary issues, making organizational changes, figuring out where new activities should be housed, and determining when a new core mission should be added. The implications of structural politics must be considered in relation to all four tasks.

WHAT ARE THE CORE MISSIONS OF THE EXECUTIVE BRANCH OF THE FEDERAL GOVERNMENT?

The first task is to identify the core missions of the federal government. Core missions are different from activities. The Volcker Commission muddles this point by emphasizing the tremendous duplication of effort across the federal government in terms of the number of agencies operating similar programs.

The report seems to suggest a bottom-up approach for identifying core missions, recommending, for example, that programs designed to achieve similar outcomes be combined within one agency. It also suggests that agencies with similar or related missions should be combined into one core department. An important challenge inherent in such an approach is that of determining the basis upon which related programs will be grouped. One program might be related to six other programs, but those six programs may or may not be related directly to one another. Without an overarching sense of core missions, it may be difficult to determine which related programs should be grouped together. Another concern with the bottom-up approach is that the entire set of Volcker Commission recommendations is based on the finding that the current structure of government is inefficient. As a result, it is possible that the restructuring process will involve pruning in addition to reshuffling and reorganization.

Finally, a bottom-up approach might misinterpret the objective of many existing activities. Labels can be misleading. For example, the Volcker report notes that the federal government operates more than 90 early childhood programs. One might be tempted to group all these activities into a Department of Early Childhood or a Department of Education. However, some, even many, of these programs exist primarily to serve objectives unrelated to education or early childhood development. For example, Department of Defense (DoD) early childhood programs may be serving an underlying workforce management objective for DoD (i.e., to better meet the specific childcare needs of military personnel so they can support and fight wars without worrying about whether their children are well cared for). Programs sponsored by the Department of Labor may be intended to facilitate full-time employment for single mothers. And programs sponsored by the Department of Education may be designed to promote school readiness for disadvantaged children. Grouping all three programs together may not yield efficiency gains or economies of scale, because the programs have different aims. Similarly, to prevent an organization with a mission that is not related to early childhood, such as DoD, from running an early childhood program if it determines that such a program is needed to help the department meet its overall mission would seem to go against the Volcker Commission's recommendations that government agencies be given the flexibility to achieve their missions. It is important to keep in mind that any department pursuing its mission may engage in a wide variety of activities in support of that mission.

There is a strong argument for creating an organizational structure that encourages awareness of similar programs across agencies and at least considers whether replication could be reduced. This could be accomplished through cross-cutting task forces on topics or issues that cut across agencies. Awareness, information sharing, and professional development might be encouraged across these programs, but such coordination need not imply reorganization or structural integration.

A more practical approach to defining the core missions of the federal government would begin by articulating those missions and only then grouping existing activities related to them into departments, as is suggested by the strategic planning literature. In his congressional testimony on the Volcker report, Frank Carlucci recalled the proposal of the Ash Commission that all domestic agencies be grouped into four departments: community development, human resources, economic affairs, and natural resources. It would seem that in today's complex world, more specific missions, and hence more departments, may be needed. The blank-slate core missions might include the following:

- Providing for the national defense
- Ensuring the security of the homeland
- Supporting the transportation infrastructure and ensuring its safety
- Representing U.S. interests in foreign countries and supporting Americans abroad
- Gathering and disseminating objective information on the U.S. population, economy, workforce, etc.

- Protecting the environment and managing public land
- Ensuring that a minimum standard of education is available to all children
- Ensuring equal opportunity (in various contexts)
- Managing the social safety net
- Enforcing the tax code, collecting taxes, and managing the federal budget
- Managing the structure of the federal government

RESTRUCTURING THE GOVERNMENT ALONG MISSION LINES

Once the core missions have been identified, the real work begins. It is unreasonable to expect that the new structure can be redesigned in a one-shot effort. Reorganizing current activities along mission lines will be a large undertaking. If the new department structure is to be truly mission-based, there will be substantial change. Some agencies will be moved wholesale into new departments; some agencies or programs will be restructured before being moved; other agencies or programs will be dissolved, with their responsibilities possibly assumed by other agencies.

In congressional testimony on the Volcker report, Donna Shalala suggested that "each of the new mission-centered departments would be composed of the agencies tasked with contributing to that mission. Programs with similar objectives would be combined in the same agency."[22] Some activities will relate to several missions. Other activities may relate to no missions. The process of restructuring the federal government must be capable of resolving conflict among departments that may lay claim to a particular agency and of placing those activities that are deemed necessary but don't have an obvious home.

MAKING MIDCOURSE CORRECTIONS

Just as framers of the U.S. Constitution could not account for all potential changes or future needs, those designing the new organizational structure cannot be expected to get everything right the first time. As a result, substantial midcourse corrections will likely be needed to adjust the new structure as departments try to deal with boundary issues or simply discover errors that must be corrected.

MAINTAINING THE MISSION-BASED STRUCTURE

Over the longer term, new activities and even new missions will emerge for the federal government. Determining where new activities should be housed within the structure and when new core missions should be added—ensuring that this is done in a manner that is consistent with the core principles of the reorganization and is not subject to structural politics—will be ongoing tasks.

In sum, the process of reorganizing the federal government according to key missions will be a long and iterative process that will require continuous effort if the new structure is to be sustained. Existing activities must be restructured according to the core missions, adjustments must be made to the new structure in the short run, and there must be active oversight to ensure that the new structure doesn't fracture under the pressures of structural politics. To accomplish these aims, the restructuring process will thus need something akin to the process for constitutional amendments in order to allow for changes and oversight in both the short and the long run. The manner in which this process is approached will influence just how difficult it is. In the next section, we propose a strategy for accomplishing these tasks in a way that might limit the difficulties.

A STRATEGY FOR ACCOMPLISHING THE TASKS

In view of the structural politics, the challenge is to allow for interested parties without creating the same political dynamic led to the current ineffective government structure. We the four tasks into two phases that are tackled separate structures. The first phase—the design phase—involves identifying the core missions. The second—the implementation and maintenance phase—involves three other tasks.

At the Congressional Hearing on the Volcker report, Paul Volcker suggested that the President be given expedited authority to recommend structural reorganization of federal departments and that those proposals should be subject to a yes or no vote within a specified time frame.[23] A comprehensive approach would be more likely to succeed than a sequential one. Weingast and Marshall argue that political exchange and coalition building on issues that are not being considered simultaneously is very difficult because of the high level of uncertainty in the political environment.[24] As Frank Carlucci noted in his congressional testimony, "Only a total approach makes sense. Doing it bit by bit stirs up just as many hornets as total overhaul. Moreover, an overarching concept is essential to mustering the necessary political support."[25] Similar arguments in favor of a comprehensive approach to major reform were advanced in the early 1990s when Eastern European governments were grappling with the question of how to transition from a communist political and economic system to a market economy.[26]

These two principles thus shape the recommendations below: (1) the initial reorganization must be simultaneous—rather than piecemeal, and (2) structural politics must be considered at each stage.

A BRAC-STYLE PROCESS COULD BE USED TO DEFINE CORE FEDERAL MISSIONS

During congressional hearings on the Volcker report, Paul Volcker likened government reorganization to base closure decisions and trade negotiations. This is an important insight for the design phase of this strategy. If a comprehensive reorganization of the U.S. government is possible, it may require a bold way to organize for reorganizing. The Defense Base Closure and Realignment Act of 1990[27] may provide a useful template.[28] The decision to close a military base has important similarities to administrative restructuring decisions. The impetus behind both types of decisions is efficiency and/or cost savings. As with the benefits of government restructuring, the benefits of base closure are diffuse, while the costs are concentrated and imposed upon groups with a strong incentive to oppose the reforms or closure. The 1990 act grew out of the perceived failure of alternative approaches over the years. Kirshenberg provides a brief history of base closure leading up to the act.[29] Base closure actions initiated by DoD in the 1970s created tremendous political controversy, leading to congressional legislation providing Congress with the authority to determine which bases would be subject to closure. Not surprisingly, given the concentrated costs and diffuse benefits, Congress recommended no bases for closure between 1977 and 1988.

The act called for the creation of an independent defense base closure and realignment commission, responsible for reviewing and approving or modifying recommendations made by the Secretary of Defense regarding the list of bases to be closed or realigned. The independent commission is to comprise eight members. The President is authorized to make recommendations for appointment to the commission but is required to consult with the Speaker of the House on two of the members, with the majority leaders of the Senate on two members, and with the minority leaders of the Senate and House on one member each. The base closure process begins with the Secretary of Defense, who must articulate a force structure plan and a list of criteria to be used in making recommendations for base closure and realignment. After opportunities for congressional and public comments, the criteria must be applied in developing a list of military installations to be closed or realigned, and those choices must be justified vis-a-vis the force structure plan and the approved closure criteria. The role of the independent defense base closure commission is then to hold public hearings, review the Defense Secretary's list, and report its findings and recommendations to the President. The President must then approve the list in its entirety before the recommendations are forwarded to Congress. The President is not allowed to pick and choose individual bases and exclude them from the list. Congress must consider the recommendations in total on a specified time schedule.

Two key features of the BRAC process would be essential in any process for identifying the core missions of the government:

1. Broad political input would be required in developing the procedures for identifying the missions and in approving the final list of missions.
2. A single list of core missions would be developed, and there would-be no opportunity for individuals or groups to demand the inclusion or exclusion of a particular mission. Congress would be responsible for passing legislation to authorize the mission determination process. An important element of this legislation would be core principles to be followed in identifying the missions. A potentially effective approach would be to appoint a commission of nine or ten individuals and task them with the responsibility of identifying the core missions. Congress could establish a limited set of guidelines regarding the characteristics of this list (e.g., there can be no more than 15 core missions and no fewer than seven) but would not specify that certain things be included as core missions.

Given the importance of this task, it would be wise to require the appointed individuals to be well respected, with high-level management experience in the federal government and/or the private sector. These individuals should be familiar with the federal government, but they must be viewed as independent parties with nothing to gain or lose from the identification of core missions. Therefore, these individuals would be required to resign from any current federal government position. Participation on the committee must be a full-time, short-term appointment. The appointment process must carefully consider conflicts of interest. Importantly, those who are part of this commission would not be eligible to play a role in phase-two efforts involving implementation and maintenance. The President would be responsible for appointing the members of the commission, subject to congressional approval. As with appointments to the BRAC commission, Congress may require the President to collaborate with party leaders in the selection of members.

This committee would be responsible for submitting a draft list of core missions along with a justification for those choices within a specified time frame (e.g., three months). The draft list would include no commentary related to which programs, agencies, or activities should or should not be attributed to particular missions. The list would be subject to comment from all existing cabinet secretaries, the House, and the Senate, as well as public hearings. After considering comments from various sources, the committee would submit a final list of core missions for congressional approval. In presenting that list, the committee might be required to explicitly respond to comments from Congress and cabinet secretaries. Congress would then consider the list in total for approval or rejection, with no opportunity for modifying it in a conference committee or through other mechanisms. If both houses of Congress approve the list, it would then be sent to the President for approval or rejection.

NOTES FOR CHAPTER 5

1. Morton Grodzins, 1961, "Centralization and Decentralization in the American Federal System," in Robert A. Goldwin (Ed.), *A Nation of States: Essays on the American Federal System,* Rand McNally & Co., Chicago, pp. 3–4.
2. This is a close paraphrase of a quotation that appears in Elizabeth Drew, 1976, *American Journal: The Events of 1976,* New York: Random House, p. 40.
3. Remarks by Mr. Harrison Wellford to a panel on Government Reorganization, 1978 Meeting of the American Political Science Association, August 31, 1978, New York.
4. Erwin Hargrove, July 1975, "The Missing Link: The Study of the Implementation of Social Policy," Urban Institute, Washington, DC.
5. Stephen K. Bailey, 1968, "Managing the Federal Government," in Kennit Gordon (Ed.), *Agenda for the Nation,* Brookings Institution, Washington, DC, p. 319.
6. National Security reorganizations have typically employed orders from a separate classified series: NSAMs (National Security Action Memoranda), NSDMs (National Security Decision Memoranda), and currently PDs (Presidential Directives).
7. William Backus, 1974, *Foreign Policy and the Bureaucratic Process,* Princeton University Press, Princeton, p. 67.
8. For a detailed historical discussion of successive reorganization acts, see Louis Fisher and Ronald C. Moe, 1980, "Delegating With Ambivalence: The Legislative Veto and Reorganization Authority," in U.S. Congress, House, Committee on Rules, *Studies on the Legislative Veto,* 96th Cong., 2d sess. (committee print), pp. 164–247.
9. Herbert Emmerich, 1971, *Federal Organization and Administrative Management,* University of Alabama Press, Tuscaloosa, AL, p. 43.
10. Many public administrators, over several decades, would pin their hopes and aspirations for a better world on Taylorism. "Our administrators of the future," John Pfiffner declared in 1940, "must be good managers. They must know the techniques of scientific management. Indeed, it may well be that the principles of Frederick W. Taylor, 1940, adopted to social ends, will some day free the world of drudgery. . . . What is needed is the development of a school of management research technicians who possess the just, wise, and omniscient qualities of Plato's guardians," *Research Methods in Public Administration,* Ronald Press, New York, p. 25.
11. Leonard D. White, 1955, *Introduction to the Study of Public Administration,* 4th rev. ed., Macmillan Company, New York, p. 21.
12. Peri E. Arnold, September 1976, "Executive Reorganization and Administrative Theory: The Origins of the Managerial Presidency," Paper presented at the 1976 Annual Meeting of the American Political Science Association, Chicago, IL.
13. Ibid., p. 12. See also Peri E. Arnold, July 1980, "The 'Great Engineer' as Administrator: Herbert Hoover and Modern Bureaucracy," *Review of Politics,* vol. 42, p. 329.
14. "Of the reorganization plans transmitted to the Congress from 1949 through 1978, only six . . . were supported by precise dollar estimates of savings. . . . Granted executive branch reluctance to offer savings estimates which can be later used in evidence by the appropriations committees, it is clear that the failure to itemize expenditure reductions reflects the reality that economies are produced by curtailing services and abolishing bureaus, not by reorganization," Harold Seidman, 1980, *Politics, Position, and Power,* 3rd rev. ed., Oxford University Press, New York, p. 13.
15. U.S. Congress, Senate, *Congressional Record,* 95th Cong., 1st sess., 1977, 123, pt. 5: 6147.
16. U.S. Congress, House, Committee on Government Operations, *Extension of Reorganization Authority: Report to Accompany H.R. 6585,* 96th Cong., 2d sess., 1980, H. Rept. 805, pp. 3–4.
17. *Opinions of the Attorney General,* vol. 37 (1933), pp. 63–64. For Hoover's veto, see U.S. Congress, House, *Congressional Record,* 72d Cong., 2d sess., 1933, 76, pt. 3, 2445–2446.

18. Quoted in U.S. Congress, Senate, *Congressional Record,* 72d Cong., 2d sess., 1933, 76, pt. 4, p. 3538.
19. Letter reprinted in *To Renew the Reorganization Authority,* hearings before the Senate Committee on Governmental Affairs, 95th Cong., 1st sess., 1977, pp. 11–12.
20. U.S. Congress, House, Committee on Government Operations, *Extension of Reorganization Authority to the President: Report to Accompany H.R.* 5045, 95th Cong., 1st sess., 1977, H. Rept. 105, p. 43. Congressman Brooks did succeed in amending the bill to require that resolutions of disapproval be introduced in both chambers. This move was intended to virtually assure a floor vote on each reorganization plan. In practice, however, the Senate in a majority of instances did not take a floor vote on the reorganization plans submitted by President Carter.
21. Harvey C. Mansfield, July/August 1969, "Federal Executive Reorganization: Thirty Years of Experience," *Public Administration Review,* vol. 29, pp. 332–345.
22. *From Reorganization to Recruitment: Bringing the Federal Government into the 21st Century,* 2003, Hearing before the Committee on Government Reform, House of Representatives, 108th Cong., 1st Sess., Government Printing Office, Washington, DC.
23. *Urgent Business for America: Revitalizing the Federal Government for the 21st Century,* Report of the National Commission on the Public Service, Volcker Report, Chapter 2, p. 56.
24. B. Weingast and W. Marshall, February 1988, "The Industrial Organization of Congress: Or, Why Legislatures, Like Firms, Are Not Organized as Markets," *Journal of Political Economy,* vol. 96, No. 1, pp. 132–163.
25. From Reorganization to Recruitment, 2003, p. 39.
26. D. Lipton and J. Sachs, 1990, "Creating a Market Economy in Eastern Europe: The Case of Poland," *Brookings Papers on Economic Activity,* No. 1, pp. 75–133.
27. Public Law 101-5 10.
28. W. M. Hix, 2001, *Taking Stock of the Army's Base Realignment and Closure Selection Process,* RAND Corporation, Santa Monica, CA, MR-1337-A; and D. Levy, J. S. Moini, T. Kaganoff, E. G. Keating, C. H. Augustine, T. K. Bikson, K. Leuschner, and S. M. Gates, *Base Realignment and Closure (BRAC) and Organizational Restructuring in the DoD: Implications for Education and Training Infrastructure,* RAND Corporation, Santa Monica, CA MG-153-OSD (2004), provide useful overviews of the base realignment and closure (BRAC) process.
29. Seth D. Kirshenberg, "Base Closings: What's Ahead in 1995?" *Public Management,* Vol. 77, February 1995.

PART II

EXAMPLES OF REORGANIZATION EFFORTS

As is clear from the range of articles that appears in Part I of this volume, most of the scholarship around the general topic of reorganization emphasizes a management approach to the subject. As a result, this literature highlights issues related to authority of the executive branch to undertake reorganizations, searches for rules and patterns of goals of reorganization that can be generalized across the federal government, emphasizes the role of commissions and other bodies as advisory mechanisms, and explores what can be viewed as the appropriate role of Congress in this endeavor.

The focus of these issues changes when one shifts the unit of analysis from the general to the specific—that is, from a general discussion of reorganization to an analysis of a specific reorganization effort—but the focus on a single reorganization brings forward a policy rather than a management lens on these issues. There is much less concern about general rules and the formal process of coming to a decision and, instead, more emphasis on the substantive effects on the policy itself. In addition, the players in the process shift to some degree in both the executive branch and in Congress. They move away from actors who emphasize general management issues (such as OMB and the congressional government reform committees) to players who are concerned about the dimensions of the policy (such as specialized congressional committees concerned about specific policies, executive branch staff, and representatives of interest groups involved in implementing the policy).

In addition, this section of the book indicates that there is a move from a focus on structure to a more functional approach that emphasizes networks, coordination, and collaborative strategies.

Part II of this book illustrates the shift from management to policy and opens up questions about the ability of structural change to deal with contemporary issues. It focuses on four different reorganizations: the Department of Homeland Security (DHS), the Department of Defense (DOD), the Department of Education (ED), and proposals to create a Department of Food Safety. Each of these reorganizations has its own story; the readings included in this book illustrating the issues involved in the four stories provide a sense of the multiple perspectives that are often found in federal reorganization decision making. In addition, the pieces that are included in three of these reorganizations move beyond the decision to reorganize to subsequent policy developments that are related to or at least affected by the reorganization.[1]

THE DEPARTMENT OF HOMELAND SECURITY

This department, created in November 2002, was established in the environment of the 9/11 disaster and is probably the most visible, public, and political example of a reorganization in the federal government. The selections included in this section not only provide a story of the creation of the department but also focus on the impact of the reorganization on the federal government's abilities to respond to the Hurricane Katrina emergency in 2005.

THE DEPARTMENT OF DEFENSE

Following World War II, DOD was created through the strengthening of a central defense organization that increased the authority and power of the Secretary of Defense. The Defense Reorganization Act of 1958 became the basis for efforts that were undertaken by Robert McNamara in the 1960s to create a centralized department that included all of the separate services under civilian control. This structure was further modified in 1986 with the Goldwater-Nichols DOD Reorganization Act that sought to increase the authority and influence of unified commands, decreasing the autonomy of the separate services.

THE DEPARTMENT OF EDUCATION

In 1979, a separate department of education was created, moving out the education programs found in the Department of Health, Education, and Welfare. The proposal to fashion a department was closely tied to the political agenda of President Jimmy Carter, and much of the debate over the plan related to differing views about the federal role in education policy. Although Republicans had attempted to kill the department, by 2001, President George W. Bush's No Child Left Behind policy actually increased federal power in education and shifted federal–state relationships.

A DEPARTMENT OF FOOD SAFETY

For more than 20 years, there have been discussions about the creation of a single agency to deal with multiple agencies and approaches to food safety. To this writing, there have been many proposals for such an agency but they have not resulted in such a department. Much of the difficulty in reaching agreement emerges from different perspectives on the issue. Over time, the debate has highlighted science questions, the relationship between food safety and terrorism, and food safety and globalization. It raises the question of whether the problems to be addressed are so complex that structural change cannot really deal with them.

NOTE FOR PART II

1. Each of the sections of the book that deal a separate reorganization is introduced with a summary of the issues involved as well as the perspective of the author included.

CHAPTER 6

The Department of Homeland Security

INTRODUCTION

It is clearly rare for reorganization politics and proposals to appear in front page articles in America's daily newspapers day after day; nevertheless, the creation of the Department of Homeland Security (DHS) held the attention of U.S. citizens in the months after the 9/11 disaster. It is not exaggerating to characterize the development and implementation of DHS as the most urgent of all creations of a federal government department.

The destruction of New York City's twin towers, the damage to the Pentagon, and the airplane crash in Pennsylvania on September 11, 2001, raised the question of what the federal government could do to assure that such a disaster would not happen again. For at least some members of Congress, the creation of a cabinet-level department was viewed as a way to respond to that public desire. The idea for a separate department started in Congress while the White House originally argued that an office in the Executive Office of the President was adequate to respond to the need. The Office of Homeland Security in the White House was established less than a month after September 11.

The initial writers that were concerned about the possibility of creating a department focused on the behaviors that allowed terrorists to plan and execute their plans. These early analyses highlighted problems related to the relationships between criminal justice agencies, intelligence agencies, and other federal government organizations. Because he was committed to keeping responsibility for these issues within the White House, President George W. Bush did not concentrate on the details of the congressional proposals, but a month after Congress introduced DHS legislation, the president changed direction and proposed a department.

At that point, both the Congress and the White House focused on the elements that would be included in a department, the authority that would be given it, and the structure of the new organization. Once enacted, the president was required to submit a reorganization plan to Congress within 60 days. A plan was presented on November 25, 2002, to go into effect in January 2003. For the next few years, the focus within DHS was on finding a way to organize its operations. During this period, changes in departmental leadership occurred. The 22 program elements that were contained in the reorganization plan were clustered into coordinating offices, and a range of implementation activities was planned and undertaken.

All of this changed in September 2005 when Hurricane Katrina struck. The Federal Emergency Management Agency (FEMA)—one of the program elements within DHS—was widely criticized for its role in responding to the hurricane. Attention was drawn to the impact of the reorganization on FEMA's ability to meet the needs of the citizens of the Louisiana and Mississippi Gulf region. Concern was raised about the relationship between activities related to terrorism and those focused on natural disasters. Soon after, the Immigration and Customs Enforcement (ICE) agency—also a part of DHS—received attention as the immigration policy issue surfaced in both the White House and in Congress. The Katrina experience has made some observers less sanguine about the possibilities of structural change and has led to an interest in the creation of networks.

The excerpts that are included in this section of the volume represent various stages of development and implementation of DHS. They include readings that discuss the crafting of the department, changes that occurred before Katrina, the experience of dealing with Katrina, and the immigration policy issue.

Ashton B. Carter's article, "The Architecture of Government in the Face of Terrorism," reviews previous approaches to the issues as well as key ingredients required to deal with the issue. He discusses what he calls four failed approaches: the command and control approach, the lead agency approach, a cabinet department, and a White House coordinator.

In "Organizing for Homeland Security," Charles R. Wise provides another perspective on the organization of homeland security and raises a number of key issues that confronted both the President and Congress. He notes that the proposals for a centrally headquartered federal organization for homeland security may be grouped under three options: executive order coordinator, statutory coordinator, and a departmental option.

Wendy Haynes' article, "Seeing Around Corners: Crafting the New Department of Homeland Security," provides a picture of the organizational elements within DHS and also gives a chronology of the events related to the crafting of the new department. She cautions readers to be wary of quick fixes and argues that organizing and operating DHS is a challenging enterprise. This complexity is illustrated by the DHS organization chart that was provided by the Congressional Research Service (**Figure 6-1**).

Harold C. Relyea of the Congressional Research Service discusses the impact of the competition between the executive branch and Congress involving homeland security. In "Organizing for Homeland Security," he argues that Bush's actions involving DHS illustrate the long-term competition. Relyea reviews the ways that Bush pushed his agenda and managed to get the legislation he wanted through the Congress.

Once DHS was in operation, analysts raised a variety of issues about the new department. Richard S. Conley highlights the relationship between 9/11 and the managerial presidency. In "Reform, Reorganization, and the Renaissance of the Managerial Presidency: The Impact of 9/11 on the Executive Establishment," he emphasizes the impact of 9/11 on the presidency, particularly the reorganization of the federal government and intelligence apparatus. This piece discusses President Bush's focus on executive control, bureaucratic coordination, and adequate funding.

The impact of a change in leadership in DHS in 2005 is discussed in Harold C. Relyea and Henry B. Hogue's CRS Report for Congress entitled "Department of Homeland Security Reorganization: The 2SR Initiative" (2SR is the Second Stage Review). They focus on the agenda of DHS Secretary Michael Chertoff and the changes in organization structure that he proposed. They emphasize the disagreement between Chertoff and members of Congress over reorganization authority.

The problems faced by DHS after Katrina are discussed in several excerpts. Henry B. Hogue and Keith Bea review the historical developments and legislative options in FEMA and DHS in a report issued by CRS. Charles R. Wise's article, "Organizing for Homeland Security After Katrina: Is Adaptive Management What's Missing?" focuses on organizational problems that were present before Katrina and the impact of the disaster on those issues. These include planning, incident management, and intergovernmental relations management. He presents two models that could address these issues: the hierarchical model and the network model.

Michael Greenberger also emphasizes the problems related to Hurricane Katrina and focuses on the role of the federal government in health emergencies. In "The Role of the Federal Government in Response to Catastrophic Health Emergencies: Lessons Learned from Hurricane Katrina," he discusses the relationship between the federal government and state and local agencies in this crisis situation.

The experience with Katrina raised serious questions about the ability of DHS to respond to emergency management responsibilities. Patrick Roberts, in "FEMA After Katrina: Redefining Responsiveness," suggests that it has been difficult for the agency to respond to both natural disasters and national security issues. He reviews the past FEMA experience and calls for more responsibility for planning by state and local agencies.

Finally, Jeffrey Manns, in "Reorganization as a Substitute for Reform: The Abolition of the INS," suggests that restructuring the INS cannot address the multiple demands of immigration policy—one of the components within DHS. He argues that a policy approach—focusing on the priorities of immigration—is a more effective way to deal with this issue than by restructuring.

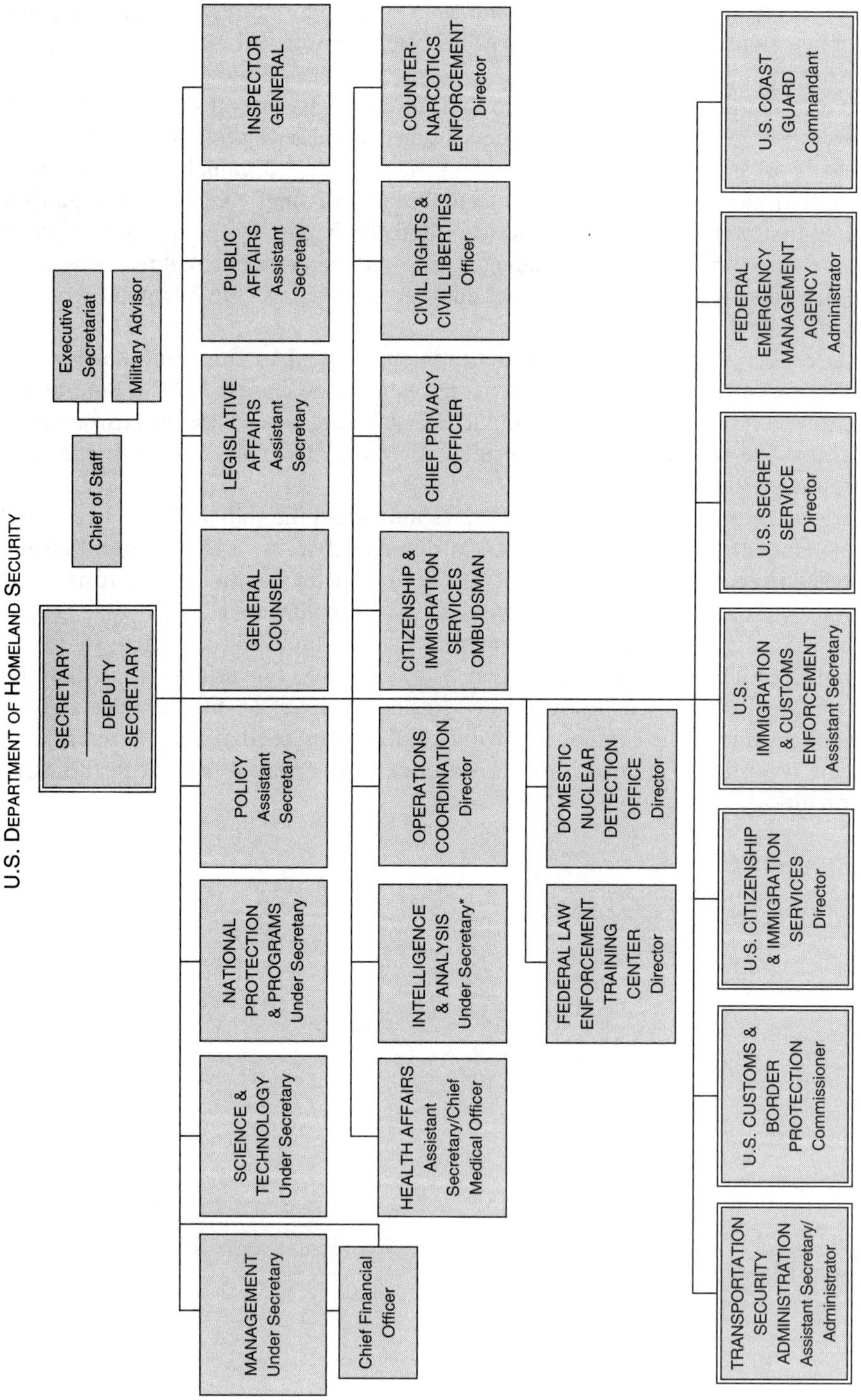

* Under Secretary for Intelligence & Analysis title created by Public Law 110–53, Aug. 3rd, 2007
Approved 4/1/2007

Source: Department of Homeland Security Organizational Charts (www.dhs.gov/xlibrary/assets/DHS-OrgChart.pdf).

FIGURE 6-1 U.S. Department of Homeland Security.

Ashton B. Carter, "The Architecture of Government in the Face of Terrorism," *International Security*, Vol. 26, No. 3. (Winter, 2001–2002), pp. 5–23.

Before September 11, 2001 . . . the U.S. government did not have a managerial approach (i.e., a framework for bringing responsibility, accountability, and resources together in sharp focus) to deliver a key public good—security in the homeland against catastrophic terrorism. This managerial deficiency was not unique to catastrophic terrorism. The post-Cold War world spawned a host of novel security missions for government: peacekeeping and post-peacekeeping civil reconstruction, counterproliferation, threat reduction, information warfare, and conflict prevention (or "preventive defense"). Although it is widely agreed that the United States needs to be able to accomplish these missions (even if debate continues over exactly when and where it should perform them), no fundamental changes have been made in the security architecture to create better institutions and capabilities for them.

Indeed, at least on paper the federal structure has changed little since the first burst of innovation in the aftermath of World War II and the onset of the Cold War. No comparable burst occurred in the 1990s. It is as though corporate America was managing the modern economy with the structures of the Ford Motor Company, the Bell System, and United Fruit. Company managements spend a great deal of thought and energy on organizing their functions to align executive authority with key products. The federal government disperses executive authority so thoroughly that few individuals believe they are accountable for any of the government's key security outputs. People rise to the top of the Washington heap because of their policy expertise, not their managerial expertise. Those senior executives who are managerially inclined find their tenures so short and precarious that there seems to be little reward in making changes in "the system" that will make it possible for their successor's successor to be more effective."[1]

Above all, the federal government in the past few decades has eschewed creating new institutions for new missions such as preparedness for catastrophic terrorism. The political climate in the United States has been hostile to "big government," and existing cabinet departments staunchly defend their heritages and authorities, many of which are enshrined in two hundred years of statute. The sense of departmental entrenchment is mirrored on Capitol Hill, where separate authorization and oversight committees protect each "stovepipe"—national security, law enforcement, disaster relief, public health, and so on—as jealously as the executive agencies themselves.

Source: Ashton B. Carter, "The Architecture of Government in the Face of Terrorism," International Security, 26:3 (Winter, 2001–02), pp. 5–23.

It is not surprising, therefore, that the specter of catastrophic terrorism occasions deep reflections on the nature and structure of governance in the United States. What needs to be done next cannot be understood without reference to these problems, and to past attempts to overcome them.

In broad outline, four approaches to managing the mission of homeland security have been proposed: the command and control approach of the Clinton administration, the lead agency approach, the establishment of a Department of Homeland Security, and the appointment of a White House coordinator or "czar." To date, the Bush administration appears to be focusing on the last, which like the other three has inherent deficiencies.

The Clinton administration defined its approach in command and control terms: Which federal agency should be in charge of dealing with catastrophic terrorism? Initially, the administration determined that the Department of Justice would "have the lead" in domestic terrorist incidents, while the Department of State would do so in incidents abroad. This approach both reinforced the false distinction between domestic and foreign terrorism and focused on acts in progress rather than on advance detection, prevention, and protection. Later, the Clinton administration promulgated two presidential directives, PDD-62 and PDD-63, which further apportioned the matter of "who's in charge" among the existing agencies according to their traditional functions.[2] Thus, for example, PDD-63 assigned protection of the financial system to the Treasury Department. The fact that this department had no funds, no technology, and little authority to regulate in the field of cybersecurity did not deter the authors of PDD-63. In fact, by focusing on the question of who is in charge, the command and control approach presumed that the government possessed the capabilities to combat catastrophic terrorism; all that was required was to marshal them effectively under a clear command system. The result was the creation of a host of unfunded mandates responsibilities assigned with no plan for providing the means to fill them. The administration made no provision to build new capability, which was—and remains—the crux of the matter.

A second approach considered was to designate a single lead agency as having the homeland defense mission. In this approach, the proposed lead was usually the Department of Defense. DOD was presumed to have already much relevant technology, an ample budget, and a reputation for carrying out its mission more effectively than most other government agencies.[3]

But this approach failed because too much of the relevant capability—for example for surveillance of potential terrorists on U.S. territory—fell beyond DOD's traditional purview. The Pentagon shared the disinclination to arrogate such sweeping new authorities to itself and proclaimed itself willing to take a strong, but follower, role if another agency would lead the effort.

A third approach called for the creation of a Department of Homeland Security.[4] This approach sought to escape the problem of interagency coordination by concentrating the catastrophic terrorism mission in a single agency. It recognized that none of the existing cabinet departments was a natural lead agency, and that their ingrained cultures would not easily incline them to adopt the new mission. The fallacy in this approach is that interagency coordination could be thus avoided. Suppose, for example, that the Department of Homeland Security sought to develop a more rapid means of determining whether someone was exposed to anthrax. It would soon discover that this effort was redundant with DOD's efforts to develop the same detector technology for battlefield exposure in accordance with its traditional mission. The problem of interagency coordination would not have been eliminated, but only complicated by the introduction of a new agency. Aggregating functions such as customs, immigration, border patrol, and coast guard into a new agency might be efficient, but it can hardly be said that such an entity should have the lead in homeland defense, or that its creation eliminates the inherently interagency nature of catastrophic terrorism.

A fourth approach to organizing the federal government for catastrophic terrorism is to appoint a White House coordinator or "czar." President Bush named Pennsylvania Governor Tom Ridge to such a post within a month of September 11. This approach is the least problematic, because it recognizes that the essence of the solution is the coordination of a wide range of government functions behind a new priority mission. White House czars, however, have usually been ineffective. With no resources or agencies of their own, they are easily reduced to cajoling cabinet departments into doing what the czar prescribes. The czar's instructions inevitably compete with other needs and tasks of the department, and the final outcome of the competition is determined by the cabinet secretary (invoking legal authorities, usually of long standing) and the relevant committees of Congress, not the czar. After the czar is thus overridden a few times, lower-level bureaucrats conclude that the czar's directives can be ignored. As the Washington saying about czars goes, "The barons ignore them, and eventually the peasants kill them."

A solution to the managerial challenge of catastrophic terrorism should have two features that the approaches outlined above lack. First, it should acknowledge the inherent and ineluctable interagency nature of the problem and abandon any idea of creating a single lead agency.[5] Second, the approach should begin the long process of providing the United States with a stock of essential capabilities—tactics, technology, and institutions—that the federal departments, state and local governments, and private sector currently lack. Interagency coordination implies a White House focus. But this focus should not be a "czar" who tries to assume or direct the daily functions of all the agencies involved but an "architect" who designs the capabilities that these agencies need to address the problem. This approach gives the architect budgetary authority (the key to his influence) and applies that influence where it is needed most: to creating needed capabilities rather than stirring up empty command and control disputes over who is in charge of capabilities that are woefully inadequate or do not exist at all. In short, the important function of the White House architect is *program* coordination, not policy coordination or command and control. The program in question is a multiyear, multiagency effort to develop tactics, technology, and where required new institutions for the ongoing struggle against catastrophic terrorism.

Charles R. Wise, "Organizing for Homeland Security," *Public Administration Review*, Vol. 62, No. 2. (March–April 2002), pp. 131–144.

The events of September 11 have prompted vastly heightened scrutiny of many aspects of government functioning, as major wars and national cataclysms have done in the past. Few aspects, perhaps, have received more attention than the question of whether government in general, and the federal government in particular, has the right organizational structure to meet the requirements for homeland security. An initial determination was made by the president that sufficient organization was woefully lacking, and he established the Office of Homeland Security by executive order on October 8, 2001, less than one month after the terrorist attacks. The establishment of the office headed by the new Assistant to the President for Homeland Security and involving the new Homeland Security Council has not ended the scrutiny and debate over the appropriate organizational system needed by the federal government to meet impending terrorist threats. . . .

Although there has been much focus on the requisite powers of the president's Homeland Security Assistant and hearings have been held on the options for structuring a central homeland security headquarters agency, Congress appears content for now to see how the office created by executive order will work before undertaking legislative action. This wait-and-see posture undoubtedly will come to an end, and Congress will once again take up the issue in a more concerted fashion.

Even though the issue of organization for homeland security involves the question of the organization of a headquarters under the president, it extends considerably beyond that. In fact, the organizational issue of homeland security implicates the organizations of various venues, including the organization of individual federal departments and agencies, state and local governmental organizations, and private-sector organizations, as well as their relationships with each other. The issues involved in the appropriate organizational structure for the presidential headquarters organization are embedded in organizational issues that pervade all of these organizations. . . .

In addressing issues of the appropriate organizational design for government organizations to meet the threats in the terrorist environment, it is necessary to guard against making facile assumptions about the type of organization required and the relationships

---

Source: Charles R. Wise, "Organizing for Homeland Security," *Public Administration Review*, Vol. 62, No. 2. (March–April, 2002), pp. 131–144, Blackwell Publishing.

that can be made to exist among organizations. Many times, recommendations for a particular organizational solution or design of an organization are made on the basis of past practice or emphasize one or two dimensions of organizational functioning. Too infrequently, such organizational prescriptions are advanced without a thorough analysis of the multiple goals required of the organization, the environment in which it will be required to operate, or the interorganizational relationships and constraints that will influence its functioning. . . .

It may be argued that, at least for a while, the current conditions of terrorism constitute "truly exceptional circumstances" that augur for some departure from the hierarchical mode that the principles imply. Nonetheless, these principles are fodder for the debate over what types of organizational modes are required. Trade-offs between such principles and the imperatives of rapid organizational adaptation are inherent in decisions about appropriate organizational design for homeland security. New organizational proposals also will inevitably confront these principles, in that several are embodied in statutes that govern the existing departments and agencies and their activities.

Prior to September 11, the General Accounting Office had identified more than 40 federal agencies involved in countering terrorism, with $11 billion programmed to be spent during fiscal year 2001.[6] As a part of this, the federal government offered almost 100 separate federal terrorism-preparedness training courses and created more than 100 federal terrorism response teams operating out of five federal agencies and departments.[7]

Following September 11, the conception of what agencies are involved in combating terrorism certainly has been expanded. Few would have included the Postal Service as a primary counterterrorism agency prior to the anthrax attack. Thus, the post-September 11 reality is that homeland security could implicate reorganizing activities of much of the government.

Numerous issues are involved in this reorganizing enterprise. Issues that arise with respect to reorienting or reorganizing particular departments and agencies have some commonality with those that arise in the context of how to organize a federal headquarters office for homeland security, but there are also significant differences. Among the issues that the president and Congress confront in addressing the headquarters design task are as follows:

- What functional and policy responsibilities are included in "homeland security"?
- Role in developing a national strategy for homeland defense
- Objectives for the headquarters office
- Emphasis on coordination of versus emphasis on directing operations
- Political accountability provisions
- Emphasis on legal authority versus political authority
- Role in directing budgetary resources.
- Relationship between continental U.S. terrorism preparation and response activities versus non-continental U.S. activities
- Relationship to state and local governments and their officials

It must be emphasized that the reorganization of federal efforts for the purposes of homeland security is not necessarily going to wait for the resolution of the headquarters organization; in fact, agencies and departments have initiated their own changes already as a result of September 11. For example, the FBI and the Secret Service, together with the Washington, D.C., police, established a joint operations center for Washington, D.C.[8] The proposals for a central headquarters federal organization for homeland security may be grouped under three options:

1. Executive Order Coordinator
2. Statutory Coordinator
3. Departmental

EXECUTIVE ORDER COORDINATOR

The executive order coordinator option is represented by the office established by President Bush in his executive order, in which he established the Office of Homeland Security and the Homeland Security Council. The office is headed by the Assistant to the President for Homeland Security. It shares the basic approach of the statutory coordinator option, in that its function is "to coordinate the executive branch's efforts to detect, prepare for, prevent, protect against, respond to, and recover from terrorist attacks within the United States." The functions to be coordinated constitute a quite detailed and ambitious list, including developing a national strategy, detecting terrorist threats and activities within the United States, preparedness, prevention, protection, response and recovery, incident management, continuity of government, executive branch communication with the public, cooperation with state and local governments, review of legal authorities and legislative proposals, and budget review. . . .

The functions of the office appear to be quite comprehensive, and it is specifically assigned the task of developing a homeland defense strategy. Precise, measurable objectives are not specified. The emphasis is on coordinating the activities of other agencies, as opposed to being given line authority to direct operations. Its location within the Executive Office of the President puts a priority for political accountability directly to the president. The advantage of this is that the director is positioned to rise above the particular interests of any one particular agency, and he is located close to the president to resolve cross-agency disagreements. One disadvantage is that the office is in a position to interfere with operations conducted by the respective executive agencies, and it could hinder direct communication between the president and the cabinet officers in charge of the respective executive agencies.[6] Another disadvantage is that there is no direct line of political accountability to Congress, and it is difficult to believe Congress is going to permit the development of a national strategy for countering terrorism to exist for very long without establishing political accountability to the legislative branch. Congress has a central role in federal administration and is heavily involved in the creation of federal agencies and supervising them.[9]

This option emphasizes reliance on the political authority of the president over the legal authority that would be established in statute. The advantage of this is that it provides flexibility by relying on the broad executive power of the president. The disadvantage is that without a legislative framework providing budgetary authority and staff, the power of the office is uncertain and subject to the vagaries of the president or future presidents' attention to homeland security, which can wax and wane over the years ahead.[10]

STATUTORY COORDINATOR OPTION

This option shares many of the same characteristics as the executive order coordinator option, with the difference that it places some key responsibilities and authorities in statute that must be approved by Congress. . . . The keys to these proposals are the establishment of the office and the director in statute, and the commitment of responsibilities, such as developing a national strategy, coordinating agency efforts to implement the strategy, budget review and certification to statute, and providing for explicit oversight by Congress.

In addressing congressional oversight . . . at least 11 full committees in the Senate and 14 full committees in the House—as well as their numerous subcommittees—have oversight responsibilities for various programs for combating terrorism, and it opined that the executive branch cannot successfully coordinate its programs for coordinating terrorism alone without Congress being better organized. . . .

DEPARTMENTAL OPTION

This option is represented by the report of the US. Commission on National Security in the 21st Century, known as the Hart-Rudman Commission[11] and by a bill introduced by Senators Lieberman and Specter. The core idea is to create a Cabinet department with both operational responsibilities and coordinating responsibilities. The Department of Homeland Security would involve the transfer of the Federal Emergency Management Agency (FEMA), the Coast Guard, the Customs Service, and the Border Patrol. It also envisions the transfer of the Critical Infrastructure Assurance Office and the Institute for Information Infrastructure Protection from the Department of Commerce, and the National Infrastructure Protection Center and the National Domestic Preparedness Office from the FBI. The Secretary of National Homeland Security would be made a member of the National Security Council, and the president would be authorized to add other departmental secretaries as well.

The option clearly assigns operational responsibilities for a portion of homeland security to the department, but it also assigns coordinating responsibilities affecting a larger portion that involves other departments and agencies. . . .

Like advocates of the statutory coordination option, proponents of the departmental option place great emphasis on the power of legal authority. They argue that without a legislative framework providing budget and staff, the power of the head of homeland security will be uncertain and subject to the vagaries of presidents' attention to homeland security, which may wax and wane in the years ahead.[10] Proponents of the departmental approach also argue that the co-location of key entities dealing with critical infrastructure protection, border security, and disaster response will provide a logical arrangement and create internal synergies and efficiencies.[12]

WHICH APPROACH TO ORGANIZING HOMELAND SECURITY: HIERARCHY OR NETWORK?

When a crisis is declared and government agency performance is found wanting, the call is heard to create a focal point at the highest level to create the needed organizational arrangement and to coordinate federal agencies. Proposals to do this are now in evidence. The notion of a single focal point is based in the hierarchical model and presumes that organizing to meet the new priority of homeland security must begin at the top and be directed down. This is not necessarily the immediate priority requirement.

The fact is the federal government has hierarchical departments and agencies, and they are infused with missions, activities, and authorities prescribed in federal law. The president is at the top of all these hierarchies, but Congress is a partner in changing how they will function to meet the newly recognized environment of homeland security. Attempts to delegate presidential power and authority to achieve coordinated action confront numerous obstacles and challenges. "Even when the will to cooperate is present, good intentions may be thwarted by the size of the federal establishment, the growing complexity and compartmentalized character of federal programs, differences among professional groups, and the absence of a clear sense of direction and coherence of policy either in the White House or in the Congress."[13] Arriving at a central-headquarters organizational form is not likely to be done quickly. Coordination is not neutral, and even when it results in a decision, it advances some interests over others, which has high potential to alienate important players.[13]

The design for a new central homeland security organization cannot be based on assumptions about how it will operate. The idea of top-down coordination rests on the notions that the organizations to be coordinated have been identified or can be readily identified by the headquarters coordinators; that the relationships of these organizations to each other are well understood; that agreement has been reached about what objectives will be accomplished by altering certain of these interorganizational relationships: and that the authority and means to effectuate desired goals exist to alter the relationships in the desired direction. It assumes the hierarchy will facilitate the implementation. The problem in the context of homeland security is that most of these assumptions are unfounded. The requisites for combating terrorism are in the process of discovery; the organizations that must be coordinated and for what purpose are the subject of deliberation and debate and will shift; objectives are being formulated and debated: and the authority is ambiguous at best.

References

Advisory Panel to Assess Domestic Response Capabilities for Terrorism Involving Weapons of Mass Destruction, 2000, *Toward a National Strategy for Combating Terrorism*, Available at http://www.rand.org/nsrd/terrpanel, accessed September 16, 2008.

Paul DiMaggio and Walter W. Powell, 1983, "Institutional Isomorphism and Collective Rationality in Organizational Fields," *American Sociological Review*, Vol. 48, No. 4, pp. 147–160.

R. H. Hall, 1996, *Organizations Structure and Process*, 6th ed., Prentice Hall, Upper Saddle River, NJ.

Donald F. Kettl, 1993, *Learning Organizations and Managing the Unknown*, Paper presented at the Conference on Rethinking Public Personnel Systems, April 16–17, Washington, DC.

Paul R. Lawrence and Jay W. Lorsch, 1967, *Organization and Environment: Managing Differentiation and Integration*, Harvard University, Cambridge, MA.

Bruce McCaffery, 2001, Organizing the United States Government to effectively protect America's homeland against terrorism, Statement prepared for the U.S. Senate, Committee on Governmental Affairs, *Hearing on Legislative Options to Strengthen National Homeland Defense*, 107th Congress, 1st session, October 12.

Ronald C. Moe and Robert S. Gilmour, 1995, "Rediscovering principles of government organization: the neglected foundations of public law," *Public Administration Review*, Vol. 55, No. 1, pp. 135–146.

J. Pfeffer, 1982, *Organizations and Organization Theory*, Pitman, Boston.

Hal G. Rainey, 1997, *Understanding and Managing Public Organizations*, 2nd ed., Jossey-Bass, San Francisco, CA.

Philip Selznick, 1966, *TVA and the Grass Roots*, Harper Collins, New York.

Thomas H. Stanton, 2001, Statement prepared for the U.S. Senate, Committee on Governmental Affairs, *Hearing on Legislative Options to Strengthen National Homeland Defense*, 107th Congress, 1st session, October 12.

U.S. House of Representatives, 2001, Subcommittee on Economic Development, Public Buildings, and Emergency Management, *Hearing on Combating Terrorism: Options to Improve the Federal Response*, 107th Congress, 1st session, April 24.

Wendy Haynes, "Seeing Around Corners: Crafting the New Department of Homeland Security," *Review of Policy Research*, Vol. 21, No. 3. (2004), pp. 369–395.

Much has happened at the federal level since the terrorist attacks of September 11, 2001. Immediately following the terrorist attacks, funding for homeland security increased dramatically, beginning with the $40 billion emergency supplemental appropriations act (Public Law 107–38), $10.7 billion of which was appropriated for homeland security initiatives. . . .

The following discussion selectively summarizes the major events depicted in the figure, as well as significant events that occurred early in 2003.

PRESIDENT ESTABLISHES OFFICE OF HOMELAND SECURITY (OHS)/HOMELAND SECURITY COUNCIL (OCTOBER 8, 2001)

By Executive Order 13228 President George W. Bush established the OHS and charged the new entity with the following mission and functions:

Sec. 2. Mission. The mission of the Office shall be to develop and coordinate the implementation of a comprehensive national strategy to secure the United States from terrorist threats or attacks. The Office shall perform the functions necessary to carry out this mission, including the functions specified in Section 3 of this order.

Sec. 3. Functions. The functions of the Office shall be to coordinate the executive branch's efforts to detect, prepare for, prevent, protect against, respond to, and recover from terrorist attacks within the United States.[14]

The executive order also created a new Homeland Security Council (HSC) as the main coordinating body, to be staffed by OHS and chaired by the Assistant to the President for Homeland Security (HS), Thomas Ridge, who also was to serve as director of the OHS.[15] . . . Ridge's role brought with it tremendous powers to influence the agenda and forge consensus through a variety of coordinating councils and interagency committees,

---

Source: Wendy Haynes, "Seeing Around Corners: Crafting the New Department of Homeland Security," *Review of Policy Research*, Vol. 21, No. 3. (2004), pp. 369–395, Blackwell Publishing.

but no formal authority over budgets, people, and programs. Slightly more than a year later, on November 25, 2002, President Bush would sign into law a bill creating a new mega-agency that would provide Ridge with much of the formal authority the OHS concept lacked.

SENATOR LIEBERMAN INTRODUCES HOMELAND SECURITY LEGISLATION (OCTOBER 11, 2001)

Even before September 11, a number of commissions had concluded that the federal government sorely lacked the organizational capacity for meaningful counterterrorism. Perhaps the best known of those examining the topic was the US Commission on National Security/21st Century, better known as the Hart-Rudman Commission. . . .

The commission's recommendations were pursued in Congress by Representative Mac Thornberry (Republican, Texas) and Senators Joseph I. Lieberman (Democrat, Connecticut) and Arlen Specter (Republican, Pennsylvania).[16] Not until June 2002, when the president filed legislation and the next month released the *National Strategy for Homeland Security*, did the notion of a cabinet-level mega-agency enjoy public support from the White House.

USA PATRIOT ACT BECOMES LAW (PUBLIC LAW 107–56, OCTOBER 26, 2001)

In the month following the September 11 terrorist attacks, Congress passed and the president signed a new antiterrorism bill, thus laying "the foundation for a domestic intelligence-gathering system of unprecedented scale and technological prowess, according to both supporters and critics of the legislation."[17]

TRANSPORTATION SECURITY ADMINISTRATION (TSA) CREATED THROUGH THE AVIATION AND TRANSPORTATION SECURITY ACT (PUBLIC LAW 107–71, NOVEMBER 19, 2001)

. . . In the aftermath of the terrorist attacks, Congress passed legislation establishing a new Transportation Security Administration in the US Department of Transportation (USDOT) as the responsible authority for assuring aviation security. Knowledgeable observers have noted that this significant change in the USDOT organizational structure was hastily cobbled together and has created significant jurisdictional confusion at the local level among staff of the Federal Aviation Administration, local airport authorities, and private carriers.

THE CONGRESS INTRODUCES DHS LEGISLATION (MAY 2, 2002)

Led by Senator Joe Lieberman, members from both houses (and both parties) of Congress again introduced legislation calling for a cabinet-level Department of National Homeland

Security to plan, coordinate, and integrate US government activities, including border security and emergency preparedness, and to act as a focal point regarding natural and manmade crises and emergency planning. The legislation would create a White House Office of Combating Terrorism to coordinate threat assessments, and exercise budget certification authority over spending to combat terrorism, among other duties and authorities.[18]

PRESIDENT PROPOSES DHS LEGISLATION (JUNE 2, 2002)

A month after the Lieberman contingent introduced DHS legislation, the president introduced a bill that, while similar to the first one, included notable differences. For instance, the Lieberman bill did not provide the management flexibility sought by the president to facilitate the new secretary's efforts to integrate 22 agencies composed of 170,000 employees, seven different payroll and benefit systems, 17 different unions, and a multitude of collective bargaining units. Moreover, the Lieberman bill would have transformed the Office of Homeland Security from a presidentially created entity to an office created by statute. Although the president had initially resisted the notion of a cabinet-level mega-agency, his proposal in June 2002, reflected a change of policy direction based on the analytical efforts of his Office of Homeland Security to craft a structure that drew on various aspects of previous proposals, including Lieberman's.[18]

PRESIDENT ISSUES NATIONAL STRATEGY FOR HOMELAND SECURITY (JULY 16, 2002)

Within a matter of weeks of filing DHS legislation, the president's Office of Homeland Security released the administration's first National Strategy for Homeland Security. The president identified three strategic objectives:

1. Prevent terrorist attacks within the United States.
2. Reduce American's vulnerability to terrorism.
3. Minimize the damage and recover from attacks that do occur.

In pursuit of those objectives, the strategy proposed creating the DHS, including an Information Analysis and Infrastructure Protection Division to access and analyze data collected by other agencies (including the FBI and the CIA), retaining the Office of Homeland Security, and engaging all 87,000 government jurisdictions in a coordinated, nationwide effort to protect the homeland.[19]

PRESIDENT GEORGE W. BUSH SIGNS A $29 BILLION EMERGENCY SUPPLEMENTAL APPROPRIATIONS ACT (PUBLIC LAW 107–206, AUGUST 2, 2002)

According to GAO estimates, approximately $4.6 billion of the $29 billion supplemental act was appropriated for homeland security activities. (The president had earlier requested $37.8

billion for funding homeland security activities in the regular FY 2003 budget, a matter to be discussed in greater detail later in this article.)

THE CONGRESS PASSES (NOVEMBER 2, 2002) AND THE PRESIDENT SIGNS THE HOMELAND SECURITY ACT OF 2002 (PUBLIC LAW 107–296, NOVEMBER 25, 2002)

Within hours of signing the department into law, Bush requested and received Senate approval for his handpicked leadership team, headed by his long-time ally, Tom Ridge, former Governor of Pennsylvania. Bush also filed the Department of Homeland Security Reorganization Plan,[20] which "starts the clock ticking" for beginning to move agencies over to the department on March 1, 2003. The FEMA, the TSA, and the Secret Service were among the first agencies slated to move.

SENATE SELECT COMMITTEE ON INTELLIGENCE AND HOUSE PERMANENT SELECT COMMITTEE ON INTELLIGENCE RELEASE FINAL REPORT ON JOINT INQUIRY INTO THE TERRORIST ATTACKS OF SEPTEMBER 11, 2001 (DECEMBER 11, 2002)

Although much of the report remains classified, lawmakers issued nineteen recommendations, many aimed at structural changes to intelligence agencies, including creating a cabinet-level director of national intelligence to oversee all US intelligence operations.

References

Brookings Institution, May 7, 2002, *Project on homeland security–Chapter 7: Organizing for success*, pp. 99–124. Brookings, Washington, DC, Retrieved from http://www.brookings.org/dybdocroot/fp/projects/homeland/orgs.html.

R. C. Shelby, December 10, 2002, September 11 and the imperative of reform in the US intelligence community: additional views of Senator Richard C. Shelby, Vice Chairman, Senate Select Committee on Intelligence (84 pages), Retrieved from http://www.shelby.senate.gov/news/record.cfm?id=188900.

U.S. General Accounting Office, December 2002b, *Homeland Security: Management Challenges Facing Federal Leadership (Report to the Chairman, Committee on Government Affairs, US Senate)*, Author (GAO-03-260), Washington, DC.

U.S. General Accounting Office, January 2003c, *Transportation Security Administration: Actions and Plans to Build a Results-Oriented Culture*, Author (GAO-03-190), Washington, DC.

Harold C. Relyea, "Organizing for Homeland Security," *Presidential Studies Quarterly*, Vol. 33, No. 3. (September 2003), pp. 602.

During the latter half of 2002, a contest was underway over the organization of the federal government for *homeland security.* It had begun in the aftermath of the terrorist attacks of September 11, 2001, when *homeland security* came into popular parlance. For several months, this phrase was a symbol, a goal-preservation of the security of the homeland. Then, as various responses to the terrorist attacks were developed, *homeland security* began to migrate from its symbolic status to that of a policy concept. When President George W. Bush released his National Strategy for Homeland Security on July 15, 2002, the concept was defined as "a concerted national effort to prevent terrorist attacks within the United States, reduce America's vulnerability to terrorism, and minimize the damage and recover from attacks that do occur."[21] By this time, however, *homeland security* was seen by some as a substitute for the Cold War-weary *national security* concept and possibly prone to the same use as a justification for the exercise of prerogative or implied powers by the president. Certainly President Bush made a strong effort to determine the organization and management arrangements for the executive branch that he perceived to be necessary for homeland security. The contest, in which he was largely successful in obtaining what he wanted from Congress, was the most recent development in a long history of interbranch rivalry regarding government organization.

Because the Constitution vests in Congress the authority to "make all Laws which shall be necessary and proper for carrying into Execution" the expressed powers of Article I, Section 8, "and all other Powers vested by this Constitution in the Government of the United States, or in any Department or Officer thereof," as well as to establish, by law, all other officers of the United States whose appointments are not otherwise mandated by the Constitution, it was long assumed that the organization of the federal government, including the structuring of the departments and agencies of the executive branch, was an exclusive responsibility of Congress. . . .

With the end of [World War II], the liquidation of most of the wartime agencies, and efforts underway to convert both the government and the economy to peace conditions, Congress renewed the president's reorganization authority with the Reorganization Act of 1945.[22]

The conversion was one of the specified purposes for reorganization. Otherwise, the new law was very similar to the lapsed act of 1939: no department could be abolished or created by a plan, a few agencies were exempted from its scope, and Congress had 60 days to veto a plan by the adoption of a concurrent resolution of disapproval by both houses. It would expire on April 1, 1948.

Thereafter, Congress, at various times—1949, 1953, 1955, 1957, 1961, 1964, 1965, 1969, 1971, 1977, and 1984—enacted modified and extended versions of the Reorganization Act.

At different junctures, qualifications were placed upon its exercise. For example, Congress initially prohibited, then allowed, then again prohibited, the abolition or creation of a department by reorganization plan, and later disallowed plans dealing with more than one logically consistent subject matter. Also, the president was prevented from submitting more than one plan within a 30-day period, and was required to include a clear statement on the projected economic savings expected to result from a reorganization.

Modification of the president's reorganization plan authority was made necessary in 1983 when the Supreme Court, in the *Chadha* case, effectively invalidated continued congressional reliance upon a simple or concurrent resolution to disapprove a proposed plan.[23] Under the Reorganization Act Amendments of 1984, which were signed by President Ronald Reagan on November 8, several significant changes were made in the reorganization plan law. Any time during the period of 60 calendar days of continuous session of Congress following the submission of a reorganization plan, the president might make amendments or modifications to it. Within 90 calendar days of continuous session of Congress following the submission of a reorganization plan, both houses had to adopt a joint resolution (which, unlike a concurrent resolution, becomes law with the president's signature-a central issue in the *Chadha* case) for a plan to be approved. This amendment, however, continued the president's reorganization plan authority only to the end of 1984, when it automatically expired.[24] Neither President Reagan nor his successors requested its reauthorization, although the initial September 1993 report of the National Performance Review recommended this course of action to President William Clinton,[25] as did the National Strategy for Homeland Security released by President George W. Bush on July 16, 2002.[21]

In the absence of reorganization plan authority, the president may propose executive branch reorganizations to be realized through the normal legislative process. The Departments of Energy, Education, and Veterans Affairs were established in this manner. This approach, however, is devoid of the action time frame and required final vote of the reorganization plan arrangement that expedites reorganization. The president might attempt a minor reorganization, such as establishing a small, temporary entity within the Executive Office of the President, by issuing a directive, such as an executive order. Operative law specifies that an "agency in existence for more than one year may not use amounts otherwise available for obligation to pay its expenses without a specific appropriation or specific authorization by law."[26] An agency created by executive order would not have a specific appropriation or authorization unless Congress provided one. The Office of Homeland Security, established by President George W. Bush with E.O. 13228 of October 8, 2001, found itself confronted by this requirement, but its situation had become irritating for Congress because its director had declined to appear before congressional committees.[27] Appropriators addressed the matter by providing the office funds and an account for FY 2003, thereby setting the expectation that the director would appear before them next year to discuss the agency's budget and activities.

During the latter half of the twentieth century, the agenda for government reorganization was fueled from time to time by recommendations and proposals resulting from expert studies. Sometimes such offerings were made by panels mandated by Congress, such as the first and second Commissions on Organization of the Executive Branch of the Government (1947–49, 1953–55) headed by former President Herbert C. Hoover. More often, they were produced by presidential groups, such as the President's Advisory Committee on Government Organization (1953–58), the President's Advisory Council on Executive Organization (1969–1970), and, more recently, the National Performance Review/National Partnership for Reinventing Government (1993–2000). Also, some such contributions have emanated from private sector bodies, such as the Brookings Institution, the Heritage Foundation, and the National Academy of Public Administration, and, occasionally, from individuals. . . .

Terrorist attacks on the World Trade Center and the Pentagon on September 11, 2001, prompted major efforts at combating terrorism and ensuring homeland security. President George W. Bush seized the initiative, and became the architect of new arrangements to coordinate these efforts. With E.O. 13228 of October 8, 2001, he established the Office of Homeland Security (OHS) and the Homeland Security Council (HSC) within the Executive Office of the President.[28] That same day, he appointed former Pennsylvania Governor Tom Ridge as Assistant to the President for Homeland Security to direct OHS.

As the coordinator of homeland security policy and practice, OHS would have to obtain the cooperation of some powerful leaders of executive entities having strong professional bureaucracies and enjoying the close support of portions of the congressional and private interest communities. . . .

(T)he director of OHS had the president's confidence and backing, enjoyed easy access to the Oval Office, and occupied office space in the West Wing of the White House. Thereafter, the comparison ends. The OHS director's mandate to "coordinate the executive branch's efforts" to combat terrorism, "work with executive departments and agencies" in this regard, and "identify priorities" concerning same did not appear to convey authority equal to that of the OWM-OWMR director. Stated in the executive order in the most general terms, the jurisdiction of OHS for performing its functions was not clear, and it is questionable if, compared with OWM-OWMR, OHS has had any jurisdiction "over" other agencies. Whereas the director of OHS was one of at least ten members of the Homeland Security Council, the relationship between OHS and the council was ambiguous. Furthermore, the order mandating OHS and the council offered no definition of the *homeland security* concept, a serious shortcoming for their coordination efforts.

The OWM-OWMR experience also warned against OHS becoming involved in operating or administrative responsibilities. Nonetheless, the assistant to the president for homeland security was designated "the individual primarily responsible for coordinating the domestic response efforts of all departments and agencies in the event of an imminent terrorist threat and during and in the immediate aftermath of a terrorist attack within the United States.[29] Such activity not only suggested the exercise of operating or administrative authority, but also a duplication of, or intrusion into, the responsibilities of the director of the Federal Emergency Management Agency.

Although Ridge contended that his close proximity and easy access to the president gave him all the authority he needed to do his job, some were not convinced and sought to reconstitute OHS with a statutory mandate and more explicit responsibilities and powers. Others favored a different course of action, consolidating relevant programs and hierarchical administrative authority in a new department. Among the first to pursue this approach was Senator Joseph Lieberman (D-Connecticut), who introduced his initial proposal (S. 1534) a few days after the establishment of OHS. He and Representative Mac Thornberry (R-Texas) later introduced more elaborate versions of this legislation (S. 2452 and H.R. 4660) in early May 2002.[30]

By late January 2002, Ridge, according to the *Washington Post*, was "facing resistance to some of his ideas, forcing him to apply the brakes on key elements of his agenda and raising questions about how much he can accomplish." OHS plans engendering opposition from within the executive branch reportedly included those to streamline or consolidate agencies responsible for border security; improve intelligence distribution to federal, state, and local agencies; and alert federal, state, and local officials about terrorist threats using a system of graduated levels of danger.[31]

At about this same time, Ridge began to become embroiled in controversy over his refusal to testify before congressional committees. Among the first to request his appearance were Senator Robert C. Byrd (D-West Virginia) and Senator Ted Stevens (R-Alaska), the chairman and ranking minority member of the Committee on Appropriations, respectively. Ridge turned down their initial, informal invitation and later formal requests of March 15 and April 4.[32] When Ridge declined the request of Representative Ernest Istook, Jr. (R-Oklahoma), chairman of the House Appropriations Subcommittee on Treasury, Postal Service, and General Government, appropriations for the Executive Office of the President were threatened, prompting Ridge to offer to meet with Istook and other subcommittee members in an informal session.[33] Thereafter, Ridge arranged other informal briefings with members of the House Committee on Government Reform and a group of senators, and agreed to a similar such session with members of the House Committee on Energy and Commerce. These informal meetings, however, did not appear to abate the controversy that Ridge's refusals to testify had generated.[34]

Assessing the situation in early May, a *New York Times* news analysis proffered that, "instead of becoming the preeminent leader of domestic security, Tom Ridge has become a White House adviser with a shrinking mandate, forbidden by the president to testify before Congress to explain his strategy, overruled in White House councils and overshadowed by powerful cabinet members reluctant to cede their turf or their share of the limelight." In support of this view, the analysis noted that the Pentagon did not consult with Ridge when suspending air patrols over New York City—a special assistant to the secretary of defense explained this action by saying, "We don't tell the Office of Homeland Security about recommendations, only about decisions"—and the attorney general unilaterally announced a possible terrorist threat against banks in April.[35] Asked about this assessment by Jim Lehrer on the PBS *NewsHour*, Ridge called it "false" and said, "I just don't think they have spent enough time with me on a day-to-day basis."[36] Shortly thereafter, a *New* York Times editorial opined that one of the reasons Ridge "lost these turf battles is that he failed to build a constituency for change in Congress. His refusal to testify before Congressional committees has not helped. . . ."[37]

The president's surprise announcement of his proposal for a Department of Homeland Security certainly had political implications. Many viewed it as an attempt by the president to regain the initiative in the nation's efforts at combating terrorism. Offering his proposal to Congress and asking for its immediate adoption also set the legislative agenda on the matter. Moreover, the proposal reflected the president's desire to move beyond the indeterminate coordination efforts of OHS to a strong administrative structure for managing consolidated programs concerned with border and transportation security, effective response to domestic terrorism incidents, and ensuring homeland security.

The proposal, however, had its shortcomings. These resulted, at least partly, from the inexperience of its principal drafters: none of the four had previously prepared legislation for a new department and only one of them, if only briefly, had headed such an entity. Furthermore, the proposal had been developed somewhat hastily and in strict secrecy. Available reorganization expertise was not utilized; input and support from the agencies and professional constituencies directly affected was not sought.

A glaring omission in the president's proposal was a definition of the organizing concept: a Department of Homeland Security was proposed, but what was *homeland security?* Without a clear understanding of this concept, there was no standard for determining which existing agencies, programs, and functions merited transfer to the new department. Then, what should be done with the non-homeland security programs and functions of an agency being transferred? OHS director Tom Ridge, in his June 20, 2002 testimony before the Senate Committee on Governmental Affairs, acknowledged that the new department would have a number of programs not directly related to countering terrorism, but did not indicate any particular concern about this development. . . .[38,39]

The president's proposal also contained provisions which, in the view of some, enhanced, in various ways, the authority of the executive to the detriment of Congress, producing a disruption of the constitutional balance of powers between the two branches. It would have authorized the unprecedented presidential appointment, without Senate confirmation, of upwards of ten assistant secretaries-their responsibilities to be determined by the president-for the new department. Article 11, Section 2, of the Constitution specifies that the president has the power, "by and with the Advice and Consent of the Senate," to appoint "all other Officers of the United States, whose Appointments are not herein otherwise provided for, and which shall be established by Law." Congress, of course, "may by Law vest the Appointment of such inferior Officers, *as they think* proper, in the President alone, in the Courts of Law, or in the Heads of Departments."

Another section of the president's proposal would have authorized the head of the new department to make certain reorganizations and reallocations of functions unilaterally, that is, without affirmation by Congress—a form of approval for presidential reorganization plans specified in the expired Reorganization Act. Also, the president's proposal would have allowed the head of the department to transfer upwards of five percent of any appropriation available to the secretary in any fiscal year to other appropriated accounts of the department with only notice to the congressional appropriations committees rather than some form of approval of such actions. Similarly, another section would have authorized the president, until the transfer of an agency to the new department, to transfer to the secretary of homeland security upwards of five percent of the unobligated balance of any appropriation available to such agency with only prior notice to the appropriations committees. It was roughly estimated that the new department envisioned in the president's proposal would have an initial budget of approximately $37.4 billion. These provisions were seen as attempts to diminish the power of the purse vested in Congress by the Constitution.

Finally, the president's proposal would have exempted the new department from the requirements of the Federal Advisory Committee Act and the Federal Property and Administrative Services Act, was silent concerning its compliance with some other general management laws such as the Administrative Procedure Act and the Government Performance and Results Act, and rejected applying existing civil service protections and collective bargaining rights for department workers, favoring instead more "flexible" human resources management arrangements. The president's proposal would have authorized the secretary of homeland security, in regulations prescribed jointly with the director of the Office of Personnel Management, to establish and, from time to time, adjust a human resources management system for some or all of the organizational units of the department. In testimony before the Senate Committee on Governmental Affairs on June 20, OHS Director Ridge indicated that the president would request for the department "significant flexibility in hiring processes, compensation systems and practices, and performance management to recruit, retain, and develop a motivated, high performance and accountable workforce."[38,39]

The provision quickly raised various issues concerning staffing requirements, such as adequate numbers of personnel and planning for the replacement of retiring staff; hiring, particularly direct hiring, which would not be merit based and free of political influence and otherwise devoid of preference for veterans; and pay, particularly pay parity or equity for employees who are performing similar jobs.[40] These matters would continue to be among the most contentious issues surrounding the establishment of a Department of Homeland Security. As envisioned in the president's proposal, the department would begin operations with almost 170,000 workers. . . .

Realizing that the leadership and coordination efforts of OHS and, to some extent, HSC were not altogether successful, President George W. Bush proposed the legislative establishment of a strong administrative structure for managing consolidated programs concerned with border and transportation security, providing effective response to domestic terrorism incidents, and ensuring homeland security. By offering his own draft bill for the creation of the new department, the president signaled his dissatisfaction with legislative models pending before Congress. Moreover, offering his proposal to Congress and asking for its immediate adoption set the congressional agenda. In the House, the majority leader gave support to the president's initiative by introducing the proposal, helping fashion the strategy for its consideration, shepherding it through the select committee, managing it on the floor, and bringing it to a final vote with bipartisan support.

Protracted discussion of the legislation in the Senate and, due to the extremely tight party ratios, failure to bring the matter to closure prompted the president to become insistent on a bill meeting the expectations reflected in his original proposal. For some Senate Democrats, the fall elections foretold that, if the president did not get the department model he wanted from the 107th Congress, he could probably expect to be far more successful in this regard in the next. The House majority leader produced a new bill, designed to have broad appeal but not compromising the president's priorities, and brought it to a final vote, which reflected slightly more support than had been evidenced for the initial House-passed measure. This model also proved to be acceptable to a bipartisan majority in the Senate. Thus, ultimately, the president largely obtained what he wanted in the legislation mandating the Department of Homeland Security.

References

Charles A. Beard, 1934, *The Idea of National Interest*, Macmillan, New York.

Morton R. Berkowitz and P. G. Bock, eds., 1965, *American National Security*, Free Press, New York.

Morton R. Berkowitz and P. G. Bock, 1968, National security, in David L. Sills (Ed.), *International Encyclopedia of the Social Sciences*, vol. 11, pp. 40–45. Macmillan-Free Press, New York.

Wilfred E. Binkley, 1947, *President and Congress*, Alfred A. Knopf, New York.

P. G. Bock and Morton R. Berkowitz, October 1966, "The emerging field of national security," *World Politics*, Vol. 19, pp. 122–136.

Louis Brownlow, Autumn 1944, Reconversion of the federal administrative machinery from war to peace, *Public Administration Review*, Vol. 4, pp. 309–326.

Robert D. Cuff, 1973, *The War Industries Board: Business-Government Relations During World War I*, Johns Hopkins University Press, Baltimore, MD.

Jeffrey M. Dorwart, 1991, *Eberstudt And Forrtstal: A National Security Partnership, 1909–1949*, Texas A&M University Press, College Station, TX.

Herbert Emmerich, 1971, *Federal Organization and Administration*, University of Alabama Press, Tuscaloosa, AL.

Paul Y. Hammond, 1961, *The American Military Establishment in the Twentieth Century*, Princeton University Press, Princeton, NJ.

Oscar Kraines, 1970, "The president versus Congress: The Keep Commission, 1905–1909," *Western Political Quarterly*, Vol. 23, pp. 5–54.

Seward W. Livermore, 1966, *Politics is adjourned: Woodrow Wilson and the Wa Congress, 1916–1918*, Wesleyan University Press, Middletown, CT.

Gene M. Lyons and Louis Morton, 1965, *Schools for Strategy: Education and Research in National Security Affairs*, Praeger, New York.

Harold C. Relyea, 1997, "Exigency and emergency." in Harold C. Relyea (Ed.), *The Executive Office of the President*, Greenwood Press, Westport, CT.

Harold C. Relyea, 2002, "Homeland security: the concept and the presidential coordination office-first assessment," *Presidential Studies Quarterly*, Vol. 32, pp. 397–411.

James D. Richardson (Ed.), 1918, *Messages and Papers of the Presidents*, Bureau of National Literature, New York.

W. W. Rostow, 1975, *How It All Began: Origins of the Modern Economy*, McGraw-Hill, New York.

Herman Miles Somers, 1950, *Presidential Agency: OWMR, the Office of War Mobilization and Reconversion*, Harvard University Press, Cambridge, MA.

U.S. Bureau of the Budget, 1946, *The United States at War: Development and Administration of the War Program by the Federal Government*, Government Printing Office, Washington, DC.

U.S. Congress, House Select Committee on Post-War Military Policy, 1944, Proposal to establish a single Department of Armed Forces, 78th Congress, 2nd session, hearings pursuant to H. Res. 465, Government Printing Office, Washington, DC.

U.S. Congress, Senate Committee on Armed Services, 1949, National security act amendments of 1949, 81st Congress, 1st session, hearings, Government Printing Office, Washington, DC.

U.S. Congress, Senate Committee on Military Affairs, 1945, Department of Armed Forces, Department of Military Security, 79th Congress, 1st session, hearings, Government Printing Office, Washington, DC.

U.S. Congress, Senate Committee on Naval Affairs, 1945, *Unification of the War and Navy Departments and Postwar Organization for National Security*, by Ferdinand Eherstadt, 79th Congress, 1st session, committee print, Government Printing Office, Washington, DC.

U.S. President's Committee on Administrative Management, 1957, *Administrative Management in the Government of the United States*, Government Printing Office, Washington, DC.

U.S. White House Office, 2002, *The Department of Homeland Security*, Government Printing Office, Washington, DC.

Woodrow Wilson, 1887, "The study of public administration." *Political Science Quarterly*, Vol. 2, pp. 197–222, 1908, *Constitutional government in the United States*, Columbia University Press, New York.

Arnold Wolfers, December 1952, "'National security' as an ambiguous symbol," *Political Science Quarterly*, Vol. 67, pp. 481–502.

Benjamin Fletcher Wright (Ed.), 1966, *The Federalist, by Alexander Hamilton, James Madison, and John Jay*, Belknap Press of Harvard University Press, Cambridge, MA.

Daniel R. Yergin, 1978, *Shattered peace: The origins of the cold war and the national security state*, Houghton Mifflin, Boston, MA.

Richard S. Conley, "Reform, Reorganization, and the Renaissance of the Managerial Presidency: The Impact of 9/11 on the Executive Establishment," *Politics and Policy*, Vol. 34, No. 2. (2006), pp. 304–342.

Bush's leadership on the resultant functional changes, bureaucratic reforms, and reorganizations is best understood from the perspective of the "managerial presidency"—the notion that implementation of the president's policy objectives is essentially a problem of effectively managing the White House and permanent bureaucracy.[41] Although rare in recent decades, successive post-World War II presidents' attempts to restructure the federal government represent "a changed conception of the role of the presidency in administration" unique to the modern office.[42] In the post 9/11 context, for Bush to signal his resolve as commander-in-chief and to win the war on terrorism required asserting optimal control over agencies with counterterrorism responsibilities.

Previous presidents have tended to approach the comprehensive reorganization of executive functions cautiously. Bush's administrative strategy immediately after 9/11 was to centralize functions in the White House. Following the lead of many of his recent predecessors, he bypassed congressional approval and circumvented the career bureaucracy. When Congress threatened to pursue reorganization on its own, Bush quickly preempted the legislature with his own plan that sought to maximize influence over, and impose his own managerial vision on, any new structure. It is in this way that 9/11 provided a unique window of opportunity for the largest reorganization of federal responsibilities since the end of World War II. . . .

Just like the unification of the armed services in 1947, the reorganization follows the rationale of the punctuated equilibrium framework. September 11 gave precisely the "push" necessary to prompt lawmakers—and ultimately the president—to take action and streamline organizational structures to wage the war on terror more effectively and fulfill public expectations. Final legislative action came on the heels of many high-profile studies and reports that had called attention to the likelihood of domestic terrorism reaching American shores before the attacks on New York and Washington.

Protecting the United States from a terrorist incident had been on presidential and congressional agendas for years before 9/11. The 1992 bombing of the World Trade Center and the 1995 bombing of the Murrah Federal Building in Oklahoma City accentuated the

---

Source: Richard S. Conley, "Reform, Reorganization, and the Renaissance of the Managerial Presidency: The Impact of 9/11 on the Executive Establishment," *Politics and Policy*, Vol. 34, No. 2. (2006), pp. 304–342, Blackwell Publishing.

country's vulnerabilities. President Clinton signed an executive order and issued several Presidential Decision Directives in 1995 to enhance counterterrorism efforts.[43] By 1997, various commissions were emphasizing the centrality of domestic security and homeland defense in the new millennium. The National Defense Panel's[44] report, *Transforming Defense National Security in the 21st Century*, gave particular weight to the need to thwart nuclear threats and streamline the Department of Defense (DOD). Beginning in 1999 and based on five reports that underscored the potential threats from chemical, biological, radiological, and nuclear attack and the importance of domestic preparedness, the Gilmore Advisory Panel to Assess Domestic Response Capabilities for Terrorism involving Weapons of Mass Destruction initiated a review of federal programs and national standards. In 2000, the congressionally mandated National Commission on Terrorism, chaired by Paul Bremer, advocated targeting state sponsors of terrorism, loosening CIA guidelines on intelligence sources, and enhancing the FBI's role in counterterrorism activities.[45] In its last 2003 report, the Gilmore Advisory Panel continued to accentuate the need for information sharing across federal agencies as well as coordination with state and local governments.[46] Finally, from 1998–2001 the Hart Rudman Commission[47] on National Security in the 21st Century identified homeland security as one of five vital capabilities that the United States needed to develop or enhance. . . .

Among its recommendations, the Hart Rudman Report called for a National Homeland Security Agency in which the Federal Emergency Management Agency (FEMA) would play a central role. All of these past reviews of domestic terrorism prevention and preparedness failed to prompt bold governmental action. The attacks on New York and Washington on September 11 made these concerns matters of the utmost urgency.[48] Through Executive Order 13228, in October 2001 Bush established an OHS, which centralized the function swiftly in the EOP. Bush's move was more than window dressing designed to show the country that he was "doing something" to fight terrorism. He appointed a well-respected and capable advisor, former Pennsylvania governor Tom Ridge, to head the OHS with the tasks of harmonizing counterterrorism efforts scattered across federal agencies and acting as "honest broker" in coordinating cabinet departments and agencies in policy making.

Problems with this "presidential advisor" model surfaced quickly. In particular, critical voices in Congress pointed to inherent weaknesses in Ridge's post. Without any budget authority, they argued, the Homeland Security czar lacked sufficient human and financial resources, had no way to enforce decisions, and relied primarily on the power of persuasion, albeit as a trusted advisor with unfettered access to President Bush.[49] Matters came to a head in early 2002 when Ridge proposed merging elements of the Border Patrol, Coast Guard, and Customs Service. The proposal met with enmity from the chairs of relevant congressional committees determined to protect their turf. Others, including Democratic senators Joe Lieberman (D-CT) and Robert Byrd (D-WV), feared that without statutory authority for his position, Ridge was beyond congressional accountability—a fear that was seemingly given weight by Ridge's refusal to testify before Congress on his office's activities.[50] President Bush had previously rejected the need for full-scale government reorganization. However, by March 2002, congressional calls for a full-scale reorganization of the federal bureaucracy became insistent. The White House reversed its position when it became apparent that the Congress would legislate with or without its blessing and in June 2002 introduced a proposal that sought to maximize presidential influence over the structure of any new cabinet-level department. Bush's plan became the centerpiece of a debate that would not be reconciled until the 2002 midterm elections.

A conflict ensued between the White House and Senate Democrats, which was as much concerning Bush's vision of managing the federal bureaucracy as it was concerning the specifics of homeland defense programs. Bush insisted on flexible personnel rules that far exceeded the latitude requested by his predecessors. In keeping with what Moynihan calls the "New Public Management" agenda targeting efficiency,[51] the president demanded unprecedented discretion over hiring, firing, and transferring employees that ran counter to traditional civil service protections. The Republican-controlled House of Representatives passed Bush's proposal in late July 2002 but when Senate Democrats who had a bare majority balked, Bush threatened to veto any measure that did not conform to his preferences. Ultimately, the legislation was resolved following the 2002 midterm elections in which Bush indefatigably reiterated the need for Republicans to win back control of the Senate and pass his bill. The GOP took back the majority and gained six seats in the House.[52] Realizing the inevitability that the 108th Congress would pass Bush's proposal, Senate Democrats dropped their filibusters and the lame duck 107th Senate agreed to the bill 90–9 in late November. The Homeland Security Act (Public Law 107–296) reorganized a host of federal responsibilities along functional lines. The major agencies transferred and renamed under various DHS directorates included Immigration and Customs Enforcement, Customs and Border Protection, the Coast Guard, the Secret Service, and the FEMA. Others comprised the National Cyber Security Division and the Transportation Security Agency, which oversees airport security.[53] Reorganization of intelligence gathering and management would be addressed through various reforms at the FBI and CIA, and through the creation of the DNI or "intelligence czar."

One of the key lessons of 9/11 is that reorganization and reform of the executive branch is not necessarily a linear process. . . . September 11 furnished a policy-making environment conducive to reforming counterterrorism programs along functional lines by creating the DHS, and to reforming the intelligence community by restructuring the FBI and establishing a DNI in a coordinating role. It also created many opportunities for strong presidential leadership. By preempting Congress on the need for a new cabinet-level department, and charging the 9/11 Commission with recommendations on intelligence reform he promised to follow, President Bush was able to leave an indelible imprint on the shape of counterterrorism programs and their management from the top. When Bush leaves office in 2008, the war on terrorism will be an entrenched component of the permanent bureaucracy.

Dramatic events such as 9/11 also can have a distinct and profound impact on decision-making processes within in the White House. Dick Cheney assumed an unprecedented role for a vice president as Bush's chief advisor who makes operational decisions, frames internal White House debates, and builds a very public case to go to war in Iraq. Perhaps interviews and archival material will cast light on whether Cheney's influence and interpretation of intelligence reports on Iraq unduly swayed Bush to launch a preemptive invasion of Iraq. If so, scholars will be able to compare the advisory processes that led to decision failures in other situations in other administrations, such as Kennedy and the Bay of Pigs, Johnson and Vietnam, with a vice-presidency-centric policymaking framework that is truly unique in the modern era.

References

Richard S. Conley, 2005, "Presidential and Congressional Struggles over the Formation of the Department of Homeland Security," in Richard S. Conley (Ed.), *Transforming the American Polity: The Presidency of George W. Bush and the War on Terrorism*, Prentice Hall, Upper Saddle River, NJ, pp. 135–148.

Gilmore Commission, 1999–2003, "Panel Reports," in *National Security Research Division*, Accessed February 19, 2006, Available online at http://www.rand.org/nsrd/terrpanel/.

National Commission on Terrorism, 2000, *Countering the Changing Threat of International Terrorism,* National Memorial Institute for the Prevention of Terrorism (Bremer Report), Accessed on February 19, 2006, Available online at http://www.mipt.org/bremerreport.asp.

David E. Sanger, June 9, 2002, "In Big Shuffle, Bush Considered Putting FBI in His New Department," *New York Times*, p. 35.

Harold C. Relyea and Henry B. Hogue, "Department of Homeland Security Reorganization: The 2SR Initiative," CRS Report for Congress RL33042, August 19, 2005.

The Department of Homeland Security (DHS) was mandated by the Homeland Security Act of 2002. The creation of DHS resulted in a reorganization of the executive branch on a scale not experienced since the establishment of the Department of Defense (DOD) half a century ago. Originally denominated the National Military Establishment at birth in 1947, DOD was given its current name and underwent the first of what would be a series of structural modifications through statutory amendments in 1949. A similarly complex organization, DHS was the product of legislative compromises, and it was anticipated that congressional overseers, as well as department officials, would monitor the management and operations of DHS with a view to adjusting its structure as conditions warranted. In this regard, Section 872 of the Homeland Security Act authorizes the Secretary of Homeland Security to reorganize functions and organizational units within DHS, subject to specified limits. In late January 2003, as components of DHS were being transferred to the department's operational control, President George W. Bush modified his original reorganization plan for DHS to reconfigure the functions of certain border security agencies into two new components—the Bureau of Customs and Border Protection and the Bureau of Immigration and Customs Enforcement—within the department's Border and Transportation Security Directorate.

In one of his first actions as Secretary of Homeland Security Tom Ridge's successor, Michael Chertoff, on March 2, 2005, the day before he was sworn in as Secretary, announced in testimony before the House Appropriations Subcommittee on Homeland Security that he was "initiating a comprehensive review of the Department's organization, operations, and policies." This effort, he said, would begin "within days." The results of that undertaking, which came to be known as the Second Stage Review or 2SR, were made public in mid-July. As Secretary Chertoff explained, 2SR involved the evaluation of a variety of operational and policy issues, and among those was "the DHS organizational structure, to make sure that our support our mission."

DHS was mandated by the Homeland Security Act of 2002.[54] The creation of DHS resulted in a reorganization of the executive branch on a scale not experienced since the establishment of the Department of Defense (DOD) half a century earlier. . . .[55] In this regard, Section 872 of the Homeland Security Act authorizes the Secretary of Homeland Security to reorganize functions and organizational units within DHS, subject to specified limits.[56] Secretary Chertoff would make initial use of this authority to implement some of his 2SR plans. For a period of 12 months after the effective date of the Homeland Security Act, Section 1502 vested the President with temporary authority to prescribe a reorganization plan for DHS, and subsequent modifications of that plan. In late January 2003, as components of DHS were being transferred to the department's operational control, President George W. Bush modified his original reorganization plan for DHS to reconfigure the functions of certain border security agencies into two new components—the Bureau of Customs and Border Protection and the Bureau of Immigration and Customs Enforcement—within the department's Border and Transportation Security Directorate (BTS).[57]

When it began operations, DHS was largely organized like a hand—the palm being the office of the Secretary Deputy Secretary with the thumb and fingers being individual directorates for (1) management, (2) science and technology, (3) information analysis and infrastructure protection, (4) border and transportation security, and (5) emergency preparedness and response. In addition, however, approximately two dozen other units within the department, but not located within one of the directorates, reported directly to the Secretary. These included program entities, such as the United States Coast Guard and United States Secret Service, and units within the office of the Secretary, such as the Office of International Affairs and Office of State and Local Government Coordination, as well as some Assistant Secretaries. At the time of its creation, DHS had about 170,000 employees, only 18,000 of whom worked in the Washington, DC, area, indicating that the new department had a considerable field organization. . . .

In his July 13, 2005, remarks concerning the results of the 2SR initiative, Secretary Chertoff explained that the work of that effort had been conducted utilizing "18 action teams—involving more than 250 DHS staff—to evaluate specific operational and policy issues." The participants were asked "how would you solve a particular problem," and "how would you take the best solutions and implement them aggressively." He noted, as well, that those immediately directing the 2SR effort also "actively sought opinions from hundreds of public and private partners at the federal, state, local, tribal and international levels." From these deliberations and consultations the following six-point agenda resulted.

1. Increase preparedness, with particular focus on catastrophic events.
2. Strengthen border security and interior enforcement and reform immigration processes.
3. Harden transportation security without sacrificing mobility.
4. Enhance information sharing with our partners, particularly with state, local and tribal governments and the private sector.
5. Improve DHS stewardship, particularly with stronger financial, human resource, procurement and information technology management.
6. Re-align the DHS organization to maximize mission performance.

"In the weeks and months to come," said the Secretary, "the Department will launch specific policy initiatives in a number of key areas" relative to the six-point agenda.[58]

In his July 13, 2005, remarks concerning the results of the 2SR, Secretary Chertoff said that he had "concluded that some structural changes are needed at DHS to improve mission performance. Modest but essential course corrections regarding organization," he said, "will yield big dividends. Most can be accomplished administratively—a few require legislation." He then announced "organization changes that include four important areas of focus: . . . (1) formation of a new, department-wide policy office; (2) significant improvements in how

DHS manages its intelligence and information sharing responsibilities; (3) formation of a new operations coordination office and other measures to increase operational accountability; and (4) an important consolidation effort that integrates the Department's preparedness mission."[59]

While the Secretary, in his July committee testimony, expressed his confidence that his 2SR reforms would "remedy the existing problems," other interested parties had raised issues concerning his plans, not the least of which concerned his means to achieve his reorganization ends. In concluding remarks at the July 14 hearing of the Senate Committee on Homeland Security and Governmental Affairs, Senator Susan Collins, the chair of the panel, made the following comment to Secretary Chertoff:

> . . . as I review your plan, you are intending to make some truly fundamental changes to the department without requesting legislative authority to do so. Your list of legislative changes is very narrow.
>
> I think you're pushing the boundaries on that. And I hope you will work with the committee so that we can draft a more comprehensive reauthorization bill. I think many of the changes you're proposing really should be done by law and not just administratively. So, that's an issue we'll be pursuing with you.[60]

The issue underlying the comment made by Senator Collins involves Secretary Chertoff's interpretation of his reorganization authority. His interpretation is seemingly revealed in the text of a footnote in his July 13 notification letter to Congress, which states: "Section 872 of the Homeland Security Act of 2002 provides *broad* reorganization authority and permits the Secretary to alter or consolidate existing organizational units, to establish new organizational units or to allocate or reallocate functions within the Department."[61] Senator Collin's comment suggests that she does not regard the reorganization authority conveyed at Section 872 to be broad in scope, or at least not as broad as the Secretary was asserting. Moreover, the expressed agreement with her closing comments by Senator Joseph Lieberman, the ranking minority member of the committee, would appear to imply that he, too, does not regard the Secretary's reorganization authority to be broad.[62]

Section 872 of the Homeland Security Act (HSA) provides that the "Secretary may allocate or reallocate functions among the officers of the Department, and may establish, consolidate, alter, or discontinue *organizational units* within the Department, but only . . . after the expiration of 60 days after providing notice of such action to the appropriate congressional committees, which shall include an explanation of the rationale for the action," and subject to certain limitations specified in the section. These limitations include no abolition of "any agency, entity, organizational unit, program, or function established or required to be maintained by the [Homeland Security] Act" or "by statute."[63] Noting that the term "organizational units" is not defined in the act, a CRS legal analysis of the section is instructive regarding its scope.

> [I]n applying canons of statutory construction to the HSA, it appears Congress intended an *organizational unit* to *be* something smaller than an agency or other statutorily created entity. In the limitation provision of $872(b)(l), for example, Congress placed the term *organizational units* after the terms *agency* and *entity*, but before the terms *program* and *function*. This placement suggests Congress may have intended an *organizational unit* to be smaller than an *agency*

> and *entity* on the general assumption that things of a higher order are named at the beginning of an enumeration and that Congress does not intend to be superfluous. In Â§471(b) of the HSA, Congress again suggests that an *organizational unit* may be a small administratively created structure. Section 471(b) authorizes the Secretary (through the President's Reorganization Plan) to reorganize the functions or organizational units *within* the Bureau of Citizenship and Immigration Services. Because the provision places an organizational unit *within* the Bureau, it appears Congress intended the term to be something smaller than a bureau.
>
> The definition of the term *organizational units*, in essence, affects the Secretary's authority to reorganize DHS. Because Â§872(a) only allows the Secretary to establish, consolidate, alter, or discontinue *organizational units* within the Department, it might be argued that the Secretary is only allowed to establish, consolidate, alter, or discontinue units smaller than an agency, entity, or bureau. An *office*, *advisory committee*, or *laboratory*, for example, might arguably qualify as something smaller than an agency, entity, or bureau. Changes to structures other than *organizational units* would apparently need to be categorized as a reallocation of *functions* among the officers of the Department or be conducted pursuant to new legislative action to avoid an unauthorized action. Nonetheless, because the term organizational units is not defined in the HSA or discussed in any relevant legislative history, the scope of the term is not completely clear.[64]

Secretary Chertoff contends that his reorganization of DHS has resulted in a "flattening" of the department.[65] However, his plan substitutes one hierarchical directorate, Policy, for another, BTS, and transforms another directorate, IAP, into one for Preparedness. Furthermore, his restructuring results in some 27 lines of reporting to the Secretary/Deputy Secretary, instead of the previous 22 lines, with seven of these new lines coming from operating agencies. This new arrangement raises two issues which the minority members of the House Committee on Homeland Security articulated in a July 2005 report.

> While reorganization of operational functions is generally a good idea, if the Secretary's office is not structured in a way that will channel the oversight of all these agencies, a Secretary less able or influential than Secretary Chertoff may become overwhelmed.
>
> Additionally, such a "flatter" structure could lead to political staff in the Secretary's office having too much control over daily operations of law enforcement and screening agencies, such as ICE, CBP, and TSA.[66]

Henry B. Hogue and Keith Bea, *Federal Emergency Management and Homeland Security Organization: Historical Developments and Legislative Options*, CRS Report for Congress RL33369, June 1, 2006.

Homeland security is an outgrowth of decades of emergency preparedness and civil defense arrangements. Since the end of World War II, Congress and Presidents have debated, formulated, and revised administrative responsibilities for emergency management. Some of the issues debated during the past 60 years have included the following:

- What should be the boundaries or limitations of the matters subject to the jurisdiction of the agency, department, or office charged with the management of emergencies? Should certain emergencies (e.g., nuclear facility incidents, transportation accidents, hazardous material spills) be the jurisdiction of agencies with specialized resources?
- Is it necessary to distinguish between natural threats (floods, earthquakes, etc.) and those caused by human action or inaction? Are all attacks on the United States, whether by military action or terrorist strikes, "emergencies" that require a coordinated response from agencies other than the Department of Defense or the Department of Justice?
- How should federal policies be coordinated with state policies? What are the boundaries between federal responsibilities and those held by the states under the 10th Amendment to the Constitution?
- How should responsibility for new or emerging threats be established? Are federal statutory policies sufficient to enable the President and Administration officials to address adequately the unforeseen emergency conditions?

From the early years of the republic to 1950, Congress enacted legislation that directed federal disaster relief, largely on an ad hoc basis. Laws unique to each disaster authorized the amount of funds to be distributed, the type of federal equipment to be sent, or the personnel to be allocated to stricken areas.[67] For the most part, federal emergency assistance consisted of disaster relief authorized to provide specific relief to victims after disasters occurred.[68] Departments and agencies holding resources and personnel most pertinent to the given emergency (often the Armed Forces or federal financing entities) were charged by Congress with providing disaster assistance. As a general rule, the Office for Emergency Management (OEM) in the Executive Office of the President (EOP) provided advice to the President on emergency responsibilities.[69]

The federal approach changed when the Disaster Relief Act of 1950[70] became the first comprehensive federal disaster relief law. The act authorized federal agencies, "[in any major disaster . . . when directed by the President, to provide assistance" to states and localities by lending federal equipment, supplies, facilities, personnel, and other resources; "by distributing, through the Red Cross or otherwise, medicine, food, and other consumable supplies;" by donating surplus federal property; and "by performing . . . protective and other work essential for the preservation of life and property, clearing debris and wreckage," repairing and temporarily replacing damaged or destroyed local public facilities, and providing grants to states and localities for these purposes. After the President determined that a natural catastrophe had overwhelmed state and local capabilities, federal aid was to be provided. The act authorized the President to coordinate related agency activities, prescribe related rules and regulations, and "exercise any power or authority conferred on him [by the act] either directly or through such Federal agency as he may designate." The President and agencies were also given budget flexibility with regard to the repair or reconstruction of damaged or destroyed federal facilities. . . .

The decentralization of some emergency functions lasted five years. Reorganization Plan No. 1 of 1958 went into effect on July 1 of that year, vesting emergency management authorities in the President and establishing the locus of related activities in the EOP.[71] The plan transferred the functions of ODM and FCDA to the President, and it consolidated these two organizations into the Office of Defense and Civilian Mobilization (ODCM) in the EOP. The plan further provided that this new agency would be led by a director, deputy director, and three assistant directors, with appointments to each made by the President with the advice and consent of the Senate. The Civil Defense Advisory Council and its functions were also folded into the new office. . . .

Driven primarily by calls to reduce the size and reach of the EOP, in 1971, President Nixon proposed the establishment of four new departments with broad areas of responsibility. These departments would have subsumed many of the functions of existing federal departments and agencies. One of the proposed departments, the Department of Community Development, would have incorporated federal disaster assistance functions, but not the civil defense functions then being performed by OCD.[72] Congress held hearings, in 1972, on legislation to implement this plan, but the legislation was not enacted.

The reorganization concept, however, did not die with the legislation. The Nixon Administration subsequently pursued more limited reorganizations, including those in Reorganization Plan No. 1 of 1973. The plan, which went into effect on July 1, 1973, transferred certain functions out of the EOP.[71] Among other provisions, the plan abolished OEP, and nearly all functions previously vested in that office or its director were transferred to the President. The plan also abolished the Civil Defense Advisory Council, which had been established in 1950.

In his message accompanying the plan, President Nixon stated his intent to delegate the transferred functions to the Department of Housing and Urban Development (HUD), the General Services Administration (GSA), and the Department of the Treasury, and he did so by executive order[73] at the time the plan went into effect. Functions delegated to HUD included those relating to preparedness for, and relief of, civil emergencies and disasters. The Federal Disaster Assistance–Administration (FDAA) was established in HUD to administer disaster relief. GSA was given responsibilities related to continuity of government in the event of a military attack, to resource mobilization, and to management of national security stockpiles—duties assigned to the Office of Preparedness, later renamed the Federal Preparedness Agency, within GSA. The Treasury Department was given responsibility for investigations of imports that might threaten national security.

Also during the Nixon Administration, civil defense responsibilities moved. In 1972, the Secretary of Defense abolished the Office of Civil Defense, then located in the Department of the Army, and established, within the Office of the Secretary CRS-13 of Defense, the Defense Civil Preparedness Agency (DCPA). As the Nixon Administration pursued a policy of detente with the Soviet Union, the leaders of the Department of Defense and DCPA envisioned a role in assisting states and localities with preparations for both any possible nuclear attack or natural disaster.[74]

The dispersal of emergency functions among federal agencies did not resolve administration challenges. In fact, the 1973 plan exacerbated problems, according to many who had to work in the decentralized environment. Most notably, a National Governors' Association (NGA) study, conducted in 1977, reported, among other findings, that emergency preparedness and response functions were fragmented at the state and federal levels. It recommended a more comprehensive approach to emergency management that would include, in addition to preparedness and response, mitigation of hazards in advance of disasters and preparations for long-term recovery. In addition to calling for such comprehensive emergency management at the state level,[75] NGA endorsed organizational changes at the federal level that would promote a more comprehensive and coordinated approach to emergency management. It adopted, on February 28, 1978, a policy position that called for "consolidation of federal emergency preparedness and disaster relief responsibilities into one office [to] make the management and operation of the federal effort more effective and efficient." The NGA paper urged that the director of this new agency be charged with "additional responsibility for coordinating the efforts of all federal agencies that deal with emergency prevention, mitigation, any special preparedness and disaster response activities in other federal agencies, and short and long-term recovery assistance.[76]

Using existing statutory presidential reorganization authority, President Jimmy Carter submitted to Congress, on June 19, Reorganization Plan No. 3 of 1978, which proposed the merger of five agencies from the Departments of Defense, Commerce, and Housing and Urban Development, as well as GSA, into one new independent agency, the Federal Emergency Management Agency (FEMA).[77] The statutory authority[78] for such a reorganization plan provided for expedited congressional consideration and action, and, under that process, Congress allowed the plan to go into effect.[79]

On March 31, 1979, President Carter issued an executive order putting Reorganization Plan No. 3 of 1978 into effect.[80] FEMA was established as an independent agency, as of April 1, and some transfers were completed at that time. The order transferred certain functions to FEMA from the Department of Commerce (fire prevention and control, certain Emergency Broadcast System functions); the Department of Housing and Urban Development (flood insurance); and the President (other Emergency Broadcast System functions).

In July, the President issued a second executive order that transferred to FEMA additional functions from the Departments of Defense (civil defense) and Housing and Urban Development (federal disaster assistance), GSA (federal preparedness), and the Office of Science and Technology Policy (earthquake hazards reduction). The order also authorized

FEMA to coordinate "all civil defense and civil emergency planning, management, mitigation, and assistance functions," in addition to dam safety, "natural and nuclear disaster warning systems," and "preparedness and planning to reduce the consequences of major terrorist incidents." In addition, the order mandated establishment of the Federal Emergency Management Council, composed of FEMA and Office of Management and Budget Directors, and others as assigned by the President. . . .[81]

By the end of the Clinton Administration, FEMA had improved in many ways. Rather than suffering constant criticism from the media and political leaders, the agency was cited as a source of best practices in agency transformation in one study. Although the agency was credited with significant improvements, however, it was not free from challenges. In the final year of the Clinton presidency, the same study identified financial management and the disaster declaration process as two areas in need of improvement. . . .[82]

In the aftermath of Hurricane Katrina, committees in both chambers of Congress and the Bush Administration conducted investigations into governmental failures during the preparation for and response to the disaster. The House Select Bipartisan Committee to Investigate the Preparation for and Response to Hurricane Katrina[83] held nine hearings and, on February 15, 2006, issues a report on its findings. . . .[84]

The complexities of the emergency management process, the lack of a consistent and generally accepted statutory definition of "homeland security" in federal policies, and the difficulty of formulating administrative structures are some of the factors that challenge Members of the 109th Congress as they consider organizational options in the wake of Hurricane Katrina. Some contend that FEMA should be removed from DHS and reestablished as an independent federal entity. Others argue that it should remain in the department because the problems encountered after Hurricane Katrina reflect leadership and operational, not organizational, challenges. The preceding historical overview indicates that reorganizing federal emergency management, civil defense, or homeland security entities may address certain shortcomings and problems, but the challenges go beyond such changes. Remaining cognizant of a maxim of H.L. Mencken,[85] congressional agreement on the "best" organizational structure will be part of the solution to the question of how to ensure the effective implementation of emergency management responsibilities. The extent to which a reorganization contributes to the improvement of problems evident after Hurricane Katrina is a matter of debate. . . .

[I]ssues concerning the scope of responsibility, types of threats, federalism concerns, and assignment of responsibility . . . and other issues will shape congressional debate over the future of FEMA. An examination of the evolution of federal emergency management (now homeland security) policy since World War II reveals that some concepts have not changed. Just as the debate over the federal role in civil defense affected executive and legislative branch decisions on organizational options 50 years ago, the current debate over whether a terrorism focus detracts from natural disaster preparedness and response is likely to affect present day policymaking.

Charles R. Wise, "Organizing for Homeland Security After Katrina: Is Adaptive Management What's Missing?," *Public Administration Review*, Vol. 66, No. 3. (May–June, 2006), pp. 302–318.

The events of 9/11 kicked off one of the most active periods of reorganization in the history of the federal government. The enactment of the law creating the DHS was itself one of the largest reorganizations ever undertaken, but the department's creation is but one milestone in an ongoing process of organizing for homeland security—a process that Hurricane Katrina intersected. Numerous proposals are now being put forward in Congress and by the executive branch to reorganize federal agencies and intergovernmental relationships for homeland security; some are a direct result of Katrina, including everything from separating the Federal Emergency Management Agency (FEMA) from the DHS to giving the Department of Defense (DOD) a stronger role in emergency response. The questions are, first, how will the reorganization proposals intersect the ongoing process of organizing homeland security functions and programs in the federal government? Second, are any of them likely to cause significant changes in the behavior of the multiple organizations that perform the homeland security function in the United States?

This analysis will first discuss events leading up to Katrina that signaled organizational problems in the response system. An analysis of performance and organizational issues revealed by the governmental response to Katrina will then be presented. The article will then review and analyze the organizational changes that have been made in the federal government to address homeland security and the stage of development of the organizing process at the time Katrina hit, followed by a presentation of several proposals for reorganization suggested by policy makers in the aftermath of Katrina. This will be followed by an analysis of two organizational models that could provide a framework for the next round of reorganization. Finally, a management approach rooted in adaptive management will be presented for use in the ongoing process of organizing for homeland security.

Following the federal response to Hurricanes Andrew and Iniki in 1992, a Government Accountability Office (GAO) report issued findings chat forecast the experience during Katrina: "The problems we found with the federal strategy for catastrophic disasters such as inadequate damage and needs assessments, miscommunication, unclear legislative authority, and unprepared, untrained state and local responders—are more systematic than agency specific. Thus, they require solutions that cut across agencies and levels of government."[86]

Source: Charles R. Wise, "Organizing for Homeland Security After Katrina: Is Adaptive Management What's Missing?," Public Administration Review, Vol. 66, No. 3. (May–June, 2006), pp. 302–318, Blackwell Publishing.

About one year before Katrina, in July 2004, a tabletop exercise that simulated a category 3 hurricane hitting New Orleans, dubbed Hurricane Pam, was conducted in Louisiana. About 250 emergency-preparedness officials from more than 50 federal, state, local, and volunteer agencies participated. It involved issues such as developing an effective search-and-rescue plan, identifying short term shelters, devising housing options, and removing floodwater from New Orleans.

The exercise assumed that in advance of the storm, pleas for evacuation would only be half-successful. That was partly a recognition that as many as 100,000 people lived in households in which no one owned a car. A University of New Orleans survey released in July 2005, the month before Katrina, which found that although 60 percent of those asked at first said they would leave if public officials recommended an evacuation, on further questioning, only 34 percent of the residents of 12 coastal parishes would "definitely" leave. The message to the numerous New Orleans residents without a car provided on the City of New Orleans' Web site under "General Evacuation Guidelines" was, "If you need a ride, try to go with a neighbor, friend, or relative."[87] The assumption presumably was that cars were equally distributed throughout the city, which was actually not the case. The House Katrina Investigation Committee found that the implementation of lessons learned from Hurricane Pam was incomplete prior to Katrina.[7]

The picture that emerged is one in which the officials of federal, state, and local governments and the private sector did not have any specification of how their functions were supposed to interrelate, and they did not understand the principles and protocols in the NRP and NIMS framework that were supposed to guide their decision making. Furthermore, without a common operational picture or an adequate information system to track and share information, the officials had difficulty achieving unified command and control of the total shared response.

Katrina was the first-large scale test of the NRP and the NIMS. Although many individuals performed skillfully under the worst conditions, as President Bush[88] stated, "the system, at every level of government was not well-coordinated, and was overwhelmed in the first few days." Organizational problems related to planning, incident management, and the management of intergovernmental relations were experienced during the response to Katrina. . . .

The basic model underlying the planned role of federal agencies seemed to be at issue. That model assumes that state and local government in disaster response, with federal forces respond in to calls for assistance and thus arriving later. This model is now under scrutiny. Scott Wells,[89] the federal coordinating officer for Hurricanes Katrina and Rita in Louisiana, testified about the bottom-up emergency-response system . . . "This system works for small to medium disasters. It does not work so well for large disasters, and it falls apart for a catastrophic disaster. I think it is a fundamental problem with the response to Katrina." The House Katrina Investigation Committee concluded that catastrophic disasters require the federal response to be more proactive and not dependent on state requests for assistance.[7]

Members of Congress raised significant questions about who was really in charge of the total response effort, and why federal authorities did not take over the total effort when it became apparent that the capabilities of the state of Louisiana and local governments were failing. Secretary Chertoff testified that under the Homeland Security Presidential

Directives, he had a responsibility as the secretary of homeland security to manage incidents of national significance, but he had delegated this responsibility to the head of FEMA, Michael Brown. Though Brown was not named as principal federal officer by Secretary Chertoff until Tuesday, when the response was fully under way, Chertoff[90] testified that this was only a formal recognition of the delegation that he had made to Brown earlier.

The House Katrina Investigation Committee found considerable confusion existed over the authority of the Principal Federal Official (PFO) and the Federal Coordinating Officer (FCO) over who was authorized to direct federal operations and that FEMA officials acknowledged that the Department of Defense frequently operated on its own outside the established unified command.[7] The White House Report recommended that the confusion over Federal Officials authority be remedied by designating the PFO as the FCO.[91]

Regardless of the interpretation of the Catastrophic Incident Annex during Katrina, the issue of under what circumstances federal authority should supersede state authority has been placed on the agenda for homeland security reorganization, as has the question of what processes should exist to designate who is in charge during emergencies. Concern about the potential preemption of state authority by federal officials was heightened by questions surrounding the authority to order evacuations. R. David Paulison,[92] acting director of FEMA, testified that evacuation is a state and local issue and that FEMA does not make evacuation decisions. In fact, the NRP lists directing evacuations as a responsibility of local chief executive officers.[93] Federal officials can help facilitate evacuation procedures when the NRP is invoked, support search-and-rescue efforts, and provide technical assistance. In the event of catastrophic incidents, the federal government is to provide public health, medical, and mental health support at evacuation points and refugee shelters.[94] Scott Wells,[89] federal coordinating officer for Louisiana, testified that FEMA had received no preland fall requests for evacuation assistance. . . .

A major issue addressed in the creation of DHS was to specify *who* is in *charge*. Proponents of the department argued that it would fix accountability for homeland security in the federal government: The secretary of the department would have the power to act and not just coordinate, and various agency activities would be integrated by means of hierarchical organization.[95] Opponents argued that the non-terrorism-related functions of the agencies that were to be merged into the department, such as those of the Coast Guard and FEMA, would be neglected or subordinated to the terrorism mission.[96] Another question raised at the time about the coordinating capacity of the proposed department was whether its own operational responsibilities would be compatible with a government-wide coordinating role.[95] Many of the federal agencies with major homeland security responsibilities were not included in the merged department, such as the DOD, the Department of Justice, and the Central Intelligence Agency, among others. The issue was how Congress could write a law giving the head of a department of homeland security what amounts to presidential authority to direct the activities or realign the resources of other cabinet departments.[97] In the end, Congress did not do that. It did not give the DHS the power to direct the activities of other cabinet departments, but instead a mandate to call on other departments for their assistance in homeland security tasks. The department, in fact, was given little new legal authority to undertake its coordinating role.

However, trying to establish a departmental super-structure and begin some degree of integration of what had been 22 separate agencies became the major preoccupation of the department, with interdepartmental coordination taking a lower priority. As was pointed out prior to the passage of the legislation establishing the DHS, digesting transferred units is a longer and more arduous process than reorganizers often plan for.[95]

The GAO designated the department's transformation in 2003 as "high risk" because it faced enormous challenges in implementing an effective transformation process and building management capacity and because it faced a broad array of operational and management challenges that it inherited from its component legacy agencies.[98] In a review update in 2005, the GAO reported that implementation and transformation of the DHS remained high risk.[99] Just integrating the management systems of the department, including financial, human resources, information, and procurement systems, has been an enormous task occupying top leadership, and though the DHS has made some progress, it does not have a comprehensive strategy, with overall goals and a timeline, to guide management integration across functions and departments.[100]

Katrina revealed significant problems with regard to planning the defined roles of various departments and officials and their interactions. The primary planning document to guide all federal activities is the NRP, which was issued on January 6, 2005, and forms the basis for how the federal government coordinates with state, local, and tribal governments and the private sector during incidents. . . .

THE WAY FORWARD FOR HOMELAND SECURITY REORGANIZATION: TWO MODELS

What many of the suggested reorganization proposals have in common is a desire for greater centralization of authority, whether that means turning over more power to the president, elevating FEMA's director to a position directly under the president, or increasing the authority of DOD and other Federal departments. Granted, the desire to use military assets involves more than a wish to centralize authority, but even there, the desire for a unitary command structure is implicated. Following the same dynamic that was set in motion after 9/11, there is a renewed desire to strengthen hierarchy and fix accountability. The cry *who is in charge?* is raised once again, this time in the context of response and recovery from natural disasters. Apparently, the idea of creating the Department of Homeland Security as the one Federal agency to be in charge has given way to a search for a new organizational solution.

Hierarchical Model

The common tendency just identified rests on the well-known hierarchical model of organization. "Hierarchy uses authority (legitimate power) to create and coordinate a horizontal and vertical division of labor. Under hierarchy, knowledge is treated as a scarce resource and is therefore concentrated, along with the corresponding decision rights, in specialized functional units and at higher levels in the organization."[101] Among the advantages of this mode of organization are that it provides a form for employing large numbers of people and preserves unambiguous accountability for the work that they do. . . .[102]

Thus, the hierarchical model speaks particularly to the recurrent desire of federal policy makers to achieve stability in homeland security operations and to fix accountability. However, the idea of top-down (i.e., hierarchical) coordination to achieve cooperative effort that provides stability in a multiorganizational environment "rests on the notions that the organizations to be coordinated have been identified or can readily be identified by the headquarters coordinators; that the relationships of these organizations to each other are well understood; that agreement has been reached about what objectives will be accomplished by altering certain of these inter-organizational relationships; and that the authority and means to effectuate desired goals exist to alter the relationships in the desired direction. It assumes hierarchy will facilitate the implementation."[95] Many of these assumptions are questionable at present. . . .

Network Model

The network model starts with the presumption that public functional fields are populated by a variety of organizations, government agencies, nonprofits, and for-profits.[103–108] "Networks are structures of interdependence involving multiple organizations as parts thereof, where one unit is not merely the formal subordinate of the other in some larger hierarchical arrangement."[107] Although networks may take many forms, the type of interest here are public management networks, which are "those led or managed by government representatives as they employ multi-organizational arrangements for solving problems that cannot be achieved, or achieved easily, by single organizations."[103] The activities of public management networks are purposeful efforts to bring parts of organizations together to access knowledge and technology and to guide, steer, control, or manage.[109]

Purposeful efforts to bring parts of organizations together place an emphasis on facilitating interorganizational arrangements in which negotiation and adjustment occur, as opposed to restructuring formal organizations in an attempt to control all future contingencies. Accomplishing this does not mean that the design or structuring of governmental organizations is immaterial. From the network perspective, the emphasis is placed on structuring organizations and organizational arrangements in government, so that government organizations can play positive roles in setting the stage for other organizations in the interorganizational field to interact to accomplish common goals.[108]

One of the weaknesses of the network model is that accountability is diffused, and assessing performance means that not only must the performance of individual agencies be measured but also the joint action of multiple agencies.[110] Thus, in an area such as homeland security, when performance gaps are experienced, it is difficult for policy makers to isolate and pinpoint fault.

Major works of modern organization theory stress that there is no one structural model that is suitable for all situations. The work of major organization researchers stresses that key determinants of effective organizational structuring and functioning include the nature of the tasks the organizations are to perform and the nature of the environment in which they are embedded.[111–115]

Adaptive management is not a panacea for solving all the problems experienced during Katrina or all the problems in homeland security more generally. It is not a substitute for sufficient professional personnel who are well trained or for astute leadership and decision making. Establishing collaborative relationships also does not mean there is no room for formal organization. On the contrary, it means putting into place a formal framework that facilitates the interpersonal interaction across agency, intergovernmental, and intersectoral boundaries and at multiple levels. What is required for homeland security is for professionals at various levels to work across boundaries, plan and negotiate future activities, and communicate during operations to resolve unanticipated problems. From this perspective, the goal of any adjustments in formal structure is to facilitate collaborative decision making at multiple levels rather than fix decision making in one person or organization at each level, which is then expected to resolve the myriad issues that arise on an unpredictable basis.

References

David Alexander, 2002, *Principles of Emergency Planning and Management*, Oxford University Press, New York.

Albert Ashwood, October 6, 2005, Statement before the House Committee on Transportation and Infrastructure, Subcommittee on Economic Development, Public Buildings, and Emergency Management, Hearing on Recovering After Katrina: Ensuring that FEMA Is Up to the Task, Available from www.house.gov/transportation/, Accessed January 19, 2006.

Warren G. Bennis and Philip Slater, 1964, "Democracy is inevitable," *Harvard Business Review*, Vol. 64, No. 2, pp. 51–59.

Kathleen Blanco, December 14, 2005, Testimony before the House Select Bipartisan Committee to Investigate the Preparation for and Response to Hurricane Katrina, Hearing on Hurricane Katrina: Preparedness and Response by the State of Louisiana, Available from http://katrina.house.gov/, Accessed January 19, 2006.

Brookings Institution, September 8, 2005, *Hurricane Katrina: Where Do We Go From Here?* Brookings Institution Briefing, Available from www.brookings.edu/dybdocroot/comm/events/20050908.pdf, Accessed January 19, 2006.

Michael Brown, September 27, 2005, Testimony before the House Select Bipartisan Committee to Investigate the Preparation for and Response to Hurricane Katrina, Hearing on Hurricane Katrina: The Role of the Federal Emergency Management Agency, Available from http://katrina.house.gov/, Accessed January 19, 2006.

Carwile, William L. 2005. Testimony before the House Select Bipartisan Committee to Investigate the Preparation for and Response to Hurricane Katrina, Hearing on Hurricane Katrina: Voices from Inside the Storm. December 7, 2005, Available from http://katrina.house.gov/, accessed January 19, 2006.

Jim Q. Chen, Ted E. Lee, Ruidon Zhang, and Yue Jeff Zhang, 2003, "Systems Requirements for Organizing for Homeland Security," *Communications of the ACM*, Vol. 46, No. 12, pp. 73–78.

Michael Chertoff, 2005a, October 19, Testimony before the House Select Bipartisan Committee to Investigate the Preparation for and Response to Hurricane Katrina, Hearing on Hurricane Katrina: The Role of the Department of Homeland Security, Available from http://katrina.house.gov/, Accessed January 19, 2006.

Ross Clayton and Dan M. Haverty, 2005, "Modernizing Homeland Defense and Security," *Journal of Homeland Security and Emergency Management*, Vol. 2, No. 1, Article 7.

Louise Comfort, 1988, "Designing policy for action: the emergency management system," in *Managing Disaster: Strategies and Policy Perspectives*, Duke Press Policy Studies, Durham, NC.

Louise Comfort, 2002, "Rethinking security: organizational fragility in extreme events, special issue," *Public Administration Review*, Vol. 62, pp. 98–107.

Richard L. Daft, 1998, *Essential Organization Theory and Design*, South-Western College Publishing, Cincinnati, OH.

Tom Davis, October 27, 2005, Opening Statement, House Select Bipartisan Committee to Investigate the Preparation for and Response to Hurricane Katrina, Hearing on Hurricane Katrina: Preparedness and Response by the Department of Defense, the Coast Guard, and the National Guard of Louisiana, Mississippi, and Alabama, Available from http://katrina.house.gov/, Accessed January 19, 2006.

Stanley J. Freedberg, Jr., December 22, 2005, Hurricane response shows gaps in public-private coordination, Govexec.com, Available from www.govexec.com/story_page.cfm?articleid=33068&dcn=todaysnews, Accessed January 18, 2006.

Amanda Carol Graham and Linda E. Kruger, 2002, *Research in Adaptive Management: Working Relations and the Research Process*, U.S. Department of Agriculture, Forest Service. Research Paper No. PNW-RP-538, Portland, OR.

Crawford S. Holling (Ed.), 1978, *Adaptive Environmental Assessment and Management*, Whey, London.

Michael Jackson, November 9, 2005, Statement before the House Committee on Armed Services, Subcommittee on Terrorism, Unconventional Threats, and Capabilities.

Barry L. Johnson, 1999, "The role of adaptive management as an operational approach for resource management agencies," *Conservation Ecology*, Vol. 3, No. 2, p. 8.

Herbert Kaufman, 1985, *Time, Chance, and Organizations*, Chatham House, Chatham, NJ.

Anne M. Khademian, 2006, "The politics of homeland security," in David G. Kamien (Ed.), *The McGraw-Hill Homeland Security Handbook*, McGraw-Hill, New York, pp. 1091–1114.

Kai N. Lee, 1993, *Compass and Gyroscope: Integrating Science and Politics for the Environment*, Island Press, Washington, DC.

Louisiana Office of Homeland Security and Emergency Preparedness (OHSEP), 2004, "In Case of Emergency," Available from www.ohsep.louisiana.gov/newsrelated/incaseofemergencyexercise.htm, Accessed January 18, 2006.

Louisiana Office of Homeland Security and Emergency Preparedness (OHSEP), 2005, Survey: Many Won't Evacuate for a Category 3 Storm, Available from www.ohsep.Iouisiana.gov/newsrelated/manywon't evacuate.htm, Accessed January 18, 2006.

Paul McHale, November 9, 2005, Testimony before the House Select Bipartisan Committee to Investigate the Preparation for and Response to Hurricane Katrina, Hearing on Hurricane Katrina: Preparedness and Response by the State of Alabama, Available from http://katrina.house.gov/, Accessed January 19, 2006.

Rebecca McLain and Roben G. Lee, 1996, "Adaptive management: promises and pitfalls," *Environmental Management*, Vol. 20, No. 4, pp. 437–448.

National Governor's Association (NGA), October 13, 2005, *NGA Statement on Federalizing Emergencies.* News release.

Laurence O'Toole, Jr., and Kenneth Meier, 1999, "Modeling the impact of public management: implications of structural context," *Journal of Public Administration Research and Theory*, Vol. 9, No. 14, pp. 505–526.

Philip Parr, December 8, 2005, Testimony before the Senate Committee on Homeland Security and Governmental Affairs, Hearing on Hurricane Katrina; Perspectives of FEMAs Operations Professionals, Available from http://hsgat.senate.gov/index.cfm?Fuseaction=Hearings.Detail&HearingID=298, Accessed January 19, 2006.

Paul L. Posner, 2003, *Homeland Security and Intergovernmental Management: The Emergence of Protective Federalism.* Paper prepared for the Annual Meeting of the American Political Science Association, August 28–31, Philadelphia, PA.

Richard J. Rowe, November 9, 2005, Statement before the House Armed Services Committed Subcommittee on Terrorism, Unconventional Threats, and Capabilities.

Claire B. Rubin and John R. Herald, 2006, National Response Plan, the National Incident Management System, and the Federal Response Plan, in David G. Kamien (Ed.), *McGraw-Hill Homeland Security Handbook*, McGraw-Hill, New York, pp. 677–688.

James M. Saveland, 1989, *Knowledge-Based Systems Approach to Wilderness Fire Management*, PhD dissertation, University of Idaho.

Bruce Shindler, Kristin A. Cheek, and George J. Stankcy, 1999, *Monitoring and Evaluating Citizen–Agency Interactions: A Framework Developed for Adaptive Management.* U.S. Department of Agriculture, Forest Service, Portland, OR, Technical Report No. PNW-GTR-452.

Jeff Smith, December 14, 2005, Testimony before the House Select Bipartisan Committee to Investigate the Preparation for and Response to Hurricane Katrina, Hearing on Hurricane Katrina: Preparedness and Response by the State of Louisiana, Available from http://katrina.housc.gov/, Accessed January 19, 2006.

Chris Strohm, October 18, 2005a, *DHS Failed to Use Catastrophe Response Plan in Katrina's Wake*. Govexec.com, Daily Briefing, Available from www.govacc.com/dailyfed/1005/101805cl.htm, Accessed January 18, 2006.

U.S. Conference of Mayors, October 24, 2005, "The US. Conference of Mayors Hold Special Meeting on Emergency Response and Homeland Security," Press release.

U.S. Conference of Mayors, 2004b, National Incident Management System, Available from www.dhs.gov/interweb/assetlibrary/NIMS-90-web.pdf, Accessed January 19, 2006.

U.S. Department of Homeland Security, Office of the Inspector General, 2005, *A Review of the Top Officials 3 Exercise*, Government Printing Office. OIG-06-07, Washington, DC.

U.S. Department of Homeland Security, Office of the Inspector General, 2005a, *Homeland Security: Management of First Responder Grant Programs Has Improved but Challenges Remain*, Government Printing Office. GAO-05-121, Washington, DC.

U.S. Department of Homeland Security, Office of the Inspector General, 2005d, *Results Oriented Government: Improvements to DHS Planning Process Would Enhance Usefulness and Accountability*, Government Printing Office. GAO-05-300, Washington, DC.

U.S. Department of Homeland Security, Office of the Inspector General, 2005e, *Homeland Security: Agency Plans, Implementation and Changes Regarding the National Strategy Homeland Security*, Government Printing Office. GAO-05-33, Washington, DC.

U.S. Department of Homeland Security, Office of the Inspector General, 2005f, *Department of Homeland Security: A Comprehensive and Sustained Management Approach Needed to Achieve Management Integration*, Government Printing Office. GAO-05-139, Washington, DC.

U.S. Department of Homeland Security, Office of the Inspector General, 2005g, *Results-Oriented Government: Practices That Can Help Enhance and Sustain Collaboration among Federal Agencies*, Government Printing Office. GAO-06-15, Washington, DC.

U.S. Department of Homeland Security, Office of the Inspector General, February 1, 2006a, *Statement* by *Comptroller General David M. Walker on GAO's Preliminary Observations Regarding Preparedness and Response to Hurricanes Katrina and Rita,* before the Select Bipartisan Committee to Investigate the Organizing for Homeland Security 317, Reproduced with permission of the copyright owner. Further reproduction prohibited without permission, Preparation for and Response to Hurricanes Katrina and Rita. Government Printing Office. GAO-06-365R, Washington, DC.

U.S. Department of Homeland Security, Office of the Inspector General, March 8, 2006b, *Hurricane Katrina: GAO's Preliminary Observations Regarding Preparedness, Response and Recovery,* Statement by Comptroller General David M. Walker before the Senate Homeland Security and Governmental Affairs Committee, Government Printing Office. GAO-06-442T, Washington, DC.

William L. Waugh, 2002, *Leveraging Networks to Meet National Goals: FEMA and the Safe Construction Networks*, PricewaterhouseCoopers Endowment for the Business of Government, Washington, DC.

William L. Waugh and Richard T. Sylves, 2002, "Organizing the war on terrorism, special issue," *Public Administration Review*, Vol. 62, pp. 145–153.

Michael Greenberger, "The Role of the Federal Government in Response to Catastrophic Health Emergencies: Lessons Learned from Hurricane Katrina," University of Maryland School of Law, Legal Studies Research Paper, No. 2005-52.

> The only mistake we made with Katrina was not overriding the local government."[116]
>
> *Karl Rove, White House Deputy Chief of Staff*

> I am going to need all the help you can send me."[117]
>
> *Kathleen Babineaux Blanco, Governor, Louisiana, to President Bush*

The recent devastation and destruction by Hurricane Katrina in August 2005 in the Gulf Coast exemplifies the critical need for better federal, state, and local government planning, communication, and cooperation to achieve a coordinated and swift response to a catastrophic public health emergency. Relying on only one or two of these governmental entities, or an uncoordinated response by all three, to spearhead disaster relief only exacerbates the disaster, costing thousands of lives and billions of dollars.

Although many criticized the federal government response to Katrina, especially that of the Department of Homeland Security (DHS) and the Federal Emergency Management Agency (FEMA) as highly disorganized,[118] is nevertheless, now clear that the federal government has an integral role to play in responding to a catastrophic public health disaster. Statements made by President Bush in the immediate wake of Katrina[119] demonstrate that the federal government may even be more prepared to superimpose itself on states and local governments during a crisis. Indeed, federal officials (including President Bush) have also acknowledged the need for a "swifter federalization of response operations and deployment of military force."[120] Accordingly, emergency response planners need to be ever more mindful and aware of the role and power of the federal government in disaster response and the interaction between federal, state, and local authorities in these emergency situations. . . .

Under direction of Congress through the Homeland Security Act[121] and of the President through Homeland Security Presidential Directive 5 (HSPD-5),[122] DHS promulgated a "National Response Plan (NRP) in December 2004 further evidencing the broad reach of the federal government. The NRP is "an all-discipline, all-hazards plan that establishes a single, comprehensive framework for the management of domestic incidents [and] provides the structure and mechanisms for the coordination of Federal support to State, local, and tribal incident managers and for exercising direct Federal authorities and responsibilities."[123] The NRP recognizes that any time the President declares an emergency under the Stafford Act, it is an "Incident of National Significance,"[124] calling into play broad federal oversight mandated by that plan. While it is now widely acknowledged that the *NRP* was triggered belatedly.[125] Secretary Michael Chertoff did finally activate it by declaring an "Incident of National Significance" as a result of the destruction caused by Hurricane Katrina.[126]

Not only does the NRP contemplate federal involvement, but the plan dictates proactive federal response even without requests for assistance from the states. It expressly provides that "[s]tandard procedures regarding requests for assistance may be expedited or, under extreme circumstances, *suspended* in the immediate aftermath of an event of catastrophic magnitude."[127] The *NRP* also provides for federal law enforcement assistance and immediate response authority for "[i]mminently serious conditions [when] time does not permit approval from higher headquarters."[128] When this situation exists, the *NRP* makes it clear that the Department of Defense (DOD) has authorized local military commanders and responsible officials from DOD to "take necessary action to respond to requests of civil authorities consistent with the Posse Comitatus Act (PCA)."[129] Indeed, President Bush recognized this power under the *NRP* in his September 15 speech in Jackson Square, New Orleans by stating that "a challenge on this scale requires greater federal authority and a broader role for the armed forces -the institution of our government most capable of massive logistical operations on a moment's notice."[130]

The NRP also emphasizes the importance of deploying the federal National Disaster Medical System (NDMS), a coordinated effort by the Department of Health and Human Services (HHS), DHS, the Department of Veteran Affairs (VA), and the DOD.[131] The NDMS works in collaboration with the states and other appropriate public and private entities in providing medical response, patient evacuation, and definitive medical care to victims and responders of a public health emergency.[132]

This federal medical assistance is deployed through Emergency Support Function (ESF) Annex #8, "Public Health and Medical Services," within the NRP. ESF #8 provides for federally directed medical assistance to supplement state and local resources in response to an incident of national significance.[133] Katrina, as the first incident of national significance under the NRP, demonstrated, even when belatedly dep1oyed,[134] the actual effectiveness of these federal mechanisms for response. . . .

Hurricane Katrina is a prime example of the impact of a catastrophic public health emergency on interstate commerce.[135] In the immediate aftermath of the hurricane, the destruction sent thousands of victims across state borders in search of food and shelter and required delivery of relief workers and supplies from across the nation.[136]

In the extended aftermath, commerce in several industries was drastically affected.[137] For example, the hurricane severely impaired substantial portions of the country's oil refineries and curtailed offshore production of oil and gas.[138] As a result, the nation is currently experiencing its highest rates in gasoline prices in recent history.[139] On August 31, the White House decided to release oil from the nation's emergency stockpiles to meet shortages caused by Hurricane Katrina.[140] In response to this announcement alone, the price of crude oil fell in trading.[141] Therefore, the suggestion that the federal government's role is limited in a catastrophic public health emergency because of commerce clause constraints is unconvincing. Moreover, the broad array of federal legislation programs that address catastrophic health emergencies itself evidences Congress' strong belief that it has the constitutional power to address these kinds of national crises.[142]

As an example, the help given by the federal government in the wake of Katrina included: deploying more than 72,000 unified federal personnel; housing approximately 89,400 people in shelters nationwide; completing roughly 55,000 housing damage inspections; rescuing more than 33,000 lives; restoring more than 73% of affected drinking water systems in Louisiana and 78% in Mississippi; and serving more than 12 million hot meals and more than 8.2 million snacks to survivors.[143] These federal actions and the implementation of policies and programs under the NRP[144] demonstrate the strong level of commitment and involvement by the federal government in preparation and response to catastrophic public health emergencies.

Accordingly, whether adopting the Model Act or using existing public health laws or other forms of new laws, states must plan for response to a catastrophic event with an eye toward the federal government. They must do so to be aware of the substantial assistance the federal government can provide. They must do so to be prepared to advise the federal government of the role the state wants it to play. In the absence of keeping federal government in mind, states will not know what to ask from the federal government for assistance, as evidenced by Governor Blanco's highly generalized request of President Bush ("I'm going to need all the help you can send me").[145] Even worse, the doctrine of Karl Rove may be followed—just take over the response and ignore the states and localities.[146] States should be prepared to fight such a takeover if they feel able to lead a response or invite federal leadership if they believe they are overwhelmed.

Hurricane Katrina has hopefully taught an important lesson—that the federal government, cannot be ignored; its resources and powers must be acknowledged by states to ensure a healthy balance between the state and federal role during a catastrophic public health emergency.

Patrick Roberts, "FEMA After Katrina: Redefining Responsiveness," *Policy Review* (June–July 2006).

Before issuing more cries for radical change at FEMA, reformers should look to the lessons of the agency's reorganization in the 1990s, which focused on natural disasters rather than national security. Its turbulent history shows that while the agency can marshal resources for natural disasters and build relationships with states and localities, it lacks sufficient resources to take on too many tasks. Today, FEMA faces a protean terrorist threat and an increasing array of technological hazards. To address contemporary threats, the agency must hone its natural disaster expertise and delegate authority for disaster response to states and localities. True, delegation runs the risk of returning to the days of ad hoc disaster preparedness, when government poured money into recovery without reducing vulnerability to disasters. Nevertheless, decentralizing response functions is the best way to prepare for an increasingly complex array of disasters, as the risks and strategies for recovery for different kinds of disasters vary so dramatically from region to region.

When viewed against the history of emergency management, the success FEMA enjoyed in the 1990s was the exception, not the rule. For most of the century, states and localities rushed to the aid of disaster-stricken citizens, and the federal government helped overwhelmed communities with recovery. As a result, the federal government sent supplies, surveyors, and money to help rebuild the same regions over and over again. Federal involvement dates from at least the San Francisco earthquake of 1906, which registered an estimated 8.3 on the Richter scale and left 478 people dead and more than 250,000 homeless. The disaster came in two parts, one natural and the other a result of poor planning. The earthquake was unavoidable, but the fires that swept through neighborhoods stuffed with wooden buildings could have been prevented had San Franciscans used other materials or not built them so close together. President Theodore Roosevelt was alarmed by the disaster and pledged federal troops to help, but local officials, not federal authorities, were always in control, if unofficially. On their own initiative, Army commanders stationed in the area ordered troops to protect the Treasury and essential services during the chaos after San Francisco burned. The mayor, not the president, issued 5,000 handbills telling citizens that he had (illegally) ordered federal troops and local police to shoot looters.[147] (Few people were actually shot on this order.) Much later, the federal government directed aid to the Bay Area through the Red Cross.

The first broad and permanent legislation defining federal authority in disasters was the Civil Defense Act of 1950, which centralized programs for defense against nuclear attack.

Source: Patrick Roberts, "FEMA After Katrina: Redefining Responsiveness," *Policy Review*, (June–July 2006). Courtesy of Policy Review, Hoover Institution at Stanford University.

Civil defense programs might have helped to scare the Soviets into thinking that the U.S. was serious about nuclear war, but they would never have been much help during an all-out attack. The federal government's involvement in natural disasters, meanwhile, was mostly ad hoc and too little, too late. A series of ferocious disasters in the 60s and 70s caused great destruction: the Alaskan earthquake (1964), Hurricane Betsy (1965), Hurricane Camille (1969), the San Fernando earthquake (1971), and Hurricane Agnes (1972). . . .[148]

FEMA owned technology that could have helped in 1992, but much of it was unavailable and restricted to national security uses. State-of-the-art satellite phones were controlled by the national security division, while FEMA's hurricane response team, with communications down, resorted to buying Radio Shack walkie-talkies.[149] FEMA kept asking the states and localities what they needed, and Florida officials kept saying that they needed everything, anything–yesterday. With the situation in chaos, President George H.W. Bush replaced the FEMA director and ordered Andrew Card, the secretary of transportation, to take charge of the recovery along with a cadre of generals. FEMA lore holds that the agency's poor performance in response to Andrew was enough to cost Bush re-election. . . .

Unlike the emergency management crises of the 1970s that spawned haphazard changes, Andrew led to a comparatively comprehensive reorganization. Academics and emergency management professionals suggested a battery of reforms that were adopted by the agency's new director, James Lee Witt, who successfully lobbied Congress and the president for patience and support. Chief among the changes was the elimination of the agency's national security functions, and with it many of the appointed positions that had made FEMA a dumping ground for political appointees with little emergency management experience. Congress streamlined its oversight accordingly, easing the agency's relationship with relevant committees. As Witt trimmed FEMA's Cold War inheritance, he built the foundation for a legacy of his own of hazard mitigation and crisis management.

Witt was, on the one hand, one of the many "friends of Bill" who accompanied Clinton from Arkansas to the White House. While previous FEMA directors might have struggled for time with the president, Witt was invited to the White House for movie nights. On the other hand, Witt was a Southern Democrat with emergency management experience and extraordinary political skill. He never attended college, but he made a career as a construction-company entrepreneur and was elected to a county judgeship at age 34. . . .

Upon taking office, Witt asked Clinton for the authority to make changes. During his first months on the job, he spoke to the chairs of the 20 committees that had a stake in FEMA's reorganization. He convinced skeptical members of Congress that FEMA could work to their advantage if it provided constituents affected by disaster with an immediate and effective response for which politicians could receive credit. Witt followed bold promises with bold actions. . . .

While the 1993 reorganization focused and improved FEMA's capacity to address natural disasters, it neglected other responsibilities. It was precisely FEMA's celebrated focus on all hazards that caused the agency to put civil defense and terrorism on the back burner. As one longtime FEMA employee put it, "Some will say he introduced all hazards. I say he reduced the importance of some hazards at the expense of others." In shifting resources to programs that could be more generally applied to natural hazards, Witt scaled back the agency's national security role and left it ill-prepared to combat the emerging terrorist threat. Between 1998 and 2001, the Hart-Rudman Commission looked for a cornerstone for a new domestic security effort but found FEMA's culture and capabilities insufficient for taking a lead role in counterterrorism.[150]

While the agency was applauded for its quick response to natural disasters, some of its acclaim came from people who simply received more money for recovery under the Witt regime than they had before. The president declared more disasters per year after 1993, including "snow emergencies" for which previous administrations had refused aid. Disaster funds were more likely to flow to politically important districts where the president or members of FEMA's oversight committee faced a competitive election.[151] Large disasters always received federal aid, but political interests determined whether smaller ones would receive federal dollars or states would be left to make do on their own. . . .

Though FEMA could have used an infusion of experienced professionals, simply repeating the Witt recipe for reorganization would not have addressed the challenges of the twenty-first century. Career FEMA employees, like civil servants across government, began to retire in droves. At the same time, oversight committees began to worry that programs for mitigation and recovery lacked proper procedures to ensure that money was being spent wisely. Terrorism posed the greatest challenge. Witt initially had refused to take on more responsibility for terrorism preparedness because he thought the threat was too unpredictable for the agency to be able to address effectively. After 9/11, the country had no choice but to consider terrorism.

Most attempts to assign blame for Katrina focus on the Bush administration or poor state and local government response. While there is plenty of blame to go around, such a focus is misdirected. Reformers must attempt to understand FEMA's shortcomings in an effort to retool for the future.

The agency dug its own hole in the decade leading up to Katrina because of ever-greater public expectations for disaster relief, ever-greater specialization of preparedness and mitigation programs, and confusion about how terrorism fit into the all-hazards model. People had not always looked to the federal government for help during disasters, but during the twentieth century the level of assistance expected from the federal government before and after a disaster ratcheted upwards. The media broadcast images of FEMA agents rushing to disaster sites and FEMA relief workers helping communities rebuild, all of which reinforced the public's belief that the federal government owed the disaster-stricken public. Stories of federal relief were far more widespread than stories of investors and local governments choosing to invest in hurricane- or flood-prone areas, gambling that the federal government would bear the cost of rebuilding.

Terrorism complicated FEMA's efforts to respond to natural disasters, not by seizing resources formerly directed to natural disasters, but by adding new considerations to preparedness efforts. The numbers and amounts of grants devoted to emergency preparedness and natural disasters increased slightly from 2001 to 2005.[152] Authoritative federal response plans invoked the all-hazards language, but the language was not reflected in organizational structures at lower levels of government. Enough resources flowed to natural disaster preparedness, but not enough attention was devoted to reconciling the different threats posed by terrorism and natural disasters, especially at the state and local levels. In a terrorist attack the FBI and law enforcement agencies take the lead because the disaster is a crime scene. In a natural disaster, however, the sole focus is rescue and recovery, tasks best left to emergency managers. When Katrina struck, states and localities had been crafting plans and procedures for terrorist attacks but in many cases had failed to refine plans for natural disaster response. . . .

After 1993, FEMA reversed course and showed that it could be both effective and popular. The agency jettisoned its civil defense legacy and crafted a focus on "all hazards, all phases" emergency management that in practice emphasized natural disasters. When forced to address new concerns, however, from terrorism to the need for more accountable disaster relief, FEMA fell short. Emergency management has become too complex for a FEMA federal agency to coordinate. Only states and localities are able to weigh many-faceted concerns about a range of disasters and develop appropriate strategies. New Orleans, for example, faces far different hazards from those facing a northeastern industrial city with a similar population and demographics. In the wake of Katrina, reformers should resist the all-too-easy temptation to centralize control in the national bureaucracy and instead grant more power and responsibility for disaster preparedness, response, and recovery to agencies further down the federal ladder.

Still, decentralization poses the risk of returning to the days when emergency management was ad hoc and the federal government provided too much, too late to communities after a disaster struck. Disasters are, by definition, rare events that overwhelm the capacity of normal public institutions and practices. States and localities have little incentive to prepare for 100-year floods, yet such floods occur with alarming frequency in the United States.

Disaster management poses a paradox: If states and localities are to take more responsibility for disaster preparedness and response, the federal government must also take more responsibility for disaster preparedness. FEMA is best equipped to assemble best practices and encourage their adoption through the granting process so that communities reduce their vulnerability before disaster occurs. Reforming emergency management should proceed along three lines: focusing FEMA's tasks on emergency management, reviving the "all hazards, all phases" process, and giving states and localities more responsibility for disaster preparedness and response. . . .

FEMA's first major organizational challenge was to transform itself from a civil defense agency into a natural disasters agency. The agency faces a similarly formidable task today as it attempts to improve its natural disasters capability while not shortchanging the terrorist threat. While the agency can learn from the past, the solutions that worked in the 1990s do not translate directly to the present dilemma. FEMA faces the challenge of handing more responsibility to states and localities while taking a greater role in preparedness and mitigation than it has ever assumed. . . .

Understanding emergency management as a process will be key to reform if two groups can be given more responsibility. First, states and localities must invest more in planning and in reducing vulnerability. The federal government can provide incentives for planning through the granting process, and it can provide disincentives for poor planning by making states and localities bear more of the cost of disasters. Second, if individual emergency managers understand their jobs as part of an "all hazards, all phases" process, they might make decisions based less on turf claims and more on a desire to reduce the damage that disasters wreak on citizens who deserve better from their governments.

Jeffrey Manns, "Reorganization as a Substitute for Reform: The Abolition of the INS," *The Yale Law Journal*, Vol. 112, No. 1. (October 2002), pp. 145–152.

September 11th and the events that followed highlighted the shortcomings of our nation's immigration policies and their enforcement. Gaffes, such as the issuance of student visas to two of the hijackers on the six-month anniversary of 9/11, reinforced public perceptions that the Immigration and Naturalization Service (INS) is an agency beyond repair.' Critics from both ends of the political spectrum have condemned the INS for its failures. As House Minority Leader Richard A. Gephardt stated, "We saw in the 9/11[153] incident some of the problems in the INS that many of us had seen before. . . . It became clear, I think, to everybody in the country and in the Congress that we needed reform."[154]

Consensus on the need for reform may be clear, but the question remains of what shape reform should take. Unfortunately, politicians have taken the path of least resistance by focusing on reorganization plans, rather than tackling the substantive issues that plague the INS.[155] The Bush Administration and both houses of Congress have differed about what form a reorganization should assume.[156] Their proposals share a misguided faith, however, in the efficacy of agency restructurings as a vehicle for reform.

These proposals are the latest variation on an old theme.[157] Reorganizations have long served as politicians' tool of choice for reforming the American administrative state.[158] Such plans do have the potential to effect widespread change by shaking up agency culture and reallocating management responsibilities and personnel. At the same time, the literature on reorganizations casts doubt on their efficacy as a vehicle for reform. . . .

The original version of the Homeland Security Act proposed by the Administration seeks to merge the INS into the new Office of Homeland Security. This proposal would vest control of the INS in the Undersecretary for Border and Transportation Security and combine the INS with the Coast Guard, the Customs Service of the Treasury Department, and the Transport Security Administration of the Department of Transportation, as well as parts of other agencies.[159] The Administration's proposal is silent as to what internal changes in the INS may be necessary to effect this merger.[160] This proposal also does not address whether this plan is designed to redress the problems facing the INS or only to address broader national security challenges. . . .

While all of the proposals have shortcomings, the Administration's Homeland Security Bill is noteworthy for the fact that it ignores the thorny problems of reforming the INS in

---

Source: Jeffrey Manns, "Reorganization as a Substitute for Reform: The Abolition of the INS," *The Yale Law Journal*, Vol. 112, No. 1. (October 2002), pp. 145–152. Reprinted by permission of The Yale Law Journal Company, Inc. and The William S. Hein Company.

favor of focusing on a macro "solution" to America's homeland security challenges.[161] A one-stop shop for point of entry controls that consists of more than 169,000 federal workers and a $37.4 billion budget looks impressive on paper.[162] Combining the Coast Guard, the Customs Service, the INS, and many other agencies signifies the Administration's commitment to homeland security concerns and may be a first step toward enhancing inter-agency communication and coordination. The creation of this superagency may result in little more, however, than forcing a host of agencies to order new letterhead and change their seals. Worse still, the Department of Homeland Security may become a bureaucratic juggernaut, whose unmanageability may magnify the shortcomings of each component agency.

As importantly, the danger exists that the relocation of the INS into the Department of Homeland Security will subordinate all other goals and functions of the INS to national security concerns. This outcome may appease the popular desire for the appearance of action on homeland security. In the long term, however, this focus may create many more problems for immigration policy than it solves, if only by obscuring the importance of other pressing concerns facing the INS.

The amended Homeland Security Bill attempts to avert this danger by retaining the service functions of the INS in a new bureau within the DOJ.[163] By "solving" one problem, this approach may create a more significant one by allowing inconsistencies to arise between the service and enforcement bureaus. Relocating only enforcement functions to the Department of Homeland Security may accentuate the shift of the enforcement focus toward national security issues by reducing internal policymakers' awareness of service concerns. September 11th helped to highlight the importance of immigration issues. In the long term, however, one ironic legacy of this tragedy may be a lower profile for immigration issues, if separate immigration bureaus are subsumed under larger agencies. . . .

Crafting an effective immigration policy requires reconsidering the extent to which economic, foreign policy, cultural, or national security interests should be the national priority. An immigration policy designed to stop potential terror threats will look very different from one designed to halt rising levels of illegal immigration. A visa policy that favors tourism and respect the need for skilled and unskilled laborers will be far different from one focused on national security or foreign policy concerns. Clarifying the priorities of our immigration policy in the wake of 9/11 will do more to enhance U.S. immigration policy than any restructuring plan.

In the short term, a reorganization plan for the INS may be a necessary evil to assuage the popular desire for action. Nonetheless, politicians should do more than make hollow promises of reform through reorganization. They should also be leading a national debate to redefine the priorities for immigration policy. September 11th provided an occasion to consider far-reaching reforms to immigration policy, and neither politicians nor the American people should be content to let reorganization substitute for reform.

NOTES FOR CHAPTER 6

1. Ashton B. Carter, 2001, "Keeping the Edge: Managing Defense for the Future," in Ashton B. Carter and John P. White, *Keeping the Edge,* MIT Press, Cambridge, MA, pp. 1–26.
2. Address by President Bill Clinton at the U.S. Naval Academy, May 22, 1998, White House fact sheet, Combating Terrorism, PDDINSC-62, Protection against Unconventional Threats to the Homeland and Americans Overseas, May 22, 1998, Available from http://fas.org/~/offdocs/pdd-62.hh; and White House fact sheet, PDDINSC-63, Critical Infrastructure Protection, May 22, 1998, Available from http://~.fas.org/up/offdws/pdd/pdd-63.hm.
3. See Joseph S. Nye, Jr., Philip D. Zelikow, and David S. King (Eds.), 1996, *Why People Don't Trust Government,* Haward University Press, Cambridge, MA, p. 9, and references therein.
4. Hart-Rudman Commission, Gary Hart, Warren B. Rudman, Anne Armstrong, et al. February 15, 2001, *Road Map for National Security: Imperative for Change: The Phase III Report of the U.S. Commission on National Security/21st Century,* Washington, D.C.
5. This does not rule out the possibility of creating an agency that combines the functions of such border-related agencies as the Coast Guard, Border Patrol, Immigration and Naturalization Service, and Customs. Accomplishing this bureaucratic feat, however useful, would require the full-time attention of a senior manager with presidential and congressional support. If Governor Ridge were to assume this task, he would have no time for anything else.
6. Raymond J. Decker, April 24, 2001, *Combating Terrorism,* statement prepared for the U.S. House of Representatives, Subcommittee on Economic Development, Public Buildings, and Emergency Management, *Hearing on Combating Terrorism: Options to Improve the Federal Response,* 107th Congress, 1st session.
7. U.S. House Select Bipartisan Committee to Investigate the Preparation for and Response to Hurricanes Katrina and Rita, February 15, 2006, *A Failure of Initiative: The Final Report of the Select Bipartisan Committee to Investigate the Preparation for and Response to Hurricanes Katrina and Rita.* Government Printing Office, Washington, DC.
8. Anthony Williams, November 1, 2001, Mayor Anthony Williams, *Online Newshour,* Available from http://www.pbs.orglnewshour/bb/terrorism/ july-dec01/williams11-1.html, Accessed January 29, 2002.
9. David H. Rosenbloom, 2000, *Building a Legislative Centered Public Administration,* University of Alabama Press, Tuscaloosa, AL.
10. Lee Hamilton, October 12, 2001, Homeland Security, Statement prepared for the U.S. Senate, Committee on Governmental Affairs, *Hearing on Legislative Options to Strengthen National Homeland Defense,* 107th Congress, 1st session.
11. U.S. Commission on National Security/21st Century (a.k.a. Hart-Rudman Commission), February 15, 2001, *Road Map for National Security: Imperative for Change: The Phase III Report of the US Commission on National Security/21st Century,* Available from http://www.nssg.gov.
12. Charles G. Boyd, October 12, 2001, Statement prepared for the U.S. Senate, Committee on Governmental Affairs, *Hearing on Legislative Options to Strengthen National Homeland Defense,* 107th Congress, 1st session.
13. Harold Seidman, 1998, *Politics, Position, and Power: The Dynamics of Federal Organization,* 5th ed., Oxford University Press, New York.
14. George W. Bush, October 8, 2001, Executive Order no. 13228, Available from http://www.whitehouse.gov/news/releases/2001/10/2001008-2.html.
15. Governor Tom Ridge of Pennsylvania was sworn in as director of OHS on October 8, 2001, Available from http://www.whitehouse.gov/news/releases/2001/10/20011008-3.html. He was later sworn in as secretary of DHS on January 24, 2003, Available from http://www.whitehouse.gov/news/releases/2003/01/20030124-5.html.

16. Senator J. I. Lieberman, May 2, 2002, National Homeland Security and Combating Terrorism Act of 2002: Bill summary, Lieberman press office, Available from http://www.senate.gov/~Lieberman/press.
17. J. McGee, November 4, 2001, "An intelligence giant in the making: anti-terrorism law likely to bring domestic apparatus of unprecedented scope," *Washington Post*, A-04, final edition.
18. The author is indebted to the expertise and assistance of Allen Lomax, senior evaluator with the U.S. General Accounting Office, who served on assignment to Congress during the crucial period of debate and negotiations over the shape and substance of the new Department of Homeland Security.
19. George W. Bush, July 2002b, National strategy for homeland security, Available from http://www.whitehouse.gov/homeland/books/index.html.
20. George W. Bush, November 25, 2002a, Department of Homeland Security reorganization plan, Available from http://www.dhs.gov/dhspublic/display?theme=9.
21. U.S. Office of Homeland Security, 2002, National strategy for homeland security, Government Printing Office, Washington, DC.
22. 59 Stat. 613.
23. See *INS v. Chadha*, 462 U.S. 919 (1983).
24. 98 Stat. 3192; 5 U.S.C. 901–12.
25. U.S. Office of the Vice President, 1993, *From Red Tape to Results: Creating a Government That Works Better and Costs Less: Report of the National Performance Review*, Government Printing Office, Washington, DC.
26. 31 U.S.C. 1347.
27. See *Federal Register* 66, October 10, 2001, 51812–51817.
28. *Federal Register* 66, October 10, 2001, 51812–51817.
29. E.O. 13228, sec. 3(g), *Federal Register* 66, October 10, 2001, 51814.
30. Representative Thornberry had introduced legislation (ILR. 1158) on March 21, 2001, to establish a National Homeland Security Agency that closely resembled his subsequent departmental proposal, but the organization was not denominated by a department and seemingly did not have Cabinet status.
31. Eric Pianin and Bill Miller, January 23, 2002, "For Ridge, Ambition and Realities Clash," *Washington Post*, pp. Al, A10.
32. Dave Boyer, February 27, 2002, "Ridge reluctant to testify in Senate," *Washington Times*, p. A4; Alison Mitchell, March 5, 2002, "Congressional hearings: letter to Ridge is latest jab in fight over balance of powers," *New York Times*, p. A1; Mark Preston, April 18, 2002, "Byrd holds firm," *Roll Call*, pp. 1, 26.
33. George Archibald, March 22, 2002, "Panel ties funding to Ridge testimony," *Washington Times*, pp. A1, A1.4; George Archibald, March 23, 2002, "White House mollifies House panel," *Washington Times*, pp. A1, A4.
34. Bill Miller, April 4, 2002, "Ridge will meet informally with 2 house committees," *Washington Post*, p. A15; George Archibald, April 11, 2002, "Ridge attends private meeting on hill," *Washington Times*, p. A4; Elizabeth Becker, April 11, 2002, "Ridge briefs house panel, but discord is not resolved," *New York Times*, p. A17; Bill Miller, April 11, 2002, "From Bush officials, a hill overture and a snub," *Washington Post*, p. A27; Amy Fagan, April 12, 2002, "Democrats irked by Ridge's closed house panel meeting," *Washington Times*, p. A6; Stephen Dinan, May 3, 2002, "Ridge briefing called 'stunt,' " *Washington Times*, p. A9; Bill Miller, May 3, 2002, "On homeland security front, a rocky day on the hill," *Washington Post*, p. A25.
35. Elizabeth Becker, May 3, 2002, "Big visions for security post shrink amid political drama," New York *Times*, pp. Al, A16.
36. *NewsHour Focus*, "Newsmaker: Tom Ridge," May 9, 2002, transcript available from *NewsHour* Index, Available from http://www.pbs.org/newsho~ir/newshourinclex.html.

37. Editorial, May 12, 2002, "Faltering on the home front," New *York Times*, p. 14.
38. U.S. Congress. Senate Committee on Governmental Affairs, 2002a, National homeland security and combating terrorism act of 2002, 107th Congress, 2nd session, S. Rept. 107–175 to accompany S. 2452, Government Printing Office, Washington, DC.
39. U.S. Congress. Senate Committee on Governmental Affairs, 2002b, President Bush's proposal to create a Department of Homeland Security, 107th Congress, 2nd session, hearings, Government Printing Office, Washington, DC.
40. See Dave Boyer, June 20, 2002, "Democrats call terror bill 'ruse' to fire civil workers," *Washington Times,* pp. Al, A14; Audrey Hudson, June 21, 2002, "Ridge defends hiring proposal," *Washington Times,* p. A14; Tim Kauffman, June 24, 2002, "Critics see few job protections at new agency," *Federal Times,* p. 5; Tim Kauffman, June 24, 2002, "Retirements threaten homeland security staffing," *Federal Times,* p. 3; Ellen Nakashima and Edward Walsh, June 7, 2002, "Unions say they will oppose consolidation; critics say reorganization may not be effective," *Washington Post,* p. A25.
41. James P. Pfiffner, 1991, "Can the president manage the government? should he?" in James P. Pfiffner (Ed.), *The Managerial Presidency,* Brooks/Cole, Pacific Grove, CA.
42. Peri E. Arnold, 1998, *Making the Managerial Presidency: Comprehensive Reorganization Planning, 1905–1996,* 2nd ed. University of Kansas Press, Lawrence, KS.
43. Annette D. Beresford, 2004, "Homeland security as an American ideology: implications for U.S. policy and action," *Journal of Homeland Security and Emergency Management,* Vol. 1, No. 3, pp. 1–21, Available from http://www.bepress.com/jhsem/vol1/iss3/301.
44. National Defense Panel, December 9, 1997, *Transforming Defense Security in the 21st Century,* Available from http://www.fas.org/man/docs/ndp/exec.htm, Accessed February 19, 2006.
45. The National Commission on Terrorism (2000) has published the full text of the report.
46. See Gilmore Commission (1999–2003) for the full version of reports 1–5.
47. Hart Rudman Commission, January 31, 2001, "Executive summary of the U.S. Commission on National Security in the 21st century, *Milnet Brief,* Available from http://milnet.com/hart-rudman/, Accessed February 19, 2006.
48. The section that follows draws heavily from Richard S. Conley, 2005, "Presidential and Congressional Struggles over the Formation of the Department of Homeland Security," in Richard S. Conley (Ed.), *Transforming the American Polity: The Presidency of George W. Bush and the War on Terrorism,* Prentice Hall, Upper Saddle River, NJ, pp. 135–148.
49. Lindsay, James, and Ivo Daalder, 2003, "Who's job is it? Organizing the federal government for homeland security," in James M. Lindsay (Ed.), *American Politics After September 11,* Atomic Dog Publishers, Cincinnati, OH.
50. Dana Milbank, April 18, 2002, "Congress, White House fight over Ridge status; compromise is likely on constitutional flap," *Washington Post,* A19.
51. Donald P. Moynihan, 2005, "Homeland security and the U.S. public management policy agenda," *Governance,* Vol. 18, No. 2, pp. 171–196.
52. Andrew E. Busch, 2005, "National security and the midterm elections of 2002," in Richard S. Conley (Ed.), *Transforming the American Polity: The Presidency of George W. Bush and the War on Terrorism,* in America Series, Prentice Hall, Upper Saddle River, NJ, pp. 40–61.
53. Bush had contemplated placing the FBI in DHS, but concluded that its law enforcement focus required that the agency remain within the Department of Justice (see Sanger, 2002).
54. 116 Stat. 2135; 6 U.S.C. Â 101 et seq.; see Harold C. Relyea, September 2003, "Organizing for homeland security," *Presidential Studies Quarterly,* Vol. 33, pp. 602–624.
55. See 61 Stat. 495 at 499.
56. 116 Stat. 2243; 6 U.S.C. § 452.
57. See Weekly Compilation of Presidential Documents, Vol. 39, February 3, 2003, p. 136; U.S. Department of Homeland Security, January 30, 2003, "Border reorganization remarks by

Secretary Ridge," Port of Miami, Miami, FX, Available from http://www.dhs.gov/dhspublic/display?theme=44&content=419&print=true; U.S. Department of Homeland Security, "DHS Announces Border Security Reorganization," Washington, DC (undated), Available from http://www.dhs.gov/dhspublic/display?theme=44&content=422&print=true; U.S. Department of Homeland Security, January 30, 2003, "Border reorganization fact sheet," Washington, DC, Available from http://www.dhs.gov/dhspublic/display?theme=43&content=4236&print=true.

58. U.S. Department of Homeland Security, "Secretary Michael Chertoff, U.S. Department of Homeland Security Second Stage Review Remarks," pp. 2–3.
59. Ibid., p. 6.
60. Congressional Quarterly, "Senate Homeland Security and Governmental Affairs Committee holds hearing on review or [sic] Department of Homeland Security Organization," p. 49.
61. U.S. Department of Homeland Security, letter from Secretary Michael Chertoff to the Honorable Christopher Cox, p. 1 note (emphasis added).
62. Congressional Quarterly, "Senate Homeland Security and Governmental Affairs Committee holds hearing on review or [sic] Department of Homeland Security Organization," p. 50.
63. 116 Stat. 2243; 6 U.S.C. § 452 (emphasis added).
64. CRS Report RS21450, Homeland Secretary: Scope of the Secretary's Reorganization Authority (August 9, 2005), p. 3 (emphasis in original).
65. Congressional Quarterly, "Senate Homeland Security and Governmental Affairs, Committee holds hearing on review or [sic] Department of Homeland Security Organization," p. 38.
66. Representative Bennie G. Thompson, et al. (minority members), n.d., House Committee on Homeland Security, *Protecting America Against Terrorists: The Case for a Comprehensive Reorganization of the Department of Homeland Security*, Government Printing Office, Washington DC, p. 7.
67. Michele L. Landis, Spring 1998, "Let Me Next Time Be Tried by Fire: Disaster Relief and the Origins of the American Welfare State 1789–1874," *Northwestern University Law Review*, Vol. 92, pp. 967–1034. A list of disaster legislation enacted by Congress from 1803 through 1943 may be found in Rep. Harold Hagen, Statement for the Record, Congressional Record, Vol. 96, August 7, 1950, pp. 11900–11902.
68. The exception to this general statement concerns flood prevention policies enacted since the late century. See CRS Report RL32972, *Federal Flood Insurance: The Repetitive Loss Problem,* by Rawle O. King.
69. The Office for Emergency Management was established in the EOP by an administrative order of May 25, 1940, pursuant to Executive Order 8248, *Federal Register*, Vol. 4, September 12, 1939, p. 3864.
70. 64 Stat. 1109. The act is also sometimes referred to as P.L. 875 after its public law number, P.L. 81–875.
71. At that time, under the Reorganization Act of 1949, as amended, reorganization plans submitted by the President went into effect unless either chamber of Congress passes a resolution of disapproval. For more on the history of presidential reorganization authority, see CRS Report RL30876, Ronald C. Moe, March 8, 2001, *The President's Reorganization Authority: Review and Analysis*, Congressional Research Service, Washington, DC.
72. For information on this initiative, see U.S. Executive Office of the President, Office of Management and Budget, 1971, *Papers Relating to the President's Departmental Reorganization Program: A Reference Compilation*, Government Printing Office, Washington, DC.
73. Executive Order 11725, *Federal Register*, Vol. 38, June 29, 1973, p. 17175.
74. Harry B. Yoshpe, 1981, *Our Missing Shield: The U.S. Civil Defense Program in Historical Perspective*, FEMA, Washington, DC, p. 377.
75. See, for example, National Governors' Association, *Comprehensive Emergency Management: A Governor's Guide,* Government Printing Office, Washington, DC, 1979.

76. National Governors' Association, 1979, "National Governors' Association Policy Position A-17: Emergency Preparedness and Response," in *1978 Emergency Preparedness Project: Final Report*, Governement Printing Office, Washington, pp. 363–364.
77. U.S. Congress, House, Message from the President of the United States Transmitting A Reorganization Plan to Improve Federal Emergency Management and Assistance, Pursuant to 5 US.C. 903 (91 Stat. 30), H. Doc. 95–356, 95th Congress, 2nd session, Government Printing Office, Washington, DC, 1978.
78. This reorganization authority is provided for in Chapter 9 of Title 5 of the US. Code. Portions of this chapter were amended in 1980 and 1984. The authority has since become dormant.
79. At that time, under the Reorganization Act of 1977, reorganization plans submitted by the President went into effect unless either chamber of Congress passed a resolution of disapproval. Such a resolution had to be introduced, at the time the plan was submitted by the President, by the chairs of the House Government Operations Committee and the Senate Governmental Affairs Committee. In this case, the House, on September 14, rejected the resolution of disapproval, and the Senate, on September 18, postponed the resolution indefinitely, by unanimous consent. For more on the history of presidential reorganization authority, see CRS Report RL30876, *The President's Reorganization Authority: Review and Analysis*, by Ronald C. Moe.
80. Executive Order 12127, *Federal Register,* vol. 44, April 3, 1979, p. 19367.
81. Executive Order 12 148, *Federal Register,* vol. 44, July 24, 1979, p. 43239.
82. R. Steven Daniels and Carolyn L. Clark-Daniels, 2000, *Transforming Government: The Renewal and Revitalization of the Federal Emergency Management Agency*, Pricewaterhouse Coopers Endowment for The Business of Government, Washington. For an additional assessment of FEMA under the Clinton Administration, see Schneider, "Reinventing Public Administration," p. 35.
83. The committee's report notes that the Democratic leadership elected not to appoint members officially to the panel but that some Democratic members chose to participate on an individual basis.
84. U.S. Congress, House Select Bipartisan Committee to Investigate the Preparation for and Response to Hurricane Katrina, 2006, *A Failure of Initiative*, 109th Congress, 2nd session, Government Printing Office, Washington.
85. "There is always an easy solution to every human problem—neat, plausible, and wrong," attributed to H. L. Mencken, 1949, "The divine afflatus," *A Mencken Chrestomathy,* A. A. Knopf, New York, p. 443, quoted in Suzy Platt (Ed.), 1989, *Respectfully Quoted: A Dictionary of Quotations Requested from the Congressional Research Service*, Library of Congress, Washington, p. 326.
86. U.S. Government Accountability Office (GAO), 1993, *Disaster Management: Improving the National Response to Catastrophic Disasters.* Government Printing Office. GAO/IRCED-93-186, Washington, DC.
87. City of New Orleans, 2005, General Evacuation Guidelines, Available from www.cityofno.com/ponal.aspx?portal=468&tabid-18, Accessed January 25, 2006.
88. George W. Bush, September 15, 2005, Address to the Nation, Available from www.whitehouse.gov/news/releases/2005/09/20050915-8.html, Accessed January 19, 2006.
89. Scott Wells, December 8, 2005, Testimony before the Senate Committee on Homeland Security and Governmental Affairs, Hearing on Hurricane Katrina: Perspectives of FEMA's Operations Professionals, Available from http://hsgac.senate.gov/index.cfm?Fuseaction=Hearings.Detail&HearingID=298, Accessed January 19, 2006.
90. Michael Chertoff, July 14, 2005b, Statement before the Senate Committee on Homeland Security and Governmental Affairs, Department of Homeland Security: Second Stage Review, Available from http://hsgac.senate.gov/index.cfm?Fuseaction=Hearings.Detail&HearingID=257, Accessed January 19, 2006.

91. White House, 2006, *The Federal Response to Hurricane Katrina: Lessons Learned*, Executive Office of the President, Washington, DC, Available from www.whitehouse.gov/reports/Katrina-lessons-1earned.pdf.
92. David R. Paulison, December 8, 2005, Testimony before the Senate Committee on Homeland Security and Governmental Affairs, Hearing on Hurricane Katrina: Perspectives of FEMA's Operations Professionals, Available from http://hsgac.scnate.gov/index.cfm?Fuscaction=Hearings.Detail&HearingID=298, Accessed January 19, 2006.
93. U.S. Department of Homeland Security (DHS), 2004a, National Response Plan, Available from www.dhs.gov/interwcb/assetlibrary/NRP_FullText.pdf, Accessed January 19, 2006.
94. Keith Bea, 2005, Disaster Evacuation and Displacement Policy: Issues for Congress, Report No. R.522235, Congressional Research Service.
95. Charles R. Wise, 2002, "Organizing for Homeland Security," *Public Administration Review*, Vol. 62, No. 2, pp. 131–144.
96. Charles R. Wise, 2002b, "Reorganizing the Government for Homeland Security: Congress Creates a New Department," *Extensions*, Fall, pp. 14–19.
97. Michael B. Donley and Neal A. Pollard, 2002, "Homeland Security: the difference between vision and wish. special issue," *Public Administration Review*, Vol. 62, pp. 138–153.
98. U.S. Department of Homeland Security, Office of the Inspector General, 2003, *Major Management Challenges and Program Risks, Department of Homeland Security*, Government Printing Office, GAO-03-02, Washington, DC.
99. U.S. Department of Homeland Security, Office of the Inspector General, 2005c, *High risk series: an update*, Government Printing Office. GAO-05-207, Washington, DC.
100. U.S. Department of Homeland Security, Office of the Inspector General, 2005b, *DHS Efforts* to *Enhance First Responders' All-Hazards Capabilities Continue to Evolve*, Government Printing Office, GAO-05-652, Washington, DC.
101. Paul S. Adler, 2001, "Market, hierarchy and trust: the knowledge economy and the future of capitalism," *Organization Science*, Vol. 12, No. 2, 215–234.
102. Elliot Jaques, 1990, "In praise of hierarchy," *Harvard Business Review*, Vol. 90, No. 1, pp. 127–133.
103. Robert Agranoff and Michael McGuire, 2001, "Big questions for public network management research," *Journal of Public Management Research and Theory*, Vol. 11, No. 3, pp. 295–327. 2003, *Collaborative Public Management*, Georgetown University Press, Washington, DC.
104. Robyn Keast, Myrna Mandell, Kerry Brown, and Geoffrey Woolcock, 2004, "Network structures: working differently and changing expectations," *Public Administration Review*, Vol. 64, No. 363–371.
105. Walter Kickert, Erik-Hans Klijn, and Joop F.M. Koppenjan (Eds.), 1997, *Managing Complex Networks and Network Structures for Public Policy and Management*, Sage Publications, London.
106. Brinton H. Milward and Keith G. Provan, 2000, How networks are governed, in Carolyn J. Heinrich and Laurence E. Lynn (Ed.), *Governance and Performance: New Perspectives*, Georgetown University Press, Washington, DC.
107. Laurence O'Toole, Jr., 1997, "Treating networks seriously: practical and research based agendas in public administration," *Public Administration Review*, Vol. 57W, pp. 45–51.
108. Charles R. Wise, 1990, "Public service configurations and public organizations: public organization design in the post-privatization era," *Public Administration Review*, Vol. 50, No. 2, pp. 141–155.
109. Robert Agranoff, 2007, *Managing in Networks: Boundary Spanning among Public and Nongovernmental Organizations*, Georgetown University Press, Washington, DC.
110. Charles R. Wise and Rania Nader, 2006, "HLS and accountability," in David G. Kamien (Ed.), *The McGraw-Hill Homeland Security Handbook*, McGraw-Hill, New York, pp. 11, 1115–1131.

111. Henry Mintzberg, 1980, *The Nature of Managerial Work*, Prentice Hall, Englewood Cliffs, NJ.
112. Henry Minzberg, 1993, *Structure in Fives: Designing Effective Organizations*, Prentice Hall, Englewood Cliffs, NJ.
113. James D. Thompson, 1967, *Organization in Action*, McGraw-Hill, New York.
114. Oliver E. Williamson, 1975, *Markets and Hierarchies*, Free Press, New York.
115. Oliver E. Williamson, 1990, "Chester Barnard and the incipient science of organization," in Oliver Williamson (Ed.), *Organization Theory*, Oxford University Press, New York.
116. "Rove Off the Record on Katrina: The Only Mistake Was Not Overriding the Local Government," *The Huffington Post*, Available from http://www.hufRn~onpost.com/2005/09/l7/rove-off-the-record-onn-7k5a1 3.html, Accessed September 23, 2005.
117. Eric Lipton, et al., "Breakdowns Marked Path from Hurricane to Anarchy," *NY Times*, September 11, 2005, Â1, at 11 ("To President Bush, Governor Blanco directed an ill-defined but urgent appeal. 'I need everything you've got,' the governor said she told the president on Monday. 'I am going to need all the help you can send me.' ").
118. See, for example, Eric Lipton & Scott Shane, September 2, 2005, "Leader of Federal Effort Feels the Heat," *NY Times*, at A17 (noting the "remarkable confession" of Michael D. Brown, former Director of the Federal Emergency Management Agency [FEMA], who had only just learned of the three-day plight of thousands of citizens without food or water at the New Orleans convention center). On September 12, Michael Brown resigned as Director of FEMA amid heavy criticism of FEMA's response to the effects of Hurricane Katrina. Richard W. Stevenson, September 13, 2005, "After Days of Criticism, Emergency Director Resigns," *NY Times*, at AS. See also Jennifer Steinhauer and Eric Lipton, September 17, 2005, "FEMA, Slow to the Rescue, Now Stumbles in Aid Effort," *NY Times*, at A1 ("Nearly three weeks after Hurricane Katrina cut its devastating path, FEMA . . . is faltering in its effort to aid hundreds of thousands of storms victims [and] serious problems remain throughout the affected region.").
119. See infra note 27 and accompanying text.
120. John M. Colmers and Daniel M. Fox, 2003, "The politics of emergency health powers and the isolation of public health," *Am J Pub Health*, Vol. 93, pp. 397. See also Matthew E. Brown, 2005, "Reconsidering the model state emergency health powers act: toward state regionalization in bioterrorism response," *Annals Health*, Vol. 14, pp. 95–97.
121. 6 U.S.C.A. 8 112 (West Supp. 2005).
122. NRP, *supra* note 16, at 1 (discussion of the NRP objectives).
123. DHS, NRP BROCHURE, Available from http://www.dhs.gov/interweb/assetlibrarv/NRP_Brochure.pdf, Accessed September 27, 2005.
124. An "Incident of National Significance" is defined as "an actual or potential high-impact event that requires a coordinated and effective response by and appropriate combination of Federal, State, local, tribal, nongovernmental, and or private-sector entities in order to save lives and minimize damage, and provide the basis for long-term community recovery and mitigation activities." *NRP, supra* note 16, at 67. There is an automatic trigger for an incident of national significance whenever major disasters or emergencies are declared under the Stafford Act. *Id.* at 4.
125. See generally Editorial, Unprepared, *Washington Post*, September 5, 2005, at A30 (critical discussion of the delay in declaring an "incident of national significance"); Spencer S. Hsu and Steve Hendrix, September 25, 2005, "Hurricanes Katrina and Rita were like night and day," *Washington Post*, at A1 (discussion of differences between delayed response of federal government after Hurricane Katrina compared to the response for Hurricane Rita). NRP, *supra* note 16, at 44 (emphasis added).
126. Press Release, Department of Homeland Security, United States Government Response to the Aftermath of Hurricane Katrina, September 1, 2005, Available from http://www.dhs.gov/dhspublic/display?content=4777, Accessed September 26, 2005.

127. DHS, National Response Plan (NRP) (December 2004), at v–viii, Available from http://www.dhs.gov/interweb/assetlibrary/NRP_FullText.pdf, Accessed August 25, 2005 (hereinafter NRP) (listing the Signatories to the NRP), at 44 (emphasis added).
128. *Id.* at 42.
129. *Id.* at 43. The Posse Comitatus Act (PCA), 18 U.S.C.A. 5 1385 (West 2000 & Supp. 2005), prohibits the willful use of the Army or the Air Force for law enforcement purposes. *Id.* This includes interdiction of a vehicle, vessel, aircraft or other similar activity; directing traffic; search or seizure; an arrest, apprehension, stop and frisk, or similar activity. U.S. NORTHERN COMMAND, FACT SHEETS, POSSE COMITATUS ACT, Available from http://www.northcom.mil/index.cfm?fuseaction=news.factsheets&factsheet=5, Accessed September 28, 2005. The PCA expressly applies to the Army and Air Force, and Congress has included the Navy and Marines through the Departments of Defense and Navy regulations. 10 U.S.C.A. Â 375 (West 1998 & Supp. 2005) (ordering the Secretary of Defense to prescribe "such regulations . . . to ensure that any activity [regarding civilian law enforcement] does not include or permit direct participation by a member of the Army, Navy, Air Force, or Marine Corps in a search, seizure, arrest, or other similar activity"). *See also* U.S. DEP'T, OF DEFENSE, DIRECTIVE NO. 5525.5, DoD COOPERATION WITHIN CIVILIAN LAW ENFORCEMENT OFFICIALS, at 21 (January 15, 1986), Available at http://www.dtic.mil/whs/directives/corres/pdf2/d55255p.pdf, Accessed August 31,2005. There are a number of statutory exceptions to the PCA. These include the Insurrection Act, 10 U.S.C.A. §§ 331–335 (West 1998 & Supp, 2005); 10 U.S.C.A. §§ 372(b), 382 (West 1998 & Supp. 2005) (emergency situations involving chemical or biological weapons of mass destruction); Stafford Act, 42 U.S.C.A. §§ 5170b (c), 5192 (West 2003) (federal emergency assistance & utilization of DOD resources); 18 U.S.C.A. §§ 831(e) (West 2000) (military assistance in emergency situations involving nuclear materials).
130. Press Release, September 15, 2005, The White House, President Discusses Hurricane Relief in Address to the Nation, Available at http://www.whitehouse.gov/news/releases/2005/09/20050915-8.html, Accessed September 26, 2005.
131. NRP, *supra* note 16, at 69.
132. *Id.*
133. NRP, PUBLIC HEALTH AND MEDICAL SERVICES ANNEX, *supra* note 16, at ESF #8-1. This support is categorized into the following areas: assessment of health/medical needs, health surveillance; medical care personnel; health/medical equipment and supplies; patient evacuation; in-hospital care; food/drug/medical device safety; worker health/safety; all-hazard consultation; mental health care; public health information; vector control; potable water/wastewater and solid waste disposal; victim identification/mortuary services; and veterinary services. *Id.* at ESF #8-6.
134. *See supra* note 3 and accompanying text.
135. HHS Secretary Mike Leavitt declared a federal public health emergency on August 31, 2005, for the states of Louisiana, Alabama, Mississippi, and Florida. Press Release, August 31, 2005, Department of Health and Human Services, HHS Delivering Medical Care to Help Evacuees and Victims, Available at http://www.hhs.gov/news/press/2005pres/2005018.3html, Accessed September 1, 2005. *See also* Associated Press, September 8, 2005, "Before Katrina, the economy was doing fine," *NY Times*, at C6 (discussing the prediction by private economists and the Congressional Budget Office that "fallout from the storm would cause overall economic activity to slow in the second half of this year by one-half to a fall percentage point on an annualized basis").
136. See James Dao, September 11, 2005, "Off the map; no fixed address," *NY Times*, at 41 (discussing "resettling evacuees" from the Gulf Coast who fled to other states after Katrina); Kirk Johnson, et al., September 12, 2005, "President visits as New Orleans sees some gains," *NY Times*, at A1 (discussing extent of relief effort from all over the nation); Robert D. McFadden and Ralph Blumenthal, September 1, 2005, "Bush sees long recovery for New Orleans; 30,000 Troops in Largest Relief U.S. Relief Effort," *NY Times*, at A1 (discussing evacuation attempts

for the city of New Orleans as well as New Orleans's Mayor C. Ray Nagin's fear that the hurricane might have killed thousands in his city).

137. August 31, 2005, "Prices for energy futures soar in the wake of Hurricane Katrina," *NY Times*, at C2 ("Economists warned that Katrina was likely to leave a deeper mark on the national economy than previous hurricanes because of its profound disruption to the Gulf of Mexico's complex energy supply network."). *See also id.* at C4 ("The airline industry felt the delayed brunt of Hurricane Katrina, with some airports running low on jet fuel and carriers canceling hundreds more flights.").

138. Jad Mouawad and Simon Romero, September 1, 2005, "Gas prices surge as supply drops," *NY Times*, at Al.

139. Associated Press, September 11, 2005, "Some states reached their highest gasoline prices ever, gasoline pricing violations," *NY Times*, at 14NJ-6 ("New Jersey's gasoline prices hit their highest levels ever on Labor Day, averaging $3.16 a gallon for regular."); Jad Mouaward, September 11, 2005, Storm stretches refiners past a perilous point, *NY Times*, at 27 ("The hurricane also knocked off a dozen refineries at the peak of summer demand, sending oil prices higher and gasoline prices to inflation-adjusted records."); Mouawad and Romero, *supra* note 63 ("While gasoline averaged $2.60 a gallon earlier in the week [of Aug. 29 to Sept. 21], unleaded regular gas was selling [on Aug. 31] at $3.09 at stations in West Palm Beach, Fla.; $3.49 in Indianapolis; and $3.25 in San Francisco. Premium fuel was going for up to $3.89 a gallon in Chicago.").

140. Press Release, August 31, 2005, The White House, President Outlines Hurricane Katrina Relief Efforts, Available at http://wvw.whitehouse.gov/news/releases/2005/08/20050831-3, Accessed September 1, 2005.

141. Mouawad and Romero, *supra* note 63. The price of crude oil fell in trading from $69.81 to $68.94. *Id.*

142. *See supra* notes 16–31 and accompanying text.

143. *See* DHS, What Government is Doing, *supra* note 16; *U.S.* Interagency Council on Homelessness, in Washington: Federal Agencies Make Additional Resources and Waivers Available to Assist Those Affected by Hurricane Katrina, Available from http://www.ich.eov/, Accessed September 28, 2005.

144. *See supra* notes 16–31 and accompanying text.

145. *See* Lipton, *supra* note 2.

146. *See* Rove Off the Record, *supra* note 1.

147. Simon Winchester, 2005, *A Crack in the Edge of the World*, Harper Collins, pp. 307–310; Doris Muscatine, 1975, *Old San Francisco: From Early Days to the Earthquake*, Putnam and Sons, New York, p. 428.

148. Peter J. May, 1985, *Recovering from Disasters: Federal Disaster Relief Policy and Politics*, Greenwood Press, Westport, CT.

149. Robert Ward, et al., 2000, "Network organizational development in the public sector: a case study of the Federal Emergency Management Administration (FEMA)," *Journal of the American Society for Information Science*, Vol. 51.

150. Frank G. Hoffman, personal e-mail correspondence, December 11, 2003, FEMA's witnesses before the Hart-Rudman Commission were Lacey Suiter and V. Clay Hollister. Notes of their briefing do not exist.

151. Garrett and Sobel note both that from 1991 to 1999 states politically important to the president had a higher rate of disaster declaration by the president and that disaster expenditures were higher in states that had congressional representation on FEMA oversight committees. They also find election-year impacts for disaster aid, controlling for the true size of a disaster measured through private property insurance claims and Red Cross assistance levels. Thomas A. Garrett and Russell S. Sobel, 2003, "The political economy of FEMA disaster payments," *Economic Inquiry*, Vol. 41. Other studies have found that the president's decision to issue a

disaster declaration is influenced by congressional and media attention. *See* Richard T. Sylves, 1996, "The Politics of Federal Emergency Management," in Richard T. Sylves and William H. Waugh Jr. (Eds.), *Disaster Management in the US and Canada*, Charles C. Thomas Publishers, Springfield, IL.

152. Patrick S. Roberts, July 2005, "Shifting priorities: congressional incentives and the homeland security granting process," *Review of Policy Research*, Vol. 22, No. 4.
153. *See* Eric Schmitt, March 16, 2002, "4 Top officials on immigration are replaced," *NY Times*, at Al; see also Cheryl W. Thompson, March 25, 2002, "Justice Dept. to probe new INS visa error," *Washington Post*, at All (investigating an INS official's decision to grant visas without following screening protocols to four Pakistanis who subsequently disappeared).
154. *See* Eric Schmitt, April 26, 2002, "Vote in house strongly backs an end to I.N.S.," *N.Y. Times*, at Al.
155. One notable exception is legislation requiring greater information sharing between intelligence agencies and the State Department, which issues visas, and mandating the creation of machine-readable, tamper-resistant visas. *See* Enhanced Border Security and Visa Reform Act of 2002, Pub. L. No. 107–173, ## 201–204, 116 Stat. 543, 547–552.
156. July 11, 2002, see "Details of Homeland Plan assailed, House panels vote to block transfers of some agencies," *Washington Post*, at Al.
157. Donald Kettl and John DiIulio framed this point best when they argued that "[r]eorganizations ye have always with you, a prophet could confidently promise." Donald F. Kettl and John J. DiIulio, Jr., Brookings Institute, 1995, CUTTING GOVERNMENT, Vol. 28.
158. *See*, e.g., Jerry Mashaw, 1996, *Reinventing Government and Regulation? Reform: Studies in the Neglect and Abuse of Administrative Law*, 57 *U.* PITT. L. REV. 405, 408 (noting that "it is safe to say that none of our Chief Executives, or their COOS, have been immune to the management fraternities' panaceas du jour").
159. *See* Homeland Security Act of 2002, H.R. 5005, 107th Cong. 95 401–403 (original version).
160. *See* id. 5 402.
161. Then-INS Commissioner James Ziglar indicated that "[the] President's plan will pre-empt all other restructuring proposals," which suggests that the INS's internal restructuring plan will be on hold indefinitely. Press Release, June 7, 2002, Message to INS Employees from Commissioner Ziglar on the President's Announcement of the Formation of the Department of Homeland Security, Available at http://www.ins.gov/graphics/publicaffairs/s~tements/securityfomation.html.
162. *See* George W. Bush, 2002, The Department of Homeland Security Report, Available from http://www.whitehouse.gov/deptofhomelandhook.pdf.
163. *See* H.R. 5005 5 421 (approved version).

CHAPTER 7

The Department of Defense

INTRODUCTION

The Department of Defense (DOD), created in 1947 through the National Security Act, is the oldest of the reorganizations that are included in this volume. As such, this reorganization activity illustrates the dynamic of constant change that frequently surrounds reorganization decisions. Organization structure in defense has not emerged from general theories about management but rather as a response to political, economic, and administrative shifts that constantly has caused modifications and redefinitions of defense policy.

The excerpts included in this section of the book begin with the creation of the Department of Defense to replace a War Department made up of separate and quite autonomous Departments of the Army, Navy, and Air Force. The structure placed a civilian secretary over these separate departments and began to move to minimize the autonomy of the separate branches.

The section moves to the reorganization defined by the Goldwater-Nichols Act of 1986—legislation that sought ways to improve the ability of U.S. armed forces to conduct joint and combined operations in the field. The act strengthened the influence and staff of the chair of the Joint Chiefs of Staff, increased the authority and influence of unified commands, and created a joint officer specialization within each service to staff the Joint Staff. It then raises questions that emerged in the post 9/11 era.

The changes that have occurred in the DOD structure represent incremental changes that address constant and familiar problems. Although the general problems in 2008 are not much different than they were in 1958, they emerge from very different settings. Technology and globalization are two of the major changes that have driven different solutions to both policy and administrative problems.

Historically, the development of defense policy has been the purview of military specialists. Unlike some other policy sectors, it often has been a relatively closed policy system. Thus, it is not surprising that decisions and debates about organization structure involved a predictable cast of characters—especially active and retired uniformed officers. Some of the organization structure decisions were based on studies, but those involved in the studies were usually part of the military establishment or its supporters within its issue network. Unlike two of the reorganizations included in this volume (DHS and ED), many of the changes were actually quite acceptable to at least some DOD staff and to their supporters within the Congress.

The first excerpts in this section provide a history of developments that led to the passage of the original Act that created the DOD. John C. Ries, in *The Management of Defense: Organization and Control of the U.S. Armed Services*, suggests that unification concerns may have dated back to the early 1920s and were linked to policy debates; however, the experience of World War II led to the drive to create such a department.

Richard C. Steadman was the author of the 1978 "Report to the Secretary of Defense on the National Military Command Structure." This report signals an interest in increasing the role of the Joint Chiefs of Staff in the context of a balance between individual service interests and the need for unified direction of the armed services.

Archie D. Barrett draws on the Defense Organization Study of 1977–1980 to suggest that it is time to revisit some of the arguments that were used to justify the original creation of the department. Issues that relate to the relationship between the military department secretaries, the Joint Chiefs of Staff, and central management under the civilian secretary continue to be heard.

David C. Hendrickson argues in *Reforming Defense: The State of American Civil-Military Relations* that the balance between centralization and decentralization has been of concern to the DOD for many years. He notes that there are arguments for both strategies; centralization brings oversight, whereas decentralization provides opportunities for military professionals to draw on their expertise.

Further emphasis on management issues is found in Fred Thompson's article, "Management Control and the Pentagon: The Organizational Strategy-Structure Mismatch." He focuses on what he calls a "gap" between the defense organization and strategic purpose and highlights three issues: the division of labor in the organization, the distribution of authority and responsibility, and the system of measuring and evaluating performance.

Following the passage of the 1986 reorganization, John G. Kester emphasizes the role of Congress in the process. His article, "The 1986 Defense Reorganization: A Promising Start," differentiates between the concerns of Congress and those of the Executive Branch. Major General Perry Smith moves to the implementation of the Goldwater-Nichols Act and provides advice for players in "Operating in the Joint Arena." He argues that it will be the experienced and skilled players who will be the most effective in this process.

Ten years after the enactment of Goldwater-Nichols, James R. Locher III called for an assessment of the legislation. In "Building on the Goldwater-Nichols Act," Locher finds that despite some reluctance within the services when enacted, the legislation improved the performance and war-fighting capabilities of the American military establishment.

After 9/11, the Center for Strategic and International Studies focused on the impact of that tragedy on the DOD and defense policy. It issued a report entitled *Beyond Goldwater-Nichols: Defense Reform for a New Strategic Era* that argues that the organizational structures and processes constructed in a Cold War environment is not appropriate for the 21st century. Drawing on the experience of former practitioners, the report emphasizes consolidation of organizational structures and department-wide efforts, strengthening civilian professionals, and improving interagency and coalition operations.

John C. Ries, *The Management of Defense: Organization and Control of the U.S. Armed Services*, Baltimore, MD: Johns Hopkins University Press (1964).

THE SEARCH FOR ORGANIZATIONAL CONCEPTS

Identification of the exact time when unification became a major organizational issue is virtually impossible. Some defense historians say that pressure began in the unanswered claim of the prewar army aviators for a commanding position in American military planning rather than with wartime experiences of inefficiency and waste. Unification was the army aviators' only "practicable avenue to independence and authority."[1] And if unification did result from attempts to establish the autonomy of air power, it became a major issue during the early 1920s. Other students of military history feel that the failure of interservice co-ordination at Pearl Harbor and the success of unified command systems developed later in the war provided the impetus for unification.[2] Other military historians point to the degree of actual unification realized by such wartime agencies as the Joint Chiefs of Staff (JCS). And they contend that these agencies provided the model for later unification plans.[3] But regardless of its exact beginning in time, unification eventually succeeded in turning defense organization through a full cycle from 1789, when the War Department was divided, and the Navy-like Adam's rib was removed and given a separate identity.

The issue of unification of the armed services is the product of at least three pressures: attempts to establish the autonomy of air power; the wartime inefficiency and duplication of effort in the Army and Navy; and the success of wartime experiments in interservice co-ordination. However, the plea of aviators for coequal status with the other service arms was, and is still, a major commitment of the proponents of unification. . . .

The lessons of World War II were that slow and costly mobilization, limited intelligence as to the designs and capacity of potential enemies, "prodigal" use of resources, lack of unity of command in the Pacific, and duplicating supply lines—all these undesirable conditions—resulted from the existence of two separate service departments. And these conditions could be eliminated by merging the two service departments.

The creation of a single service department would bring many advantages. One department meant one department head. One department head meant unified direction. The argu-

---

Source: Ries, John C. The Management of Defense: Organization and Control of the United States Armed Services, pp. 3–5, 7–8, 15–16, 23, 35, 45, 47.

ment was simple, logical, and compelling, especially to wartime field commanders who saw their plans for victory deterred by delay, wrong decision, or no decision at all. Grafted on to this argument was one supported by the Army Air Forces that the role of air power was so irrefutably demonstrated during the war that it must never again risk domination by either land or sea power. Therefore, unification must "triplify" as well as "unify." If the independence of air power and the lessons of wartime "disunity and duplication" were accepted, only one answer was possible: three services, land, air, and sea, under one department. So the argument ran, and such was the thinking during the summer of 1945. . . .

Between June 30, 1941, and December 12, 1945, three major proposals were made for consolidating the two service departments under a single military staff headed by a single chief of staff.[4] And during congressional hearings on one of these proposals, the McNarney plan,[5] most military witnesses testified in favor of merger as a concept of unification. Those who did not asked only for postponement of a final decision and further study, not for rejection.

In October, 1945, when the Senate Military Affairs Committee opened hearings on two bills[6] for the creation of a single department of armed forces composed of three equal services, air, land, and sea, witnesses invariably equated unification with a single department headed by a single chief of staff. Furthermore, they equated unification with the results they expected such centralization would bring. In addition to establishing air power in its proper role, ten other benefits were cited in support of unification. 1) It would insure the required teamwork of all components of the armed forces in wartime.[7] 2) It would provide the peacetime training for exercising and operating unified commands.[8] 3) It would give the military establishment an organization prepared for the events of war.[9] 4) It would make possible the speed and flexibility required in modern warfare fought with modern weapons.[10] 5) It would assure the necessary impetus for adequate research and development of weapons.[11] 6) It would bring about the proper co-ordination of military programs with other governmental programs.[12] 7) It was necessary for the development of comprehensive military plans and programs.[13] 8) It would provide the best means for over-all presentation and consideration of the budget.[14] 9) It would reduce the waste inherent in the present duplication of services and facilities.[15] 10) It would eliminate undesirable interservice competition and rivalry for goods and man power.[16] These benefits were alleged to be the direct consequences of creating a single service department headed by a chief of staff. . . .

In many respects the problems facing reformers of the organization of the War Department at the beginning of the twentieth century were not unlike those facing reformers of the organization of local, state, and national government. In each case, at that time, responsibility was dispersed, authority disintegrated, and organization consisted of many layers of independent or semi-independent bureaus and agencies. The analogy cannot be carried too far, however, because the War Department had certain peculiar problems. In wartime it was the focus of attention, appropriations, and highest national policy. In peacetime it was subject to almost no public notice. In peacetime, the department carried out essentially nonmilitary functions: feeding, clothing, curing, arming, and housing troops. These functions were divided among various bureaus or divisions (the special staff) such as Ordnance, Engineers, Signal Corps, and Quartermaster.[17] Officers who had spent their entire careers within the bureau and who served as commanders without limit of time commanded the bureaus. "Some of them had lived in Washington and presided over their separate duchies for two or three decades. . . ."[18]

The War Department entered World War II within this environment and with this doctrinal heritage. The first problem facing the department was a series of command breakdowns.[19] It became apparent that top echelons would need extensive reorganization of the immediate needs of the war effort were to be handled. Not only were delays in execution of orders occurring, but it was impossible to discover the reason for them.[20] The alternatives included strengthening the General Staff or substantially changing its concept of operation. . . .

Another factor must also be considered. Tradition has been found to play a major role in both organizational operation and organizational change.[21] There is little doubt that tradition has had a deep influence on War Department thinking. For forty years the Chief of Staff and the General Staff had been the symbols of hope that the chaotic bureau system might someday be overcome. Reverence and devotion to symbols can be quite unrelated to the actual operation which the symbol represents. The association, developed in practice and codified in theory, between the notion of General Staff and the hope of central control, probably played a large role in early unification proposals.

A symbol such as the General Staff is easy to represent and locate on an organizational chart. Its functions can be readily defined, and rules can be formulated to insure its position as an agency of control. This approach to organization can lead to an oversimplification of organizational operation, to an overemphasis on formal control, and to a neglect of actual organizational behavior. The elaboration of formal controls which characterized the general staff system before the war, when measured against the operation of the department, indicates that there is no necessary relation between formal roles and organizational behavior. In fact, the elaboration of controls resulted from the very resistance of the bureaus to central control. In this context, the prewar organizational charts which showed 390 commands reporting to the chief of staff was really a picture of what in practice was a very decentralized structure. Although it may be no more than a commonsense observation that formal structure and organizational behavior may vary sharply, the notion that centralization equates with control does not allow for this. . . .[22]

The hierarchical general staff concept of organization relies heavily upon the principle of subordination. Varying amounts of power are distributed throughout the system, and each subordinate reports to one superior. The superior being higher, presumably has more power; he at least has more legal authority. This tendency to equate hierarchical position with power, as seen earlier, leads to the myth that a junior officer on a high-level staff does not give orders to a superior officer who occupies a lower position in the command hierarchy. He either coordinates, advises, or acts in the name of the chief of staff. In addition to ignoring the real power of staff agencies, this notion tends to view organization as a dosed system.[23] But authority is a much more complex phenomenon. Legal authority (the right to demand obedience), cannot be confused with influence or power (the ability to obtain obedience).[24] The chief of staff in the War Department reorganization of 1903 held the highest position in the Army. He was to be obeyed when he acted in the name of the secretary of war. Yet both the highest military authority and the highest civilian authority in the department suffered many defeats at the hands of subordinate bureau commanders.

If the experience of the chief of staff proves anything, it proves that "simply being in an executive hierarchy does not mean that one can direct freely those below him."[25] Since the bureaus could gain control over the chief of staff by their alliances in Congress, the chief of staff had to make his own alliances to fight a recalcitrant subordinate. . . .

To appreciate the significance of means in pursuing organizational goals, reference must be made to the point at which this discussion of the assumptions of the hierarchical model began, namely, are goals obvious, consistent and generally accepted? If an executive can expect to influence only minimally the discretion of his subordinates, line or staff, how can he be sure they understand the goals as he does? Can he safely assume that his goals will be somehow translated into specific actions at lower echelons?[26] The hierarchical concept would seem to answer affirmatively. As noted above, the staff is supposed to translate goals into specific actions; the line is supposed to perform these actions. This attitude puts enormous demands on the staff, for they are expected to come up with a program that will, for example, bring about a maximum of deterrent force for a minimum cost.[27] Yet even when goals are consistent and generally agreed upon, the instruments of policy, the conduct of it, the form it takes and the assignment of credit for it, all matter as much as the policy objective.[28]

Goals, such as those involved in defense, are frequently non-operational. They do not contain measuring rods for comparing alternative solutions, "but can only be related to specific action through the intervention of subgoals."[29] Now the relation of these subgoals to the broader goals is usually not subject to proof.

Richard C. Steadman, *Report to the Secretary of Defense on the National Military Command Structure*, Washington, DC: U.S. Government Printing Office (July 1978).

INTRODUCTION

The present National Military Command Structure was created by the National Security Act of 1947, as amended. It has evolved, through a series of amendments up to 1958, from a decentralized National Military Establishment of separate Military Departments to today's Department of Defense (DoD) headed by a Secretary of Defense with full authority and responsibility for its operation. This authority has permitted central and coherent management of the Department, and its exercise is a major reason why DoD, while it has its failings, is among the best managed departments in the Executive Branch.

The Military Departments organize, train, and equip the forces of their Services. They have no role in the operational employment of these forces. Combatant forces which have completed their initial training are assigned to the operational command of Unified and Specified (U & S) Commanders. The 1958 Amendment made these commanders directly responsible to the Secretary of Defense and the President.

As a matter of policy, the Secretary generally exercises his command authority through the Joint Chiefs of Staff, who include the Chairman, the Army and Air Force Chiefs of Staff, and the Chief of Naval Operations. The Commandant of the Marine Corps participates with the JCS on matters of direct concern to the Corps. Their primary statutory function is to be the principal military advisers to the Secretary, the National Security Council (NSC), the President, and also the Congress. They have accordingly been charged by the President with presenting in governmental councils the military viewpoint for the effective formulation and conduct of national security policy. OSD and the JCS both provide staff assistance to the Secretary and, though separately identified and organized, are formally charged to function in full coordination and cooperation. The Joint Staff is the staff of the JCS and is managed for them by the Chairman.

The structure, which emerged in 1958 and which remains essentially the same today, was a compromise between a recognized requirement for unified direction of the armed forces and for military advice rising above individual service interests, on one hand, and the natural desire of our military services organized separately for land, naval, and air warfare to preserve their historic autonomy, on the other. It is not surprising, then, that we find some of the fundamental problems of the NMCS today to be products of the tensions inherent in that basic compromise. The central issue today is whether the NMCS, as presently organized, can work well enough to cope with the national security problems of the future.

The world has become both more complex and more dangerous for the United States than it was in 1958, and the need for sound planning of defense policy and resources and their coordination with foreign and economic policy is even more essential. The period of American preeminence following World War II has given way to one of precarious strategic nuclear balance. Other elements of national power are more widely diffused throughout the world, with our preponderance correspondingly reduced. New problems have arisen, such as the proliferation of nuclear capabilities at one end of the spectrum of violence and terrorism at the other, shortages of natural resources, and major changes in the international economic structure. Moreover, defense budgets are tight, weapon systems are expensive, and technological changes are providing new possibilities which may result in altered roles for various elements of the armed forces.

This Report divides the National Military Command Structure into two broad areas. The first addresses the organization for war-fighting, as well as command and control of forces in the field. The strengths and weaknesses of the Unified and Specified Commands as now established and the experience of recent crisis situations those aspects which relate to policy, planning, and advice. It. discusses the interactions and functions of the Secretary of Defense, OSD, JCS, Joint Staff, and the field commanders in these areas. . . .

They are mainly directed at ways to enhance the joint and unified military contribution to the national security decision-making process. Hopefully, they will stimulate discussion of the fundamental philosophies underlying our Defense organization.

Whatever recommendations are adopted, it is important that, within the framework of clearly defined authorities and responsibilities, the National Military Command Structure remain flexible enough to respond to different leadership, different circumstances, and different events in an unpredictable future. . . .

ROLE OF THE CHAIRMAN, JCS

The Chairman is key to the superior functioning of the command system. He is, in practice, the link between the operational commands and the NCA. As such he passes NCA directives in the field and is the CINCs' primary point of contact in Washington.

Nevertheless, DoD directives now in force do not provide the CINCs with a single military superior in Washington. This has two negative aspects. First, the CINCs do not have a formal spokesman in the Washington arena to assure that their viewpoints are part of the decision-making process. Second, there is no single military officer responsible for overseeing and directing the activities of the CINCs: they have no military boss *per se*. These are both functions which the Chairman now informally, and in part, fulfills, but he is naturally inhibited by not having a clear formal mandate. We believe the Chairman should now be given authority to play a more active role with the CINCs, and that this authority should be formally delegated to the Chairman by the Secretary. The CINCs would continue to be directly responsible to the Secretary, as required by law, but the Chairman would become both their spokesman in Washington and the Secretary's agent in managing the CINCs.

It is important that the JCS as a body continue to act as the immediate military staff of the Secretary. This insures that he will be directly exposed to differing judgments and advice where they exist. However, a committee structure is not effective for the exercise of military command or management authority. Such authority could be more effectively exercised by the Chairman, who in being so empowered, should also be directed to act in consultation with the other JCS members when time permits.

An expanded and formalized role for the Chairman in managing the Unified and Specified Commands would include a responsibility for advising the Secretary on the war-fighting capabilities (readiness) of the forces and for assuring that the CINCs' views on resources required to correct identified deficiencies are adequately addressed in the allocation process.

There are now many detailed reports on the operational readiness and war-fighting capability of the combatant forces. However, these reports are focused on unit, not joint combatant force, capabilities; they use differing standards among Services; they are not designed to tie into the resource allocation process; and they do not focus on alternative corrective action possibilities. . . .

Constrained resource recommendations combining the various aspects of war-fighting capability, such as readiness, modernization, and force structure, are provided only in the Service Program Objectives Memoranda (POM) submitted annually to the Secretary. There are, however, no constrained joint recommendations on the Service POMs. The continuing refinement of the DoD program and budget subsequently involves the joint process only on selected major issues, rather than on alternatives, trade-offs, or a total program approach. Thus, the CINCs have no direct input into the budget process and no joint spokesman in the PPBS to represent their views on improvements to the capabilities of their forces. Moreover, the Secretary lacks joint military advice on resource allocation issues regarding readiness, except to the extent that it is provided informally by the CJCS. These gaps represent serious limitations in the NMCS in the planning and management procedures for maximizing the war-fighting capability of the combatant forces within the limitations of fiscal realities.

Because the CINCs and the JCS now have a minimal role in the corrective decisions, the initiation of corrective action is left largely to the Services. Because such actions relate mostly to expenditures on forces in being they are particularly important to the CINCs. The process should be changed to provide a formal input from the CINCs to the Chairman regarding the CINC's assessment of deficiencies of forces assigned to him and resource actions required to correct these deficiencies. With appropriate staff support, the Chairman could analyze inputs from the CINCs and then assure that these assessments of priority actions are considered by the Services and the Secretary of Defense in the budget decision process. Some of this now goes on in a continuing and generally informal manner. But the role of the CINCs and the Chairman in the resource allocation process should be expanded and formalized. . . .

THE SECRETARY OF DEFENSE AND OSD

Civilian Control

Civilian control over the military has been a basic tenet of our Nation since its founding, and the effectiveness of this control has been a basic question in the evolving legislation on DoD organization. We find that the concept of civilian control over the military is unquestioned throughout the Department. It is a non-issue. Our military forces are fully responsive to the command and control of the duly constituted civilian authorities; the President, the Secretary of Defense, and the Deputy Secretary.

Problems do exist in the relationship between other OSD officials and the military. There is a perception among many military officers that OSD officials below the Secretary and Deputy Secretary, sometimes improperly attempt to direct the Joint Chiefs, the Joint Staff, or the field commands. The military feel this is an extension of the concept of civilian control beyond the intent of the law. A different and more important problem is the manner in which civilian control is sometimes exercised. Many military officers believe that OSD's increasing involvement over the last thirty years in details of implementation—the "how"—as well as the establishment of the policies—the "what"—represents an intrusion into details beyond that needed for the legitimate exercise of policy direction. Moreover, they contend that detailed "how" directions from OSD authorities tend to stifle military initiative which will, over the long run, result in degraded performance.

Organizational adjustments cannot deal with these issues. It is a matter of attitudes, management styles, and perceptions of the proper role and level of OSD direction. Officials in OSD should be sensitive to these issues and careful to exercise only such authority as has been clearly delegated to them by the Secretary.

On the operational side OSD should limit its "how" directives and encourage military initiatives to the extent compatible with reasonable exercise of OSD policy direction. Field commanders are responsible for the security of their forces and are sensitive to the possibility that detailed "how to" orders may so limit their flexibility as to jeopardize their discharge of this responsibility. On the other hand, military actions have political implications, and the Secretary of Defense thus must be able to monitor JCS messages which provide operational instructions that derive from mission-type orders.

Policy Direction

Policy direction is the primary responsibility of OSD. Such direction naturally encompasses all areas of DoD activities. That which relates to the NMCS includes guidance for strategic planning, both in the near term, to include the preparation of contingency plans, and future force plans.

In the area of force planning, effective policy direction requires the statement of policy and objectives which can form the basis for military planning and from which derive the DoD program and budget. Most military officers believe that more clear and definitive national security policy guidance is needed for strategic planning. If adequate policy guidance is not given to military planners, they must prepare their own, as a necessary starting point. Some argue that previous national security policy guidance was too general to be useful, and it certainly is true that vague or all-encompassing statements of defense policy objectives are of little help in detailed force planning. On the other hand, programs constructed without clear policy directives can only be prepared on the basis of policy goals determined by the programmer himself, but often not made explicit for senior decision makers to accept or reject. Policy goals and alternatives should be made as explicit as feasible and subjected to the test of scrutiny and debate. This procedure would insure rigor in their formulation, consistency with the goals of the NCA, and better understanding of the policy by those who are charged with its execution. We believe, therefore, that a serious effort must be made to provide policy guidance which defines the national security objectives we expect our military forces to be able to attain.

In the area of policy guidance for operational plans there is a need for at least an annual review by the Secretary and selected key assistants of the principal military plans to assure that their political assumptions are consistent with national security policy. Such briefings also would broaden the understanding of key policy makers of military capabilities and options in the event of crisis or conflict.

The JCS are sensitive to the fact that only the Secretary and the Deputy Secretary are in the operational chain of command and, thus, strictly interpreted, only they have a "need to know" regarding operational plans. While security of operational plans is critical, present arrangements place too great a burden on the Secretary and Deputy Secretary for assuring that there is sufficient continuing policy guidance in these areas. This responsibility should be delegated to the Under Secretary for Policy. . . .

Alternatives for Improving Military Advice to the NCA Enhancing the Role of the Joint Staff

Several adjustments to current JCS procedures, which could be made within existing legislative statutes, would, we believe, lead to improving the effectiveness and impact of the joint institutional product. One is to enhance the role of the Joint Staff and to reinforce its capability to provide the kind of integrated national planning and advice envisioned by President Eisenhower in submitting the 1958 legislation:

> Strategic and tactical planning must be completely unified, combat forces organized into unified commands, each equipped with the most efficient weapons systems that science can develop, singly led and prepared to fight as one, regardless of Service.

Adjustments to JCS procedures which have most promise in this connection are: more guidance from senior levels prior to formal staffing; reduced requirement for the Joint Staff to "coordinate" with the Service staffs, substituting a requirement merely to include differing views in the body of its paper; increased use of analysis of pros and cons of alternative courses of action in JCS papers; and Service assignment of their most qualified officers to Joint Staff duty.

Unproductive conflict, particularly at lower staff levels, could be reduced if the Chairman or the JCS provided the Joint Staff with general guidance, when appropriate, on difficult and important issues *prior* to the initiation of staff action. In addition to reducing lower-level conflict, early guidance could also result in a final product more closely reflecting the position(s) of the senior officers. Another advantage would be that, because the principals would address the issues without responsibility to support previously prepared staff efforts, they would be better able to agree on a genuine national approach. A disadvantage is that the complexity and multiplicity of modern military problems preclude principals from being expert on all simultaneously, and that therefore, such initial high-level guidance may not lead in all cases to more thorough or less negotiated solutions and/or may preclude innovative initiatives by the staff experts.

Another path to a more focused product would be for the Joint Staff to be relieved of any requirement for Service coordination and for it to present its product directly to the Operations Deputies. Under this procedure Joint Staff officers would solicit Service inputs, while informing them of the development of the paper. This procedure would sharpen the presentation of JCS views and place greater emphasis on a joint military perspective. Since it would eliminate the lower committees, time spent on minor issues of an editorial or non-substantive nature would diminish. Disadvantages of this procedure include an increased number of issues faced by the Operations Deputies. Moreover, their negotiations might not improve the final product. However, reducing the number of lesser issues and limiting the Operations Deputies' deliberations to major issues might overcome these disadvantages. . . .

If the Joint Staff is to perform the staff leadership role envisioned by the adjustments suggested in this paper, it must be staffed with the best qualified officers available. Historically, the Services have most often assigned such officers to the Service staffs and not to the Joint Staff, although recently the Services have, on their own, taken commendable actions to attempt to upgrade the quality of officers assigned to the Joint Staff. . . .

Emphasizing joint duty as a promotion criterion is important but will not in itself develop a Joint Staff with the standard of excellence it would rewire if it is to provide the best possible support for the JCS and the Secretary in the national security decision-making process. To assemble the best officers from each Service on the Joint Staff on a continuing basis will require extraordinary measures. We suggest the Chairman be empowered to obtain assignment to Joint Staff duty of any requested officer, with due consideration for rotation requirements and the officer's career development. The criteria for such selection should be excellence in performance of staff duty as well as capacity for approaching problems from a national outlook. Exceptions would naturally have to be made, but these should be granted by the Chairman, for the Secretary, and not by the Services. Such exceptions should be recorded by the CJCS to insure that these officers are requested at a later date when they become available. By so empowering the CJCS, the Secretary would assure an upgrading of the Joint Staff.

Archie D. Barrett, *Reappraising Defense Organization: An Analysis Based on the Defense Organization Study of 1977–1980*, Washington, DC: National Defense University Press (1983).

What is the best way to organize the Department of Defense? That question concerned the architects of the National Security Act from the mid-1940s until its last major revision in 1958. This inquiry revisits the question in the context of the 1980s.

The most recent study of defense organization provides the rationale for retracing ground long ago traveled by some of the foremost national security thinkers of the post-World War II era. The Defense Organization Study of 1977–1980 (DOS 77–80) suggests the Joint Chiefs of Staff (JCS) and the military department secretaries are weak, ineffectual, and sterile institutions dominated by the Army, Navy, Air Force, and Marine Corps. Significant Department of Defense decisions, the study intimates, derive from the interplay between the secretary of defense, whose control is tenuous at best, and each of the services, whose unflagging, skillful, and effective pursuit of their interests is deservedly legendary. How best to configure the major organizational elements of the defense establishment, it turns out, remains a valid, significant–and, to many, unanswered–question.

Treatments of organization usually address mission or purpose, structure and function, process, management, and personnel. All of those subjects find their way into the following pages from time to time. But the principal focus is on that aspect of organization which comes to the fore when considering reorganization, the overall structure of the Department of Defense (DOD).

During the two decades since the last major reorganization in 1958, DOD organizational efforts followed directions other than structural. They focused on consolidating the performance of common functions in defense agencies and building and adjusting processes to regulate major activities, most notably the planning, programming, and budgeting system (PPBS) and the procedures for acquiring weapon systems and equipment. That activity continues apace.

Structural changes, on the other hand, have been relatively insignificant in recent times, as compared to the dozen years prior to 1958. During that period, Congress established the Department of Defense and refined its creation repeatedly. Successive reorganizations transformed the secretary of defense from a weak policy broker to a powerful department head, the position of chairman of the Joint Chiefs of Staff was established, unified and specified commands took shape, and service secretaries lost cabinet status.

Is reorganization needed? In addition to the DOS 77–80, a number of responsible commentaries over the last two decades have criticized the present structure and recommended changes. The first section of this chapter demonstrates this position cannot be lightly dismissed. Why has restructuring as an organizational technique for achieving improved performance subsided since 1958? The second section suggests intangible political and bureaucratic boundaries exist that limit viable reorganization proposals. Recommendations which breach the bounds have little chance of being accepted. Past studies, nevertheless, have consistently advanced proposals beyond the pale. Recognizing that this explanation of past inaction does not justify neglecting reorganization if the structure is flawed, the third section advances the recent Defense Organization Study of 1977–80 as a vehicle for exploring DOD reorganization alternatives. . . .

The slackening of structural changes has not occurred because the United States has reached the millennium in organizing its defense structure, if government studies and academic treatments in the years since 1958 are given any credence. Such works have consistently criticized the structure and recommended changes to the basic framework of defense organization. The Defense Organization Study of 1977–1980 continues that tradition. It contains a trenchant critique of the present organization.

The thesis of the critique is that the dominant organizations in the Department of Defense are the military services and the central management, the secretary of defense and the Office of the Secretary of Defense (OSD).[30] The Army, Navy, Air Force, and Marine Corps exercise preponderant influence over the joint military structure-the Joint Chiefs of Staff (JCS) and the unified and specified commands. Consequently, no authentic, independent joint military presence exists to advise civilian leaders from a national point of view and employ the unified forces of the United States in the field. The relationship between central management and the services is the anvil on which the major national security decisions involving the military instrument are hammered out in the Department of Defense. . . .[31]

The DOS 77–80 critique implies that the time has come to consider modifying the present Department of Defense structure. Although a few actions have addressed the study concerns, none which would significantly alter the structure of the Department have been initiated, nor apparently are they in the offing.[32] Thus the latest study effort is in danger of suffering the same fate as earlier studies which substantially agreed with its critique. Why have structural weaknesses been unattended since 1958? Why has this facet of DOD organization been so unresponsive to the findings and recommendations of critics, while relative flexibility has been evident in adjusting processes, management techniques, and even personnel policies?

One reason is that many proposals have been too far-reaching to attract committed and powerful proponents. Proposals run the gamut from recommending complete centralization to championing a return to decentralized service preeminence. Acceptance of any one of those proposals would result in changes as wrenching as any of the sweeping reorganizations of the past.

The Symington Report, for example, suggested eliminating the present military departments and placing the services, as separate organizational units, under the secretary of defense within a single Department of Defense. In addition, the report recommended replacing the Joint Chiefs of Staff with a single officer who would act as the principal military advisor to the president and secretary of defense, preside over a military advisory council unaffiliated with the services, and direct the combatant commands.[33] The Blue Ribbon Defense Panel proposed completely regrouping the functions of DOD under three deputy secretaries of defense to whom service secretaries and a revamped military operations structure would be subordinate.[34] Paul Y. Hammond recommended conferring authority and responsibility for the military program of all of the services upon the chairman of the Joint Chiefs of Staff, who would head a formally established general staff.[35] Finally, John C. Ries' treatise favoring a return to decentralized organization suggested the possibility of consolidating the unified and specified commands into four mission-oriented services which would absorb the existing military department.[36]

After the strident conflicts of the early post-World War II years, the erstwhile combatants had little energy and no enthusiasm for further battles along these lines. Furthermore, less provocation existed. The secretary of defense emerged with such sweeping authority he could hardly continue to claim to be too weak to run the Department. The Army, Navy, Air Force, and Marine Corps found they had successfully defended the separate identities and relative autonomy they sought. Finally, the external factors which had fanned the reorganization fires subsided with the election of President Kennedy. Parsimonious Truman and Eisenhower defense budgets, which gave rise to intense service competition and corresponding public reaction in support of greater unification, gave way to an expanding defense posture and subsequently to the plentiful Vietnam budgets. Nor did succeeding presidents share Eisenhower's penchant for personal involvement in Department of Defense reorganization. In these circumstances, despite the periodic proposals for major realignments, none of the powerful potential demonstrated sufficient interest to make structural change a viable issue.

Thus the later years have confirmed what the early years demonstrated: structural reorganization of the Department of Defense is, first and foremost, a political process, involving the clash and adjustment of bureaucratic, legislative, and private interests. Restructuring is not, as many studies implicitly assume, an academic exercise in organizational optimization. Studies are simply too prone to advance far-reaching proposals while remaining insensitive to possible sources of support and opposition in the bureaucracy, White House, Congress, and public. If they are to influence the shape of public institutions such as the Department of Defense, organization studies and other literature of this genre must advance reorganization proposals developed with an informed appreciation of the likely boundaries of the politically possible.[37]

A second reason for the absence of significant structural changes is the relative ease and apparent effectiveness of alternative organizational approaches. Since 1958, if not before, the authority of the secretary of defense to establish processes for deciding resource allocation, acquisition, and similar issues has been unchallenged. Organizational processes, after all, in one respect are merely rules defining who figures, and to what degree, in a decision. The power to establish a process is the power to slice through the structure of an organization, bypassing certain elements regardless of their position in the hierarchy, and including others, even though they may be formally subordinate. Thus, processes can be used to avoid direct conflict and facilitate action by defining, and redefining when necessary, the rules of the game for making decisions.

And process changes are less dolorous for secretaries of defense than reorganizations. Although the formal authority of the secretary of defense to reorganize his department is comparable to his authority to create and modify processes, the *de facto* circumstances differ markedly. A secretary who proposes significant reorganization of the military departments or Joint Chiefs of Staff can be certain he will be strongly challenged both from within the Department of Defense and from powerful segments of the Congress and the general public. Faced with inevitable, unremitting opposition to significant restructuring, secretaries focus on modifying processes. . . .

Examination of the Army budget controversy succinctly illustrates several advantages of limited reorganization. Many controversies now inaccurately couched in terms of "vertical" civil-military conflicts would assume their genuine dimensions as disagreements between competing military perspectives. The reorganized DOD would resolve a large proportion of those issues at levels below the secretary of defense, or at least transform them into broad questions more suitable for his attention.

The structural realignments would also enhance the capability to resolve issues the present organization avoids. The Army budget controversy involves resource allocation, an area the National Military Command Structure (NMCS) Study Report finds particularly troublesome for the present Joint Chiefs of Staff.

> The nature of the organization virtually precludes effective addressal of those issues involving allocation of resources among the services, such as budget levels, force structures, and procurement of new weapons systems-except to agree that they should be increased without consideration of resource constraints. . . .[38]

Would the proposed reorganization be approved by Congress? Yes, probably. The outcome would depend on the circumstances at the time, of course. But as this volume is being completed early in the 1980s, the situation appears to be more favorable to change than usual for several reasons. A new President elected with an overwhelming electoral margin occupies the White House. His secretary of defense enjoys broad congressional support as a result of the strong national security posture advocated by President Reagan during his winning campaign. Those factors reinforce an underlying tendency of Congress to defer to a secretary on organization matters, particularly when its prerogatives are not threatened and the specific proposals call for moderate, incremental change as in the case of the limited reorganization alternative.

An equally important, if less apparent, circumstance is the increasing realization, in the public at large as well as among legislators, that organizational reform may be necessary. Congress might be receptive to proposals which reflect a growing public sentiment favoring institutional change.

David C. Hendrickson, *Reforming Defense: The State of American Civil-Military Relations*, Baltimore, MD: The Johns Hopkins University Press (1988).

It has long been recognized that an appropriate pattern of civil-military relations requires some attention to the fact that the military services are extremely large organizations. Over two million men and women are in uniform and the influence of the services reaches far beyond that. The theorist of civil-military relations must therefore be concerned with a set of issues that go beyond those involving the level, scope, and unity of civilian and military authority. Of those issues, three stand out in importance: whether organizations should be structured along purposive or functional lines; the appropriate degree of centralization (or decentralization); and responsiveness to change. . . .

The problem of centralization is best understood as one of competing virtues (or vices), for there must be some measure of both centralized oversight and decentralized initiative in any organization; to carry one or the other principle to an extreme normally leads to pernicious consequences. The degree of centralization will affect the extent to which accurate or misleading information is transmitted from higher to lower echelons and vice versa; and the character and effectiveness of any organization, in turn, will be affected by the specificity of the orders given to lower units as well as the amount of initiative expected of them. . . .

That military organizations have the resources and incentive to resist and frustrate change forced upon them "from the outside" ought at least to make us wary of the attempt. It serves, on the whole, to reestablish the presumption in favor of deferring to the professional expertise of the military in matters that concern its professional function—a presumption most organizational theorists have sought to demolish. It also points to three other factors that ought to be borne in mind in the contemporary debate over defense reform. One is the value of services whose functions in some degree overlap and that are therefore competitive with one another. Another is the danger that civilian intervention, over time, will reflect a variety of inconsistent proposals and may work at cross-purposes. And the third is the importance of effecting reform at least partly "from the inside"—that is, through promotion rather than continual outside pressure. . . .

In the postwar era, the United States has never lacked proposals for reforming the institutions that govern civil-military relations. Until recently, virtually all reforms had been successfully resisted. In 1986 however, Congress passed a Defense Reorganization Act that

---

incorporated many of the proposals of the organizational reformers. Although it is still too early to say how the reforms will work out in practice, the Goldwater-Nichols bill was a substantial accomplishment. As might have been expected, Congress made far greater headway in reforming the Joint Chiefs of Staff than in changing its own internal procedures—many of which have had a deleterious effect on how efficiently the Pentagon is managed. Still, the changes made in 1986 were for the most part for the better, and it is not clear that the impulse toward organizational reform has been fully spent. The present moment, indeed, recalls the situation at the end of the 1950s when a consensus existed among many Republican and Democratic leaders on the need for change which yielded, in turn, the Eisenhower reforms of 1958 and the McNamara revolution of the early 1960s.

Most of the institutional reforms that have been considered . . . have been around for a long time. In general, they address the feature of American civil-military relations that is least conducive to objective civilian control—the lack of unified direction on both sides of the civil-military divide. This lack of unity is deeply embedded in the American governing system: on the one side it stems from the separation of powers between the president and the Congress; on the other, from the existence of separate military services. The reforms that would be most effective in overcoming the lack of unified direction, however, are usually difficult to bring about and sometimes are of questionable desirability. Congress is most unlikely to surrender its detailed review over line items: were it to do so it would also surrender its power of distributing the loot among its varied constituencies. But it would also lose much of its power as a check on the excesses of both the executive branch and the military. It is very difficult to deprive Congress of the power to make mischief without simultaneously reducing its power to do good. Reforms that combat the lack of unified direction on the military side have proved themselves much more of a practical possibility, but not all are desirable. The extensive reallocation of roles and missions of the services would probably make matters worse. Even the reform of the JCS accomplished in 1986, though it offers the prospect of a much-needed improvement in the conduct of operations, will probably yield only modest benefits. Interservice rivalry has never lost us a war; nor has it ever prevented us from winning one. Institutional reforms are no substitute for sensible political and strategic choices, and it is a mistake to believe that they are.

The current wave of proposals for institutional reform therefore seems likely to issue only in the most modest of improvements. It is probable that some reforms, such as the extensive rewriting of the Key West accord, would actually make matters worse. The two reforms that do offer some hope of improvement are the strengthening of joint institutions within the present military structure and the establishment of biennial budgeting. The former has already been adopted; the latter remains on the table. Biennial budgeting would bring much-needed stability to the acquisition of military systems and would focus more attention on longer range issues of strategy and force structure; strengthening the joint capability of the officer corps offers the prospect of improvements in the conduct of operations. It goes without saying that such reforms—and the more far-reaching measures that have been considered here—would not guarantee wise choices in the great issues of war and peace the United States will confront in the coming years. They might even magnify error and deepen our predicament. But they would help restore to political deliberation and military command a measure of the "energy" that is now so sorely lacking, and such a result is not to be despised.

Fred Thompson, "Management Control and the Pentagon: The Organizational Strategy-Structure Mismatch," *Public Administration Review*, Vol. 51, No. 1. (January–February, 1991), pp. 52–66.

Planning, organizing, staffing, and organizational development are the key functions of top management in any organization. It is my thesis that the top managers in the Department of Defense (DOD) have failed to perform these functions satisfactorily. Because of this failure, they have been forced to devote their attention to lower level tasks-operating, controlling, and budgeting. Overwhelmed by administrative detail, they have allowed the DOD to become turgid and ineffective. Furthermore, I argue that this failure largely reflects the incomplete implementation of organizational and budgetary reforms initiated over thirty years ago. . . .

By organizational structure I mean three distinct but related things. First is the division of labor in the organization. This is the organization's administrative structure–the structure depicted in organization charts, including tables of organization and equipment. Second is the distribution of individual authority and responsibility within the organization. This is the organization's responsibility structure. Third is the organization's system of measuring and evaluating performance–how it organizes information on inputs, costs, activities, and outputs. This is the organization's account or control structure. An account structure should be oriented to administrative units or responsibility centers–optimally to both, since the information provided by these accounts can be used both to coordinate unit activities and to control the behavior of responsibility center managers.

Two basic rules govern organizational design. First, strategy should determine structure. Strategy means the pattern of purposes and policies that defines the organization and its missions and that positions it relative to its environment. Single-mission organizations should be organized along functional lines; multimission organizations should be organized along mission lines; multimission, multifunction organizations should be organized along matrix lines. Where a matrix organization is large enough to justify an extensive division of labor, responsibility centers ought to be designated as either mission or support centers, with the latter linked to the former by a system of internal markets and prices.

The second basic rule is that the organization should be as decentralized as possible. It has been demonstrated to the satisfaction of most students of management that the effectiveness of large, complex organizations improves when authority is delegated down into the organization along with responsibility.[39] Authority must not be arbitrarily or capriciously delegated, however. Decentralization requires prior clarification of the purpose or function of each administrative unit and responsibility center, procedures for setting objectives and for monitoring and rewarding performance, and a control structure that links each responsibility center to the goals of the organization as a whole. Centralization is *not* policy direction from the top, hierarchically established goals, and central control procedures. These are characteristics of *all* well-managed organizations. Rather, centralized authority is characterized by the use of *ex ante* controls—by rules and regulations that specify what must be done, as well as how, when, where, and by whom. Decentralized authority is characterized by *ex post* controls—rewards and performance targets that are high enough to elicit the best efforts from an organization's responsibility center managers.[40]

Mission attributes constrain the degree of decentralization possible within an organization.[41] Some missions require precise orchestration and coordination of complex bundles of tasks. The existence of reciprocal dependence (i.e., activities that must be carried out simultaneously to be successful) severely limits the degree to which the responsibility structure of an organization can be decentralized. Goal ambiguity, i.e., ambiguous administrative boundaries and roles and mission responsibilities, also constrains decentralization. Unlike reciprocal dependence, however, goal ambiguity is often a self-inflicted wound.

At the other extreme, where organizational missions or activities do not directly impinge upon each other, decentralization is not at all constrained. Mission performance may be constrained by the pool of resources available to the organization—top management attention, production capacity, or space, for instance. Hence, even in a decentralized organization, it may be necessary for top management to evaluate the organization's missions and to ration the limited resource among them.

The significance of common pool or common property resources is a function of the organization's time horizon. In the short run, nearly every resource is constrained. In the Management Control and the Pentagon long run, there are few if any real resource constraints, at least not this side of total mobilization of the nation's capacity to produce. Military strategy has two aspects—raising, equipping, and organizing armed forces and using them in support of political objectives. Preparing forces for combat is governed primarily by longer-run considerations. The implication is that in peacetime, at least, there may be few if any common pool resources that have to be rationed by DOD's top management. In contrast, where combat is concerned, short-run considerations obviously predominate.

Finally, there is the intermediate case in which mission performance depends upon the sequential performance of a series of tasks or functions; i.e., there is one-way movement of work from one administrative unit to the next. Sequential interdependence need not constrain decentralization, however. The relationship between sequentially dependent administrative units is essentially bilateral in nature. Where bilateral relationships are concerned, it is usually possible to set up some kind of transactional arrangement to eliminate or internalize spillovers. In most cases, these relationships can be governed satisfactorily via buyer-seller arrangements and, where they occur within the organization, by appropriate transfer prices.[42]

The failure to think these structural relationships through is highly inimical to decentralization. It produces an organization that is rife with externalities and common property resources, one in which everything depends upon everything else—in other words, an organization in which effective decentralization is impossible. Organizations that fail to sort out the relationships between their component units—i.e., that fail to align their administrative structure with their responsibility and control structures—must choose between centralization and organizational chaos. Given that choice, centralization is probably the preferable alternative.

This article contends that the DOD in general and the Office of the Secretary of Defense (OSD) in particular have failed to clarify administrative boundaries, roles, and mission responsibilities and to delegate authority accordingly. Instead, the DOD has alternated between delegating authority to the uniformed services and centralizing authority in the hands of the Secretary of Defense. Each swing of this pendulum has led to failures and excesses, in some cases arising out of the pursuit of parochial interests on the part of the uniformed services. These failures have in turn led to renewed centralization, to a further proliferation of rules and regulations aimed at preventing error, to auditors charged with monitoring compliance with the rules, to overstaffing, and, ultimately, to inflexibility and immobility. The point is not that anyone in the OSD ever consciously chose the extreme centralization that characterizes the DOD. No one ever consciously chooses obesity; it is acquired, bite by bite, over an extended period. . . .

Effective decentralization of DOD would have required more than the installation of a results-oriented operating budget, however. At a minimum, responsibility budgeting and decentralization would have required prior clarification of the purpose of the major administrative units and responsibility centers in the DOD and of their relationships to each other. Thinking organizational purpose through and reorganizing to bring the DOD's structure into line with U.S. defense strategy was the singular challenge facing its top management in the postwar era. For one reason or another the OSD consistently failed to recognize or meet this challenge. . . .[43]

From this vantage point one fact stands out: the combatant commands are the principal instruments of U.S. defense policy. Flexible response requires organizational responsibilities to be divided along geographic lines. This fact is now widely acknowledged to be the key to closing the gap between defense organization and strategic purpose that appeared in the wake of the Eisenhower/McNamara reforms. One manifestation of this belief is Jacques Gansler's recommendation that the budget process be restructured to provide spending authority to the combatant commands, rather than by object of expenditure classes to the uniformed services.[44] Gansler refers to this concept as mission budgeting, but he does not explain how budgeting by mission area would work, or how it would make things better. . . .

(T)he conceptual foundations of intraorganizational decentralization and their application to the DOD are fairly well understood. First, align strategy with structure. An appreciation of the distinction between mission centers and support centers is central to a resolution of the DOD's strategy-structure mismatch. Mission centers contribute directly to the organization's objectives. They are the principal instruments of organizational policy. Support centers supply goods or services to other responsibility centers in the organization—i.e., they perform functions for other support or mission centers.

According to contemporary military doctrine and strategy, the combatant commands are the principal instruments of U.S. defense policy. Contemporary military doctrine and strategy assigns supporting roles to the uniformed services. They are supposed to supply combat and support units to the combatant commands. The units they supply to the combatant commands are organized along functional lines, but the combatant commands are not. In other words, the DOD's mission structure does not follow functional lines. The DOD is a multimission, multifunction organization. . . .

Aligning structure with strategy is of fundamental importance for any organization. This conclusion holds a fortiori for an organization as large and complex as the DOD. If the DOD is to transform itself into a more effective and efficient organization, it must think through its structural relationships, clarify its administrative boundaries, functional roles, and mission responsibilities, and develop an accounting system that links each administrative unit and responsibility center to the overall defense policies of the United States. The DOD's failure to sort out these relationships has produced an organization that is rife with externalities and common property resources, one in which everything depends upon everything else-an organization in which effective decentralization is impossible. Consequently, this failure has led to centralization, to a proliferation of rules and regulations aimed at preventing error, to auditors and inspectors general charged with monitoring compliance with the rules, to overstaffing, and, ultimately, to organizational inflexibility, and immobility.

Organizational strategies should reflect environmental risks and opportunities. When the constellation of risks faced by an organization changes, so too should its strategy and, along with its strategy, its structure. American military strategy has to be affected by the changes now taking place in the realm of international politics. Consequently, military doctrine will likely undergo major changes. New doctrines call for new organizational designs. Does this mean that the diagnosis Management Control and the Pentagon 63 and prescriptions presented here are largely moot, that administrative control theory has nothing to offer save belated advice on how to organize the DOD to fight the late, unlamented cold war? The candid answer is both yes and no. The specifics of the DOD's organizational structure will certainly have to change to accommodate the new reality. It would not be surprising, for example, if in the new era the combatant commands lost their place as the principal instruments of American defense policy. But the fundamental logic of organizing and budgeting the DOD on a mission basis remains sound. This course of action reflects proposals made by Fredrick C. Mosher and Robert N. Anthony thirty years ago or more, under an earlier, narrower doctrinal regime. The broad organizational template they outlined—a matrix structure, with mission and support centers linked by transfer prices, responsibility budgeting, and accrual accounting should serve the national interest well under almost any conceivable set of circumstances, at least so long as military strategy continues to call for the deployment of multifunctioned forces on behalf of multiple missions.

Moreover, change can be accommodated far more readily by a decentralized organization than by a bloated bureaucracy. The critical defense policy issue of the next decade is likely to be managing a drastic reduction in the scale of America's force structure and its defense industrial base, without threatening its creativity, flexibility, or efficiency. Such an outcome is hardly imaginable under the DOD's existing centralized organizational arrangements.

John G. Kester, "The 1986 Defense Reorganization: A Promising Start," in *Bureaucratic Politics and National Security: Theory and Practice*, David C. Kozak, James M. Keagle (Eds.), (1988).

On October 1, 1986, Congress went further in telling the Pentagon how to do its job than at any time since the fundamental defense organizational statutes of 1947, 1949, and 1958. The movement was bipartisan: The law carries the names of retiring Senator Barry Goldwater and House Armed Service Subcommittee Chairman Bill Nichols.[45] It could just as well have borne the names of Senator Sam Nunn and some diligent committee staffers on both sides of Capitol Hill who had pushed the effort for many years.

What strikingly distinguishes the new legislation from its predecessors is that it was unquestionably the child of Congress, not the Executive Branch. It was enacted not with Secretary of Defense Caspar Weinberger's blessing, but, figuratively, over his dead body. It became law in the face of protests by the sitting Joint Chiefs of Staff (who were disputed by some of their predecessors) that it was not needed-protests that finally became so strident and exaggerated that they were self-defeating.

Coming on the heels of flamboyant complaints about defense procurement–the allegedly overpriced hammers, coffee machines, and toilet seats–these long-needed organizational reforms secured passage partly on their merits and partly as a congressional vote of no confidence in the way the Pentagon had (or had not) been managed for the past six years. The Reagan administration understood the bill in the latter sense. The bill was quietly approved by the president without the usual signing ceremony that trumpets legislation drawing executive enthusiasm.

Congress, however, remains the Legislative Branch. It can pass laws, occasionally investigate, and intermittently micromanage. But it is up to the Executive Branch, under the Constitution, to enforce the laws that Congress passes. The armed services committees have vowed to keep an eye on how well the reluctant targets of this legislation are saluting and moving out. The first promised checkup hearings were held in May 1987. "The devil," someone once observed, "is in the details." It will take a year or two of examining details of implementation before anyone will know for sure whether the 1986 Goldwater-Nichols Act is really, as House Armed Services Committee Chairman Les Aspin described it,

---

"probably the greatest sea change in the history of the American military since the Continental Congress created the Continental Army in 1775."[46]

The new reorganization law is fundamental legislation. It addresses longstanding dissatisfaction with the way the U.S. military functions. The law has potential, if not sabotaged or ignored, to change permanently the way the armed forces are planned and the way they operate, and, in the process, it could reshape military careers. . . .

However, and ironically, while Capitol Hill was opening its eyes to Pentagon reorganization issues, a totally opposite shift had taken place in the Pentagon. Caspar Weinberger, the new secretary of defense, soon revealed that he had no interest whatsoever in management. (Indeed, he quickly undid many of Brown's small reforms. The number of assistant secretaries of defense swelled from six to eleven, while Congress continued to add even more in a sort of interest-group approach to defense management.) Weinberger's answer to all organizational questions-and for a time his president's answer also-was to leave budget and policy decisions to the three military departments and to give the uniformed leadership whatever it wanted. The three military departments, not surprisingly, did not rise to the challenge; instead, they, predictably, pushed their pet programs (for example, fifteen carrier battle groups) without regard to overall capability.

The uniformed advocates of change were soon out of office. Jones retired in 1982 and Meyer in 1983. Jones was replaced by General John W. Vessey, Jr., not the least of whose attractions to the new administration was that he had been rejected for army chief of staff by Jimmy Carter. Vessey and the new chiefs spent the next four years assuring everyone that the JCS were one of nature's most nearly perfect creations since mother's milk. If the JCS were to be changed at all, they explained, it needed only minor adjustments of their own concoction-such as making the chairman a statutory member, coequal with his boss the secretary of defense, on the National Security Council (NSC).

Weinberger, egged on by the chiefs and following his hands-off management style, dug in his heels against meaningful change—to the point that his intransigence finally became an administration embarrassment. Meanwhile, public complaints about high-priced flukes of spare-parts pricing, and a growing desire to save money on defense, deepened loss of confidence in Weinberger's judgment. . . .

The reorganization arrow almost hit the wrong target. The biggest problem in the DoD structure was that the four military services were too dominant, and the central military organization—the JCS and particularly its chairman—too institutionally weak. Yet some earlier House versions of the reorganization bill, as well as proposals pushed by the Weinberger administration at the behest of the JCS, would have cut back on the power of the secretary of defense, while leaving the service bureaucracies unscathed. The JCS chairman would have been made a military commander of all the forces, instead of simply head of the senior uniformed staff, and would have been added to the political leaders on the NSC (which he had always attended in a proper advisory role). All those bad ideas finally were eliminated. . . .

Continuing a trend begun under the secretary's own authority by Secretary of Defense Harold Brown, the new law removes many functions from the service-dominated JCS—the corporate body—and reassigns them to the chairman alone. It is he, not they, who advises the president and secretary of defense, and it is to him that the joint staff now will answer.

The law also gives the chairman a four-star deputy. No longer will one of the service chiefs fill in as acting chairman on the frequent occasions when the chairman is out of town. Simple as it sounds, creation of this new second-ranking officer for the U.S. armed forces is a striking measure of the seriousness of the legislation, and of Congress' determination to change the present system.

The current service chiefs pulled out all the stops to lobby against this provision. Partly because no one likes to lose a chance to visit the White House, they urged that the new vice chairman should rank below them and never be acting chairman. They argued that the responsibility of acting as chairman gave each of them incentive to keep abreast of joint matters (which they are supposed to do anyway). They did not object to creation of a new office—but as they conceived it, the incumbent would have ranked behind them and never acted as chairman. In effect, Congress simply would have awarded the chairman's existing three-star assistant a fourth star. . . .

Assignments and promotions are the currency of power in the U.S. military organization. Over the long run they shape the services far more than quibbles about who attends meetings at the White House.

Thanks to the stubborn insistence of the House conferees, the new law at last lays the foundation for a real U.S. general staff. Finally, by Congress' direction, there will be a career specialty for officers in joint-duty assignments. Their promotions are to be monitored to make sure able officers get into the field. (A House provision that went further and called for numerical quotas was wisely dropped.) Their big daddy will be the chairman of the JCS, and he will have what it takes to protect them. Unlike some of the passing enthusiasms that crop up every so often for one career field or another, this policy favoring joint duty is written into law and so will be difficult to ignore.

Perry Smith, "Operating in the Joint Arena," in *Bureaucratic Politics and National Security: Theory and Practice*, David C. Kozak, James M. Keagle (Eds.), (1988).

Of all the bureaucratic structures within the U.S. government, the Organization of the Joint Chiefs of Staff is clearly one of the most complex, most structured and most difficult to explain to outsiders. On the other hand, it is in the joint arena, both in Washington and in the Unified Commands in the field, that important planning and policy making take place. Anyone wishing to understand how national security policy is made must understand the rules of thumb for operating in the joint arena. The participants in the policy making and decision making processes within the joint arena tend to be hard-working, dedicated, and quite sophisticated individuals. The majority are military officers with anywhere from twelve to thirty-four years of service, mostly in the field and not in Washington. This lack of long-term Washington experience is quite unique since almost all other federal bureaucracies are staffed by long-term Washington hands.

Most military officers serving in Washington in the Office of the Joint Chiefs of Staff and in the military service staffs (army staff, navy staff, air staff, Marine Corps staff) serve for no more than four years and return to operational jobs in this country (or overseas) at the completion of two-, three-, or four-year tours in Washington. Although short in Washington experience, these officers are highly educated (a master's degree is common as is completion of one or more professional military colleges), and they have an excellent grasp of the operational aspects of their particular service. Those who serve in the Office of the Joint Chiefs of Staff are vastly outnumbered by those who serve on the military service staffs, and, as a result, the military service staffs are often able to overwhelm those serving in a joint position because they have ready access to more people, to more analytical resources, and so on.

Anyone examining the joint arena must understand that parochialism and provincialism are common phenomena at work at many levels and in complex patterns. For instance, an army lieutenant colonel from the infantry branch with a great deal of experience in airborne operations who works in the plans and policy area of the Joint Chiefs of Staff (JCS) has a number of loyalties. He must be loyal to the chairman of the JCS, who in most cases will be a four-star general or admiral from another service; he must be loyal to the director of the joint staff and the director of plans and policy, both three-star officers from different services; he must maintain his loyalty to the U.S. Army, the infantry branch, and the airborne infantry subbranch of the infantry, to which he will return in a few years; he must often represent and be loyal to a commander of a unified or specific command (such as the US. Commander of Europe or the Commander of the Strategic Air Command) since the paper he may be responsible for concerns one or more of these commands; and, of course, he must be loyal to both the secretary of defense and the president, to whom he has constitutional, legal, and traditional responsibilities.

An officer serving on the staff of a military service in Washington also has a hierarchy of loyalties, although this hierarchy is somewhat different in crucial areas. For instance, an officer from the staff of a military service often is expected to hold loyalty to his or her service higher than his or her loyalty to the chairman of the JCS or to a commander of a unified or specified command.

Hence, when the five key players (a joint staff officer and an officer from each of the service staffs) sit down to thrash out a study, action paper, message, and so on, these officers not only have different backgrounds but also different loyalties. If any of these five officers takes a parochial position favoring his or her individual service, the other officers normally feel obliged to take corresponding, but conflicting, parochial positions. Often the joint staff officer must work hard to draft a position that serves the overall interest of the nation and not just the narrower interest of one or two of the military services. Usually the result is a carefully crafted compromise that is not the best, or even nearly the best, solution to the problem, but is one that all can agree upon. Since the power of the joint staff officer is quite limited in the shaping and coordination of joint staff papers, the final papers are often disappointing to the chairman of the JCS, to the secretary of defense, and to the unified and specified commanders in the field. . . .

One of the worst mistakes an officer working in the joint arena can make is failing to stay in close contact with relevant agencies and individuals in the field. If, for instance, an officer is assigned to the Middle East Division of a service or the joint staff, he or she should travel often to the Middle East, should make contact with both foreign and U.S. officials visiting Washington from the Middle East, should get to know foreign officials who serve in Washington, and should spend much time on the telephone, sharing insights from the Washington scene and gaining information and insights from the Middle East. Officers may think they are creating superb policy on the Middle East in Washington, but, if they do not check their work often with people in the field who have the advantage of being totally immersed in the issues and the culture, they are making a grave mistake. The same is true of individuals who are working in more technical areas: Contact with laboratories, think tanks, and field agencies is an essential part of the job. The Washington-based staff officer must realize that with each passing day he or she becomes more and more removed from past experiences in the field and, hence, becomes more and more likely to err on the side of old experiences and outdated insights. After about four years, most military officers need to return to the field to reestablish currency, expertise, and contacts. However, a few officers in Washington have such a knack of staying in touch with the field that they can remain effective well beyond this four-year mark.

One of the dysfunctional aspects of joint activities is a phenomenon known as "kicking the can." When one or more military services have a major objection to aspects of a joint paper, they try to change the paper to satisfy their concerns. If they succeed, as is often the case, they will try a number of delaying tactics so that the decision will not be made for months, years, or, preferably, ever. The postponement of a decision is common in the joint arena. In fact, it is probably the worst offense in the committee system known as the Joint Chiefs of Staff.

One way to postpone a decision is to initiate a study. Many studies are started, not because more complete data or analyses are needed by decision makers, but because one or more military services object to a decision being made. There are a number of unfortunate aspects of this tendency: First, a decision that should be made relatively quickly is not made for many months or even years; second, much time and money is spent, wastefully in many cases; third, the people involved often realize that they are participating in a sham, which leads to discouragement and cynicism. The JCS should work to overcome their propensity to postpone decisions. . . .

Although most attention is paid to the decision-making process, the implementation process is equally important. Decisions that cannot or will not be carried out are of little value; too many decision papers lead nowhere. Actors in the joint arena have a responsibility to insure that they find solutions that can be implemented with a minimum of agony. Hence, decision papers must be written with clarity and precision and must contain the funding, manpower, logistics, and communications wherewithal to insure implementation. Once they realize they cannot prevent a decision by the Joint Chiefs of Staff, manipulative officers from various services will sometimes work to make the decision impossible to implement. In the vernacular of the joint arena, "Let's make this paper a real turkey so it will never fly." In other words, if an action officer cannot make the paper come out in favor of his or her service's position, he or she will often work to make the paper weak, confusing, and incapable of being implemented.

James R. Locher III, "Building on the Goldwater-Nichols Act," in *The Goldwater-Nichols DOD Reorganization Act: A Ten-Year Retrospective*, Dennis J. Quinn (Ed.), Washington, DC: National Defense University Press (1999).

When Congress passed the Goldwater-Nichols Act, Les Aspin, then Chairman of the House Armed Services Committee, declared, "This is one of the landmark laws of American history. It is probably the greatest sea change in the history of the American military since the Continental Congress created the Continental Army in 1775."

Barry Goldwater, Chairman of the Senate Armed Services Committee, also measured the 1986 legislation in historic terms. He judged that the bill "will possibly be the most significant piece of defense organization legislation in the nation's history.... For the first rime, we will have organizational arrangements that will lead to true unity of effort in the Pentagon and in the warfighting commands in the field."

In 1986, few understood why Aspin, Goldwater, and key colleagues–including Congressman Bill Nichols and Senator Sam Nunn–had such high expectations for the Goldwater-Nichols Act. Many in the Pentagon held an opposite view. Navy Secretary John Lehman said the legislation would "make a hash of our Defense structure." General P. X. Kelley, its Commandant of the Marine Corps, argued that the reforms "would create chaos ... to the point where I would have deep concerns for the future of the United States." Air Force Secretary Russ Rourke warned, "The bill would have very adverse consequences for our national defense."

The extent to which the Pentagon resisted and misjudged the Goldwater-Nichols Act is instructive. It reveals that the majority of military officers were then giving priority to service interests over genuine national interests and somehow had come to believe that their behavior in doing so was correct. Although both World War II and postwar experiences had clarified the need for an effectively integrated military establishment, resistance to a more unified approach continued to be the orientation of officers deeply immersed in their service cultures. Despite overwhelming evidence of the need, military officers resisted the creation of viable joint institutions that would lessen service independence and prerogatives. In 1985, Senator Goldwater lamented, "As someone who has devoted his entire life to the military, I am saddened that the services are still unable to put national interest above parochial interest."

The Pentagon's unyielding opposition to the Goldwater-Nichols Act also demonstrated that it knew little about organization issues. In line with the song, "Don't Know Much About History, Don't Know Much About Geography," DOD could have written "Don't Know Much About Organization." Historical factors created this situation. For more than a century, the military was denied the initiative to reorganize itself. Not surprisingly, this off-limits area permanently disappeared as a topic of serious interest. . . .

Now that we know how the act came about, was it worth it? Has Goldwater-Nichols worked? In the broad sweep of American military history, recent years have been remarkable for the number and scope of significant achievements and successes by the Department of Defense. Superb leadership played an important role as did doctrine, training, education, and hardware developments that preceded the Goldwater-Nichols Act. Nevertheless, a significant body of evidence and numerous public assertions by senior defense officials and military officers argue that the act enormously contributed to the positive outcomes of recent years. The act validated the 1983 prediction of former Defense Secretary Jim Schlesinger: "Sound structure will permit the release of energies and of imagination now unduly constrained by the existing arrangements."

During the last 10 years, the Goldwater-Nichols Act transformed and revitalized the American military profession. Overwhelming successes in operations Just Cause in Panama and Desert *Shield/Storm* in the Persian Gulf region provided visible evidence of the act's effect. Secretary Perry reported, "All commentaries and after-action reports on Operation Desert. *Shield/Storm* attribute *the* success of the operation to the fundamental structural changes in the chain of command brought about by Goldwater-Nichols."

Shortly after the Gulf War, Forbes magazine commented, "The extraordinarily efficient, smooth way our military has functioned in the Gulf is a tribute to . . . the Goldwater-Nichols Reorganization Act, which shifted power from individual military services to officials responsible for coordinating them. . . . The extraordinary achievements of Secretary Cheney and Generals Powell and Schwarzkopf would not have been possible without Goldwater-Nichols."

Secretary Perry recently used an historic yardstick to praise the legislation: "The Goldwater-Nichols Act is perhaps the most important Defense legislation since World War II." While serving as Vice Chairman of the Joint Chiefs of Staff, Admiral Owens saw the legislation in even larger terms: "Goldwater-Nichols was the watershed event for the military since the second World War. It changed significantly the culture of the U.S. military. In the last seven or eight years, we've progressed from a reluctant standing up of the Goldwater-Nichols reforms, to a fall acceptance by the services that this is the future of warfighting." In line with congressional expectations, it is clear that the Goldwater-Nichols Act has profoundly improved the performance and warfighting capabilities of the American military establishment. . . .

Although DOD has a full agenda of internal organization issues, an outside set of organization issues demands priority attention. This set centers on the need for improvements in interagency planning and coordination. This is the province of the National Security Council system, but the ability of the Pentagon to execute assigned missions now depends to a greater extent on the contributions of other departments and agencies. And increasingly, deployed forces find themselves in supporting roles in operations other than war.

The Pentagon has been slow to recognize this growing interdependence. Traditionally, DOD wanted to be assigned the entire mission and then be left alone. As Senator Nunn noted, "The old days of the Pentagon doing the entire mission are gone for good." But past habits are difficult to overcome.

Center for Strategic and International Studies (CSIS), *Beyond Goldwater-Nichols: Defense Reform for a New Strategic Era, Phase I Report*, (March 2004).

EXECUTIVE SUMMARY

The Beyond Goldwater-Nichols (BG-N) study team concludes that the U.S. national security apparatus requires significant reforms to meet the challenges of a new strategic era. As part of its transformational efforts, the Department of Defense (DOD) must adapt not only to the post-Cold War, post-9/11 security environment but also must cope with many "hidden failures" that, while not preventing operational success, stifle necessary innovation and continue to squander critical resources in terms of time and money. Many organizational structures and processes initially constructed to contain a Cold War superpower in the Industrial Age are inappropriate for 21st century missions in an Information Age.

In taking a problem-centric approach to reform issues, the BG-N study team relied heavily on the experience of esteemed former practitioners for both identifying problems and justifying pragmatic recommendations. It also looked beyond the scope of the original Goldwater-Nichols Act in addressing problems that significantly affect how DOD operates today, including the conduct of interagency and coalition operations as well as its relationship with Congress. In making its recommendations, we believed it was essential to give organizations the capacity to carry out new mandates and not simply exhort a better performance from all relevant parties.

In its approach to defense reform, the BG-N study team formulated a set of six guiding principles that would guide its search for recommendations to solve the most serious problems. First, we recognize that preserving civilian control over the military is a paramount value in the American political system and is a prime responsibility of the Secretary of Defense (SecDef). The President relies on the SecDef to assume ultimate authority over the affairs of the department. Though the Defense Under Secretaries act as the principal means for exercising SecDef control of the military, the Service Secretaries continue to perform a meaningful role. Second, we believe that the institutional vitality of the Military Services must be maintained. In a real sense, the Military Services are the most enduring institutions in DOD and maintaining their health is a paramount concern. Third, while it is important to maintain the institutional vitality of the Military Services, jointness needs to be extended as a means to achieving superior military, interagency and coalition operations.

Source: *Beyond Goldwater-Nichols: Defense Reform for a New Strategic Era, Phase I Report*, by Clark A. Murdock, et al.

Fourth, despite the "seams" and the elaborate processes that inevitably result, we base our recommendations on the premise that defense resources should continue to be organized, managed and budgeted along Service lines. The Military Services remain the single best source for coherent and integrated budgets within their respective domains and are increasingly coordinating allocation structures to compensate for the inter-service "seams." Fifth, our recommendations attempt to conform to the basic organization formula that the Combatant Commanders (CoComs), Military Services and defense agencies are the operating elements of the Department of Defense. The Office of the Secretary of Defense and the Joint Staff, in large part, are the staffs that oversee these operations. Our sixth and final guiding principle is to ensure a healthy competition of ideas on major issues among the CoComs, Military Services, the Joint Staff and OSD. A balance must be struck, however, between processes that ensure a diversity of views on the most critical issues, and processes that create too many competing power centers and unnecessary friction.

We have taken a broad view of defense reform, as is necessary in the new strategic era. No longer can defense reform be confined simply to the institutions and functions of the Department of Defense. Rather, *Beyond Goldwater-Nichols* recognizes that for the United States to fully seize opportunities and confront dangers in the 21st century, both DOD and its partners in the U.S. government (USG) must adapt to new strategic circumstances. It is in this collaborative spirit that we hope our recommendations will be received and acted on by the leadership.

RATIONALIZING ORGANIZATIONAL STRUCTURES IN DOD

Too often, the current organizational structure of the Military Departments, the Joint Staff, and the Office of Secretary of Defense (OSD) unnecessarily overlap, resulting in duplicative and, in some instances, overly large staffs that require wasteful coordination processes and impede necessary innovation.

Forcing a renewed focus on the core roles and responsibilities of each of DOD's principal actors exposes those organizations whose contributions are outweighed by the inefficiencies in process and structure that they perpetuate. A targeted consolidation of DOD organizational structures can thus preserve a diversity of ideas where it is warranted, and do so in a way that strengthens civilian oversight without undermining the value of independent military advice on matters of great interest to U.S. policy makers.

We therefore recommend the merging of most of each Service Secretariat into a single, smaller integrated staff that reports to both the Service Secretary and the Chief of Staff. A more integrated civilian and military staff would reduce friction-generating coordination mechanisms, increase the coherency of Service positions, and provide clearer lines of accountability. As the responsibility for civilian oversight of the military has increasingly shifted to the Office of the Secretary of Defense, the nature of the Service Secretary's job has evolved from a staff function to a "line" function. The Service Secretary no longer needs a large, separate secretariat and would be better served by a more integrated team.

The Joint Staff enables the Chairman to provide oversight of the Combatant Commands and the Military Departments and fulfill his role as the principal military advisor to the National Command Authority.[47] OSD is the apparatus that provides managerial oversight and independent analysis to the Secretary of Defense on issues he deems critical. In line with those key roles and responsibilities, we recommend the integration of military and civilian staffs with respect to managerial functions and retaining as separate organizations those Joint Staff directorates that are most directly within the Chairman's military purview. For the personnel and logistics function, we recommend, therefore, that J-1 (Manpower and Personnel) and J-4 (Logistics) be merged into integrated civilian and military offices under a military deputy who reports directly to its respective Under Secretary. 3-7 (Operational Plans and Joint Force Development), whose responsibilities have migrated steadily to the Joint Forces Command (JFCOM), should be disbanded. J-7's planning function should go to J-5 (Strategic Plans & Policy).

JOINT PROCUREMENT OF COMMAND AND CONTROL (C2)

The armed forces are increasingly waging joint and interdependent combat operations. Yet, as seen in Operations Enduring Freedom and Iraqi Freedom, DOD is still failing to acquire and field joint interoperable command and control capabilities. Therefore, we recommend that J-6 (Command, Control, Communications and Computers or C4) be converted into the core of a department-wide, joint task force (with budgetary and acquisition authority) for Joint C2. This military task force would be commanded by a 3-star (the former J-6) and augmented by appropriate elements of the Defense Information Systems Agency (DISA) as determined by the Secretary of Defense upon the recommendation of CJCS. A new Under Secretary of Defense for C31, which would be created by elevating the C3 function to the Under Secretary level and combining it with Intelligence, would provide oversight of the new JTF for C2. We support the recent elevation of the intelligence function to the Under Secretary level, but believe that leaving C3 at the Assistant Secretary level understates the importance of the C3 function in modem warfare.

We further recommend that OSD renew its focus on policy formation and oversight, resist the temptation to manage programs and consolidate DOD housekeeping functions under an Assistant Secretary of Defense for Administration.

TOWARD A MORE EFFECTIVE RESOURCE ALLOCATION PROCESS

The Department of Defense's resource allocation process often stifles innovation by making it extremely difficult for defense leaders to make important trade-off decisions across mission areas. Strategic planning, essential in a world of finite resources and shifting priorities, is poorly connected to program decisions and budgeting. And though the Department is adept at allocating resources for its programs, it pays inadequate attention to program execution and policy implementation.

The BG-N study team salutes the substantial effort Secretary Donald Rumsfeld and his team have made to strengthen strategic direction and the building of joint capabilities in the resource allocation process.

The changes made during 2003 have considerable promise, but more, we believe, is necessary for them to be fully implemented. As a consequence, we recommend building capacities in the Combatant Commands for a stronger role in the resource allocation process.

We further recommend building a strong Office of Program Analysis and Evaluation (PA&E) capable of providing independent analysis to the Secretary on broad strategic choices facing DOD, as a necessary hedge against those occasions when there is too little jointness in the options generated by the Military Services and the Joint Staff.

Finally, the Secretary of Defense should create an independent, continuous policy implementation/execution review process under a new office within OSD. This office also would be responsible for gathering all authoritative and directive guidance to establish a single, unified statement of the strategies, policies and programs to be followed, implemented and executed. This would provide a clear standard to which all DOD components could be held accountable.

STRENGTHENING CIVILIAN PROFESSIONALS IN DEFENSE AND NATIONAL SECURITY

Civilian professionals in the Defense Department, and the national security agencies more broadly are losing the ability to provide strategic guidance and policy oversight. DOD, in particular, must confront a looming crisis in its ability to attract and retain top-level talent to the career civil service. While the passage of the new National Security Personnel System legislation gives the Secretary of Defense significantly broadened latitude to reshape the future of DOD's civilian workforce, substantial additional steps are needed to attract, retain, motivate and reward a quality and high performing corps of defense professionals.

We recommend therefore that Congress establish a new Defense Professionals Corps to attract the best and brightest civilians to serve in DOD and to provide greatly expanded opportunities for professional development and career advancement. Training, education, and required interagency rotations for senior-level career appointments should become centerpieces of the new personnel system.

We further recommend that the Secretary of Defense should create a "personnel float" over the next five years of about a 1000 career civilian billets (GS-12 through SES) in OSD and defense agencies to enable education, training and rotations. Congress should also reassess overly restrictive ethics rules to enable defense professionals to more easily move in and out of government service over the course of their careers and limit the number of political appointees to enhance the incentives associated with career service.

IMPROVING INTERAGENCY AND COALITION OPERATIONS

Complex U.S. contingency operations over the past decade, from Somalia to Iraq, have demonstrated the necessity for a unity of effort not only from the armed forces but also from across the U.S. government and an international coalition. In most cases, however, such unity of effort has proved elusive, sometimes with disastrous results. The U.S. national security apparatus requires significant new investments in this area. Otherwise, the United States' ability to conduct successful political-military contingency operations will continue to be fundamentally impaired.

A critical first step is for the President to give greater organizational emphasis to this issue by designating the Deputy Assistant to the President on the NSC staff as having lead responsibility for integrating agency strategies and plans and ensuring greater unity of effort among agencies during execution, and by establishing a new office in the National Security Council with this mandate. Each President, early in his tenure, should review the guidance establishing standard operating procedures for the planning of complex operations.

We further recommend that the Secretaries of all agencies likely to be involved in complex operations abroad (e.g., State, Treasury, Commerce and Justice) set up small, proprietary planning offices to lead the development of agency plans and participate in the interagency planning process. For each contingency operation, the president should designate one senior official to be in charge of and accountable for integrating U.S. interagency operations on the ground once major combat operations have ceased.

Congress has a significant part to play in developing the U.S. government's capacity for conducting successful interagency and coalition operations. It should establish a new Agency for Stability Operations, with a Civilian Stability Operations Corps and Reserve charged with: assessing and preparing for stability operations; organizing, training and equipping civilian capabilities for such operations; and rapidly deploying civilian experts and teams to the field. To facilitate this overall effort, we further recommend the establishment of a new Training Center for Interagency and Coalition Operations, to be jointly run by DOD's National Defense University and the State Department's National Foreign Affairs Training Center.

Finally, Congress must devote increased funds for programs that enhance peacetime opportunities for civilian planners and operators to work with their counterparts from various countries. It should also increase U.S. funding for programs that support building the operational capabilities of allies and partners in priority task areas in complex operations.

STRENGTHENING CONGRESSIONAL OVERSIGHT

Congressional oversight of the defense establishment, critically important to the nation's ability to identify and defeat extant and emerging threats to our security and that of our friends and allies across the globe, is languishing. Congress is engaged in too much of the wrong kind of oversight—too few national debates on major issues and far too much time and energy spent on relatively minor and parochial issues. The decline in Congressional oversight has clearly contributed to deteriorating relations between Congress and DOD.

To create the conditions for reinvigorating Congressional oversight of the Defense Department, we recommend that Congress establish a process similar to the one created for the base realignment and closure (BRAC). Congress could establish an independent group—perhaps made up of former Congressional leaders from both Houses and both parties—to assess current committee membership, structures and jurisdictions and to make recommendations on how to enhance Congressional oversight. While the BG-N study team believes that the Armed Services committees should be encouraged to elevate their focus on strategic and policy issues and should be reduced in size, only Congress can decide how to reform itself.

NOTES FOR CHAPTER 7

1. Walter Millis, Harvey C. Mansfield, and Harold Stein, 1958, *Arms and the State: Civil-Military Elements in National Policy*, The Twentieth Century Fund, New York, p. 149. R. Earl McClendon describes the origin and history of the movement to gain equality with the traditional services by air power enthusiasts in "The Question of Autonomy for the United States Air Arm," *1907–1945*, Maxwell AFB, Alabama: Documentary Research Division, Air University Library, 1950. *See also* Paul Y. Hammond, 1963, "Super Carriers and B-36 Bombers: Appropriations, Strategy and Politics," in Harold Stein (Ed.), *American Civil-Military Decisions, A Book of Case Studies*, Twentieth Century Fund, University of Alabama Press, Tuscaloosa, AL, p. 467.
2. Timothy W. Stanley, 1956, *American Defense and National Security*, Public Affairs Press, Washington, DC, p. 11.
3. Millis, Mansfield, and Stein. *Arms and the State*, p. 105.
4. For a detailed account of all U.S. unification attempts up to 1947, refer to Lawrence J. Legere, Jr., 1951, "Unification of the Armed Forces," PhD dissertation, Harvard University.
5. This plan was submitted by Air Force General Joseph T. McNarney, with War Department approval, before a select committee on postwar military policy. The plan called for a single department and a single chief of staff. Further description of this and the other two early unification proposals can be found in Paul Y. Hammond, 1981, *Organizing for Defense: The American Military Establishment in the Twentieth Century*, Princeton University Press, Princeton, p. 191; Millis, Mansfield, and Stein, *Arms and the State*, p. 146; and Stanley, *American Defense and National Security*, p. 72.
6. Senator Edward C. Johnson of Colorado introduced a bill for creation of a Department of Armed Forces (Senate 84) and Senator Lister Hill of Alabama introduced a bill for the creation of a Department of Military Security (Senate 1482). Discussion of these bills gave way to consideration of a War Department proposal submitted at the hearings by Lt. General J. Lawton Collins and a Navy Department proposal submitted by Secretary of Navy James Forrestal.
7. Senate Committee on Military Affairs, Hearings, 1945, See the testimony of General Dwight D. Eisenhower, p. 363; General Douglas MacArthur, pp. 24–25; and General George Kenney, p. 234.
8. Ibid. See the testimony of Secretary of War Robert A. Patterson, p. 17; General J. L. Devers, p. 312; General Henry H. Arnold, p. 80; and former Secretary of Navy Josephus Daniels, p. 183.
9. Ibid. See the testimony of General Dwight D. Eisenhower, p. 36, and General Carl Spaatz, p. 342; General Omar N. Bradley, p. 355; and Secretary of War Robert A. Patterson, p. 17.
10. Ibid. See the testimony of Secretary of War Robert A. Patterson, p. 22; General Henry H. Arnold, p. 77; General Carl Spaatz, p. 341; and former Secretary of Navy Josephus Daniels, p. 181.
11. Ibid. See the testimony of General J. Lawton Collins, p. 313; Secretary of War Robert A. Patterson, p. 14; and General J. L. Devers, p. 313.
12. Ibid. See the testimony of Secretary of War Robert A. Patterson, p. 18.
13. Ibid. See the testimony of Secretary of War Robert A. Patterson, p. 12; General George C. Marshall, p. 50; and General J. L. Devers, p. 314.
14. Ibid. See the testimony of General J. L. Devers, p. 314; Secretary of State James F. Byrnes, p. 191; and General George C. Marshall, pp. 52, 59–60.
15. Ibid. See the testimony of Secretary of War Robert A. Patterson, p. 15; General George C. Marshall, p. 51; and General Brehon Somervell, pp. 371, 639.
16. Ibid. See the testimony of Secretary of State James F. Byrnes, pp. 190–191; General J. Lawton Collins, p. 160; General Dwight D. Eisenhower, p. 371; and General M. G. White, pp. 322–323.
17. Combat forces (infantry, cavalry, and artillery, and so on) were organized into seven geographical departments: East, Missouri, Dakota, Colorado, California, Texas, and Platte. These seven geographical departments bear a striking resemblance to the eight unified commands within the present Defense Department. See infra, Chapter X, pp. 188–190.

18. Elting E. Morison, 1960, *Turmoil and Tradition: A Study of the Life and Times of Henry L. Stimson*, Houghton Mifflin, Boston, p. 148.
19. Cline, *Washington Command Post*, pp. 75–78.
20. Ibid., p. 73.
21. Eli Ginzberg and Ewing W. Reilly, 1957, *Effecting Change in Large Organizations*, Columbia University Press, New York, pp. 5, 132; and Pfiffner and Sherwood, *Administrative Organization*, p. 198.
22. Herbert Kauffman, 1960, after studying the U.S. Forest Service made this observation: "The elaboration of formal controls may indicate only that field men in the organization in question are not responsive to central leadership to influence their behavior have failed, necessitating still more and tighter efforts at direction; thus, the seemingly centralized organization may, from a behavioral standpoint, be more decentralized that one lacking the traditional procedural manifestations of centralization," *The Forest Ranger: A Study in Administrative Behavior*, Johns Hopkins University Press, Baltimore, MD, p. 231. One should consider the recommendations of the Simpson Board in light of this statement.
23. As Simon put it, "They seem to assume that organizations are antiseptically clean of influences from outside." Quoted in Pfiffner and Sherwood, *Administration Organization*, p. 334.
24. Here and throughout the book the term authority is used to mean "legal" authority or "right" to command. The usage roughly corresponds to Max Weber's concept of rational authority and to Harold Lasswell's, Abraham Kaplan's, and Herbert Simon's concepts of influence based on legitimacy. No distinction will he observed between the terms real authority, power, control, or influence. They will be used interchangeably, and they will approximate Herbert Simon's concept of power. See Max Weber, 1947, *Theory of Social and Economic Organization*, The Free Press, Glencoe, IL, pp. 324–391; Harold D. Lasswell and Abraham Kaplan, 1950, *Power and Society*, Yale University Press, New Haven, pp. 83–92; and Herbert A. Simon, November 1953, "Notes on the Observation and Measurement of Political Power," *Journal of Politics*, Vol. XV, No. 4, pp. 500–516.
25. Simon, Smithburg, and Thompson, *Public Administration*, p. 404.
26. See Kaufman, *The Forest Ranger*, p. iv.
27. For a full discussion of this problem of conflicting goals in defense, see Alain Enthoven and Henry Rowen, July 1959, "Defense Planning and Organization," The RAND Corp., p. 1640, *passim*; and Charles J. Hitch and Roland N. McKean, 1960, *The Economics of Defense in the Nuclear Age*, Harvard University Press, Cambridge, pp. 158–177.
28. Neustadt, *Presidential Power*, p. 46.
29. James G. March and Herbert A. Simon, 1958, *Organizations*, John Wiley and Sons, Inc., New York, p. 156; and Hitch and McKean, *Economics of Defense*, pp. 128–131.
30. Except in the case of direct quotations, documentation of the DOS 77–80 critique is omitted in this section. The material here summarizes the thoroughly documented, detailed survey in chapter 3.
31. Readers who may be unfamiliar with some of the DOD officials and organizations discussed in this section are invited to peruse the first section of chapter 2, which briefly describes the present organization of the Department. Also, for quick reference, an explanation of the overwhelming helping of acronyms, an unavoidable part of the diet of anyone dealing with the Defense Department, has been included in the glossary.
32. This statement holds true despite developments too recent to be included in the text, completed in early 1982. For example, the book does not discuss the movement for JCS reorganization that emerged in 1982 and the resulting 1983 Reagan administration/DOD recommendation to change the legislation governing the JCS. The 1983 DOD legislative proposal is so mild that it would not "significantly alter the structure of the Department."
33. 107 Cong. Rec. 1831, February 9, 1961, Remarks of Senator Symington followed by Report to Senator Kennedy from Committee on the Defense Establishment.

34. Blue Ribbon Defense Panel, 1970, *Report to the President and Secretary of Defense on the Department of Defense*, U.S. Government Printing Office, Washington, DC.
35. Paul Y. Hammond, 1961, *Organizing for Defense*, Princeton University Press, Princeton, NJ, pp. 384–385.
36. John C. Ries, 1964, *The Management of Defense: Organization and Control of U.S. Armed Services*, Johns Hopkins University Press, Baltimore, MD, p. 208.
37. The political nature of reorganization is a phenomenon repeatedly encountered and discussed in this book. In its reference to the "clash and adjustment of . . . interests," this paragraph conveys the intended meaning of "political" in what follows. Thus, "politics" is not limited to the activities of elected officials; the processes which adjust and accommodate the inherent contradictions among the myriad interests present in a modern society are found throughout the governmental apparatus, and elsewhere as well.
38. Richard C. Steadman, 1978, *Report to the Secretary of Defense on the National Military Command Structure*, U.S. Government Printing Office, Washington, DC, p. 52.
39. *See* Mayer N. Zald, July/August 1964, "Decentralization–Myth vs. Reality," *Personnel*, Vol. 41, pp. 19–26; and Richard Vancil, 1979, *Decentralization: Management Ambiguity by Design*, Dow Jones Irwin, Homewood, IL.
40. Fred Thompson and L. R. Jones, 1986, "Controllership in the Public Sector," *Journal of Policy Analysis and Management*, Vol. 5, No. 3, pp. 547–571.
41. Discussion of the logic of interdependence and its implications for organizational design are due to James D. Thompson, 1967, *Organizations in Action*, McGraw-Hill, New York, Chapters 3 to 6.
42. Martin J. Bailey, 1967, "Defense Decentralization through Internal Prices," in S. Enke (Ed.), *Defense Management*, Prentice-Hall, Inc., Englewood Cliffs, NJ, pp. 337–352; Charles J. Hitch and R. McKean, 1960, *The Economics of Defense in the Nuclear Age*, Harvard University Press, Cambridge, MA, pp. 396–402.
43. Charles A. Perrow, Spring 1977, "The Bureaucratic Paradox: The Efficient Organization Centralizes in Order to Decentralize," *Organization Dynamics*, pp. 3–14.
44. Jacques S. Gansler, 1989, *Affording Defense*, The MIT Press, Cambridge, MA, pp. 135, 325–330. Gansler also recommends multiyear budgets and consolidation of line items and criticizes Congress' endless tinkering with authorizations and appropriations bills, its propensities to earmark funds for specific recipients, and its insatiable appetite for reports.
45. *Goldwater-Nichols Department of Defense Reorganization Act of 1986*, P.L. 99433,100 Stat. 992 (1986).
46. "House and Senate Reach Accord on Military Command Structure," *The New York Times*, September 12, 1986, p. A25, col. 1; "The Greatest Bill Since . . ." *The Washington Post*, September 24, 1986, p. A22, col. 1.
47. This report uses the masculine pronoun for the major DOD institutional actors purely for convenience, not as an expression of support for current practice. The BG-N study team believes that opportunities for women in DOD should be expanded and expects that more women will be appointed or promoted to the most senior levels as part of that process.

CHAPTER 8

The Department of Education

INTRODUCTION

Until the passage of the law creating the U.S. Department of Education in October 1979, the United States was the only industrialized country in the world that did not have a separate national organization at a cabinet level dedicated to education. Despite efforts to create such a department, proposals were thwarted, and the limited federal role in education was tucked into the large Department of Health, Education, and Welfare (HEW). For many opponents of a separate department, the possibility of the elevation to cabinet status was closely tied to their fear that such an organization would lead to an increase in federal control over state and local authority in education. Thus, the proposals to create a department were linked to policy changes, especially those related to the appropriate federal role in education.

The actual creation of the Department of Education was linked to a political agenda. It began during Jimmy Carter's presidential campaign in 1976 and the courting of the National Education Association's support for Carter's candidacy. Although the arguments for the department were posed in many different terms, politics turned out to be the most important dynamic in the story. Politics not only involved the support of a candidate but also the dynamics of interest group agendas and powers. As the process unfolded, the debate about the structure of a new department was entangled in questions related to specific aspects of federal education policy.

The crafting of the proposal that eventually moved to closure began in the White House in the Office of Management and Budget. Despite the commitment of the Office of Management and Budget–based staff known as the Presidential Reorganization Project and significant planning and strategizing by that staff, there was conflict within the executive branch to the proposals. It was not surprising that top HEW staff did not want to see a part of their departmental portfolio moved to another setting. Similarly, as proposals to include specific program components within the new department emerged, not all program officials supported that departure.

As the proposal for a department moved out of the White House and to the Congress, the debate moved from a general commitment to a department to focus on the specific components that would be placed in the department. Congressional consideration involved a large number of committees and subcommittees with jurisdiction over the specific programs and policies being considered. Opposition to the creation of a department not only came from those specific program advocates but also from conservative Republicans who opposed a department because they saw it as acknowledgment that there would be significantly increased federal control over education. The Department of Education Reorganization Act that passed was a pale shadow of the proposals that had originally emerged from the White House. The final legislation transferred 152 education programs from HEW and five other federal agencies. With a few exceptions, the new department effectively transferred the education programs out of HEW and did not really touch other program elements.

When Ronald Reagan won the 1980 election, the proposal to eliminate the department became a part of the new administration's platform, reflecting the agenda of conservative Republicans. Despite this, the department continued to exist through the support of moderate Republicans and most Democrats. The department largely continued as it had in the past, and the impact of the new department did not seem significant. This continued until President George W. Bush proposed the No Child Left Behind program. Despite past political arguments, the structure of a separate department actually gave a Republican president the opportunity to increase the federal role in education. No Child Left Behind changed federal–state relationships in education and posed issues in policy not in administrative terms.

The excerpts that are included in this section of the book begin with pieces that address the need for a cabinet Department of Education, move to the political environment in the mid-1970s, focus on the arguments for the department, and include analyses of the process of developing the department proposals. They then move to the enactment of No Child Left Behind and the impact of that program on federal–state relationships.

Rufus E. Miles, Jr., in "The Case for a Federal Department of Education," makes an early argument for the creation of a separate department in 1967. An article entitled "President Carter, the Congress, and NEA: Creating the Department of Education," by David Stephens, focuses on the 1976 campaign and also discusses the role of Congress in the process.

Discussion found in Beryl A. Radin and Willis D. Hawley's *The Politics of Federal Reorganization: Creating the U.S. Department of Education* analyzes past efforts, discusses goals for creating the department, and focuses on the authority to reorganize and the role of the Presidential Reorganization Project. This excerpt also presents a picture of the conflict within the executive branch, particularly over decisions about what should be transferred to the new department.

Ronald P. Seyb, in "Reform as Affirmation: Jimmy Carter's Executive Branch Reorganization Effort," also places the education effort in the context of Carter's governing strategies.

Paul Manna, in *School's In: Federalism and the National Education Agenda*, reviews the organizations that were designed to give advice to federal officials and represent different approaches to the changing federal role in education.

Gary Orfield's foreword to Gail L. Sunderman and Jimmy Kim's report, *Expansion of Federal Power in American Education: Federal-State Relationships Under the No Child Left Behind Act, Year One*, focuses on the federal role in American education. He argues that No Child Left Behind (NCLB) is a departure from the history of this topic.

Another excerpt examines different aspects of the federal role in education. Although it does not directly focus on the impact of reorganization, it does indicate the importance of the policy issue of the federal role in education and its ability to resurface over time. Patrick J. McGuinn, in "The National Schoolmarm: No Child Left Behind and the New Educational Federalism," focuses on policy issues rather than structure and details the shift of bedfellows among players in the education policy world.

Rufus E. Miles, Jr., "The Case for a Federal Department of Education," *Public Administration Review*, Vol. 27, No. 1. (March 1967), pp. 1–9.

In theory, the composition of the Cabinet should change as the role of the Federal government changes in national and international affairs. Yet in a half-century of seismic social and political change, only four belated adjustments have been made in the make-up of the President's Cabinet. A unified Department of Defense was created in 1947; a Department of Health, Education, and Welfare was created in 1953; a Department of Housing and Urban Development was authorized in 1965; and a Department of Transportation was authorized in 1966. The national interest would have been much better served if each had come into being earlier.

Delay in creating a new Department of Housing and Urban Development was particularly unfortunate. Two decades of urban decay, culminating in a series of social explosions, preceded recognition that the cities' problems deserved the kind of national attention and spotlight which accompanies Cabinet status. It will be remarkable and fortunate if, in the decade ahead, HUD is able to develop rapidly and imaginatively enough to overcome much of the damage done by this organizational lag.

The subject of departmental structure is usually viewed as a managerial problem. The basic question asked is whether the creation of a new department will facilitate or impede the effective and economical management of the United States Government. This question should be asked second, not first. The *first question* should be whether the creation of the new department would be advantageous to our society as a whole. In this broader perspective, significant additional considerations come into play. The most important of these is the interaction between the organizational structure of the Federal government and the value system of our national society.

Whether the Federal government intends it or not, the status of an organization within its hierarchy communicates clearly and strongly to the public the degree of importance which the government accords the functions of that organization. And that status profoundly influences the attitudes and social values of the American public.

The effect of organizational status upon social attitudes was clearly illustrated in April 1953, when the Department of Health, Education, and Welfare was "created" by changing the name and status of the former Federal Security Agency. Nothing was added to the functions of the Federal Security Agency and no added powers of consequence were given the new Secretary. Only title and status were new; yet the action was hailed throughout the nation as a great step forward. All communications media stepped up their coverage immediately. The writers of high-school and college textbooks suddenly gave great attention to the "newly created" department. Federal, State and local governments, and private citizens showed a surprisingly rapid increase in their interest in health, education, and welfare programs.

Withal, education is still not accorded adequate prestige by the American people in the terms that really count. Elementary and secondary school teaching is not well-enough remunerated to attract many competent persons who are heads of families. Until it is, the most difficult of our educational problems will get worse instead of better. Even with its new Federal aid program for elementary and secondary education, the United States Government has not given education the first class status essential to making education a central focus of American concern. Consciously and unconsciously, students making occupational choices incorporate into their own values the second-echelon status which the United States Government has accorded education. Creation of a new Cabinet-level Department of Education would not suddenly overcome these and other educational deficiencies, but it would help more than is generally realized.

The psychological advantages of a separate Department of Education in the achievement of our international objectives are also clear and substantial. No other country in the world combines health, education, and welfare activities in a single department of government, thus relegating each to a second echelon status. . . .

To some thoughtful persons, the most important reason for creating a Department of Education is that it would place in the highest councils of government a full-time spokesman for the educational needs of the American people, thereby assuring that in the never ending competition for limited resources the comparative claims of education would be stated by a top-ranking official whose concern and efforts were undiluted by other competing concerns. It would increase the likelihood that the top spokesman for education would be sufficiently well-informed (both because of the presumed selection of a man or woman with recognized knowledge of the field and his or her subsequent full-time concentration on educational matters) to be able to present the claims of education persuasively.

President Johnson has made clear on a number of occasions that he regards education as the most basic single prerequisite to progress in a democratic society, a view shared by a substantial number of distinguished and thoughtful Americans. In the long run we are faced with two primary strategic alternatives: the strategy of education in breadth, in depth, and in length as a way of life, or the strategy of massive containment of social ills accentuated by educational deprivation. Conscious choice by intelligent citizens must opt for a strategy in which the dominant emphasis is on education. Refusal to face the alternatives and the sluggish action which result from such refusal, are a vote for massive containment and all the dangers of social explosion inherent in this repressive approach. Long delay in the elevation of education within our governmental hierarchy can only contribute to the inadequate pace of educational progress.

If education is to become the central focus and concern of the American people, as President Johnson has indicated is his desire, then the President should reflect his values and his convictions in the organizational status he accords them.

Viewed in this broad societal perspective, the case seems strong for such elevation unless there are compelling negative arguments from a managerial or other standpoint. Five sub-questions will help to illuminate the main question:

1. Would the creation of a new Department of Education aid or hinder the President in improving the management of the federal government?
2. How difficult to manage is the Department of HEW?
3. What would the effect be of a super Department of HEW, with three subcabinet Departments?
4. Is a new Department of Education the most logical split-off, if one should occur?
5. If a Department of Education is concluded to be desirable, what should be the scope of its functions?

From the standpoint of management theory, apart from all social and political considerations, large and small, there is no question that the President's effective span of control is being exceeded. He has small agency heads reporting to him whose representatives he almost never sees. He is unable personally to identify and dispose of the numerous problems of interdepartmental and interagency coordination which require, under present organization, supradepartmental leadership and action if they are to be effectively handled. The span-of-control problem is frequently used to support a case for fewer and larger departments, and is always used to oppose the creation of any more new departments. It is a factor which needs to be weighed in a total balancing of the pros and cons, but a factor which must be considered in political as well as managerial context.

The President's broad span of organizational supervision is rooted in the basic political consideration that Congress, the President, and numerous organized constituencies want it known that various concerns represented by departments and agencies are sufficiently important that their top-officials should have direct access and responsibility to the President. Wide span of control satisfies many constituencies; narrow span of control satisfies few.

Wide span of control has a significant managerial advantage in the Federal government. Large corporate enterprises can attract and hold first class managers who are two or three echelons below the company president by paying them whatever it takes to get them and by providing working conditions within which a manager can thrive. The Federal government can not do this. The salaries it pays Cabinet officers and agency heads and their chief lieutenants are notoriously low—less than half of corresponding salaries in the business world. In consequence, one of the most important factors in attracting to top posts in the Federal service men of outstanding ability and demonstrated competence is the status and consequent opportunity for influencing policy on the national scene. Wide span of control provides many positions which have, in either fact or appearance, the status and the "leverage" needed to attract outstanding executives; narrow span of control provides few. . . .

Departmental structure tends to be a belated adaptation to current need. It may be hoped that we are now sophisticated enough to look ahead and consider how the Federal government will have to be used to meet our most acute needs and problems of the future.

As we attempt to sense the deepest urges of the members of our society, both individually and in organized groups, and predict the manner in which these urges will demand expression, it seems highly likely that the need to maximize educational opportunity, especially for the socially and personally disadvantaged, linked with some form of assured employment, will rank near the top. Such a linkage will not be a one-time linkage when each individual completes his formal education and enters the job market. The rate of technological change in our society—even at its present rate, without any allowance for further acceleration—is so rapid that the great majority of workers will need several periods of either "refresher training" or substantial retraining in another skill. We will require, therefore, a much closer organized relationship between our educational institutions and the institutions which employ the individuals and use their skills in producing the goods and services demanded by society. We will need imaginative ways of achieving these linkages. We will need to shake up old relationships which have become anachronistic and defensive and replace them with a new partnership between education, labor, and business, dedicated to discovering the most fruitful ways of using the private sector of our society to give jobs, adequate income, and dignity to the whole of our society, not just the upper four-fifths.

To achieve such a partnership, Federal leadership and reasonable financial stimulus and support are unavoidable. And since they are unavoidable, it is best to make a virtue of necessity and create as effective an instrument for this purpose as can be both conceived and approved by the Congress.

In my judgment, the form of organization which is suggested by the logic of this analysis is a Cabinet-level Department of Education and Employment (or Department of Human Resources if there is preference for that name). The purpose of the Department should be fourfold: (1) to aid in strengthening the educational institutions of the nation, including the development of new techniques and approaches by old institutions, and the creation of new institutions, (2) to enlarge the educational opportunity of citizens of all ages, with particular emphasis on the provision of opportunities to those segments of society for whom the existing system is conspicuously inadequate, (3) to enlist, on a more imaginative basis and much larger scale than heretofore, the aid of American business and labor in developing refresher, retraining, and placement programs, which will make maximum use of the private sector for retraining and re-employment, and (4) to support flexible programs of public employment of such size as may be needed to employ (and simultaneously retrain, in many instances) those persons who are not employed in the private sector after all reasonable steps have been taken.

Under such a concept, the Department of Education and Employment would have the functions of the following organizations transferred to it:

- Office of Education, HEW
- All educational and employment programs of the Office of Economic Opportunity
- Manpower development and training programs of the Department of Labor, including the Neighborhood Youth Corps
- U.S. Employment Service (but not Unemployment Insurance) of the Department of Labor
- Work experience program (Welfare Administration, HEW)
- Educational TV and other educational functions now conducted by the Office of the Secretary, HEW

This is neither a precise nor a complete list of the functions which might be performed by a new Department of Education and Employment, but it is sufficient to illustrate what I believe should be the main thrust of the new Department. . . .

A new department, organized around the preceding program purposes, should not be overloaded with extraneous programs merely because they have an educational label. There are numerous educational programs scattered throughout the government which were designed to give support to noneducational missions, ranging from the military academies to the fellowship and training grant programs of the National Institutes of Health created to produce more and better research manpower in the biological and medical sciences. These should, in my judgment, be kept where they are unless and until there is a more compelling reason than now appears to transfer any one of them to a new Department of Education and Employment. Using, again, the test as to how important the relationships are between those programs and their existing parent organizations, as compared with the potential relationships between them and the other programs of the Department of Education and Employment, I suggest that most educational activities which serve in a supporting role to another broad program purpose of the government belong with that program purpose.

It seems inconceivable that President Johnson does not nurture the desire and the intent, before he leaves the Presidency, to create a new Department of Education (or Education and Employment) as the capstone of his leadership in enlisting the support of the Federal government to undergird the nation's educational institutions and broaden educational opportunity for all citizens, particularly those with limited educational horizons. If he does nurture such an intent, he had better get on with the job. It is now part of the same job as that of improving the administration of the Great Society, and time is of the essence.

David Stephens, "President Carter, the Congress, and NEA: Creating the Department of Education," *Political Science Quarterly*, Vol. 98, No. 4. (Winter 1983–1984), pp. 641–663.

Reorganizing the machinery of government in Washington is not a job for presidents alone, however much they might like it to be. Most presidents have wanted to bend the executive branch closer to their wishes, but all have found it difficult to do so. While procedural requirements have varied from time to time, presidents invariably have had to work with Congress, either because a new arrangement required legislation or because executive reorganization authorities were subject to a legislative veto.

Giving Congress a role opens Pandora's Box: myriad interests must be channeled through a Congress in which party discipline is usually weak; the rules of debate are generous; and public participation is encouraged. Such is inevitably the case when institutions, groups, and individuals share power, but it can lead to much anguish for a president committed to reorganization, as was Jimmy Carter. Like other presidents before him, he discovered that his plans had to accommodate many other actors. In this article, I will examine how the Department of Education emerged from the relationships among the president, his officials and his party, the Congress, and an important interest group, the National Education Association (NEA).

In the mid-1970s, the idea of a federal department of education was common in a limited circle, but it was hardly an idea whose time had come. Calls for a separate cabinet department had been heard intermittently for over a century, ever since a tiny subcabinet department had existed briefly in 1867–68. The department had become a bureau and ultimately the Education Division of the Department of Health, Education, and Welfare (HEW). Meanwhile, few of the dozens of bills referring to a separate department had aroused much congressional enthusiasm. Since 1953, not one of them had received a hearing in a House or Senate committee.

Perhaps the greatest obstacle faced by the supporters of a federal department was the American tradition that education was a state and local matter. Although Washington was spending some $25 billion annually on education by the early 1970s, this represented less than ten percent of total education spending by all levels of government. Many federal programs were meant to supplement state and local ones or to achieve noneducational goals of the federal government, such as civil rights, defense, rehabilitation of veterans,

---

Source: David Stephens, "President Carter, the Congress, and NEA: Creating the Department of Education," *Political Science Quarterly*, Vol. 98, No. 4. (Winter 1983–1984), pp. 641–663. Used with permission from the Academy of Political Science.

and equality of opportunity for the disadvantaged. The programs were spread over more than twenty federal departments and agencies.[1]

The base for Jimmy Carter's long and successful campaign for the presidency was not the traditional Democratic party machine, but a widespread ad hoc grass-roots organization of politically active people. The time was ripe for such an organization. . . . In two campaigns for the governorship of Georgia, Jimmy Carter made contact, either personally or through his family and close lieutenants, with hundreds of thousands of people. As governor after 1971, he further broadened his organization. He angled unsuccessfully for the Democratic nomination for vice president in 1972, but secured election as chairman of the Democratic campaign committee for the 1974 congressional elections. This job allowed him to travel widely and meet many possible future supporters. One of the groups he and his staff courted along the way was the National Education Association (NEA), the nation's largest union of elementary and secondary teachers.

Carter, the NEA, and the Democratic party's new rules were well suited to one another. In 1976, the NEA had about 1.8 million members spread across every state, averaging 4,000 members to every congressional district. No other union was at once so large and so widely spread.[2] If, as William J. Crotty and Gary C. Jacobson have suggested, the decision over the nomination was indeed in "the hands of those who take the trouble to participate in the process," the NEA's teachers were ideal potential participants.[3] They had free time, were well educated, were accustomed to speaking in public, and were experienced at organizing and at working by rules and under discipline. Since sixty percent of them were women, they were also well placed to take advantage of affirmative action rules for the election of Democratic delegates. The NEA also had some 300 full-time and over 1,000 part-time organizers outside Washington, a staff of 1,000 in Washington, good connections with other large unions, and long experience of legislative 1obbying. . . .[4]

Not surprisingly, the NEA expected to be rewarded for helping to secure the nomination for Carter. The association had many goals, among them increasing the federal government's share of national education spending to one-third, collective bargaining legislation for public employees, affirmative action, and integrated schools. A separate education department was only one of a number of NEA objectives, but it was one that Carter could easily endorse. As early as the end of 1974, he agreed with the NEAs leaders that a separate department was a good idea. He repeated his support for the concept at education forums and in position papers late in 1975 and throughout 1976. Some observers suggested later that Carter saw the department as an alternative to promising to increase federal education spending to the extent desired by NEA. Still, the idea of a separate department had been around for a long time and clearly appealed to Carter. His own experience might have encouraged him to support it even without the need far the NEA alliance. As a state senator and governor interested in education, he had seen how federal education programs were fragmented among various agencies and how slow moving the HEW machine was in delivering services to the states and localities. While he promised to clear up the bureaucratic "mess" in Washington by slashing the number of federal agencies, he tried to justify a new department on the grounds of consolidation of programs and efficiency of management.[5]

The NEA at all levels had spent some $3 million supporting Carter and Mondale during the 1976 campaign, and NEA members had worked hard getting out the vote for the Democrats.[6] The NEA might reasonably have expected early fulfillment of the commitments it believed the new administration had made. Instead, the Carter administration was so slow to deliver that some of the strongest supporters of the separate education department feared that it might have been forgotten. The NEA found that campaign promises do not become pieces of legislation through their own momentum alone.

The problem was not so much President Carter as his chief advisers. The secretary of HEW, Joseph A. Califano Jr., had worked in Lyndon Johnson's White House and had become convinced that presidents should have as few people as possible reporting directly to them. Controlling access to the Oval Office conserved the president's precious time and avoided the need for him to umpire battles between departments representing relatively narrow interests. Large departments like HEW allowed adjustments to be made internally. Califano also argued that locating education with health and welfare allowed better coordination of programs for children, such as immunization, health care, and drug education. He believed that any necessary improvements in the delivery of health, education, and welfare could be made by internal reorganization of HEW. Califano urged Carter to look at other options rather than to proceed directly to a new department. . . .[7]

The difficulties of gaining agreement on what should go into the new department, as well as the lack of time to spare from more pressing executive business, stayed the administration's hand through the early weeks of 1978. Meanwhile, Senator Abraham Ribicoff (D-Conn.), a former HEW secretary and the Senate's staunchest supporter of the separate education department, had commenced hearings before his own Governmental Affairs Committee on the most recent of many bills he had introduced to establish an education department. The White House decided not to introduce its own bill but to support the Ribicoff bill in a submission at the hearings. The fear that interest groups and government agencies would carry their fight to preserve the status quo into Congress had persuaded OMB, now headed by James T. McIntyre, Jr., to agree with Jordan and the president's Domestic Policy Staff (DPS) that the administration should seek a department based on the Education Division of HEW with a few noncontroversial additions, rather than risk a long and debilitating battle to include many other programs. While McIntyre himself would have preferred a broader department for management reasons, the more immediate consideration in the view of the White House strategists was to fulfill the commitment to the NEA and its allies.[8]

A few hours before McIntyre was to testify to the Ribicoff committee, the president was at last able to give thorough consideration to the proposed submission. He insisted on the department having more responsibilities than his advisers suggested, asking McIntyre to add more non-Education Division programs to the list in the submission. After some rapid rewriting, the list that McIntyre presented to the committee ran to 167 programs from 7 departments and agencies. Ribicoff, who had been expecting a narrower department than the one proposed in his own bill, found that his and the administration's lists were almost identical.

Neither list included all of the education-related programs of the federal government—far from it. The White House bill embraced only about 30 programs from outside the Education Division, leaving untouched between 100 and 200, depending on how one defined "education-related." The PRP team had looked at some 40 programs and decided to leave them out because they were too closely connected with the "missions" of other federal departments and agencies. It also looked at the clients the programs served and the functions performed. Judgments were made in each case whether a program served primarily educational purposes or whether it merely provided education to serve another purpose. Thus, while Califano complained later that only 1 of 55 student aid programs outside HEW that had been identified by PRP had been included, PRP staff could argue that these schemes were serving non-educational goals, such as veterans' rehabilitation and equality of opportunity for the disadvantaged. Of course, the vehemence of the opposition to transfers also influenced PRP's decisions.

Despite such omissions, the supporters of the bill argued that the new department would improve management coordination by bringing together previously scattered programs. They argued, too, that education could no longer be the "poor relation" in HEW. Education bore a disproportionate share of HEW budget cuts, mainly because many federal education programs involved discretionary expenditure rather than expenditure to which recipients had a continuing entitlement. The placing of education with health and welfare was illogical anyway, the critics argued, since the three areas had little operational connection. Education in HEW also suffered from continual organizational upheavals, unclear lines of authority, and rapid turnover at the top. Education policy was in the care of third- and fourth-rank bureaucrats who had little claim on the time of HEW secretaries, let alone presidents.

These arguments were echoed by many of the Senate committee's witnesses, representatives of education groups (including the NEA), legislators, public administration experts, and former commissioners of education. In addition, supporters of the department argued that a separate department in the cabinet would bring education the national prestige and "visibility" it deserved. The secretary of education would be an advocate before the president for the 65 million Americans who were connected in some way with education. But some people, opponents as well as supporters, believed that the department would also be a trophy that the strongest supporter—the NEA—could use to show off its new power in national politics.

The main casualty of the legislative battle of 1978 was the administration's goal of coordination. Important non-Education Division programs were whittled away, first in the Senate, then in the House, through the combined efforts of client groups and the legislators to whom they spoke. The biggest skirmish was over Head Start, the social and educational development scheme for disadvantaged children, which was a HEW responsibility outside the Education Division. President Carter had insisted that Head Start be included in the new department, apparently against the arguments of most of his advisers. . . .[9]

While the president was wary of being seen to pander to education groups, he knew that the creation of an education department—any education department—might hinge on the ability of the most powerful of those groups, the NEA, to deliver the votes of wavering legislators. The NEA, for its part, knew it had to become a less conspicuous supporter of the administration to avoid the charges that the new department would be a puppet of the NEA and that the legislation was a "payoff" for NEA help to Carter in 1976. (The latter charge worried many people in the administration as well.) NEA knew arguments along these lines might dissuade lukewarm supporters of the department just as easily as its own persuasion could win them. Consequently, the association tried to submerge its public lobbying efforts in a loose coalition of some 100 education and other groups. It kept firm control of the coalition's Washington lobbying, however, and provided most of the coalition's finance and staff, as well as most of its lobbying infantry outside Washington. About twelve groups in the coalition worked hard for the department, but NEA still worked hardest of all.

In addition, the White House began to devote more resources to the fight for the new department. A task force was established to lobby legislators. It comprised members of the White House's legislative liaison team, the DPS, other White House units, and OMB, and could call on the president and vice-president when a member of Congress required special attention to ensure his or her vote. The task force was to cooperate closely with Ribicoff and Brooks (the floor leaders of the legislation), with NEA, and with the other leading supporters of the separate department. As the legislative activity intensified, representatives of the task force met the interest groups two or three times weekly to discuss tactics and exchange information. Vice-president Mondale devoted part of almost every working day to the battle, and the president reviewed progress with the task force at least weekly. Ultimately, the president was to devote more time to lobbying for the bill than to any other lobbying effort of his administration, except for the Panama Canal treaties.

The House and Senate committee hearings on the 1979 bills and the subsequent legislative sessions raised few new issues, but they saw some altered emphases. On the prodepartment side, the main task was to allay fears of federal control, the bogey that had loomed ever larger in 1978; on the antidepartment side, it was to add amendments to the legislation that would cripple it. So worrisome had the federal control issue become that the Senate committee went out of its way to play down the likely effects of the legislation. The department, it said, "should not directly . . . improve American education. It is not intended to do so, because that is really the province and duty of the States and localities."[10] The committee added yet more amendments to the bill to guard against federal encroachments. On the staffing side, the Senate committee limited the number of high-level employees the department could employ and required Congress to establish each year a staff ceiling for the whole department. No other federal department had faced such a restriction on its size.

Once the bill reached the Senate floor it almost stumbled over an unexpected obstacle when Senator Jesse Helms (R-N.C.) tried to attach an amendment that effectively would have allowed voluntary prayer in public schools. Helms was opposed to a greater federal role in education, but he also saw the education department bill as a chance to gain ground for a moral and religious cause. His amendment was so unpalatable to some Senate liberals, who were only tepid supporters of the education department in any case, that it might have turned them against the bill. However, the amendment was removed from the bill by 53 votes to 40 after adroit maneuvers by the Democratic leadership (assisted by NEA officials) and telephone calls to wavering senators from Carter and Mondale.[11] Once the amendment was removed, the bill passed comfortably through the Senate by 72 votes (48D, 24R) to 21 (5D, 16R).

At every stage in two years of struggle for the education department, the House provided a sterner test than the Senate. House members were closer than senators to antifederal control sentiment at the grass roots and, facing elections every two years, they were more likely to respond to it. But they were also closer to the prodepartment lobbyists, who worked hard to pick up the few votes that might mean victory. Early in 1979, great interest centered on how the four new members of the House Government Operations Committee would vote. The NEA and other supporters of the department had established contact with the new men soon after their arrival in Washington, and they were believed to have secured the votes of the three Democrats. The new Republican, Lyle Williams of Ohio, was still undecided, along with two old members. The committee was neatly balanced, with eighteen votes for the bill and eighteen against. . . .

The story of the creation of the department of education is, first of all, a study in the dynamics of coalitions. A coalition is a sharing and joint use of resources to influence a decision or series of decisions, in this case a series of decisions in relation to a bill before Congress.[12] A coalition is not an alliance among organizations with similar goals. Fellow contributors of resources to one coalition may contribute to opposing coalitions on another decision. They may simultaneously be allies and opponents, as the AFT and NEA were on tuition tax credits and the education department, respectively. Because the goals of the contributors to a coalition may be diverse, the contributors often have different sets of reasons for seeking to influence the decision the coalition is trying to achieve. The desire to, for example, have a bill passed or defeated may be the only thing on which all contributors can agree unequivocally. All contributors believe passage or defeat will do something for them or their organizations, but one contributor's "something" may be nothing like another's.

The proposed education department was supported and opposed by shifting, loose coalitions that comprised interest groups, elected politicians, bureaucrats, newspapers, and television stations. All parts of each coalition agreed at least that the department should or should not exist, but beyond that they differed. They differed over what were the issues in the contest and they had differing goals. On the prodepartment side, some were always most interested in "status" and "visibility" for education in Washington. Others gave more weight to improving the quality of education administration at the center. Still others wanted most of all to reduce the burden of federal red tape and regulation on classroom teachers.

Few of the participants in the prodepartment coalition saw only one issue or sought a single goal. Rather, they perceived a number of issues and pursued a number of goals, but some issues and goals were given a higher priority than others. Similarly, contributors to the anti-department coalition gave different degrees of importance to goals like "local control," "curbing bureaucracy," "freedom of choice," and "defeating NEA." Many protagonists redistributed their priorities over time as circumstances changed. The rhetoric of the battle reflected these shifting balances. "Coordination" became less important in the OMB lexicon as the likelihood of great coordination being achieved receded. Perhaps by 1979, the president's desire for reelection outweighed everything else in the White House's approach to the legislation, and the president's lieutenants used the arguments that seemed most likely to achieve this goal. Among the department's conservative opponents, "federal control" and "controlling the bureaucracy," even "protecting the family" (the abortion and prayer amendments), became more important as debating points once they were perceived to be somehow connected with the proposed department. Indeed, so anxious were some of the department's supporters to placate its opponents that some apparently conservative goals—such as the limits on staffing and the congressional veto on regulations—became important on both sides of the fight. Supporters were forced to seek the same goals as opponents, but with less enthusiasm. . . .

The final concluding point recalls the lack of proportion between the efforts of the supporters of the legislation and the extent of the reorganization that the legislation achieved.

The original bill proposed a fairly narrow department; the legislative process whittled away even this modest conception. Yet it seems that in the White House, where the deployment of resources in proportion to benefits should have been of the highest concern, the question "Is it worth it?" was never seriously asked or considered. Or if the question was asked, the answers of those who looked at the costs and benefits from a management perspective alone were outmaneuvered by those who raised other considerations. Indeed, the force of these other considerations was the very reason why the administration refused to be deterred by the changes in the department's conception during 1978 and 1979, and why it gladly accepted the department that emerged.

These other considerations were three. First, there was the strong commitment of the president and vice-president to a separate department as a symbol of the administration's determination to raise the status of education in Washington and to increase the attention devoted to it by the federal government.[13] The "visibility" argument rather sank from view in the committee rooms and chambers of Capitol Hill, but it remained important for both Carter and Mondale. Carter had the stubbornness and Mondale the contacts in Congress to continue the fight for the extra chair at cabinet meetings, regardless of the powers its occupant might wield.

Second, while the White House had not worked as hard in 1978 to pass the legislation as it did in 1979, it had invested too many resources to pull back. The obvious time to assess costs and benefits was the turn of the year. To the extent that such an assessment was made, it was concluded that giving up the department would reduce the administration's ability to fight and win other battles in Congress. Potential allies would not trust it; potential foes would gain confidence; waverers would remain in their tents. Then, as 1979 wore on, the impossibility of retreat became the pressing need for a victory. The president was unpopular in the country, a challenge from Senator Edward M. Kennedy was looming, and the administration had gained a reputation for ineptitude in its relations with Congress. A win might boost the president's prestige and build up his resources for the last third of his term. It was no coincidence that the strongest push for the department came during one of the crises of the Carter presidency–the reappraisals and reprisals at Camp David in July 1979.

Third, the White House fought so hard for the reduced department because the likely political rewards seemed worth the effort. Among the many influences on the outcome of the battle, there stands out the relationship–past, present, and future–between the Carter camp and the National Education Association. Other presidents have had strong interests in government reorganization but few can have been so locked into a concept that eventually made so little difference to the structure of the federal government. Carter was locked in so securely because of the nature of his power base and the need to retain it. The new nomination rules of the Democratic party effectively replaced the old power structure in the party with the power of large, disciplined, and, most of all, dispersed organizations like the NEA. Carter, "everybody's second-best candidate" in 1976, whose support was "a mile wide but an inch deep," joined forces with an organization that was also thinly spread everywhere, to support something that aroused strong emotions among few Americans and made little difference to the machinery of their government. Many other groups supported the separate department of education but none had so much influence with the Carter White House as the NEA. Its skill in organizing the grass roots continually reminded Carter's team that the NEA was useful, powerful, and indeed indispensable.

Beryl A. Radin and Willis D. Hawley, *The Politics of Federal Reorganization: Creating the U.S. Department of Education* (1988), New York: Pergamon Press.

The reorganization issue was placed in the context of a broader policy environment which has historically been one characterized by controversy over the role of the federal government in education. This controversy is long-standing and we are no closer today to a political agreement on this issue that we were in 1954 with the historic *Brown v. Board of Education* Supreme Court decision. Since that decision, the federal role has broadened to promote equal opportunity on many fronts and to encourage change in education through the use of financial awards or incentives in what are essentially closed systems (local school systems). Most federal education programs were developed because states and localities were unwilling or unable to meet the requirements of students with special needs. Indeed, paradoxically, some federal programs provided funds to localities only because they had inadequately served the disadvantaged. Many state and local officials saw federal education programs as a necessary evil—at best that represented a constant threat to the effective functioning of schools. They resented the imposition of explicit federal requirements that implied that federal officials knew better than the local officials how the needs of children could best be served. This built-in conflict between the levels of government meant that educational policy decisions almost always reflected a set of compromises about the appropriate federal role. Even the period of great federal activity in the 1960s did not produce a resolution of this basic problem. Adding further to the intergovernmental tension was the fact that the various federal programs were instituted piece by piece with little concern in the Congress or the bureaucracy about possible conflicts between the various pieces of legislation.

The controversy surrounding the appropriate role of the federal government[14] was never far from the debate about the creation of a federal department of education. This created both rhetorical and substantive problems for the Carter administration as it pushed the proposal through the policy process. Because it wanted to avoid charges that it was supporting national control of education (departing from the historical reliance on state and local control), the Carter administration attempted to straddle the line carefully. Carter's disposition was to play a leadership role in education through changes in organization structure without dictating education policies and avoiding proposals to increase expenditure on new or old federal programs. . . .

Efforts to reorganize are often initiatives that seek to reorder priorities or power. Although issues of efficiency and program effectiveness frequently dominate the public discourse about reorganization, other questions may actually be more salient to the reorganization agenda. Underlying much of the debate about the establishment of the Department of Education was a concern about the appropriate role of the government in the education field and the relative importance of the Congress and the executive branch in defining that role. . . .

Herbert Emmerich has written that "the desire for autonomy characterizes the operating administrations and bureaus."[15] Programs—and their supporters both inside and outside government—appear to operate under the belief that the condition of being subsumed within a broader bureaucratic organization means that they are less than fully developed, almost a childlike condition that requires bureaucratic parental supervision. Emmerich notes that this desire for autonomy "is an apparently innate characteristic of administrative behavior."

For more than a century—even at a time when the federal responsibilities in education were extremely limited—calls for a separate cabinet-level department were heard. Some of these calls were in remembrance of things past-a time in 1867–68 when the few federal education efforts found a bureaucratic home in a tiny, subcabinet department. Soon, however, the department was downgraded to a bureau and that program eventually became the Office of Education (OE) (also known as the Education Division of the Department of Health, Education and Welfare [HEW]).

When the short lived Department of Education was moved in 1868, it was assigned to the Department of Interior and given the status of a small bureau. It stayed in this location for more than 60 years until President Harding attempted to raise its status in 1922. Harding requested the preparation of a bill creating a cabinet-level department of education, but his Commissioner of Education, Philander Claxton opposed this move. He prepared the bill to submit to Congress but spoke out against it. He was forced to resign even though the bill was never considered by the legislative body. Nearly ten years later, a commission appointed by President Herbert Hoover recommended the creation of a cabinet-level department of education, but Hoover did not request action on it.

In 1939 the Office of Education was taken out of the Department of Interior by President Franklin Roosevelt and was made a part of the Federal Security Agency, the predecessor of HEW. Roosevelt used his newly acquired reorganization authority in making this transfer. It has been argued that Roosevelt preferred the establishment of a separate education department but did not have the authority early in his administration to propose a new department under the reorganization authority given him by Congress. The move to create the Federal Security Agency followed the recommendation of Roosevelt's advisers on organization: Louis Brownlow, Charles Merriam, and Luther Gulick. Although the President did have authority to create a new department later in his administration, he did not make such a recommendation.

After World War II a recommendation was made to establish a National Board of Education answerable to the President but without cabinet status. Ironically, the proposal was similar to that made by Philander Claxton some 30 years earlier.[16]

There continued to be advocates of a separate cabinet-level department over the years but serious attention to such a structure did not develop until the growth of federal education programs in the 1960s. Writing in 1968, Bailey and Mosher noted that "the recent emergence of education as a major national concern has raised insistent questions about the appropriate level and authority of USOE in the overall structure of the Federal government. The essential issue is this: is bureau status for OSOE commensurate with the importance of the functions it performs, and adequate to enable it to exert government-wide leadership in the field of education?"[17]

At that time, Bailey and Mosher described three alternative ways of dealing with that question. First, holding on to the present arrangement because raising the visibility of education in the federal structure would increase the fear of federal domination in education policy. Second, raising the Office of Education to a departmental status but keeping it within a superdepartment of HEW. This model would follow the design of the Department of Defense where a separate department would be subsumed under a broader cabinet-level umbrella. The third alternative would involve splitting HEW into two parts—health and welfare on the one hand and education on the other. . . .[18]

In summary, the arguments that were given to justify the creation of a separate department of education were remarkably similar over the years. Five main arguments were used to support the prodepartment position:

1. A department would give education increased status and visibility. The United States is the only civilized nation in the world without an education ministry or department. Without a departmental status, education was viewed as inferior to other sectors in the society, such as agriculture, labor or business. From this perspective, simply the creation of a department—no matter in what form—would bring the education policy sector to an increased status in the American society.
2. A department would provide better access to the president in matters of education policy. It was difficult for education interest groups to push the executive branch toward a coherent position on budget or programmatic matters when it had to compete with other HEW concerns. From this perspective, the creation of a separate cabinet department would give both a chief executive as well as the education interest groups increased political advantage—in opportunity and access if not always in substance.
3. A department would allow for coordination of education programs that were scattered across agencies of the federal government. Coordination would provide the mechanism to reduce overlap and duplication. It would also allow for programmatic reforms through a more integrated organizational structure. It was assumed that more efficient administrative practices would result from these opportunities for coordination.
4. A department of education would serve as the vehicle for a president to develop a coherent set of policies in education. The scattered authorities made it difficult to have more than a reactive presidency. A department would make it easier to develop proactive policy strategies. From this perspective, it would be possible for a president and the executive branch to devise programs and policies that were more effective than efforts that had been undertaken before.
5. Cabinet-level status for education would provide the vehicle for the federal government to induce change in the highly decentralized educational system. Those who advocated change—of any sort—saw the creation of a department as an opportunity to turn those proposals into reality.

The arguments that were used against the creation of a separate department also tended to be relatively consistent over the years:

1. Creation of a department of education would signal a dramatic increase in the federal role in education. This would counter the traditional American belief in education as a state and local matter.
2. Creation of a separate department of education would politicize an important national issue and force education policy to be dominated by special interest groups with narrow and self interests in maintaining the status quo.
3. Finally, the creation of a department of education would disrupt the precarious balance that had been struck in the U.S. between private and parochial schools. A separate department would create a new set of legal and political issues regarding the separation of church and state and other civil rights and civil liberties concerns.

Both sets of arguments about the impact of the creation of a separate department were speculative. Political as well as "intellectual" arguments could be mustered on both sides of the issue. The gurus of the public administration field were full of speculations about the conditions necessary to assure the successful drive for the creation of a department. For some, there was a set of ideal conditions to be met before a department would be created. Herbert Emmerich has written that "a program must be thoroughly accepted to win departmental status, and its components must have some plausible relationship to begin with. No matter how diverse the components, they must form a visible image when combined or related, so that a department head can be chosen who can identify with them and in turn be identified as their spokesman by the public, the press, and by Congress."[19] Although this line of argument in favor of a department of education was somewhat persuasive, neither they, nor the arguments that were used to support the creation of HEW, HUD, and the Department of Transportation, were noncontroversial in nature. . . .

CARTER'S INTEREST IN REORGANIZATION

Carter's interest in reorganization was not surprising. As Joel Havemann of the *National Journal* reported on January 1, 1977:

> When Jimmy Carter moved into the Georgia governor's mansion in 1971, he quickly pushed through the state legislature a bill giving him broad powers to reorganize state agencies. He proceeded to use those powers to turn the Georgia bureaucracy upside down. Now Carter is about to move into a new home—the White House—and he is preparing to try to do to the federal bureaucracy what he did to Georgia's.[20]

Although Carter's authority in Georgia was broad enough to allow him to create and abolish cabinet departments, early conversations with leaders of Congress had indicated that there was reluctance to give him such powers at the federal level. Texas Democratic Congressman Jack Brooks, Chairman of the House Government Operations Committee, was particularly reluctant to extend such authority to the White House. Brooks was reflecting the traditional congressional skepticism about reorganization. Between 1949 and 1973, presidents had used reorganization authority 74 times to make changes in bureaucratic structures; Congress rejected these proposals 19 times. While Lyndon Johnson had been successful in getting two new departments created, he was stymied in his attempt to consolidate Commerce and Labor into a single department. Nixon's proposals for super-departments were completely rejected by the Congress.

Congressional reluctance to accept reorganization plans was also perceived to be related to the organization of Congress itself. Although congressional committee organization is independent of any changes in executive branch organization, a number of members believed that reorganization in the executive branch would be followed by reorganization of the congressional committee system—a shift that would potentially create changes in committee and subcommittee leadership positions. Interest groups also feared this kind of change, believing that it would undermine coalitions and their bases of support.

In Washington, as in Georgia, Carter's approach to reorganization centered on consolidation of governmental units with overlapping functions and reduction of the number of department and agency heads who report directly to the President. Carter's goal was to reduce the number of federal agencies to 200 from 1900,[21] a figure that included some 1400 federal advisory committees. Although the clear thrust of Carter's proposals went toward consolidation, there was a notable exception to that direction: his campaign promise to create a separate department of education, disaggregating the large Department of Health, Education and Welfare (HEW).

As Carter set about to begin his reorganization effort, there was no lack of advice from both academic as well as political quarters. Rufus E. Miles, long time HEW staff member, offered the new President 13 criteria by which to evaluate his reorganization activities:

1. Recognize that "organization is an important expression of social values" within the nation.
2. Place organizations "in a favorable environment for the performance of their central missions."
3. Remember that "organization affects the allocation of resources."
4. "Organization by reasonably broad purpose serves the President best." It should not be so narrow "as to be overly responsive to specific clientele groups, nor so broad as to be unmanageable."
5. "Wide span of control has significant advantages in improving administration and reducing unnecessary layers of bureaucracy."
6. "Organizational form and prestige are especially important at the federal level in attracting and retaining first-rate leader-managers."
7. Balance is important in government organization: "excessive concentration of important responsibilities in one agency diminishes the effective performance of most of them."
8. "When purposes overlap, one must be designated as dominant; otherwise responsibility is unclear."
9. A system of coordination must be established when purposes overlap.

10. "Programs should be grouped on the basis of their affinity or the potential for cross-fertilization."
11. "Reorganizations have traumatic effects which should be carefully weighed. Reorganizations that require congressional approval or acquiescence should be carefully weighed to make sure that they are worth the expenditure of political capital required and have a reasonable chance of approval."
12. "Economy as a ground for major reorganization is a will-o'-the-wisp."[22]

This advice did inform the reorganization staff (if not the President). But analysts disagreed about the operational implications of these views while acknowledging that they reflected the prevailing wisdom of the public administration field.

Slightly more than a month after Carter took office, the new administration appeared before a House subcommittee with its supplemental budget request for money to support the reorganization effort. Harrison Wellford appeared on behalf of OMB Director Bert Lance before the House Appropriations Subcommittee responsible for the Department of Treasury, Postal Service and General Government on the 1977 Supplemental Request for the Office of Management and Budget.[23] The request submitted by Wellford was for an additional $1.6 million dollars and 62 additional full-time positions for the reorganization activities.

Wellford's statement noted that the reorganization staff would be located within OMB, with OMB Director Bert Lance as the leader of the effort. (Lance had been Carter's most essential strategist and ally in Georgia for that reorganization activity.) A new role of Executive Associate Director for Reorganization and Management would be created in OMB with a full-time commitment to planning and directing the reorganization program, reporting to the Director and Deputy Director of OMB, and "accessible to the president and advisory Group as necessary on reorganization matters."[24]

Wellford, the individual named to the new Executive Associate Director role spelled out in the supplemental budget request, was a lawyer as well as a Ph.D. in American history who had worked previously in Congress and for consumer advocate Ralph Nader. He did not have previous experience in the executive branch. His background led him to emphasize the political nature of the reorganization issue.

In his testimony, Wellford noted that the new administration had studied the reorganization efforts of the last three administrations and identified three major problem areas:

> First, to a large degree, reorganization plans were developed in a political vacuum. Consultation with Congress, affected interest groups, agency personnel, State and local government officials and the public generally was either superficial or after the fact.
>
> Second, the scope of reorganization was too narrow and failed to address the problems at the program level where government meets the people. Recent reorganization attempts have focused primarily on box shuffling at the cabinet level and neglected improvements in administrative management and intergovernmental relations that determine the effectiveness of policy decisions within those boxes.
>
> Third, reorganization efforts have been conducted by study commissions, located in the Executive Office, without any ongoing institutional base of their own. There has been little connection between the formulators of reorganization policy and those who must implement it in the rest of the government.[25]

According to Wellford, Carter planned to prevent these problems from repeating themselves by taking the following steps:

- He will consult Congress, the Cabinet and the public at every stage of the development of our reorganization plans and proposals. This consultation is already under way in a number of areas. The President will establish a reorganization advisory group to coordinate public hearings on his reorganization proposals before final submission to Congress. This outreach to the public may be expensive, but we feel it is essential to the integrity of the reorganization effort.
- The President has defined the scope of reorganization to include a comprehensive effort to increase the competence and responsiveness of government in three broad areas.
- *Structural consolidation and streamlining* to reduce the waste, duplication, overlap, and complexity of government.
- *Implementation of "sunshine" and other openness initiatives and improvements in intergovernmental relations* to make government more responsive and compassionate in meeting public needs.
- *Development of an administrative management program for the President* to provide guidance for internal management reforms in the agencies and departments. Obviously, the President does not intend to manage the departments from the White House or OMB. He has emphasized managerial expertise in his cabinet selections and has made clear that the cabinet will be held accountable for the efficiency of their departments. The President, through management devices such as Zero Base Budgeting will provide guidance and encouragement to the cabinet effort but responsibility will remain with the agency heads. . . .[26]

With a staff in place and a sense that they had been told to go ahead with their analysis activity, the PRP education study anticipated submitting a proposal to the President at the end of November. As they prepared to complete the first phase of the study, however, some dramatic shifts were occurring within the White House.

Carter's plans to proceed with a reorganization had been constructed on an assumption that one of his closest and most trusted associates—Bert Lance—would be the key figure involved. The location of the reorganization activity within the OMB could be justified on a number of compelling grounds—but probably none was as compelling as the presence of Lance at its helm. Carter himself noted that "it is difficult for me to explain how close Bert was to me or how much I depended on him. . . . I did not hesitate in making Bert Lance the first person I asked to serve at the top level within my administration after the election. He was the only one of the Cabinet-level members with whom I had ever worked before, and I planned for him to be the leader on matters dealing with the budget and government reorganization."[27]

On September 21, 1977, OMB Director Bert Lance resigned, responding to allegations about his financial dealings involving an Atlanta bank. Lance was replaced as OMB Director by James McIntyre, his deputy, who also came with Carter from Georgia. Although McIntyre was trusted by Carter (indeed, he was named Deputy to Lance at Carter's personal insistence), he had neither Lance's personal relationship to the President nor his status in dealing with other actors inside the White House and on the Hill. Within OMB itself, the shift of top leadership affected the plans to integrate reorganization, management improvement efforts, and the traditional budget role of the agency. Because of the short period of time that Lance served in the position, it was not clear whether he would have been able to juggle the various agendas subsumed within OMB's mission statements. . . .

McIntyre was less able to deal with the complexity of the agency. Although the original plans for the PRP conceived of the effort as a regular operating arm of OMB, as the months progressed it appeared that McIntyre was preoccupied with the budget side of OMB and that budget concerns were driving both his interests and his time. Because the budget process had its own momentum and schedule, it almost always pushed out competing claims for time. A budget had to be submitted to the Congress and the budget process itself required rapid timing and quick turnaround time for response. . . .

When Carter prepared to assume the presidency, one could identify five general concerns or goals that were associated with the proposal for a new department. These goals reflected the range of actors and issues that were involved in the advocacy of the department and, as they were played out, shaped the organizational alternatives that were considered. The expectations about the possible impact of ED varied tremendously, depending on which goal was predominant. As we have noted, each of these goals–symbolic status, political advantage, efficiency, effectiveness, and change–contained arguments that had been made in favor of a new department for many years. The nature of goals (or combination of goals) shaped the character of the political activity through which they were produced.

SYMBOLIC STATUS

Those who argued for the creation of a separate cabinet-level structure for education because of the symbolic status of a department were attempting to address what they believed to be a simple problem: the U.S. was the only nation in the world that did not have an education ministry or department. For some, thus, creation of ED was a political end in itself. For others, the status of a department would have instrumental value. The creation of a cabinet-level department would provide the education sector with a status comparable to other sectors in the society which did have their own place in the president's cabinet. Some advocates of this position believed that higher status, visibility, and a place at the cabinet table would translate into future federal funding for education and, in general, greater public attention to the needs of students and educators. . . .

This case indicates that symbolism is alive and well in the *substance* of specific policy proposals. The value of the symbolic status argument as a political goal is that it can encompass many actors at once in a way that allows them to imagine different consequences of their support. As long as the issue remains at a symbolic level, the consequences of these differences are muted.

Sometimes the symbolic status goal was the sole motivation for activity and some of the department's proponents were willing to invest simply in the attainment of ED, believing that status and visibility were important enough to warrant such an effort. Others combined the symbolic status goal with other goals; indeed, they believed that the symbolic status goal did not warrant the expenditure of political capital and (particularly for analysts) achieving this goal alone was worse than doing nothing at all.

POLITICAL ADVANTAGE

The advocates of reorganization of the federal education programs often linked the symbolic status arguments to their calculation of political advantage for personal, partisan and interest group agendas. It is clear that Carter's interest in the department was motivated by his interest in attaining the support of the NEA during the 1976 campaign. The political know-how and resources of the NEA were (and continue to be) considerable and provided Carter with a unique political machine that had functioning parts throughout the country. After the campaign, this goal appeared to be less important to the Carter administration—until the time came to plan a reelection strategy. And, once again, during the 1980 Democratic convention, Carter's support from the NEA was essential to his political fortunes.

The White House also attempted to calculate political advantage as it worked with the Congress on this issue. Carter's team had difficulty maintaining the support of a Democratic Congress on a broad range of issues. As the proposal for ED developed, the White House analysis could not be limited to simple vote counts on various proposals related to the structure and functions of the department. . . .

Political advantage was also an essential goal for members of Congress as they determined their positions on ED. As long as the issue could be posed in general terms (simply a department), the organization and power of the NEA and its supporters played an important role in securing the votes of many members of Congress. However, as soon as the question before the members focused on specific programs and structures to be included or excluded from ED, then a range of other issues came to the fore. Members were, understandably, more concerned about the disruption of their long term support from various groups than they were about the short term advantage they might gain in supporting the President's position. . . .

EFFICIENCY

It is not surprising that supporters of ED argued that a cabinet-level department would make the federal education bureaucracy more efficient. Arguments based on increases in efficiency (assertions of reduced costs and more expeditious action) are the most common public positions taken to justify administrative reorganization. This position asserts that reorganization is needed because of overlap and duplication of functions; these result in complex and slow decision processes that produce costly and inadequate services.

This set of arguments focuses only on the *process* of the agencies, not on their substantive output. This approach was the path that justified the existence of a free standing PRP, theoretically connected to the substantive decision-making process but, in reality, separate from the substantive aspects of the Domestic Policy Staff or even from the budget staffs of OMB. It was also the reason for the existence of the congressional government operations committees—bodies that focused on the *how* not the *what* of federal government operations. As long as these arenas were the location of decision-making, the efficiency arguments would have some salience. In addition, in a budget-cutting environment, arguments that promise to achieve "more bang for the buck" take on some prominence. Moreover, they go down well in public because of the widespread belief that government is inefficient and wasteful.

The venue of decision-making, therefore, explains much of the attractiveness of the efficiency argument for ED's proponents. Indeed, this argument was one of the major reasons for support from the two congressional government operations committees. Efficiency arguments allowed the committees to differentiate their approach from that of the substantive committees and to justify their "meddling" in education matters. However, as has been shown, it is difficult to make a case for the creation of a department such as ED resting only on arguments of efficiency. . . .

Although the PRP always attempted to include efficiency arguments in its analysis, the particular group of individuals assembled to work on ED did not find these arguments to be particularly convincing. The reorganization group was a part of the management "side" of OMB but many of the PRP staffers did not believe that management questions–unlike budgets–were important. . . .

The PRP did recognize the arguments for improved efficiency were good public relations ploys and it was difficult for anyone to argue against them. The PRP position was not unlike that of the transition group and the strategists within ED. While they used the efficiency argument, it did not represent their major case for change. The emphasis on efficiency in the House deliberations left the administration with a weak case. The efficiency arguments used to support ED were innocuous and somewhat vapid; they did not point to scandals, examples of gross misspending or other forms of "horror" stories about management of federal education programs.

EFFECTIVENESS

Advocates of ED who argued from this goal rested their case on the belief that the creation of a separate department would improve the quality of educational services within the existing structure and level of resources already found in the federal government. Focusing on the growing skepticism within the U.S. about the ability of existing programs to address education problems, those who argued this position alleged that a new department would be able to take the programs that were already in place and make them work "better."

The effectiveness arguments were difficult to sustain in the ED decision process. First, advocates of this position were implicitly criticizing the status quo, even if they looked only to marginal and incremental changes. Proponents of the status quo were often the very groups who supported the concept of ED on other grounds. The education interest groups–especially the NEA–were found in this position. This argument also appeared to be an attack on the ability of the Washington career bureaucrats–important allies of the interest groups–to do their job.

Second, the argument often seemed trivial. If the problems in American education were significant, the effectiveness argument seemed to be placing a small band-aid on a large wound. If there were problems, it was argued, why not address them in more comprehensive ways? Those who were attracted to this argument (particularly the PRP staff and Hufstedler's staff) did find it difficult to rest with the scope of this approach. While they did want to appear to be improving American education, they were also aware of the political constraints and did not want to cause a large scale disruption of the system. This was not an easy position to hold.

Third, because the jurisdiction for the reorganization proposals was in the government operations committees in the Congress, substantive arguments (no matter how modest) were difficult to raise without violating the boundaries of the authority of those committees. Indeed, to raise some of these questions was perceived to be opening a Pandora's box. Once open, that box let loose criticisms of federal education programs, civil rights policies and other requirements that seemed to constrain state and local policy-makers.

For these reasons, the effectiveness arguments had only limited power to influence the development of ED. Despite Carter's own personal attraction to this type of argument (it acknowledged problems but did not suggest large scale action by the federal government), the decision process contained neither the arenas nor the actors to make this argument a major rallying point (**Figure 8-1**).

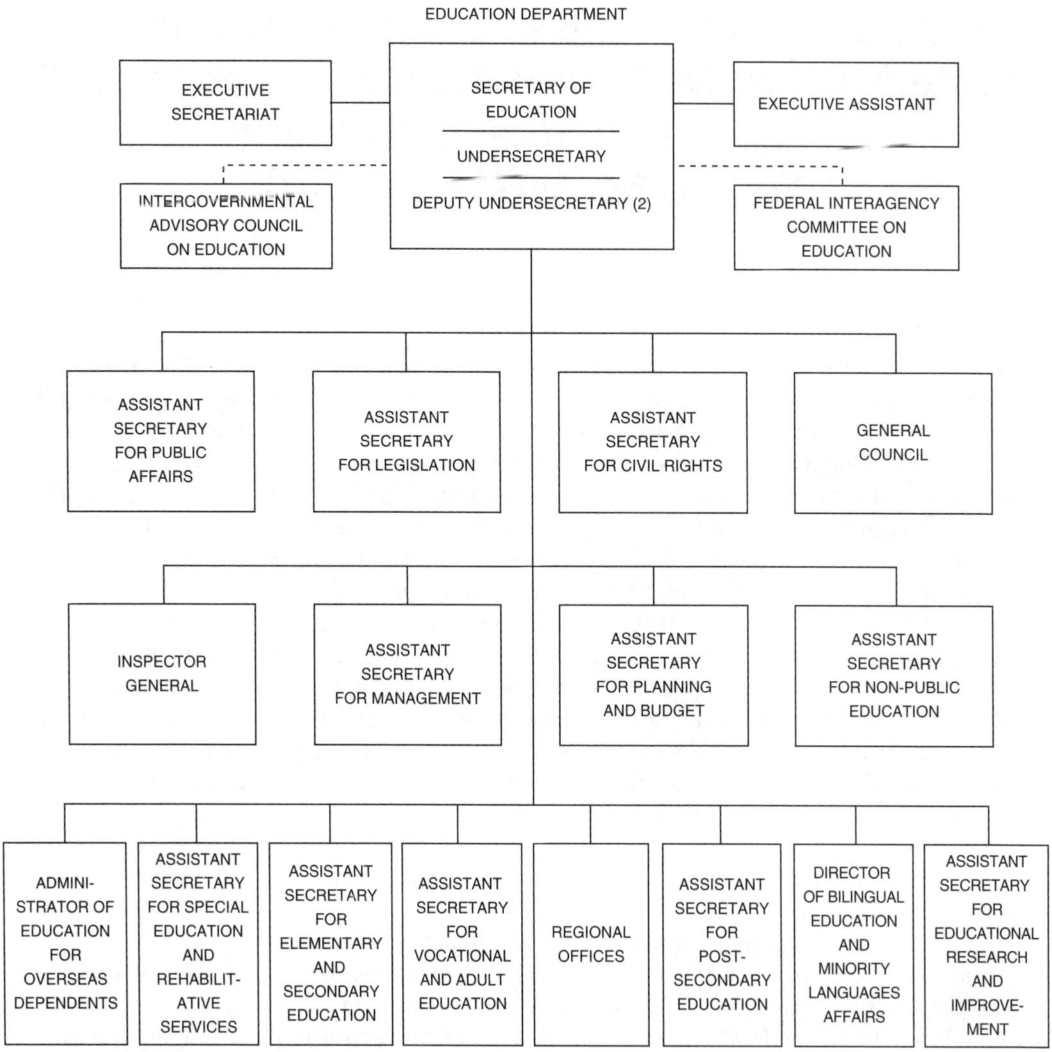

Source: Beryl A. Radin and Willis D. Hawley, *The Politics of Federal Reorganization: Creating the Department of Education*, (New York: Pergamon Press, 1988).
FIGURE 8-1 Education Department, May, 1980

Ronald P. Seyb, "Reform as Affirmation: Jimmy Carter's Executive Branch Reorganization Effort," *Presidential Studies Quarterly,* Vol. 31, No. 1. (March 2001).

Carter's executive branch reorganization proposals were the product of a nonlinear decision-making process that took Carter to an unanticipated destination. Carter and his aides' initial impulse was to pursue a novel "bottom-up" approach to reorganization. They intended to tailor their proposals to fit the problems identified in a thorough review and analysis of the executive branch's performance rather than impose a "one-size-fits-all" structural reform on every department and agency. But the participants in the President's Reorganization Project (PRP) quickly gravitated to the "top-down," structural approach to administrative reform favored by previous administrations. . . .

The Carter reorganization planning team's discussions treated structural reform not as merely one among many possible instruments for addressing the idiosyncratic problems of individual departments and agencies. They instead characterized structural reform as the linchpin of their reorganization package and spent much of their time casting about for "problems" that structural reforms could address. Carter readily accepted the recommendations of his planning group and displayed surprising flexibility in his negotiations with Congress, acceding to compromises in a way that was out of character for such a dogmatic president. . . .

Structural reform's appeal to the Carter administration stemmed from its singular ability to provide symbolic benefits that were unattainable via a bottom-up, "problem- and program-oriented"[28] approach to reform.[29] argue that "politics and governance are important social rituals" that affirm community values and beliefs. Comprehensive reorganization proposals contribute to this process by confirming Americans' belief in "progress through intentional action."[30] Carter could use structural reform to demonstrate to both a skeptical public and Washington community his "fundamental confidence in the possibility of directing and controlling human existence, or, more specifically, the government."[30] What began as an effort to tailor solutions to fit the problems unearthed by a review of specific programs became instead a campaign to discover a rationale for a reform proposal that promised little change in agency performance but could make a statement about Carter's "mastery of government." Carter's willingness to compromise away some central elements of his reorganization plans is understandable from this perspective. If the important goal is to achieve some kind of visible reorganization, then even the most rigid president can be flexible on the details. . . .

Jimmy Carter voiced a strong commitment to administrative reform during his campaign for the presidency in 1976. Carter made clear as early as the New Hampshire primary that comprehensive reorganization of the executive branch would constitute the centerpiece of this reform effort, stating at one of his early campaign rallies, "Don't vote for me unless you want to see the executive branch of government reorganized."[31] This promise to reorganize the executive branch quickly became a leitmotif of Carter's campaign speeches, as President Carter readily conceded in an interview conducted soon after his election:

> I think of all the campaign speeches that I made throughout the Nation, the most consistent commitment that was made to the American people was that I would move as quickly as possible to improve the efficiency and the effectiveness and the sensitivity of the Federal Government bureaucracy in dealing with the needs of the American people. . . . We'll begin the process as quickly as we can.[28]

The first presidential candidate to make executive branch reorganization a major campaign theme wasted little time after his election in putting together a reorganization planning group.[28] Carter chose to reject the traditional "commission" model of reorganization planning adopted by most of his predecessors in favor of installing the planning operation in the Office of Management and Budget (OMB) and manning it with members of his administration. Carter's reorganization proposal thus would be cobbled together by young professionals and political activists rather than the "wise men" who had been enlisted by past presidents.[28] This decision provoked some debate within the administration. Richard Pettigrew, a Carter adviser who had been instrumental in Florida's reorganization of its executive branch in the early 1970s, drafted a memorandum to Hamilton Jordan that, while pretending to offer a dispassionate assessment of the pros and cons of the "OMB option" and the "Commission option," clearly favored the latter over the former. Pettigrew argued that the OMB option would result not in comprehensive reorganization but in a "piecemeal, incremental effort [that] will respond to pressures, present plans without adequate public consultation or input and run a high risk of rejection in Congress except where 'pabulum' revisions are proposed." Pettigrew averred that the commission option, in contrast, would give the recommendations the kind of public visibility and credibility that would impress Congress while ensuring that these recommendations would be based on "an in-depth look at all aspects of the executive branch."[32]

Pettigrew's recommendation, however, did not persuade Carter to abandon the OMB option. Soon after Pettigrew's memo, Carter established the PRP within the OMB and placed Harrison Wellford, who had headed the reorganization planning group during the transition, in charge of the new division. . . .

The administration believed that the success of this incremental approach to comprehensive reorganization hinged on winning congressional reauthorization of presidential reorganization authority. The Reorganization Act of 1949 had provided presidents with the prerogative to submit reorganization plans to Congress that would go into effect if they were not vetoed by either the House or Senate within sixty days of submission. The act was amended in 1964 to prohibit presidents from using reorganization plans to consolidate, abolish, or create cabinet-level departments, and it was amended again in 1971 to limit the president to one plan in a thirty-day period and to require that each plan deal with only one "logically consistent subject matter." Congress, however, had allowed this presidential reorganization authority to lapse in 1973. The Carter White House initially believed that the need to win congressional reauthorization of reorganization authority provided it with an opportunity to expand the president's prerogatives to restructure the executive branch. Members of the administration debated whether to pressure Congress to allow the president to use reorganization plans to create new departments, present omnibus plans rather than "logically consistent" proposals, submit more than one plan within a thirty-day period, and oblige both houses of Congress rather than a single house to veto reorganization plans. The most dramatic of these options, and the most important for the future success of the Carter reorganization effort, was fighting to gain the authority to create executive departments by reorganization plan....

(Staff) maintained that winning this battle with Congress was critical not only for the success of Carter's reorganization effort but also for convincing the public that Carter was serious about working with Congress to fulfill his campaign promises:[33]

> Reorganization plan authority legislation meets an immediate political need both with the public and with Congress.
>
> Given the expectations about government reorganization that have been raised by your campaign, it is important that you take the initiative on this issue as quickly as possible to show the American people that they can depend on your promises. As one of the first initiatives of your administration, RPA legislation will be viewed as the initial test of whether you can work effectively with Congress. You must act swiftly, but you must also act successfully, because it is unthinkable that you would not prevail on an issue to which you have given such high priority.[34]

This analysis suggested that the Carter White House would cease its campaign to expand the president's reorganization authority at the first hint of congressional opposition. This hint was quickly dropped by Representative Jack Brooks, the chair of the House Government Operations Committee, who objected to the legislative veto provision in the reorganization statute. In 1971, Brooks had proposed an amendment to the Reorganization Act that would have required both houses of Congress to approve presidential reorganization plans within sixty days of their submission. Brooks had promised to present a new version of this amendment when Carter presented his proposal for reauthorization of the Reorganization Act.[35] Brooks's skepticism about reorganization authority promised a politically costly fight in the House if the administration pushed to expand reorganization authority in ways that further impinged on Congress's prerogatives.

The Carter administration responded to Brooks's threat by ending its flirtation with the notion of broadening reorganization authority to encompass the creation of executive departments and concentrating instead on defeating the Brooks amendment and winning more modest concessions from Congress. Carter traded an agreement to endorse a provision that would allow the president to amend his reorganization plans within thirty days of submission in return for Brooks's withdrawal of his amendment. Brooks believed this would give Congress more input into reorganization plans by allowing it to pressure the president to modify his or her plans as a condition of congressional support.[28] The Carter administration, however, won some significant victories of its own. Congress agreed to allow presidents to submit more than one plan within a thirty-day period, permit omnibus reorganization plans, and extend reorganization authority for four years instead of the two years past presidents had enjoyed.[28]

Harrison Wellford encouraged Carter to treat his reorganization authority as one instrument among many for prosecuting a bottom-up approach to administrative reform. Wellford had described this approach in congressional testimony supporting the supplemental appropriation needed to fund the PRP. . . . Wellford suggested that the administration would use its reorganization authority only when it offered the best approach to a particular administrative problem. Structural reform thus would be merely one instrument among many the administration might use to improve government performance. This approach would ensure that the administration's reorganization efforts would not be "box-shuffling" exercises but would be tailored to solve discernible managerial and service delivery problems.[28]

Reference

Harry Eckstein, 1975, Case Study and Theory in Political Science, in Fred I. Greenstein and Nelson W. Polsby, *The Handbook of Political Science*, Vol. 7, Addison-Wesley, Reading, MA.

Paul Manna, *School's In: Federalism and the National Education Agenda* (2006), Washington, DC: Georgetown University Press.

Examining the organizations that federal officials have designed to help them create, manage, and implement policy also sheds light on how federal involvement in education has changed. This section focuses on four institutions in particular: the Gardner Education Task Force of 1964; the U.S. Department of Education, formed in the late 1970s; the NCEE, which produced the famous 1983 report, *A Nation at Risk*; and the National Education Goals Panel (NEGP), formed after the first national education summit in 1989. The character of these institutions and the issues they have addressed provide insights about the changing federal role in education. They also reveal that the federal-state relationship in education has changed dramatically since the 1960s.

During the summer of 1964, incumbent Lyndon Johnson was anticipating a November victory over Republican presidential opponent Barry Goldwater. In July of that summer, LB J announced to his cabinet that he was creating fourteen policy task forces to help him build on his Great Society speech that he had delivered on May 22 at the University of Michigan's commencement. The task forces would operate in secret, develop ideas for the president's domestic and international agenda, and report their findings to the president no later than November 10. John Gardner, president of the Carnegie Corporation, chaired the president's task force on education. Overall, its members included three federal, one state, "and two local officials; six academics; and two members each from the private and non-profit sectors.

The relatively low profile of the states, with their lone representative in the group, was consistent with general feelings that existed inside the Johnson administration and on the task force itself. As former Johnson adviser Samuel Halperin described to me in a personal interview, "The people who you could call the Kennedy and Johnson elites—I don't use that term negatively—didn't think that we could get educational justice from the states. Some of them said that the states were actually the problem." In his oral history, which is available at the LBJ presidential library, U.S. Commissioner of Education Francis Keppel, a member of the task force, said many of its members "felt that the state departments of education were the feeblest bunch of second-rate, or fifth-rate, educators who combined educational incompetence with bureaucratic immovability."[36]

Despite this criticism, Keppel also recognized the Johnson education program could not succeed without state government capacity. "Having sat on that educational bureaucracy

---

in Washington," he said, "the last thing in the world I wanted was all those 25,000 school districts coming in with plans with my bureaucrats deciding whether to approve them or not. I wanted that stuff done out in the states. And to make it work in the states, you have to improve the state departments in making grants."[36] My interviews with Halperin and Gordon Ambach, a veteran of federal and state policy arenas dating to the 1950s, confirmed this view. Comments from both illustrated how important Keppel saw the states' role even as these governments remained marginalized during the actual development of the first ESEA.[37]

By late September 1964, Gardner summarized the group's top priorities in a memo to task force members. The memo stressed an overall antipoverty theme and included proposals for supplementary educational centers, educational research and development labs, and higher education. Gardner's memo reflected Keppel's view that state departments of education were too weak at the time and that the U.S. Office of Education, which Keppel headed, would likely not be able to effectively manage the new Johnson education program. To address that potential problem, the Gardner memo proposed removing the Office of Education from the Department of Health, Education, and Welfare, and creating a stand-alone federal education department instead.[36]

On November 15, Johnson received the task force's final report. It was a much expanded but essentially unchanged version of Gardner's memo and it provided the basis for titles I, III, IV, and V of the first ESEA. The president reportedly read the report from cover to cover and was pleased with its contents. Shortly after Thanksgiving, he met with his advisers and instructed them to press on with a legislative program for education based on the Gardner task force report.[36] The first ESEA became law roughly five months later.

Even though a federal education department did not emerge in 1965, the Gardner group's recommendation for one was actually not new. During the first half of the twentieth century, members of Congress had introduced more than fifty bills that would have established such a department and given education cabinet-level status.[38] The vision for a department finally became reality when, on October 17, 1979, President Jimmy Carter signed into law the Department of Education Organization Act (P.L. 96-88).

Creating the department was a notable legislative accomplishment. But in substantive terms, it is perhaps a less significant achievement than passage of the first ESEA and, by implication, the work of the Gardner task force. That is because the ESEA of 1965 represented a major break with past federal education policy and overcame persistent concerns about race, religion, and federal intrusion that had torpedoed past proposals for greater federal involvement in the nation's schools. The Carter initiative that created the Department of Education, while certainly criticized for unduly increasing federal control, did not represent this kind of substantive breakthrough. Exploring the rationale that motivated Carter's advocacy for the department reveals why.

Carter and his allies offered reasons for creating the new department but neither overhauling the nation's education system nor altering the major substantive thrust of federal programs was part of their rationale. In short, an education reform agenda did not animate their efforts. In an interview with Arthur Wise, a former Carter administration official whose "pen wrote most of the legislation [to create the department], at least the first drafts," Wise said this about the early stages of the process: "Other than saying that we should have an education department, the president and others behind it hadn't given much thought to what that actually meant." Perhaps that lack of foresight is one reason why White House groups assigned to develop the original proposal basically ignored the issue of federal-state relations.[38] Wise continued in our discussion by noting that most people in the White House who worked on the initiative "had a very unsophisticated approach. Many of them argued that what needed to be done was to gather up everything remotely related to education and put it in the department."

As the effort unfolded, the primary rationale that emerged was a perceived need for bureaucratic reorganization. Much evidence supports this conclusion. First, Carter's team lodged its effort to create the department in a broader initiative called the President's Reorganization Project, which was designed to improve the work of many government agencies. Education was but one part of this overall reorganization effort.[38,39] Second, despite his remarks at the signing ceremony for P.L. 96-88, both during the legislative process and after leaving office, Carter emphasized organizational concerns when focusing on why the nation needed the department.[40,41] Finally, some of the department's supporters and members of Congress actually argued that this new federal agency would produce little policy change. To minimize fears of growing federal control, the Senate committee that considered the bill in 1979 stated in its report, somewhat remarkably, that the new department "should not directly . . . improve American education. It is not intended to do so because that is really the province and duty of the States and localities."[40,42]

The U.S. Department of Education opened its doors on May 4, 1980. Less than one year later, Ronald Reagan entered the White House with promises to abolish the fledgling department. Despite Reagan's animosity, the institution survived and created an effective bully pulpit for his own and subsequent education secretaries. Perhaps one of the most effective uses of the department's platform was by Terrell "Ted" Bell who served as its secretary during Reagan's first term.

Gary Orfield, "Foreword," in *Expansion of Federal Power in American Education: Federal-State Relationships Under the No Child Left Behind Act, Year One*, Gail L. Sunderman and Jimmy Kim (Eds.), (February 2004).

The federal role in American education has been an issue of great sensitivity in American politics. Traditionally, policy makers have supported state and local control rather than federal directives and federal education legislation has normally contained strong prohibitions against federal control of education. It was largely because of concern about a potential abuse of federal power that the U.S. lagged generations behind other nations in the development of a national department of education. As is often true in the American system, concerns about liberty and local autonomy far outweighed concerns about policy objectives.

Part of the vigorous defense of local autonomy historically, of course, was rooted in the struggle to preserve local traditions of minority group separation and subordination. Fear of racial change, concern about subsidies to religious groups, and general support for state and local control of the schools delayed federal education legislation for many years after national surveys showed public support.

Normally conservatives were the most suspicious about federal power. They constantly warned against the danger of federal control of the schools when liberals and moderates tried to create federal programs that supported the growth and improvement of American schools or that challenged state and local practices of exclusion and discrimination. Others have been less opposed to a federal role in education. American civil rights supporters and researchers supported an extension of federal power to deal with local discrimination and exclusion from educational opportunity. Public education supporters have for many decades favored a larger federal role in equalizing funding of schools and providing programs for poor children in schools. This was the central impulse behind the creation of the Elementary and Secondary Education Act in 1965, which led to an important federal role in public education.

The No Child Left Behind Act is a startling departure from this history, both in terms of its requirements and in terms of its sponsors. It requires specific large changes in the basic assessment systems of states, sets requirements for education progress in two specific subjects only, contains unusual and large sanctions, and commands many forms of specific state action. It clearly moves to the very heart of the educational process. When the fate of schools and faculties rests solely on achieving a nationally specified rate of progress

---

Source: Courtesy of The Civil Rights Project/Proyecto Derechos Civiles, UCLA.

on two tests, those tests will drive curriculum and instruction in the schools that are clearly at risk, and, in this way, the federal mandates will control the center of the educational process.

The implementation of the law proceeded with very little time for states to prepare for some of the provisions, without the resources that school districts believed they would receive at a time of serious cutbacks in state and local funding, and without the normal diplomacy of federal-state relationships. This has produced a unique combination of critics, ranging across ideological and political spectrums.

From a civil rights perspective there are parts of this law that are clearly positive, at least in principle—the insistence on accountability for racial and ethnic minorities, the policies for more qualified teachers, the requirement to offer choices to students in failing schools, and the aspirations for substantial progress for all groups of students. However, testing mandates are central to NCLB and there is a long history of serious civil rights concerns about the racial impacts of inappropriate use of standardized tests.

The law is particularly important because many of the high poverty schools that Title I programs target are minority schools with many minority teachers and administrators, often working inside overwhelmingly minority districts. In these schools, which deal with the consequences of very serious social and economic problems in their communities, it is extremely important that reforms not make things worse. Many of these schools and teachers have been subjected to a long succession of reforms imposed from the outside that have failed. The worst kind of reform would further demoralize already overburdened staffs, undermine the kind of reforms that produce lasting change, drive qualified teachers and administrators out of the most needy schools, and take resources from them when they cannot meet standards that no school district has ever met. Critics, including some leading researchers, believe that an ill-considered enforcement of some NCLB requirements will have those consequences.

Moreover, many educational leaders in poor urban and rural schools are concerned that the law oversimplifies the problems of educational improvement, underestimates the necessary preconditions and time required for serious reform, provides no reliable increase in resources, contains the wrong mix of sanctions and incentives, and relies on the wrong theory about how educational reforms are actually implemented. These doubts and the virtual exclusion of educational leaders from the legislative drafting process mean that the law is up against serious resistance on many levels within the professional community. The conflict, which has erupted even in the early stages of enforcing the law, suggests that a strong reaction to the change in educational federalism is developing among state and local officials and educators.

The U.S. has fifty different state systems of education and there are enormous variations in size, expertise, capacity, beliefs, and traditions of state–local relationships. States are at the center of the history and finance of public education in the U.S. and they have always been accorded wide autonomy. NCLB curtails this autonomy. It creates many new requirements that states must meet and assumes that state agencies have the capacity, skill, and desire to intervene very powerfully in local school districts. Though we have a generation of experience with state interventions in failing schools, state powers have generally been used sparingly and with only limited impact. The new law will require drastic state interventions on a huge scale in the near future. State officials are not used to federal mandates that change their basic functions, particularly mandates they believe ignore regional differences and undermine state policy priorities.

Although opinion is certainly divided, when many state and local officials, experts, and journalists are skeptical or opposed to a new policy, that disquiet quickly enters national politics in Congress and elsewhere. Because the U.S. political system is one dominated by officials elected from states and localities, there is normally a strong reassertion of state and local power when federal officials try to intervene too directly. Since state and local constituencies elect all officials except the President and Vice President, the national parties have very little sway over Senators or Representatives when those officials believe that local voters and leaders are angry about a federal policy. During the 1960s, a very strong counterpressure against the expansion of direct federal intervention in the schools rapidly emerged in Congress, even under Lyndon Johnson, an extremely powerful President at that time. It is wholly predictable that the current federal directives will be the center of ongoing controversy.

The two most important changes in the history of federal education policy were the 1965 Elementary and Secondary Education Act and the 2001 No Child Left Behind Act.

Both expanded federal power and promised large new resources. The 1965 law required no particular educational approaches but it and the related 1964 Civil Rights Act forced opening the schools to previously excluded groups of students and forbade discrimination. This was a huge change in traditional relationships and was very strongly opposed by conservatives whose basic goals were state and local autonomy and vouchers or other forms of market-like competition.

In the 2000 election the Republicans won the presidency with a candidate who ran in good measure on the success of education reforms in Texas, reforms which he promised to implement on the national level. Bush's reforms involved central educational functions like assessment and sanctions, something very unusual in federal grant programs, which tend to offer incentives to try new things rather than sanctions.

Another highly unusual factor in the No Child Left Behind legislation was that school officials and experts on educational reform were largely excluded from the process of designing the law. Traditionally educational leaders have been highly influential at both the federal and state level in making education policy. Beginning in the 1980s, conservatives developed more and more biting critiques of the public schools and their leaders and supporters. They claimed that schools were failing because officials and teachers did not care enough and had to be disciplined by an external force which would expose their records, hold them accountable, label their failures, and create interventions. This critique, believed by many, facilitated the exclusion of educators from the federal legislative process.

The law did not reflect what has been learned from research about educational change. It assumed that schools were extremely powerful and families relatively insignificant in determining outcomes on standardized tests. This is in sharp contrast to many studies showing the exact opposite. The law also assumed that effective reforms could be rapidly imposed from outside of schools and that negative sanctions were highly effective. Research suggests that serious reform of schools is long and hard and requires agreement from the staff adopting the reform. It also shows that most reforms have no measurable results and that the school effects are relatively modest compared with the impact of family background.

The likelihood of conflict over the law was greatly increased when the promised increases in the educational budget occurred only during the first year. School systems lost what many believed to be the most important advance under the new law—more adequate funding. Growth in the federal education budget fell far below the agreement and far below the level achieved during the Clinton Administration. At the same time, virtually all states and a great many localities were experiencing serious budget cutbacks stemming from a recession. This meant that the federal government was trying to impose an unprecedented level of control while many school districts and schools did not even have the money to maintain their existing programs and staffs.

This was the situation during the first year of implementing the new law. Advocates of the law might describe the period as the confrontation between tough-minded federal reformers, who appropriately strengthened accountability for all districts and schools, and failing local officials, most of whom had not held themselves strictly accountable. Opponents might describe it as a radical effort to tell state and local educators how they must evaluate their students and their schools, what subjects really count for the success of a school and its staff, when public funds must be transferred to activities outside the school whether or not they are coordinated with the school's goals, and under what conditions local schools and school districts shall lose all control over their future for failing to meet goals that are wildly inconsistent among the states and have never been fully achieved in any district with a significant population of low income students.

Patrick J. McGuinn, "The National Schoolmarm: No Child Left Behind and the New Educational Federalism," *Publius*, Vol. 35, No. 1. (Winter 2005).

The No Child Left Behind (NCLB) law of 2002 represents the most significant overhaul and expansion of the federal role in education since the Elementary and Secondary Education Act of 1965 (ESEA).[43] The centerpiece of the new law is the requirement that states, as a condition of accepting federal funds, establish academic standards to guide their curricula and adopt a testing regime that is aligned with those standards.[44] States will have to test all students in math and reading in grades 3–8 every year (as well as once in high school), beginning with the 2005–6 school year.[45] Since 2002–3, states have been required to test annually the English proficiency of students for whom English is not their first language, and by the 2007–8 school year, states must also test all students in science at certain grade levels. States are free to develop and use their own standards and tests, but every school, school district, and state will have to make student test results publicly available and disaggregated for certain groups of students, including major racial and ethnic groups, major income groups, students with a disability, students with limited English proficiency, and migrant students. States also have to administer the math and reading portions of a national test, the National Assessment of Educational Progress (NAEP), every other year to a sample of their students in grades 4 and 8 to check the effectiveness of state standards and to provide a measure of comparability of student performance across states.

NCLB also requires states to have a "highly qualified teacher" in every classroom where core academic subjects are taught by 2005–6. States must establish a timetable of intermediate steps to reach this goal and all new teachers hired with Title I funds were to be highly qualified by 2002–3.[46] "Highly qualified" is specified as meaning that a teacher must be fully certified or licensed, have a bachelor's degree, and show competence in subject knowledge and teaching skills. NCLB mandates that every state and school district issue report cards that detail student test scores and identify those schools that have failed to meet proficiency targets and are in need of "program improvement." The law also gives parents, for the first time, the right to request information from schools about teacher qualifications. This wealth of school information has never before been made widely available on a consistent basis, and it is certain to provide parents and education reformers alike with a large amount of new data from which to make judgments about the progress of school improvement efforts. NCLB explicitly requires that states use this information to track their efforts to close the achievement gaps in reading and math between different

---

racial, ethnic, and income groups. States are required to establish a timeline (with regular benchmarks) for making "adequate yearly progress" toward eliminating these gaps and moving all students to state proficiency levels within twelve years (by 2014). . . .

The new federal focus on accountability and the extension of federal policy to cover every student and every school in the country marks a major shift in the governance of elementary and secondary education in the United States. Richard Elmore calls NCLB "the single largest expansion of federal power over the nation's education system in history," and Andy Rotherham, a former Clinton education advisor, says that it "represents the high water mark of federal intrusion in education.[47] The breadth and depth of the new federal involvement in schools is a remarkable development, and the impact of the legislation on state and local educational leaders and public schools has been and will continue to be substantial, whether or not it ultimately succeeds in improving school performance.

The development of such a sizable and reform-oriented federal role in education is remarkable when placed in the context of the nation's history of decentralized school governance. It is also extraordinary given the longstanding opposition of conservatives and states' rights advocates to federal influence over schools, the desire of most liberals to keep the federal role narrowly focused on providing funds for disadvantaged students, and the widespread push for deregulation and privatization that dominated the national policy-making climate in the 1980s and 1990s. To understand how No Child Left Behind and the expanded federal role in education came to pass and the political dynamics that continue to shape federal education policy, this article places the evolution of the federal role in schools within the context of broader institutional, ideational, and political changes in American politics between 1965 and 2002. . . .

Bob Sweet, the Senior Republican Staff Member on the House Committee on Education and the Workforce, observed that by 1996:

> All of the polls showed that the public saw Republicans as anti-education even as education was becoming a more important national political issue. Things changed from that point on. The public equated the decline of the quality of public education with a lack of federal funding for education because it was successfully portrayed this way by Democrats.[48]

As a result, in the late 1990s, congressional Republicans dropped their proposals to eliminate the Department of Education and to cut federal education spending, and put forward their own vision for federal educational leadership.[49] In effort to appear more pro-education to voters, Republicans also appropriated more money for education than Clinton even requested and the 1996–2001 period witnessed the most dramatic increases in federal K-12 education spending since the 1960s.[50] The increased spending went to support existing federal education programs but also to fund a wide variety of new initiatives that brought the national government into many areas of school policy where it had never before ventured.

Republican activism on education during the late 1990s represented a major political and policy challenge for Democrats, who were forced to respond to a comprehensive alternative national reform plan for the first time. The Democrats' response to this challenge was shaped by a growing recognition that money was a necessary but not sufficient condition for improving educational opportunity and increasing pressure from minority groups and voters generally for more meaningful reform. These factors, along with Clinton's leadership and his centrist New Democratic philosophy, led the Democratic Party during the 1990s to move away from its traditional focus on inputs and equity and to embrace standards, accountability, and (public) choice. As a result, the positions of both the Democratic and Republican parties moved toward the center on education over the course of the decade as support grew for tying expanded federal investment in education to state accountability for school improvement efforts.[51] In a question and answer session with education reporters in April 2000, for example, Clinton emphasized that "the fundamental lesson of the last seven years, it seems to me, is that education investment without accountability can be a real waste of money. But accountability without investment can be a real waste of effort. Neither will work without the other. If we want our students to learn more we should do both."[52] By the end of the decade, both the liberal and conservative approaches to federal education policy had been discredited and there was growing consensus around a grand bargain of greater federal investment in education in exchange for increased accountability.

If congressional Republicans and Democrats had softened their opposition to a new reform-oriented federal role in education by the late 1990s, it would take the election of a former Republican governor, George W. Bush, as president to cement the foundation of a new policy regime. Bush became convinced of the efficacy of accountability reforms in education while observing the effect of TAAS (Texas Assessment of Academic Skills) tests as governor.[53] However, a "federalist dilemma" on education emerged because "achieving Republican objectives involves more federal intervention into core areas of traditional local control, such as curriculum, testing, and teacher qualifications. . . ."[54] This federalist dilemma was ultimately subsumed by political considerations because by 2000 education had moved from an important but secondary national issue to the very top of the public agenda.[55]

Where earlier Republican presidential candidates had either ignored the issue of education or run in opposition to a federal role, Bush made education the number one issue of his campaign and a crucial part of his compassionate conservative philosophy.[56] In an effort to close the gap on education and appeal to swing voters—for whom education was a top issue—Bush adopted a pragmatic and centrist education agenda that called for an active but reformed federal role in promoting school improvement. Bush's success on the education issue was widely viewed by both Democratic and Republican strategists as key to his election victory. Republican pollster David Winston noted, for example, that "education was THE deciding issue in 2000. The groups that were most interested in education were the key swing voters—independents, Catholics, married women with children. It was an issue that you clearly saw a dramatic shift on. Going from minus 62 to minus 8 [on education] and you barely win the election, you have to assume that's the gap that closed. . . .[57]

Legislation to make minor changes to NCLB was introduced by Kennedy in September 2004, but he stated at the time, "It's important to acknowledge what this bill does not do. It does not make fundamental changes to the requirements under No Child Left Behind. Those reforms are essential to improving our public schools.[58] Perhaps the clearest sign of the continued strength of the bipartisan consensus behind NCLB was the joint statement by Boehner and Miller in response to Secretary Spellings's 2005 speech announcing new flexibility for states. They wrote that "the integrity of the law must be maintained . . . [although] every effort must be made to ensure smooth and effective implementation . . . we firmly believe that the effort must be based on the law as it is written, not on a smorgasbord of different waivers for different states and districts."[59] Far from being prepared to abandon the NCLB accountability system. there appears to be strong support in Congress for applying it to Head Start and the Higher Education Act.

Presidential politics will also continue to play a major role in the direction of federal education policy. Observers of education politics have remarked that the major story of the 2004 presidential election was that education was not a major story. In fact. however, the major story was that in the first presidential election following the passage of the most transformative national education law in forty years, there were remarkably few differences between the parties and candidates on NCLB and the federal role in schools. Bush's support for NCLB is widely credited—by Democrats and Republicans alike—with improving voters' views of the GOP's position on the education issue. Public opinion surveys from 2004 revealed that the education gap between the parties continues to close: although a plurality (42 percent) of respondents in 2004 believed that the Democratic party was more interested than Republicans (35 percent) in improving education, the GOP has narrowed that gap by 5 percent in each of the past two elections. When respondents were asked which of the presidential candidates they would support if they were voting solely on education issues, Kerry and Bush each drew the same level of support (41 percent).[60]

NOTES FOR CHAPTER 8

1. A summary of the history of the federal education function can be found in Senate Committee on Governmental Affairs, *Department of Education Act of 1978: Report of the Committee on Governmental Affairs to Accompany* S. *991 to Establish a Department of Education and for Other Purposes Together with Additional Views*, 95th Congress, 2nd session, 1978, Report No. 95-1078, 13–15.
2. The Teamsters No. 1 union is larger, but its membership is more concentrated.
3. William J. Crotty and Gary C. Jacobson, 1980, *American Parties in Decline*, Little Brown and Company, Boston, p. 250.
4. For a debate between the NEA's executive director and a critic, which touches on the association's recent history, see Eugene H. Methvin and Terry Herndon, 1979, "Annotating a *Reader's Digest* Article–'The NEA: A Washington Lobby Run Rampant,'" *Phi Delta Kappan*, Vol. 60, pp. 420–423.
5. Carter developed a particular vocabulary early in the campaign and used it repeatedly: Jimmy Carter, 1976, "If I am Elected," *Change*, Vol. 8, p. 11; 1978, *The Presidential Campaign 1976 Volume 1: Jimmy Carter*, Government Printing Office, Washington, DC, pp. 251-252, 609, 841.
6. See Michael J. Malbin, March 19, 1977, "Labor, Business and Money–A Post-election analysis," *National Journal*, pp. 412–417; Methvin and Herndon, "Annotating a *Reader's Digest* Article," 421; James W. Singer, July 28, 1979, "Carter in 1980–Not Ideal, but Maybe Labor's Best Hope," *National Journal*, pp. 252–255.
7. Joseph A. Califano, Jr., 1981, *Governing America: An Insider's Report from the White House and the Cabinet*, Simon and Schuster, New York, pp. 276–277.
8. For two versions of events in the administration, see Califano, *Governing America*, 282; Havemann, "Carter's Reorganization Plans," 791.
9. See the exchange between Senator Percy and OMB witnesses in Senate Committee on Governmental Affairs, *Department of Education Act of 1977: Hearings before the Committee on Governmental Affairs*, pt. 2, 95th Congress, 1st session, 20–21 March, 14, 18, 27 April, and 8, 16–17 May 1978, 671–674. Hereafter cited as *Senate Hearings* 1978, pt. 2.
10. Senate Committee on Governmental Affairs, *Department of Education Act of 1979: Report of the Committee on Governmental Affairs to Accompany S. 210 to Establish a Department of Education Together with Additional and Minority Views*, 96th Congress, 1st session, 1979, Report No. 96-49, 15.
11. Harrison H. Donnelly, April 14, 1979, "Education Department Survives Prayer Fight," *Congressional Quarterly Weekly Report*, pp. 694–695.
12. See William A. Gamson, 1968, "Coalition Formation," in David L. Sills (Ed.), *International Encyclopedia of the Social Sciences*, 17 vols. Macmillan Co., New York, pp. 2530–2531.
13. For a similar argument, see Willis D. Hawley and Beryl A. Radin, September 3, 1981, "Reorganization Goals, Political Processes, and Organizational Outcomes: Understanding the Organization of the U.S. Department of Education," Paper presented at the Annual Meeting of the American Political Science Association, New York. See also Murray Edelman, 1964, *The Symbolic Uses of Politics*, University of Illinois Press, Urbana, IL, p. 63.
14. See Rufus E. Miles Jr., 1974, *The Department of H.E.W.*, Praeger Publishers, New York; Normal C. Thomas, 1975, *Education in National Politics*, David McKay Co., Inc., New York; Steven Bailey and Edith K. Mosher, 1968, *ESEA: The Office of Education Administers A Law*, Syracuse University Press, Syracuse, New York; and Beryl A. Radin, 1977, *Implementation, Change and the Federal Bureaucracy*, Teachers College Press, Columbia University, New York.
15. Herbert Emmerich, 1971, *Federal Organization and Administrative Management*, University of Alabama Press, Tuscaloosa, AL, p. 17.
16. Rufus E. Miles, Jr., 1976, *A Cabinet Department of Education: Analysis and Proposal*, American Council on Education, Washington, DC, pp. 39–40.

17. Bailey and Mosher, p. 227.
18. Ibid., pp. 227–28.
19. Thomas, p. 232.
20. Joel Havenman, January 1, 1977, "Reorganization–how clean can Carter's Broom Sweep?" *National Journal*, p. 4.
21. Ibid., p. 6.
22. Rufus E. Miles, March/April 1977, "Considerations for a President Bent on Reorganization," *Public Administration Review*, pp. 156–162.
23. Harrison Wellford, February 24, 1977, Testimony to House Appropriations Subcommittee on Department of Treasury, Postal Service and General Government, "Supplemental Request for OMB."
24. President's Reorganization Project, March 1977, "Plan for Conducting Federal Government Reorganization and Management Improvement Program, Discussion Outline."
25. Wellford Testimony, pp. 2–3.
26. Ibid., pp. 3–5.
27. Jimmy Carter, 1982, *Keeping the Faith–Memoirs of a President*, Bantam Books, New York, p. 128.
28. Peri Arnold, 1998, *Making the Managerial Presidency: Comprehensive Reorganization Planning, 1905–1996*, 2nd ed., University of Kansas Press, Lawrence, KS.
29. James G. March and Johan P. Olsen, 1984, "The new institutionalism: organizational factors in political life, *American Political Science Review*, Vol. 78, No. 3, pp. 734–749.
30. James G. March and Johan P. Olsen, 1983, "Organizing political life: what administrative organization tells us about government," *American Political Science Review*, Vol. 77, No. 2, pp. 281–296.
31. John R. Dempsey, 1979, "Carter reorganization: a midterm appraisal," *Public Administration Review*, Vol. 39, No. 1, pp. 74–86.
32. Memorandum from Richard A. Pettigrew to Hamilton Jordan, March 3, 1977, Jimmy Carter Presidential Library, Hamilton Jordan Papers, Box 52, Reorganization (IF 01A 646): pp. 1–3.
33. Ibid., 2.
34. Ibid., 2.
35. Ibid., 10–11.
36. Hugh Davis Graham, 1984, *The Uncertain Triumph: Federal Education Policy in the Kennedy and Johnson Years*, University of North Carolina Press, Chapel Hill, NC.
37. Halperin told me that "Keppel was a strong believer in [Title V of the ESEA]. He pushed the idea that the states needed to be built up." In my interview with Ambach, he reflected on his work in the Kennedy administration from 1961 to 1964 and recalled that Keppel used to say that the order of the ESEA titles was essentially backwards–Title V should have come earlier–because creating state capacity was such an important feature of the law.
38. Beryl Radin and Willis D. Hawley, 1988, *The Politics of Federal Reorganization: Creating the Department of Education*, Pergamon Press, New York.
39. My interview with Arthur Wise also confirmed that bureaucratic reorganization was the driving factor. "So you are right in your general characterization that it was mainly nothing but a rearrangement of the boxes," he told me.
40. David Stephens, Winter 1983–1984, "President Carter, the Congress, and NEA: Creating the Department of Education," *Political Science Quarterly*, Vol. 98, No. 4. pp. 641–663.
41. Carter, *Keeping the Faith.*
42. See also Radin (1988, 218) and Richard F. Elmore and Milbrey Wallin McLaughlin, 1983, "The Federal Role in Education: Learning from Experience," *Education and Urban Society*, Vol. 15, No. 3, pp. 309–330.

43. For the full text of NCLB, see Department of Education, "*No Child Left Behind Act*," www.ed.gov/nclb. For a detailed analysis of the provisions of the Act, see Learning First Alliance, "*Major Changes to ESEA in the No Child Left Behind Act*," www.learninefirst.org.
44. For detailed analyses of the NCLB from the viewpoint of state implementers, see Education Commission of the States, "*State Requirements under NCLB*," January 2003, www.ecs.org, and National Governors Association, "*NGA Summary of the Timeline Requirements of NCLB*," www.nga.org.
45. Thirty-five states did not have such testing at the time of passage. Crucially, however, after much debate, the final bill did not require states to adopt nationally designed tests, allowing them instead to design their own as well as to set their own levels for student proficiency.
46. Title I was the centerpiece of the 1965 Elementary and Secondary Education Act and remains its single largest program. It provides federal funds to communities (many of which are located in urban areas) with a high concentration of low-income families.
47. Richard Elmore, Spring 2002, "Unwarranted Intrusion," *Education Next*, pp. 31–35; Andy Rotherham, August 22, 2002, interview with the author.
48. Interview with the author, April 30, 2003.
49. The Republican "Straight A's" plan railed for giving states greater discretion in the use of federal education funds in exchange for states' annual public reporting of student achievement data and their agreement to meet certain student performance targets.
50. The large increases in the late 1990s contributed to a 69 percent increase in Federal on-budget funds for elementary and secondary education in constant dollars between Fiscal Year 1990 and FY 2001. National Center for Education Statistics, Federal Support for Education: 1980–2001, U.S. Department of Education, Office of Educational Research and Improvement, NCES 2002-129, Washington, DC, p. 3.
51. This was apparent in the overlap of parts of the different ESEA reauthorization proposals—Clinton's "Educational Excellence for All Children" plan, the Republican "Straight A's" plan, and the New Democrats' "Three R's" proposal—debated in Congress in 1999 and 2000.
52. Remarks and a Question and Answer Session with the Education Writers association in Atlanta, Georgia, vol. 1, Public Papers of the President: William J. Clinton—2000, Government Printing Office, Washington, DC, 2000.
53. Kenneth Godwin and Wenda Sheard, Summer 2001, "Education Reform and the Politics of 2000," *Publius: The Journal of Federalism*, p. 31.
54. John Kincaid, Summer 2001, "The State of U.S. Federalism, 2000–2001: Continuity in Crisis," *Publius: The Journal of Federalism*, Vol. 31, p. 32.
55. See Melissa Marschall and Robert McKee, January–March 2002, "From Campaign Promises to Presidential Policy: Education Reform in the 2000 Election," *Educational Policy*, Vol. 14, No. 1, p. 101.
56. As Bush advisor Sandy Kress noted, "There is no question that education was central to Bush's 2000 campaign strategy, to his compassionate conservative philosophy—it was a big issue to him and to the campaign . . . clearly the president was mindful, as were Karl Rove and others, that the Bush approach to education was a more popular and more generally supportable position than some of the earlier Republican positions in the past." Interview with the author, May 23, 2003.
57. Interview with the author, May 9, 2003.
58. As quoted in Erik Robelen, September 22, 2003, "Kennedy Bill Would Give States, Districts Leeway," *Education Week*.
59. House Committee on Education and the Workforce press release, April 7, 2005.
60. Lowell Rose and Alee Gallup, 2004, *The 36th Annual Phi Delta Kapp/Gallup Poll of the Public's Attitudes Toward the Public Schools*, Available from http://ww~.pdkintl.org/kappan/k0309~ol.pdf.

CHAPTER 9

Proposals to Create a Department of Food Safety

INTRODUCTION

The final example that is included in this book focuses on proposals to create a Department of Food Safety. At this writing, despite attention to this topic by a range of both executive branch and congressional players, there has not been agreement on current legislative proposals. This example provides a picture of the complexity of reaching agreement on the creation of a new cabinet department. It illustrates the diverse agendas of agencies with a role in the subject area, as well as their response to political and economic changes in the external environment. It also indicates the limits of the structural approach in situations in which functional strategies (such as coordination and networks) might become more effective.

The possibility of pulling together the various agencies involved in food safety programs and policies has hovered around the policy agenda for nearly 20 years, and the creation of a separate department has been an active proposal for a decade. The main federal agencies involved in the food safety process involve the Food and Drug Administration and the Centers for Disease Control and Prevention in the U.S. Department of Health and Human Services; the Food Safety and Inspection Service, the Cooperative State Research, Education, and Extension Service, and the National Agricultural Library in the U.S. Department of Agriculture; the U.S. Environmental Protection Agency; and the National Oceanic and Atmospheric Administration in the U.S. Department of Commerce.

Each of these agencies (as well as others) has its own approach to the food safety problem, and most of them have distinct interest groups, congressional committees and subcommittees, and issue networks that support their unique positions. A number of the advocates for creation of a department containing all of these players assume that reorganization and structural shifts will bring policy changes that minimize these differences. The excerpts that are included from the Government Accountability Office (GAO) reflect this approach. Others, however, argue that the creation of a single department does not assure policy coordination on this issue. Rather, they emphasize the very different policy frames that emerge from the separate agencies: science issues in some, food production in others, and regulation in still others.

In addition to the diverse policy frames found in the separate agencies, as the issue has moved over time, it has emerged in different forms. Prominent in this process of change was a series of crises that brought the food safety issue to public prominence and to the front burner of interest. The first crisis emerged after 9/11 when fear of terrorism involving food was discussed; the second crisis came about when problems with spinach safety created major concerns. The third was related to fears about safety with imports from China. Despite this and the introduction of proposed legislation in Congress, at this writing, there has not been an agreement on this issue.

The first group of excerpts in this section of the book date from the late 1990s. The list of agencies involved in food safety is provided by a document issued by the U.S. Food and Drug Administration entitled "Food Safety: A Team Approach." This listing includes the agencies involved and their mission and roles.

Sections from the National Academy of Sciences' book, *Ensuring Safe Food from Production to Consumption*, provide the science approach to these issues. It argues that science is driving the concerns of the system and develops alternative approaches to the issue. Testimony given to Congress by an official of GAO entitled *Food Safety: U.S. Needs a Single Agency to Administer a Unified, Risk-Based Inspection System*, sets out an organization structure approach to this issue.

A report issued by the President's Council on Food Safety represented the Clinton administration's approach to the issue. The Food Safety Strategic Plan that was presented in 2001 acknowledges the problems in the food safety area but recognizes the limitations of a structural approach to the problems. The Plan finds that that no single approach can deal with all aspects of the problem but presents a range of structural options to consider.

In contrast, in "It Is Time to Designate a Single Food Safety Agency," Timothy M. Hammonds, the President of the Food Marketing Institute, presents the organization's support for changes in the regulatory system and calls for the creation of a single agency.

Less than a month after 9/11, a GAO official related food safety to bioterrorism and testified on *Food Safety and Security: Fundamental Changes Needed to Ensure Safe Food.* This testimony calls on Congress to rationalize the structure and system. This testimony, as well as that given in *Federal Food Safety and Security System: Fundamental Restructuring is Needed to Address Fragmentation and Overlap*, highlights the results of the fragmented jurisdiction between the FDA and the USDA.

By 2005, testimony by GAO responded to the global nature of the food safety problem. In *Overseeing the U.S. Food Supply: Steps Should Be Taken to Reduce Overlapping Inspections and Related Activities*, GAO staff focused on the inspection process within a globalized system. In 2007, the GAO added food safety to its list of "high-risk" areas. In its study, *Federal Oversight of Food Safety: High-Risk Designation Can Bring Needed Attention to Fragmented System*, the GAO told the Congress that this policy area is one that required serious attention.

In February 2007, members of both the House and the Senate responded to the food safety issue, and identical bills were introduced in both houses to establish the Food Safety Administration to protect public health by preventing food-borne illness, ensuring the safety of food, improving research on contaminants leading to food-borne illness, and improving security of food from intentional contamination. The proposed legislation sought to consolidate separate services and agencies into one structure.

Around the same time, a legal note appeared in the Harvard Law Review, suggesting that dangers to the food supply were not resolvable through consolidation. "Note: Reforming the Food Safety System: What if Consolidation Isn't Enough?" argues that a structural response to the issue is not adequate.

Michael R. Taylor, a former Deputy Commissioner at the FDA, as well as a former official in the USDA, provided a different take on the issue. In "Lead or React? A Game Plan for Modernizing the Food Safety System in the United States," Taylor writes that the food safety system is not in crisis but does require change. He argues that modernization and reform require leadership from the White House.

The Center for Science in the Public Interest, a nonprofit consumer organization that seeks to represent consumer interests in the policy process, issued a white paper on food safety. "Building a Modern Food Safety System: For FDA Regulated Foods," written by Caroline Smith DeWaal and David W. Plunkett, describes the position of this organization.

U.S. Food and Drug Administration, *Food Safety: A Team Approach*, Center for Food Safety and Nutrition, Department of Health and Human Services.

SEPTEMBER 24, 1998

The United States maintains one of the world's safest food supplies, thanks in large part to an interlocking monitoring system that watches over food production and distribution at every level—locally, statewide and nationally.

Continual monitoring is provided by food inspectors, microbiologists, epidemiologists, and other food scientists working for city and county health departments, state public health agencies, and various federal departments and agencies. Their precise duties are dictated by local, state and national laws, guidelines and other directives. Some monitor only one kind of food, such as milk or seafood. Others work strictly within a specified geographic area. Others are responsible for only one type of food establishment, such as restaurants or meat-packing plants. Together they make up the U.S. food safety team.

The Clinton administration's Food Safety Initiative, begun in 1997, strengthens the efforts of all the members of the nation's food safety team in the fight against food-borne illness, which afflicts between 6.5 million and 33 million Americans every year. One of the initiative's major programs got under way in May 1998 when the Department of Health and Human Services (which includes FDA), the U.S. Department of Agriculture, and the Environmental Protection Agency signed a memorandum of understanding to create a Food Outbreak Response Coordinating Group, or FORC-G. The new group will:

- Increase coordination and communication among federal, state and local food safety agencies
- Guide efficient use of resources and expertise during an outbreak
- Prepare for new and emerging threats to the U.S. food supply

Besides federal officials, members of FORC-G include the Association of Food and Drug Officials, National Association of City and County Health Officials, Association of State and Territorial Public Health Laboratory Directors, Council of State and Territorial Epidemiologists, and National Association of State Departments of Agriculture.

The following table offers a closer look at the nation's food safety lineup. The agencies listed in the table also work with other government agencies, such as the Consumer Product Safety Commission to enforce the Poison Prevention Packaging Act, the FBI to enforce the Federal Anti-Tampering Act, the Department of Transportation to enforce the Sanitary Food Transportation Act, and the U.S. Postal Service to enforce laws against mail fraud.

U.S. DEPARTMENT OF HEALTH AND HUMAN SERVICES

FOOD AND DRUG ADMINISTRATION

Oversees

- All domestic and imported food sold in interstate commerce, including shell eggs, but not meat and poultry
- Bottled water
- Wine beverages with less than 7 percent alcohol

Food Safety Role

Enforces food safety laws governing domestic and imported food, except meat and poultry, by

- Inspecting food production establishments and food warehouses and collecting and analyzing samples for physical, chemical and microbial contamination
- Reviewing safety of food and color additives before marketing
- Reviewing animal drugs for safety to animals that receive them and humans who eat food produced from the animals
- Monitoring safety of animal feeds used in food-producing animals
- Developing model codes and ordinances, guidelines and interpretations and working with states to implement them in regulating milk and shellfish and retail food establishments, such as restaurants and grocery stores. An example is the model Food Code, a reference for retail outlets and nursing homes and other institutions on how to prepare food to prevent food-borne illness.
- Establishing good food manufacturing practices and other production standards, such as plant sanitation, packaging requirements, and Hazard Analysis and Critical Control Point programs
- Working with foreign governments to ensure safety of certain imported food products
- Requesting manufacturers to recall unsafe food products and monitoring those recalls
- Taking appropriate enforcement actions
- Conducting research on food safety
- Educating industry and consumers on safe food handling practices

CENTERS FOR DISEASE CONTROL AND PREVENTION

Oversees

- All foods

Food Safety Role

- Investigates with local, state and other federal officials sources of food-borne disease outbreaks
- Maintains a nationwide system of food-borne disease surveillance: Designs and puts in place rapid, electronic systems for reporting food-borne infections. Works with other federal and state agencies to monitor rates of and trends in food-borne disease outbreaks. Develops state-of-the-art techniques for rapid identification of food-borne pathogens at the state and local levels.
- Develops and advocates public health policies to prevent food-borne diseases
- Conducts research to help prevent food-borne illness
- Trains local and state food safety personnel

U.S. DEPARTMENT OF AGRICULTURE

FOOD SAFETY AND INSPECTION SERVICE

Oversees

- Domestic and imported meat and poultry and related products, such as meat- or poultry-containing stews, pizzas and frozen foods
- Processed egg products (generally liquid, frozen and dried pasteurized egg products)

Food Safety Role

Enforces food safety laws governing domestic and imported meat and poultry products by

- Inspecting food animals for diseases before and after slaughter
- Inspecting meat and poultry slaughter and processing plants
- With USDA's Agricultural Marketing Service, monitoring and inspecting processed egg products
- Collecting and analyzing samples of food products for microbial and chemical contaminants and infectious and toxic agents
- Establishing production standards for use of food additives and other ingredients in preparing and packaging meat and poultry products, plant sanitation, thermal processing, and other processes
- Making sure all foreign meat and poultry processing plants exporting to the United States meet U.S. standards
- Seeking voluntary recalls by meat and poultry processors of unsafe products
- Sponsoring research on meat and poultry safety
- Educating industry and consumers on safe food-handling practices

COOPERATIVE STATE RESEARCH, EDUCATION, AND EXTENSION SERVICE

Oversees

- All domestic foods, some imported

Food Safety Role

- With U.S. colleges and universities, develops research and education programs on food safety for farmers and consumers

NATIONAL AGRICULTURAL LIBRARY

USDA/FDA FOOD-BORNE ILLNESS EDUCATION INFORMATION CENTER

Oversees

- All foods

Food Safety Role

- Maintains a database of computer software, audiovisuals, posters, games, teachers' guides and other educational materials on preventing food-borne illness
- Helps educators, food service trainers and consumers locate educational materials on preventing food-borne illness

U.S. ENVIRONMENTAL PROTECTION AGENCY

Oversees

- Drinking water

Food Safety Role

Foods made from plants, seafood, meat and poultry

- Establishes safe drinking water standards
- Regulates toxic substances and wastes to prevent their entry into the environment and food chain
- Assists states in monitoring quality of drinking water and finding ways to prevent contamination of drinking water

- Determines safety of new pesticides, sets tolerance levels for pesticide residues in foods, and publishes directions on safe use of pesticides

U.S. DEPARTMENT OF COMMERCE

NATIONAL OCEANIC AND ATMOSPHERIC ADMINISTRATION

Oversees

- Fish and seafood products

Food Safety Role

- Through its fee-for-service Seafood Inspection Program, inspects and certifies fishing vessels, seafood processing plants, and retail facilities for federal sanitation standards

U.S. DEPARTMENT OF THE TREASURY

BUREAU OF ALCOHOL, TOBACCO AND FIREARMS

Oversees

- Alcoholic beverages except wine beverages containing less than 7 percent alcohol

Food Safety Role

- Enforces food safety laws governing production and distribution of alcoholic beverages
- Investigates cases of adulterated alcoholic products, sometimes with help from FDA

U.S. CUSTOMS SERVICE

Oversees

- Imported foods

Food Safety Role

- Works with federal regulatory agencies to ensure that all goods entering and exiting the United States do so according to U.S. laws and regulations

U.S. DEPARTMENT OF JUSTICE

Oversees

- All foods

Food Safety Role

- Prosecutes companies and individuals suspected of violating food safety laws
- Through U.S. Marshals Service, seizes unsafe food products not yet in the marketplace, as ordered by courts

FEDERAL TRADE COMMISSION

Oversees

- All foods

Food Safety Role

- Enforces a variety of laws that protect consumers from unfair, deceptive or fraudulent practices, including deceptive and unsubstantiated advertising.

STATE AND LOCAL GOVERNMENTS

Oversees

- All foods within their jurisdictions

Food Safety Role

- Work with FDA and other federal agencies to implement food safety standards for fish, seafood, milk, and other foods produced within state borders
- Inspect restaurants, grocery stores, and other retail food establishments, as well as dairy farms and milk processing plants, grain mills, and food manufacturing plants within local jurisdictions

Embargo (stop the sale of) unsafe food products made or distributed within state border.

National Academy of Sciences, *Ensuring Safe Food from Production to Consumption*, Washington DC: The National Academies Press (1998).

Ensuring a system to provide safe food within the United States is a common goal, and legislative mandates should direct the components of that system. The mission should be focused on using public health resources and management to perform risk analysis and research and at the same time on optimizing coordination and planning of prevention, intervention, control, response, and communication mechanisms. . . .

An effective food safety system is an interdependent system composed of government agencies at all levels, businesses and other private organizations, consumers, and supporting players. The system is dynamic and aligned to the unified mission of improving food safety so as to maintain and improve the public's health and well-being. . . . Although the players have key, independent functions, they must implement many of their actions through strong partnerships. The system is built on the flexibility and adaptability of the players and on the nature and course of their relationships, and these affect their ability to prevent, identify, and resolve food safety issues in the most efficient, effective, and cost-beneficial manner. The system is responsive to the expedient issues of today but also evolves strategically to meet future challenges. It must be effective in both the domestic environment and the new global food environment, with increasing international trade.

Figure 9-1 indicates that an Effective Food Safety System includes partners in the system including government, private industry, and consumers. Supportive players, who are critical to the integration of the attributes of research, education, and information, include universities and colleges, the news media and focused special interest organizations, among others.

The system is science-based with strong emphasis on risk analysis and the use of data. It is attentive to learning through the use of feedback loops and continuous improvement. Although responsiveness to and coordination of food safety crises are critical attributes, the system is designed to stress prevention and detection of emerging problems.

The system has adequate funding, is supported by strong research and education components, uses technology adequate to the task, and is integrated to achieve its mission. Statutory and regulatory authority promotes the system's horizontal and vertical integration. Because integration is such a critical attribute, the system requires strong, centralized leadership. The system champions a culture of capacity building. With the transition toward a new scientific and risk-based foundation, agencies will encourage and fund retraining and further development of their employees, and they will initiate plans for the

---

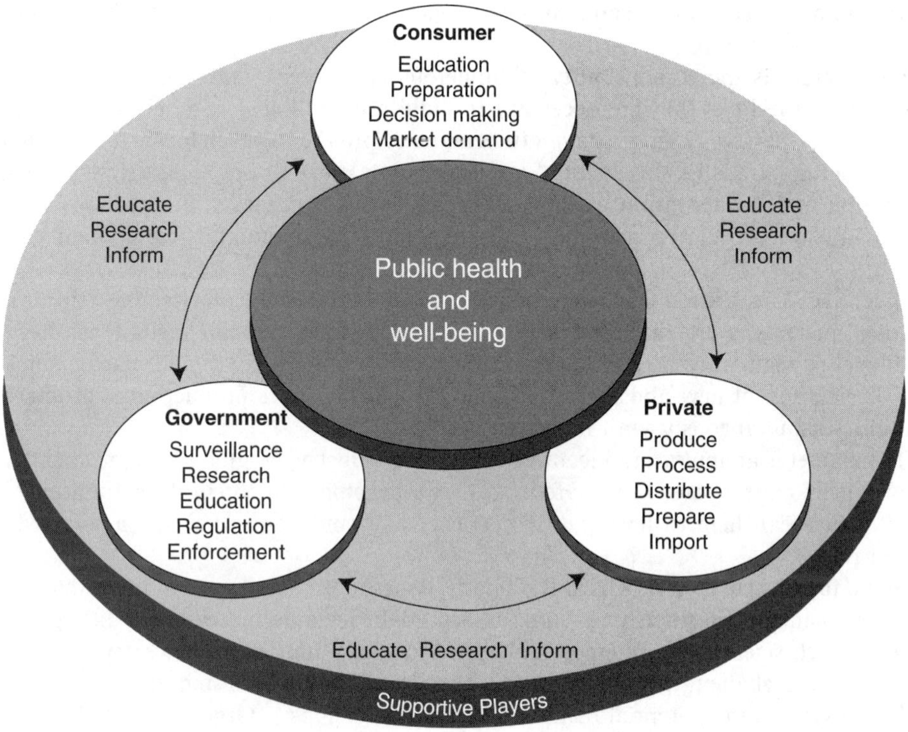

Source: National Academy of Sciences, "Ensuring Safe Food from Production to Consumption," National Academies Press, 1998.
FIGURE 9-1 Attributes of an Effective Food Safety System

recruitment and retention of high-quality staff with the skills and knowledge to enhance the new system and its changing operations and focus. Capacity must also include consumer knowledge and practices, taking into account cultural sensitivities and practices.

An effective system is commensurate with today's driving forces, trends, and societal expectations. Partnerships will expand with the growing recognition that government cannot abandon our food safety problems to private industry and consumers.

The effective system stresses the inclusion of its players in their roles but also acknowledges the need for effective regulation, compliance, and enforcement. Although some of the roles will need to change, the system functions in an environment of trust and respect. The globalization of the food system and other factors that can increase the risk of foodborne incidents mandate urgency in adopting the system.

The effective food safety system is focused on public health, and its many actions are aligned to achieve a safer food supply, improve public health, and instill consumers' confidence in both the system and their role in improving it. Finally, the dynamic interconnectiveness also promotes the attainment by all of the players of both responsibility and accountability for making the food safety system perform optimally.

The following sections describe in more detail the attributes of an effective food safety system.

Food safety is the responsibility of numerous and diverse stakeholders, and partnerships provide the links that are necessary to build a coordinated and cohesive framework for action. Partnerships can improve efficiency and provide a mechanism for information and technology transfer. Interaction and communication through partnerships lead to cooperation and collaboration among public and private interests. Partnerships can also help to integrate regulated activities with important non-regulatory components of the system.

Incentives can greatly influence and facilitate the building of effective partnerships. "Positive" incentives are often financial. "Negative" incentives can include the desire to avoid legal or regulatory action or media attention. Another incentive for partnerships can be the generation of new and useful information that improves production and processing capabilities simultaneously with improved control of risk.

The market is an important incentive for private industry. As global markets and domestic consumers expect safer food, safety itself can become a factor in differentiating products. Retailers can help to leverage this concept as brand names become associated with reduced risks.

Some factors, such as intellectual property issues, pose challenges to the establishment and maintenance of partnerships. These issues might become increasingly difficult in the future, as such sciences as the microbiology of food continue to advance rapidly.

Despite the challenges posed by the diversity of the players and changing priorities within the system, the potential realm of strong partnerships is large and includes all partners: government, the private sector, consumers, and support players, as shown in Figure 9-1. Partnerships should be formed and function in an open process that is independent and protected from political, economic, and social pressures. Partners must have clear delineations of responsibility and the authority to make decisions to meet responsibilities. They must have the resources to work together effectively. Successful partnerships are based on close, detailed, and accurate communication and collaboration.

In the public sector, the federal government is in the best position to influence how the other components of the food safety system work together. Its actions, which often take the form of regulation, originate in federal food law. The federal government must guide the system with national food law that is clear, rational, and based on scientifically determined risk. A few principles form the basis for ideal food law, which can be conceptualized by the philosophical structure of food safety. This structure includes a process that is fair and open to participation by all without political, economic, or social pressures and that provides for adequate authority and budgetary considerations.

Legislation must be flexible and enforceable, and it must comprehensively address all aspects of the entire system from production to consumption. The authority and responsibility of the federal government and its interface with private and other partners must be well-articulated. Definition of a broad federal role is promoted by the similarities of food safety issues across states and demographic groups. Other levels of government have a role in shaping federal activities if they are to be effective in implementing national standards and in dealing separately with local issues.

With a sound food law in place, partnerships between the federal government and others in the system can establish a framework to provide several important functions. For instance, partnerships of federal, state, and local governments with industry, universities, private organizations, and consumers can ensure that the system is science-based and risk-focused, that surveillance and monitoring efforts provide sufficient information to maintain and improve effectiveness, that research and education efforts are properly focused, that regulation and enforcement are effective and consistent, that the system is responsive to new technologies and changing consumer needs, that a continuous process of evaluation can respond to the queries and problems of all stakeholders, and that resources are adequate and appropriately allocated throughout the system. . . .

The recognition that food-borne illnesses and deaths cost this country billions of dollars a year coincides with an apparent lack of public trust in government and gives rise to the suggestion that government is the problem, not a solution. That is a disconcerting depiction and, in one important respect, it is inaccurate. Officials who direct or carry out diverse functions under the multiplicity of statutory mandates are capable and dedicated, as are their state and local counterparts. They perform remarkably well, given their budgetary and statutory constraints, but they operate within an institutional framework that is out of date and poorly designed to accomplish the critical goals that regulation in this field must achieve. The increasing complexity of food production and delivery and the exploding internationalization of the US food supply impose added pressure on the federal regulatory apparatus which was constructed in simpler times.

Given the challenges, the US food safety system has several strengths. Problems are addressed at many points from production to consumption and from many different perspectives (for example, federal or state, public or private, top-down or investigator-initiated, basic or applied, and combined or separated from regulatory pressures). There are significant efforts to improve the current structure through implementation of systems with multiple critical control points to address hazards and increase safety. There is a shared sense of urgency and commitment arising from the current national emphasis on food safety which has resulted in extensive communication and coordination efforts throughout the system (interagency, agency and industry, and state and federal).

There is also substantial private funding in support of food safety research. In spite of these strengths, the current food safety system that the committee studied displays several fundamental weaknesses. . . .

No single federal official can be said to be responsible for the government's food safety efforts. Instead, several officials have responsibility for parts of the system that are organizationally separate and individually funded. Many of the separate programs have other responsibilities as well. They are in different parts of the executive branch and they report to different congressional oversight and appropriation committees. Sometimes they compete for resources and for public attention. None of the heads of these agencies has direct access to the White House, and several report through more than one administrative level. *Food Safety from Farm to Table: A National Food Safety Initiative* . . . has given more prominence to the federal government's role generally, but it has not fundamentally or permanently altered the underlying balkanized structure.

Fulfillment of the federal role in protecting the food supply requires central management of now-dispersed efforts. Central management is essential if resources are to be allocated in accord with science-based assessments of risk and potential benefit. It is necessary to assume cooperation among dispersed, sometimes competing, programs. It is important for coordination among the states and between the states and localities and the federal government. It is also die only way to ensure that a focused federal entity responsible for food safety policy.

The major shortfalls regarding leadership in the current system include

- There is no single federal entity that is both responsible for the government's efforts and that has the authority to implement policy and designate resources toward food safety activities.
- There is a lack of a unified mission among the various agencies with regard to food safety. . . .

A lack of coordination on several levels seems to be one effect of the lack of strong focused leadership and the lack of a unified mission. The lack of coordination has resulted in a lack of national standards and a lack of focus on food safety. There appear to be no mechanisms to sustain expanding interagency coordination after the current national concern abates and the attention of Congress, the president, and agency leadership is directed to other issues.

Several examples of coordination deficiencies include

Lack of federal agency coordination. Surveillance information is ultimately communicated among the agencies and organizations involved, but there is (except for the recent creation of FoodNet) no integration of the various programs included in the current structure. Neither routine surveillance programs, special projects, nor emerging issues are addressed in a coordinated interagency manner. There is no comprehensive national strategy or system for surveillance. Human and animal studies and analyses of foods are for the most part, conducted independently without a common goal or design, even though they may impact the same food safety issues. Another example is the lack of coordination between FDA and USDA regarding the regulation and clearance of packaging materials. For instance, catalyst systems used to make polymers do not appear in the FDA food additive regulations because they are understood to be proprietary information. However, USDA now requires companies to file a food additive petition with FDA for catalyst systems.

Lack of federal and state coordination. Federal, state, and local authorities must work with varied amounts of resources, skills, and legal authority. Lack of coordination and consistency between federal and state governments is problematic. Some states have initiatives requiring more stringent standards than those required by the federal government. Under California's Proposition 65, warnings may be required for products, including foods, that are not required under federal law. Another example of a lack of federal and state coordination is that food retailers with stores in multiple states must deal with many regulatory entities at the federal, state, and local levels. The committee heard testimony from the Food Marketing Institute (FMI) indicating that one food retailer with stores in several states must report to 88 different regulatory authorities.[1] These conflicting requirements create an additional burden on industry and may confuse consumers.

Lack of public and private coordination. As described by the United Food and Commercial Workers Union, implementation of HACCP programs in meat packing plants is often required and attempted without allowing time to perform proper cleaning or to conduct effective employee training.[2]

Lack of international coordination. Currently, sampling of imported foods takes place at the port-of-entry.[3] This method of inspection does not allow for the timely identification of potential food-borne hazards. There is a need to identify and correct problems at the point where food is produced and processed, and this requires international government coordination and cooperation. . . .

SUMMARY FINDINGS: WHERE THE US FOOD SAFETY SYSTEM FALLS SHORT

- Inconsistent, uneven and at times archaic food statutes that inhibit use of science-based decision-making in activities related to food safety, including imported foods;
- A lack of adequate integration among the 12 primary federal agencies that are involved in implementing the 35 primary statutes that regulate food safety;
- Inadequate integration of federal programs and activities with state and local activities;
- Absence of focused leadership: no single federal entity is both responsible for the government's efforts and given the authority to implement policy and designate resources toward food safety activities;
- Lack of similar missions with regard to food safety of the various agencies reviewed;
- Inadequate emphasis on surveillance necessary to provide timely information on current and potential food-borne hazards;
- Resources currently identified for research and surveillance are inadequate to support a science-based system;
- Limited consumer knowledge, which does not appear to have much impact on food-handling behavior; and
- Lack of nationwide adherence to appropriate minimum standards. . . .

The committee believes that the creation of a centralized and unified federal framework is critical to improve the food safety system. Many members of the committee are of the view that the most viable means of achieving the goal would be a single, unified agency headed by a single administrator—an agency that would incorporate the several relevant functions now dispersed, and in many instances separately organized, among three departments and a department-level agency. However, in the time frame given the committee, it was not possible to determine whether this is the only sound approach or whether the costs of achieving it would be too high. Nor was it the committee's charge to resolve these issues.

The committee did discuss some possible structures; while it ruled out some, it certainly did not examine all possible configurations and thus the examples provided below are only illustrative of possible overall structures that could be considered. The committee does not believe that the type of centralized focus envisioned can be achieved through the appointment of an individual with formal coordinating responsibility but without legal authority or budgetary control for food safety, a model similar to a White House-based "czar". Nor, in the committee's view, can this goal be achieved through a coordinating committee similar to that currently provided via the National Food Safety Initiative. Experience indicates that any ad hoc administrative adjustments and commitments to coordinate will not suffice to bring about the cultural changes and collaborative efforts needed to create an integrated system.

In evaluating possible structures, the committee realized that past experience with other structures or reorganizations, including the creation of new agencies, such as the Environmental Protection Agency, should inform any final judgment. Further, it is quite possible that other models may now exist in government that can serve as templates for an improved structure. It thus proposes that a sequential, detailed examination of specific organizational changes be a major component of future study, in keeping with the Congressional appropriations language.

BOX 9-1. Some Examples of Possible Organizational Structures to Create a Single Federal Voice for Food Safety

- A Food Safety Council with representatives from the agencies with a central chair appointed by the President, reporting to Congress and having control of resources,
- Designing one current agency as the lead agency and having the head of that agency be the responsible individual,
- A single agency reporting to one current cabinet-level secretary, and
- An independent single agency at cabinet level.

Note: These examples are provided for illustrative purposes and many other configurations are possible. It is strongly recommended that future activities be directed toward identifying a feasible structure that meets the criteria outlined.

INTEGRATION OF FOOD SAFETY EFFORTS

This report specifically addresses the federal role in the food safety system, but the roles of state and local government entities are equally critical. For integrated operation of the food safety system, officials at all levels of government must work together in support of common goals. The federal government must be able to ensure nationwide adherence to minimal standards. The work of the states and localities in support of the federal mission deserves better formal recognition and appropriate financial support.

U.S. Government Accountability Office, *Food Safety: U.S. Needs a Single Agency to Administer a Unified, Risk-Based Inspection System*, GAO/T-RCED-99-256, Washington, DC (1999).

The federal regulatory system for food safety evolved haphazardly. As the understanding of food-borne hazards grew, food safety concerns changed. Addressing one new worry after another, legislators amended old laws and enacted new ones. Programs emerged piecemeal, typically in response to particular health threats or economic crises. The laws not only assigned specific food commodities to particular agencies but also provided the agencies with different authorities and responsibilities, reflecting significantly different regulatory approaches. The resulting inflexible and inconsistent oversight and enforcement authorities, inefficient resource use, and ineffective coordination efforts have hampered and continue to impede efforts to address the public health concerns associated with existing and newly identified food safety risks. The following examples represent some of the problems we have found in reviewing the nation's food safety system:

- Federal agencies are not using their inspection resources efficiently. Because the frequency of inspection is based on the agencies' regulatory approach, some foods and establishments may be receiving too much attention while others may not be receiving enough. Firms that process food products posing similar health risks to the public are inspected at widely different frequencies, depending on which agency—and thus which regulatory approach—governs them. Although the level of health risk is similar for all animal products, meat and poultry plants regulated by FSIS are inspected at least daily, while firms that are under FDA's jurisdiction such as, processors of rabbit, venison, and quail, are generally inspected, on average once every ten years. Furthermore, food establishments are sometimes inspected by more than one federal agency because they participate in programs or process foods that are under the jurisdiction of different agencies.
- Responsibilities for the oversight of chemical residues in foods are fragmented among FDA, USDA, and EPA. As a result, chemicals posing similar risks may be treated differently by the agencies because they operate under different laws and regulations. Furthermore, the states use different methodologies for determining the amount of fish that can be safely consumed. For example, under the Clean Water Act, EPA is required only to consider risks to human health and aquatic life when conducting water quality assessments. However, under the Federal Food, Drug, and Cosmetic Act, FDA is allowed to consider both health risks and benefits in establishing tolerances

for chemical contaminants in food. Therefore, as we reported in 1994,[4] FDA standards for some chemicals are often less stringent than those developed by EPA. This inconsistency is often reflected in the methodology the states use to determine the levels of fish consumption considered safe. According to EPA officials as of 1998, about 30 states use a methodology similar to EPA's and about 20 states use a different methodology such as one similar to FDA's.[5] Thus a fish considered unsafe to eat in one state may become safe to eat if it swims to another state.

- Enforcement authorities granted to the agencies also differ. USDA agencies have the authority to 1) require food processors to register so that they can be inspected, 2) presume that food firms are involved in interstate commerce and are thus subject to regulation, 3) prohibit the use of processing equipment that may potentially contaminate food products, and 4) temporarily detain any suspect foods. Conversely, FDA, without such authority, is often hindered in overseeing food processors.
- Oversight of imported food is inconsistent and unreliable.[3] To ensure the safety of meat and poultry imports, FSIS has a statutory mandate to require that each of the countries exporting meat and poultry to the United States demonstrate that it has a food safety system that is equivalent to the United States' system. Under the equivalency requirement, FSIS has shifted most of the responsibility for ensuring product safety to the exporting country. The exporting country performs the primary inspection, allowing FSIS to leverage its resources by focusing its reviews on verifying the efficacy of the exporting countries' systems. In contrast, FDA lacks the legal authority to require that countries exporting foods to the United States have food safety systems equivalent to ours. Without such authority FDA must rely primarily on its port-of-entry inspections, which covered less than 2 percent of shipments in 1997, to detect and bar unsafe foods. Such an approach has been widely discredited as resource-intensive and ineffective.
- Fragmented federal responsibilities also cause problems for the food industry because communication about health risks associated with contaminated food products is impaired. As we reported in April 1998,[6] nearly every day during May, June, and early July 1997, officials from FDA, FSIS, and the Environmental Protection Agency participated in conference calls to discuss the latest developments in the investigation of animal feeds contaminated with dioxin (a suspected carcinogen) to determine 2 EPA officials stated that further review of the 20 states using a methodology different than EPA's may reveal that some of them are actually using a methodology similar to EPA's. what actions, if any, the agencies needed to take to protect consumers. While FDA and FSIS worked together to make decisions on the preferred course of action, each agency was responsible for communicating its decisions to the producers or processors under its jurisdiction. However, complete information was not communicated to all affected parties. For example, when officials from FDA, the agency responsible for regulating animal feed, met with meat and poultry producers, their primary concern was with the contaminated feed, not with the animals that had consumed it. Thus, they did not necessarily tell these producers of the actions they should take for their affected animals. FSIS, the agency responsible for regulating meat and poultry processors, sent word of the testing requirements to meat and poultry processors and to trade associations, but it did not notify

meat and poultry producers. FSIS has jurisdiction over processing plants, but not producers.

- The agencies have made attempts to coordinate their activities to overcome the fragmentation and avoid duplication or gaps in coverage, but history has shown that as time passes, such efforts frequently prove to be ineffective. We have reported in the past that unsafe conditions in food processing plants have gone unaddressed because the notifications required by coordination agreements do not always take place or the problems referred to the responsible agency are not promptly investigated.[7] As we testified before this Subcommittee last month, egg safety remains questionable, despite FSIS' and FDA's efforts to coordinate their activities on egg and egg product safety—a shared responsibility between the two agencies.[8] In 1991, an amendment to the Egg Products Inspection Act mandated that federal regulations be issued requiring the refrigeration of shell eggs. Eight years later, FSIS regulations, effective August 27, 1999, set refrigeration requirements for eggs from the packing plant through transportation to the retail level. However, FDA, which has responsibility for egg safety at the retail level has not enacted similar regulations; therefore, refrigerating eggs at the retail level is not yet required.[9]

President's Council on Food Safety, *Food Safety Strategic Plan*, Washington, DC: Government Printing Office (January 19, 2001).

Over the course of the past seven years the Clinton Administration has done much to help ensure that the United States has one of the safest food supplies in the world. . . . In just the last three years, there has been a 20% decrease in illnesses due to the major bacterial food pathogens across the United States. Despite this progress, however, food-borne illnesses continue to take a staggering toll on public health. Every year, millions of Americans become sick and many die from food-borne pathogens. Our vulnerable populations are growing, with increased longevity and increasing numbers of immune-compromised individuals. Now nearly a quarter of the population is at higher risk for food-borne illness. The public has become increasingly aware and concerned about the health risks posed by both these pathogens and by potentially hazardous chemicals in food.

Changes in the ways food is produced, distributed, and consumed present new challenges for ensuring the safety of our food.

- Americans are eating a greater variety of foods, particularly poultry, seafood and fresh fruits and vegetables. This is beneficial to our health, but presents new food safety challenges, as shifting dietary preferences may lead to different patterns of exposure to chemicals and pathogens.
- More consumers desire a wide variety of foods year round, making food safety issues surrounding transportation and refrigeration increasingly important.
- As international trade expands, shifting regional commerce and products to a global marketplace, we face the challenge of ensuring the safety of imported food.
- Americans are also eating more of their meals away from home. In fact, fifty cents of every food dollar is spent on food prepared outside the home. This food is purchased not only from grocery stores and restaurants, but also is consumed in institutional settings such as schools, hospitals, nursing homes, and day care centers. As a result, a comparatively few people are involved in preparing large numbers of meals for others, so the potential impact of disease-producing errors increases.

As food safety problems have arisen over the past century, the Federal government has responded in a variety of ways. Beginning early in the 1900s with the creation of the earliest regulatory programs to the creation of the President's Council on Food Safety in 1998, the Federal government, working in concert with its state, tribal, and local counterparts, has continuously endeavored to improve the safety of the American food supply (see appendix A for accomplishments during the Clinton Administration).

In addition to Federal efforts, our nation's food safety system is significantly affected by the work of state, tribal, and local public health, agriculture, and food regulatory officials. Individually and together they perform many different roles on the front lines for food safety. From initial recognition of outbreaks and their investigation, to laboratory work, to farm and retail oversight, to communications with the public, these officials and their representative groups and organizations are key participants in the national system.

Federal food safety officials, therefore, operate in a complex system of statutes, agencies, coordinating bodies, and interactions with state, tribal, and local governments; industry; and other stakeholders. The following list provides a summary of the major Federal food safety agencies and coordinating mechanisms:

Regulatory Agencies: At the Federal level, three agencies currently have major responsibilities for regulating food and substances that may become part of food:

- Food Safety and Inspection Service (FSIS) within the U.S. Department of Agriculture (USDA) ensures the safety of all domestic and imported meat, poultry, and some egg products in interstate commerce except game meat.
- Food and Drug Administration (FDA) within the Department of Health and Human Services (HHS) has in its purview all domestic and imported foods that are marketed in interstate commerce (except for meat, poultry, and some egg products) as well as game meat, food additives, animal feed, and veterinary drugs.
- Environmental Protection Agency (EPA) licenses pesticide products and establishes maximum allowable limits (tolerances) for pesticide residues in food and animal feed. (FDA and FSIS enforce pesticide tolerances for the commodities under their jurisdiction.) In addition, EPA has regulatory and research programs related to water and food-borne toxic chemicals such as dioxin.

The three primary regulatory agencies are supported by a number of other government organizations:

- Centers for Disease Control and Prevention (CDC), in HHS leads Federal efforts to gather data on food-borne illnesses, investigate food-borne illnesses and outbreaks, and monitor the effectiveness of prevention and control efforts. CDC also plays an ongoing role in identifying prevention strategies and building state and local health department epidemiology, laboratory, and environmental health skills to support food-borne disease surveillance and outbreak response.
- USDA Agricultural Research Service (ARS), Cooperative State Research, Education and Extension Service (CSREES), and the Economic Research Service (ERS) conduct food safety research.
- Animal and Plant Health Inspection Service (APHIS) provides surveillance of zoonotic diseases, traces affected animals to herds of origin, and conducts risk assessments.
- National Marine Fisheries Service (NMFS) within the Department of Commerce conducts a voluntary seafood inspection and grading program to ensure the quality and safety of commercial seafood. (Mandatory regulation of seafood processing is under FDA's jurisdiction.)

OTHER SUPPORTING AGENCIES

- National Institutes of Health (NIH), which is part of HHS, play important roles in conducting food safety research.

- Agricultural Marketing Service (AMS) within USDA conducts voluntary dairy, poultry, fruit and vegetable inspection and grading programs to ensure the quality of commercial products in both the domestic and international marketplace. . . .

Due, in part, to the complexity of the food safety system and the fact that millions of Americans continue to suffer annually from food-borne illnesses, numerous calls have been made to examine the existing system and modify it to improve the protection of the public's health through enhanced efficiency, better coordination, and more risk-based allocation of resources. . . .

As part of the Administration's continuing efforts to improve the safety of the nation's food supply and building on the recommendations of the NAS report, the President issued Executive Order 13100 creating the "President's Council on Food Safety" (Council). The Council's goal is to make the food supply safer through a seamless, science-based food safety system supported by well-coordinated research, surveillance, sound risk assessment, regulation, enforcement, and education. The President specifically instructed the Council to develop a comprehensive 5-year Federal food safety strategic plan to improve the current system and to anticipate future needs. To address the President's directive, the Council established its Strategic Planning Task Force. . . .

In the Fall of 1998, the Council held a series of meetings to obtain the public's views on a long-term vision for food safety in the United States, to identify the important food safety challenges for the Plan, and to solicit public comment on the NAS report. Based on these meetings, the Strategic Planning Task Force developed draft goals and objectives, which were the basis for a public meeting in July 1999, and for discussions with stakeholders at scientific and professional meetings during subsequent months. In the fall of 1999, Task Force interagency working groups revised the draft Plan based upon comments from stakeholders. In January 2000, the Task Force engaged interested stakeholders in a discussion of the revised goals, objectives, and action items.

From the outset, the overarching goal has been to protect public health by reducing food-borne hazards. Thus, a Plan has been developed that helps set priorities; improves coordination and efficiency; identifies gaps in the current system and ways to fill those gaps; enhances and strengthens prevention and intervention strategies; and identifies reliable measures to indicate progress. Consistent with the NAS recommendations, the Plan calls for food safety priorities to be based on risk and aims to create an integrated seamless food safety system.

In response to the NAS report and many public comments, the Council's Task Force also examined the legal authorities under which Federal food safety programs operate and the organizational structure within which they are carried out.

. . . Several inter-related themes guided the development of the plan. First and foremost among these is the recognition that the success of the plan must be evaluated on the basis of improvements in public health.

Second, consistent with NAS recommendations, the Council recognized that "the food safety system must rest on sound science." A critical dimension of each of the Plan's goals is to collect, analyze, disseminate, and fully use objective, scientific information about the nature and extent of food safety hazards and the means of preventing them.

Third, the Council recognized that assessment of food safety risks must play a critical role in setting priorities and determining the most effective use of our resources. Priorities must be based on where the scientific data show the greatest food safety risks. Risk-based priority setting will continue to be the most defensible way to shape budget choices, research agendas, risk management targets—indeed to guide every aspect of the effort to strengthen food safety programs.

The fourth theme shaping the Plan is that proactive strategies to prevent food safety problems are more effective than strategies that respond to food safety problems as they occur. Decades of experience have taught that it is more effective, and less expensive, to prevent food safety problems before they occur than to respond to outbreaks after they have happened. By swiftly applying a science-based understanding of the causes of food-borne hazards, government can encourage and direct the adoption of practices that will prevent harm, rather than responding only after people become ill as a result of something they ate.

The fifth theme focuses on the regulatory approaches used to protect the food supply. Government at all levels has a role in oversight of regulated industries and the enforcement of laws and regulations. Federal agencies and our state, local, and tribal counterparts must work together more closely to assure comprehensive and efficient regulation of the food industry and to create an integrated, seamless food safety system that protects the U.S. consumer. Responsible government oversight has to be a key element of any plan to prevent food-borne illnesses and hazards.

Finally, the Plan recognizes that increased coordination and action by all stakeholders is essential to the Plan's success. Given the breadth of the farm-to-table continuum—from hundreds of thousands of farms and processors, to millions of restaurants and supermarkets, to tens of millions of homes—assuring the safety of the nation's food supply is a shared responsibility. Partnerships among Federal, state, tribal, and local governments, as well as governments of other countries, academia, and the private sector are vital to the success of the Plan. And, action by industry, food handlers, health professionals and consumers—by everyone in the farm-to-table chain—is needed to reduce risk and ensure the safety of our food supply. . . .

Strengthening Federal Food Safety Laws

Today seven statutes provide HHS, USDA, and EPA with the primary tools to regulate food safety:

- The Federal Food, Drug, and Cosmetic Act (FDCA);
- The Public Health Service Act (PHSA);
- The Federal Meat Inspection Act (FMIA);
- The Poultry Products Inspection Act (PPIA);
- The Egg Products Inspection Act (EPIA);
- The Federal Insecticide, Fungicide, and Rodenticide Act (FIFRA); and
- The Food Quality Protection Act (FQPA)

These statutes were enacted and amended over a span of 90 years, starting in 1906 and 1907 with the first Federal food safety statutes, the Food and Drugs Act and the Meat Inspection Act. From their inception, however, these laws focused on different areas of the food supply, and they take varying approaches to food safety.

Enhancing the System's Structure

The NAS report *Ensuring Safe Food from Production to Consumption* recommended that Congress "establish, by statute, a unified and central framework for managing Federal food safety programs, one that is headed by a single official and which has the responsibility and control of resources for all Federal food safety activities." The report acknowledges that there may be many organizational approaches for implementing the "single voice" concept, and recommended further analysis. Over the years, other organizations also have called for restructuring the Federal food safety system, while still others point out the disadvantages of major restructuring. In general, advocates of restructuring see it as a means to improve the efficiency and effectiveness of the system as well as to establish a more risk-based approach to the allocation of resources. Opponents of restructuring view it as potentially damaging to a system that already has a good track record of public health protection.

To address this issue, an interagency team identified evaluation criteria and examined a broad range of organizational options. Comments were solicited from the public on the range of options and the evaluation criteria, and were considered in the analysis. Based on this analysis and other inputs, the Council considered whether existing Federal structures and approaches need to be refined, strengthened, or changed. This chapter summarizes the Council's analysis and recommendations for enhancing the existing Federal food safety system.

There are a large number of variables to be considered in examining organizational structures for the Federal food safety system. These include

- The numerous agency functions (e.g., research, surveillance, standard setting, inspection) and the interdependence of food safety and non-food safety functions;
- The breadth and depth of the farm-to-table production system that brings food to the American consumer;
- The different types of food (e.g., meat, fruits and vegetables, beverages);
- The multiple hazards that can be present in food (e.g., pathogens, chemicals, pesticides, physical hazards);
- The differing approaches to achieving food safety (e.g., prevention, pre-market review, post-market surveillance, risk-based inspection);
- The various departments/agencies which make up the current U.S. food safety system and their statutes (e.g., FMIA, FFDCA, FQPA); and
- The different mechanisms available for creating a seamless food safety system (e.g., stronger executive leadership, facilitating mechanisms such as Memoranda of Understanding and partnerships, and reorganization including a single food agency). . . .

In conducting the review, organizational options were examined by the interagency team based on the attributes of a desirable food safety system. One key evaluation criterion was an option's ability to facilitate implementation of the Plan's strategic goals. Additionally, the team's evaluation criteria reflected the view that the Federal food safety system must be: effective, efficient, science-based with a strong emphasis on risk analysis, comprehensive, and must instill public confidence.

Implementation considerations with both long- and short-term consequences were also weighed, including long- and short-term costs to full implementation; short-term disruptions and lapses in efficiency; the potential for short-run adverse impacts on public health; the impact on state, tribal and local food safety agencies; and the implications for relationships with critical stakeholders (e.g., Congress, other Federal agencies, international organizations, industry, consumer groups, affiliated associations, etc.).

ORGANIZATIONAL OPTIONS

A broad range of organizational options was examined. The options were based on the NAS report, legislative proposals over the last few years, food safety consolidation efforts in other countries, Government Accountability Office (GAO) and Congressional Research Service (CRS) reports, public comments and testimony, and other resources.

The team considered four major options, and a variety of sub-options, encompassing the major regulatory responsibilities for food safety, and in some cases food safety research and food-borne illness surveillance funded by the U.S. government. The major options represent a continuum from strengthening the current system, to designating a lead agency, to creating a consolidated agency for most or all food safety functions.

In addition to these organizational options, the Council assumed that agencies would continue to streamline or consolidate existing regulatory programs. The Council has already proposed streamlining the agencies' approach to the oversight of egg safety. Similar efforts will be pursued in other areas where there is overlapping jurisdiction or where improvements in public health protection can be made.

The options analyzed include the following:

I. Coordinated Federal Food Safety System—Utilize the existing organizational structure, but provide a coordination mechanism to create centralized, executive leadership.
II. Lead Agency Approach—Provide centralized executive leadership and a "single voice" either through a lead agency or separate agencies with discrete responsibilities.
III. Consolidated Agency within Existing Organization—Consolidate food safety regulatory and some related functions in one agency reporting to either a current Cabinet Secretary, or the management of an existing independent agency.
IV. Stand-Alone Food Safety Agency—Create a new, stand-alone food safety agency to facilitate achievement of food safety and public health goals.

. . . Several key findings of the analysis influenced the Council's decisions. These findings were:

- The existing organizational structure:
  - reflects statutory mandates that have evolved over the past 100 years;
  - allows for a greater diversity of agency input into food safety problems;
  - reduces the ability to allocate resources based on risk;

  - impedes coordination of food safety efforts targeted to certain types of foods, technologies, or consumers; and
- Reorganization, by itself, will not significantly change the food safety system's capability to assure public health protection. Reform of the existing statutes and implementation of the Plan, which focuses on utilization of science and risk assessment, risk management, and risk communication are the key to improving public health protection.
- The Plan can be successfully implemented under any organizational option.
- No single structure for the food safety system provides the perfect solution.
- Although certain elements of the Plan may be facilitated by one or more of the organization structures, many potential changes will also create difficulties elsewhere in the Plan. For example, if only regulatory functions are consolidated, such a consolidation may not facilitate targeting these resources to the highest risks, and would divorce the regulators from the researchers.
- Options I through IV are progressively more likely to be costly and disruptive in the short term, but potentially more efficient in the long-term. Potential improvements in efficiency and efficacy need to be weighed against the costs, disruptions, and other effects experienced during reorganization and implementation.
- Attempts to coordinate within existing or slightly modified structures (Options I and II) may lead to marginal improvements but do little to address the fragmentation of the food safety system, and fail to eliminate duplication and conflict inherent in the current system.
- Consolidation (Options III and IV) could eliminate duplication and fragmentation, create a centralized leadership and single voice for food safety, clarify lines of authority, facilitate priority setting and resource allocation based on risk, and provide greater accountability.
- Consolidation (Options III and IV), coupled with statutory reform, could take many forms. Determining what responsibilities to include or not include is critical to maximizing efficiency and effectiveness of the federal food safety system. For example, separating food safety surveillance from other types of public health surveillance could be inefficient and detrimental to both. Similarly, separating research from food safety regulation could make research agencies less responsive to regulatory needs.
- A stand-alone agency (Option IV) focused on food safety and public health eliminates any perception of inherent bias or competing missions.
- A stand-alone agency might create new problems and inefficiencies in the oversight of dietary supplements and other food-related issues not included in the new agency.

Timothy M. Hammonds, "It Is Time to Designate a Single Food Safety Agency," *Food and Drug Law Journal*, Vol. 59, No. 3. (2004), pp. 427–432.

The Food Marketing Institute (FMI) is a nonprofit association conducting programs in research, education, industry relations, and public affairs on behalf of its 2,300 members and their subsidiaries–food retailers and wholesalers and their customers in the United States and around the world. FMI's U.S. members operate approximately 26,000 retail food stores with a combined annual sales volume of more than $340 billion–three-quarters of all grocery store sales in the United States. FMI's retail membership is composed of large multistore chains, regional firms, and independent supermarkets. Its international membership includes 200 members from sixty countries.

The time has come to consider a major change in the way foods are monitored and regulated in the United States in order to ensure that the American food supply remains, without question, the safest, most wholesome, and least expensive in the world. FMI has proposed the creation of a single food safety agency because we believe new challenges have arisen that, taken together, threaten to overwhelm the ability of the current regulatory system to respond effectively. FMI believes that designating a single agency responsible for food safety is essential if the United States is to continue to maintain a food supply that remains the envy of the world.

The U.S. regulatory system charged with maintaining the safety, integrity, and wholesomeness of the food supply has evolved piecemeal over a full century. Changes to this system have been made in response to problems as they have arisen one-by-one, not as part of a well-thought-out strategic plan. It should be no surprise that a system begun in the early 1900s would now find itself facing very different challenges that require very different responses.

These challenges include diets vastly different than was the case in the early 1900s, accompanied by a dramatic expansion of foods prepared and eaten away from the home; new breeding, processing, and preservation technologies unknown when the current system was designed; true globalization of the food supply, presenting challenges reaching beyond U.S. borders; and the emergence of new, virulent food-borne pathogens that require a coordinated prevention and control strategy reaching across all commodity groups.

The current U.S. regulatory system is ill-equipped to deal with these challenges. More than a dozen federal agencies have jurisdiction over various parts of the food supply. This patchwork quilt creates inconsistencies, gaps, overlaps, and duplication of effort that are

Source: Excerpted with permission of the Food and Drug Law Institute, Washington, DC. From Food and Drug Law Journal, Volume 59, Number 3, 2004.

becoming increasingly unworkable. As these agencies struggle to cope with the many inconsistent statutes and regulations under which they operate, more than fifty interagency agreements have been negotiated in an attempt to bring some degree of order to the process. The deficiencies that remain become glaringly obvious, however, in times of crisis.

The public is never in more need of assurance than when a food safety crisis arises. It is precisely at those times that the current regulatory structure prevents effective action. Because it is rare that a single agency has complete jurisdiction over the entire scope of a major food safety problem, it becomes impossible to find a spokesperson who can rapidly clarify the facts and reassure the public. Far more typically, the public is faced with a lengthy delay while overlapping bureaucracies creak into some attempt at a coordinated response. While the search for who knew what and when goes on, the crisis worsens and public confidence erodes. As this occurs, the public may be exposed to risk longer than necessary and the reputations of companies, and sometimes companies themselves, can be destroyed needlessly.

Congress has made several attempts to address modernizing the food regulatory oversight system. Congress asked the National Academy of Sciences (NAS) to assess the effectiveness of the current food safety system in the United States and to provide recommendations on scientific and organizational changes needed to ensure an effective science-based food safety system. The resulting Committee to Ensure Safe Food from Production to Consumption, formed by the Institute of Medicine and the National Research Council, issued its report in 1998.[10]

Key conclusions reached by the NAS committee in assessing the current system of regulating food safety in the United States include the following:

Officials who direct or carry out diverse functions under the multiplicity of statutory mandates are capable and dedicated, as are their state and local counterparts. They perform remarkably well, given their budgetary and statutory constraints, but they operate within an institutional framework that is out of date and poorly designed to accomplish the critical goals that regulation in this field must achieve. The increasing complexity of food production and delivery and the exploding internationalization of the U.S. food supply impose added pressure on the federal regulatory apparatus, which was constructed in simpler times.[11]

The major statutory shortfall of the current system is that: There are inconsistent, uneven, and at times archaic food statutes that inhibit use of science-based decision-making in activities related to food safety, and these statutes can be inconsistently interpreted and enforced among agencies.[12]

This report presents a damning assessment of the current system for regulating the U.S. food supply. As this system has evolved piecemeal over almost a full century, it has become primarily reactive rather than being designed to anticipate and prevent problems before they become critical. Statutory and budgetary limitations prevent the application of scientific risk assessments across all foods that would allow the flexible assignment of resources to the areas of greatest need. The result is that resources tend to become dedicated to solving yesterday's problems, and only with great difficulty can they be redirected to meet tomorrow's challenges. Even when one agency rises to an emerging challenge, there is seldom the ability to coordinate an approach across all of the agencies. . . .

As effective as these agencies may have been [in the past], they now face challenges very different from those they were originally created to solve. Today's world is increasingly complex with a resulting need for integrated policies balanced across the domestic and international issues of health, safety, trade, economic viability, scientific validity, political realities, and social concerns. It is not just that the current complex and fragmented system creates gaps and overlaps. It is that each one of these agencies uses a very different approach—often mandated by law—to address the very same issues depending on jurisdiction. Products that are perceived as identical in the minds of consumers often are regulated by different agencies administering different approaches because jurisdiction frequently is split. One well-known example is pizza. FDA regulates pizza until the toppings reach two percent or more of cooked meat or poultry. At that point, the pizza falls under the jurisdiction of the USDA. Thus, a plant that produces only cheese pizza is subject to inspection by FDA, which is likely to occur only infrequently; while a plant that produces pepperoni pizza is subject to daily inspection by the USDA, even though the agency already has inspected the animal from which the pepperoni is made and the processing of the meat into pepperoni. To complicate matters further, inspectors from both the USDA and FDA, operating under two very different sets of guidelines, simultaneously regulate an integrated pizza processing plant. . . . If these and hundreds of other examples of inconsistency, duplication, and inertia that could be cited are not yet enough to make a persuasive case for reform, there are three clear examples of growing challenges that do. The first is the arrival of modern food biotechnology. While this technology holds great promise, it does blur the current regulatory boundaries and, in an increasing number of cases, actually erases the line between food and drugs. Treating the so-called "super salmon" as a drug for the purposes of regulatory approval is only one example. Companies are left wondering just how the regulatory process is going to work and just what standards will be applied; the public is left wondering as well.

The second example of the pressing challenges facing regulators and the regulated community is the arrival of what have come to be called "functional foods" or "nutraceuticals." It is becoming increasingly difficult to fit today's products into the neat boxes of foods, drugs, or dietary supplements that existing U.S. laws create. Under the existing system, the classification of a product will determine the extent of premarket regulatory oversight. The controversy surrounding new products that are marketed as replacements for margarine or butter, but include substances that are intended to provide enhanced nutritive properties, is one example of this phenomenon.[13] The third example that dramatically illustrates the need for reform is the regulation of foods imported into the United States and our parallel export negotiations with other countries. Authority for ensuring the safety of imported foods is split between FDA and the USDA, and these agencies rely, in part, on Customs' statutory authority over imports. Yet, both FDA and the USDA use very different approaches for foods under their jurisdiction. . . .[14]

The system by which the United States regulates the safety of its food supply must be redesigned to address the current and future challenges of the rapidly evolving food system. FMI believes it is time to consider the designation of a single food agency as the appropriate vehicle to meet those challenges. FMI does not believe an appointed "czar" within the existing structure, or even an appointed coordinating committee, would carry sufficient authority to allocate budgets and resources appropriately, nor would an appointed coordinator or committee eliminate the inevitable rivalries that exist between different agencies charged with essentially the same functions. FMI believes the only way to carry out meaningful, long-lasting reform of the U.S. food regulatory system is to designate a true single agency with total regulatory authority for the safety of the entire food system. Because the resources needed for such an agency already reside within extant agencies, the challenge primarily is one of reallocation. FMI believes that this reallocation could be done at a minimum of expense. Indeed, we believe it is likely that eliminating current duplication would result in substantial budget savings, while improving overall performance. FMI recognizes the difficulties inherent in a change of this magnitude, however, we believe it is something that can be—should be—done. In considering how best to make decisions about a single food safety agency, the FMI suggests five guiding principles:

First, the single food safety agency must build on the credibility already enjoyed with U.S. international trading partners and the American shopping public. Although the current system is in serious need of reform to meet the challenges of the future, the United States is still the standard of excellence for the world. Great care must be taken not to erode the confidence of the public or of the international community.

Second, total authority for all federal food safety oversight activities must be centralized including approval, inspection, labeling, standard setting, risk assessment, research, education, and responsibility for monitoring and managing disease outbreaks. Eliminating duplication, closing the gaps that exist, and resolving inconsistencies among the various existing agencies would be given top priority.

Third, a commitment must be made to integrate federal food safety activities with those of state and local agencies. This includes speaking with one voice on safety standards to encourage each state to adopt the Model National Food Code[15] and collaboration with state and local authorities to ensure uniform enforcement.

Fourth, oversight from production to consumption must be based on scientific risk assessments that flexibly allocate inspection, research, and regulatory resources to maximize effectiveness. Sound science must be the guiding principle for aligning scarce resources with the most pressing consumer food safety needs.

Fifth, a domestic single food safety agency must be equally dedicated to ensuring the safety of all foods imported into the United States. Consumers have every right to expect domestic foods and imported foods to be equally safe. Now that a new millennium has been entered, it is time to move to a modern food safety regulatory system that is truly able to address today's challenges and fully capable of preparing for the future.

U.S. Government Accountability Office, *Food Safety and Security: Fundamental Changes Needed to Ensure Safe Food*, GAO-02-47T, Washington, DC (2001).

We are pleased to be here today to discuss the federal food safety system and whether the system's current design can meet the food safety challenges of today. While the food supply is generally safe, each year tens of millions of Americans become ill and thousands die from eating unsafe foods, according to the Centers for Disease Control and Prevention (CDC). As we have stated in previous reports and testimonies, fundamental changes are needed to ensure a safer food supply. My testimony today provides an overview of the nation's fragmented food safety system, the problems that it causes, and the changes necessary to create lasting improvements. In addition, I want to bring to your attention some work GAO has done addressing deliberate food contamination and federal research on and preparedness for bioterrorism in light of the tragic events of September 11, 2001. . . .

It is now widely recognized that food safety issues must be addressed comprehensively—that is, by preventing contamination through the entire food production cycle, from farm to table. A single, food safety agency responsible for administering a uniform set of laws is needed to resolve the long-standing problems with the current system; deal with emerging food safety issues, such as the safety of genetically modified foods or deliberate acts of contamination; and ensure a safe food supply. While we believe that an independent agency could offer the most effective approach, we recognize that there are short-term costs and other considerations associated with setting up a new government agency. A second option would be to consolidate food safety activities in an existing department, such as the U.S. Department of Agriculture (USDA) or the Department of Health and Human Service (HHS). Regardless, however, choosing an organizational structure only represents half the job. For any single food safety agency to be ultimately successful, it will also be necessary to rationalize the current patchwork of food safety legislation to make it uniform and risk-based.

Despite spending more than $1 billion annually on the federal food safety system, food safety remains a concern. For example, between May and November 2000, sliced and packaged turkey meat contaminated with Listeria monocytogenes caused 29 individuals in 10 states to become ill. In April and May of this year, imported cantaloupes contaminated with a pathogenic strain of Salmonella were linked to 54 illnesses and 2 deaths in 16 states, and in June six people in California were sickened, two of whom died, from eating oysters contaminated with Vibrio vulnificus. CDC estimates that food borne diseases cause approximately 76 million illnesses, 325,000 hospitalizations, and 5,000 deaths each year. In medical costs and productivity losses, food-borne illnesses related to five principal pathogens cost the nation about $6.9 billion annually, USDA estimates.[4]

Twelve different agencies administer as many as 35 laws that make up the federal food safety system. Two agencies account for most federal food safety spending and regulatory responsibilities: the Food Safety and Inspection Service (FSIS), in USDA, is responsible for the safety of meat, poultry, and processed eggs, while the Food and Drug Administration (FDA), in HHS, is responsible for the safety of most other foods. Other agencies with food safety responsibilities and/or programs include HHS' Centers for Disease Control and Prevention; USDA's Agricultural Marketing Service (AMS), Animal and Plant Health Inspection Service (APHIS), Agricultural Research Service (ARS), and Grain Inspection, Packers and Stockyards Administration (GIPSA); the Department of Commerce's National Marine Fisheries Service; the Department of the Treasury's U.S. Customs Service and Bureau of Alcohol, Tobacco, and Firearms; the Environmental Protection Agency (EPA); and the Federal Trade Commission (**Figure 9-2**).

Because the nation's food safety system evolved piecemeal over time, the nation has essentially two very different approaches to food safety—one at USDA and the other at FDA—that have led to inefficient use of resources and inconsistencies in oversight and

	FDA	AMS	APHIS	EPA	FSIS	GIPSA
Inputs						
Animal Feed	•					
Seeds		•	•			
Chemicals (e.g., fertilizers and pesticides)				•		
Animal Drugs	•					
On Farm						
Cows (milk), Hogs	•		•			
Wheat	•		•	•		•
Lettuce	•	•	•	•		
Tomatoes	•	•	•	•		
First-Level Processors						
Ham					•	
Cheese	•	•				
Flour	•					

→ **Second-Level Processors**

Open-face sandwich
Processor inspected daily by FSIS (USDA)

INGREDIENTS: Bread, Ham, Cheese, Lettuce, Tomato

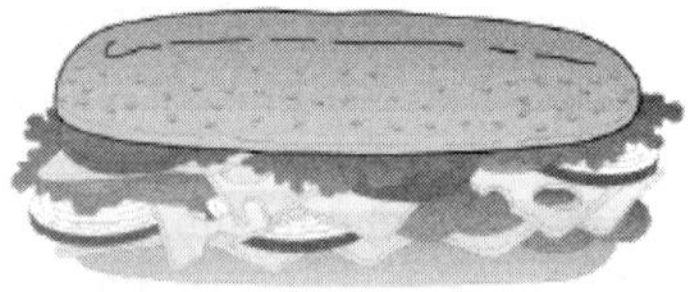

Closed-face sandwich
Processor inspected on average once every 5 years by FDA

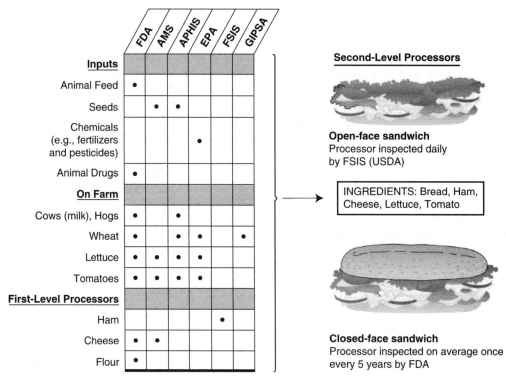

Source: U.S. Government Accountability Office, "Food Safety and Security: Fundamental Changes Needed to Ensure Safe Food," GAO-02-47T, (Washington, DC; 2001).

FIGURE 9-2 Federal Agencies Responsible for Safety of Packaged Ham and Cheese Sandwich

enforcement. These problems, along with ineffective coordination between the agencies, have hampered and continue to impede efforts to address public health concerns associated with existing and emerging food safety risks. The following examples represent some of the problems we identified during our reviews of the nation's food safety system.

- Federal food safety expenditures are based on legal requirements, not on risk. As shown in Figure 9-2, funding for ensuring the safety of products is disproportionate to the level of consumption of those products because the frequency of inspection is based not on risk but on the agencies' legal authority and regulatory approach. Likewise, funding for ensuring the safety of products is disproportionate to the percentage of food-borne illnesses linked to those products. For example, to ensure the safety of meat, poultry, and processed egg products in fiscal year 1999. . . .
- Federal agencies' authorities to enforce food safety requirements differ. USDA agencies have the authority to (1) require food firms to register so that they can be inspected, (2) prohibit the use of processing equipment that may potentially contaminate food products, and (3) temporarily detain any suspect foods. Conversely, FDA lacks such authority and is often hindered in its food oversight efforts. For example, both USDA and FDA oversee recalls when foods they regulate are found to be contaminated or adulterated.[16] However, if a USDA-regulated company does not voluntarily conduct the recall, USDA can detain the product for up to 20 days while it seeks a court order to seize the food. Because FDA does not have detention authority, it cannot ensure that tainted food is kept out of commerce while it seeks a court-ordered seizure. As another example, while FDA is responsible for overseeing all seafood-processing firms operating in interstate commerce, the agency does not have an effective system to identify the firms subject to regulation because there is no registration requirement for seafood firms. As a result, some firms may not be subjected to FDA oversight, thus increasing the risk of consumers' contracting a food-borne illness from unsafe seafood.[17]
- USDA and FDA implementation of the new food safety approach is inconsistent. Since December 1997, both USDA and FDA have implemented a new science-based regulatory approach—the Hazard Analysis and Critical Control Point (HACCP) system—for ensuring the safety of meat, poultry, and seafood.[18] The HACCP system places the primary responsibility on industry, not government inspectors, for identifying and controlling hazards in the production process. However, as we discussed in previous reports,[19] FDA and USDA implemented the HACCP system differently. While USDA reported that in 1999, 96 percent of federally regulated plants were in compliance with the basic HACCP requirements for meat and poultry, FDA reported that less than half of federally regulated seafood firms were in compliance with HACCP requirements. In addition, while USDA collects data on *Salmonella* contamination to assess the effectiveness of its HACCP system for meat and poultry, FDA does not have similar data for seafood. Without more effective compliance programs and adequate performance data, the benefits of HACCP will not be fully realized.
- Oversight of imported food is inconsistent and unreliable. As we reported in 1998, the meat and poultry acts require that, before a country can export meat and poultry to the United States, FSIS must make a determination that the exporting country's

food safety system provides a level of safety equivalent to the U.S. system.[20] Under the equivalency requirement, FSIS has shifted most of the responsibility for ensuring product safety to the exporting country. The exporting country performs the primary inspection, allowing FSIS to leverage its resources by focusing its reviews on verifying the efficacy of the exporting countries' systems. In addition, until FSIS approves release of imported meat and poultry products into U.S. commerce, they generally must be kept in an FSIS registered warehouse. In contrast, FDA lacks the legal authority to require that countries exporting foods to the United States have food safety systems that provide a level of safety equivalent to ours. Without such authority, FDA must rely primarily on its port-of-entry inspections to detect and bar the entry of unsafe imported foods. Such an approach has been widely discredited as resource-intensive and ineffective. In fiscal year 2000, FDA inspections covered about 1 percent of the imported food entries under its jurisdiction. In addition, FDA does not control imported foods or require that they be kept in a registered warehouse prior to FDA approval for release into U.S. commerce. As a result, some adulterated imports that were ultimately refused entry by FDA had already been released into U.S. commerce. For example, in 1998 we reported that in a U.S. Customs Service operation called "Bad Apple," about 40 percent of the imported foods FDA checked and found in violation of U.S. standards were never redelivered to Customs for disposition. These foods were not destroyed or reexported as required and presumably were released into U.S. commerce.

- Claims of health benefits for foods may be treated inconsistently by different federal agencies. Because three federal agencies are charged with enforcing different statutes, a product's claim of health benefits might be denied by one agency but allowed by another.[21] FDA, the Federal Trade Commission, and USDA share responsibility for determining which claims regarding health benefits are allowed in labeling and advertising of foods and dietary supplements. FDA has authorized only a limited number of specific health claims for use on product labels. However, the Federal Trade Commission may allow a health claim in an advertisement as long as it meets the requirements of the Federal Trade Commission Act, even if FDA has not approved it for use on a label. Furthermore, USDA has not issued regulations to adopt any of the FDA approved health claims for use on the products that it regulates, such as pot pies, soups, or prepared meals containing over a certain percentage of meat or poultry. Rather, USDA reviews requests to use a health claim, including those approved by FDA, on a case-by-case basis.
- Effective enforcement of limits on certain drugs in food-producing animals is hindered by the regulatory system's fragmented organizational structure. FDA has regulatory responsibility for enforcing animal-drug residue levels in food producing animals. However, FDA in conjunction with the states have only investigated between 43 and 50 percent of each year's USDA animal-drug residue referrals made between fiscal year 1996 and 2000. According to FDA officials, the agency lacks the resources to conduct prompt follow-up investigations and does not have an adequate referral assignment and tracking system to ensure that investigations are made in a timely manner. FDA has relied on the states, through contracts and cooperative agreements, to conduct the bulk of the investigations. FDA only has resources to investigate repeat

violators. As a result, animal producers not investigated may continue to use animal drugs improperly putting consumer health at greater risk. In the absence of a unified food safety system, federal agencies have attempted to coordinate their efforts to overcome fragmentation and avoid duplication or gaps in coverage. While we believe that interagency coordination is important and should be continued, history has shown that such efforts are difficult to conduct successfully. The following examples represent some of the coordination problems we have found.

- Fragmented organizational structure poses challenges to U.S. efforts to address barriers to agricultural trade. The organizational structure for food safety complicates U.S. efforts to address foreign sanitary and phytosanitary (SPS) measures. SPS measures are designed to protect humans, animals, or the territory of a country from the spread of a pest or disease, among other things. However, the U.S. Trade Representative and USDA are concerned that some foreign SPS measures may be inconsistent with international trade rules and may unfairly impede the flow of agricultural trade. In 1997, we reported that the federal structure for addressing foreign SPS measures was complex because 12 federal agencies had some responsibility for addressing problems related to SPS measures and that no one agency was directing federal efforts.[22] We found, among other things, that the involvement of multiple agencies with conflicting viewpoints made it difficult to evaluate, prioritize, and develop unified approaches to address such measures. While, the U.S. Trade Representative and USDA took some actions to respond to our report, including establishing mechanisms to improve interagency coordination and decision-making, it remains to be seen whether such actions will effectively address the coordination problems over the long run.
- Different statutory responsibilities may limit the ability of agencies to coordinate successfully. As we reported in August 1998, because FDA and FSIS have different statutory responsibilities, important information about animal feed contaminated with dioxin (a suspected carcinogen) and animals that had consumed this feed was not effectively communicated to the food industry.[23] FDA and FSIS worked together to decide on the preferred course of action for handling the contaminated feed and animals, and each agency was responsible for communicating its decisions to producers or processors under its jurisdiction. However, the agencies did not necessarily communicate all required actions to all affected parties. For example, when officials from FDA, the agency responsible for regulating animal feed, met with meat and poultry producers, their primary concern was with the contaminated feed, not with the animals that had consumed it. Thus, they did not necessarily tell these producers about the actions they should take for their affected animals. FSIS, the agency responsible for regulating meat and poultry processors, sent word of dioxin-testing requirements to the processors and trade associations but did not notify meat and poultry producers, over which it has no jurisdiction.
- The need for extensive coordination may impede prompt resolution of food safety problems. Despite FSIS' and FDA's efforts to coordinate their efforts on egg safety, more than 10 years have past since the problem of bacterial contamination of intact shell eggs was first identified and a comprehensive safety strategy has yet to be implemented. In 1988, for the first time, some intact shell eggs were discovered to

be contaminated internally with the pathogenic bacteria *Salmonella enteritidis*. In 1992, we reported that due to coordination difficulties resulting from the split regulatory structure for eggs, the federal government had not agreed on a unified approach to address this problem.[24] In July 1999, we reported that the federal government still had not agreed on a unified approach to address the problem.[8] In July 2000, FDA and FSIS issued a "current thinking" paper identifying actions that would decrease the food safety risks associated with eggs. However, as of September 2001, comprehensive proposed regulations to implement these actions had not yet been published.

- Continuity of coordination efforts is hampered by changes in executive branch leadership. The President's Council on Food Safety, created in 1998, was tasked with developing a comprehensive strategic plan for federal food safety activities. In August 2000, the council agreed to initiate an interagency process to address our recommendation that FDA and the Department of Transportation,[25] among others, enhance food safety protections by developing a strategy to regulate animal feed while in transport. While the council published its strategic food safety plan in January 2001 that included numerous "action items" and recommendations for improving the federal food safety system, the council did not address a transport strategy for animal feed. Moreover, the council has not met since publishing the strategic plan, and it remains to be seen whether the new administration will act on the council's recommendations. For example, the council's strategic plan included an action item to allocate enforcement resources based on the potential risk to public health, but the President's fiscal year 2002 budget showed little change in the allocation of food safety resources among agencies. . . .

Former key government food safety officials at USDA and FDA have acknowledged the limitations of the current regulatory system. As shown in Table 1, many former government officials recognize the need for and support the transition to a single food safety agency. Some of these officials believe the single agency could be consolidated within an existing department, and others favor an independent agency. Regardless, they all recognize the need for legislative overhaul to provide a uniform, risk-based approach to food safety. . . .

Although in the past the U.S. food safety system has served as a model for other countries, recently Canada, Denmark, Great Britain, and Ireland have taken the lead by consolidating much of their food safety responsibilities in a single agency in each country. As we reported in 1999,[26] responding to heightened public concerns about the safety of their food supplies, Great Britain and Ireland chose to consolidate responsibilities in agencies that report to or are represented by their ministers of health. The British consolidated food safety activities into an independent agency, represented before Parliament by the Minister of Health, largely because of the agriculture ministry's perceived mishandling of an outbreak of *Bovine Spongiform Encephalopathy* (commonly referred to as "mad cow" disease). Public opinion viewed the agriculture ministry, which had the dual responsibilities of promoting agriculture and the food industry and regulating food safety, as slow to react because it was too concerned about protecting the cattle industry. . . .

Recent events have raised the specter of bioterrorism as an emerging risk factor for our food safety system. Bioterrorism is the threatened or intentional release of biological agents (viruses, bacteria, or their toxins) for the purpose of influencing the conduct of government or of intimidating or coercing a civilian population. These agents can be released through food as well as the air, water, or insects. To respond to potential bioterrorism, federal food safety regulatory agencies need to be prepared to efficiently coordinate their activities and respond quickly to protect the public health. Under the current structure, we believe that there are very real doubts about the system's ability to detect and quickly respond to any such event. To date, the only known bioterrorist act in the United States involved deliberate contamination of food with a biological agent. In 1984, a religious cult intentionally contaminated salad bars in local restaurants in Oregon to prevent people from voting in a local election. Although no one died, 751 people were diagnosed with food-borne illnesses. Since then federal officials identified only one other act of deliberate food contamination with a biological agent that affected 13 individuals in 1996, but numerous threats and hoaxes have been reported. Both FDA and FSIS have plans and procedures for responding to deliberate food contamination incidents,[27] but the effectiveness of these procedures is largely untested for contamination involving biological agents. Therefore, we recommended in 1999 that FDA and FSIS test their plans and procedures using simulated exercises that evaluate the effectiveness of federal, state, and local agencies' and industry's responses to various types of deliberate food contamination with a biological agent.[28]

U.S. Government Accountability Office, *Overseeing the U.S. Food Supply: Steps Should Be Taken to Reduce Overlapping Inspections and Related Activities*, GAO-05-549T, Washington, DC (2005).

The four agencies we examined—USDA, FDA, the Environmental Protection Agency (EPA), and NMFS—are involved in key program functions related to food safety. These functions include inspection and enforcement, research, risk assessment, education and outreach, rule making and standard setting, surveillance and monitoring, food security, and administration. These agencies spend resources on similar food safety activities to ensure the safety of different food products. **Table 9-1** illustrates similar activities that these agencies conduct. . . .

USDA and FDA have new tools that could help reduce overlap in inspections. Under the Bioterrorism Act, FDA could commission USDA inspectors, who are present every day at these jointly regulated facilities, to inspect FDA-regulated food.[29] In doing so, FDA could reduce overlapping inspections and redirect resources to other facilities for which it has sole jurisdiction. While they did not disagree in principle with the benefits of such an arrangement, FDA officials said that the savings would be somewhat offset because FDA would likely have to reimburse USDA for the costs of those inspections. Furthermore, FDA officials said that they do not currently plan to pursue this option and have not conducted any analyses of the costs or savings associated with it. USDA officials commented that their inspectors are fully occupied and that they would need to be trained before conducting joint inspections. . . .

We identified 71 interagency agreements that the principal food safety agencies—USDA, FDA, EPA, and NMFS—have entered into to better protect the public health by addressing jurisdictional boundaries, coordinating activities, reducing overlaps, and leveraging resources. About one-third[26] of the agreements highlight the need to reduce duplication and overlap or make efficient and effective use of resources. However, the agencies cannot take full advantage of these agreements because they do not have adequate mechanisms for tracking them and, in some cases, do not effectively implement them. Agency officials had difficulty identifying the food safety agreements they are party to, and in many instances, the agencies did not agree on the number of agreements they had entered into. In addition, for the two comprehensive inspection-related agreements that we examined in detail, the agencies are not ensuring that their provisions are adhered to or that the overall objectives of the agreements are being achieved. For example:

TABLE 9-1 Example of Similar Food Safety Activities

Food safety program function	*Activity*	*USDA*	*FDA*	*EPA*	*NMFS*
Inspection/ Enforcement	Inspection of domestic food-processing facilities	•	•		•
	Visits to foreign countries or firms to conduct inspections and/or evaluate foreign food safety systems	•	•		•
	Inspection of imported food at ports of entry	•	•		
	Training inspectors	•	•		•
	Maintenance of inspection record database	•	•		•
	Support to state enforcement efforts (retail-level food safety)	•	•	•	
	Laboratory analysis of samples collected at food-processing facilities (to identify potential contamination)	•	•		•
Research	Research on pathogen reduction	•	•		•
	Research on foodborne chemical contaminants (such as pesticides or dioxins) or biological contaminants (such as e-coli or salmonella)	•	•	•	•
Risk assessment	Risk assessment of food contaminants	•	•	•	•
	Sample collection and/or analysis of pesticide residues to inform risk assessment	•	•		•
Education/Outreach	Development and delivery of consumer education (such as consumer hotlines or pamphlet)	•	•	•	•
	Development and delivery of industry guidance (such as guidance regarding regulations)	•	•	•	•
	International harmonization of standards	•	•	•	•
Surveillance/ Monitoring	Participation in FoodNet (active surveillance for foodborne diseases)	•	•		

TABLE 9-1 (*continued*)

Food safety program function	*Activity*	*USDA*	*FDA*	*EPA*	*NMFS*
	Participation in PulseNet (early warning system for food illness outbreak)	•	•		
Rulemaking/Standard setting	HACCP rule development and promulgation[a]	•	•		•[b]

Source: GAO analysis of documents obtained from, and discussions with, USDA, FDA, EPA, and NMFS officials.

[a]Hazard Analysis and Critical Control Point (HACCP) regulations require food processors to maintain a plan identifying critical points in the production line where contamination is more likely to occur and adopt control techniques to prevent or reduce contamination. Currently, USDA requires all meat- and poultry-processing facilities to comply with mandatory HACCP regulations, and FDA requires that seafood- and juice-processing facilities comply with mandatory HACCP regulations.

[b]NMFS participated in developing FDA's seafood HACCP rule.

Source: U.S. Government Accountability Office, "Overseeing the U.S. Food Supply: Steps Should Be Taken To Reduce Overlapping Inspections and Related Activities," GAO-05-549T, (Washington, DC: 2005).

- USDA and FDA are not fully implementing an agreement to exchange information about jointly regulated facilities in order to permit more efficient use of both their resources and contribute to improved public health protection. Under this agreement, the agencies are to share inspection information, but FDA does not routinely consider compliance information from USDA when deciding how to target its inspection resources. Also, the agreement calls for the agencies to explore the feasibility of granting each other access to appropriate computer monitoring systems so that each agency can track inspection findings. However, the agencies maintain separate databases and the inspectors with whom we spoke continue to be largely unaware of a facility's history of compliance with the other agency's regulations. Inspectors told us that compliance information might be helpful when inspecting jointly regulated facilities so they could focus on past violations.
- An agreement between FDA and NMFS recognizes the agencies' related responsibilities at seafood-processing establishments. The agreement details actions the agencies can take to enable each to discharge its responsibilities as effectively as possible, minimizing FDA inspections at these facilities. However, we found that FDA is not using information from NMFS inspections, which could allow it to reduce the number of inspections at those facilities.

U.S. Government Accountability Office, *Federal Oversight of Food Safety: High-Risk Designation Can Bring Needed Attention to Fragmented System*, GAO-07-449T, Washington, DC (2007).

We have cited the need to integrate the fragmented federal food safety system as a significant challenge for the 21st century, to be addressed in light of the nation's current deficit and growing structural fiscal imbalance.[30] The traditional incremental approaches to budgeting will need to give way to more fundamental reexamination of the base of government. While prompted by fiscal necessity, such a reexamination can serve the vital function of updating programs to meet present and future challenges within current and expected resource levels. To help Congress review and reconsider the base of federal spending, we framed illustrative questions for decision makers to consider. While these questions can apply to other areas needing broad-based transformation, we specifically cited the myriad of food safety programs managed across several federal agencies. Among these questions are the following:

- How can agencies partner or integrate their activities in new ways, especially with each other, on crosscutting issues, share accountability for crosscutting outcomes, and evaluate their individual and organizational contributions to these outcomes?
- How can agencies more strategically manage their portfolio of tools and adopt more innovative methods to contribute to the achievement of national outcomes?

Integration can create synergy and economies of scale and can provide more focused and efficient efforts to protect the nation's food supply. Further, to respond to the nation's pressing fiscal challenges, agencies may have to explore new ways to achieve their missions. We have identified such opportunities. For example, as I already mentioned, USDA and FDA spend resources on overlapping food safety activities, and we have made recommendations designed to reduce this overlap. Similarly, regarding FDA's seafood inspection program, we have discussed options for FDA to use personnel at NOAA to augment FDA's inspection capacity.

Many of our recommendations to agencies to promote the safety and integrity of the nation's food supply have been acted upon. Nevertheless, as we discuss in the 2007 High-Risk Series, a fundamental reexamination of the federal food safety system is warranted. Such a reexamination would need to address criticisms that have been raised about USDA's dual mission as both a promoter of agricultural and food products and an overseer of their safety. Taken as a whole, our work indicates that Congress and the executive branch can and should create the environment needed to look across the activities of individual programs within specific agencies and toward the goals that the federal government is trying to achieve.

To that end, we have recommended, among other things, that Congress enact comprehensive, uniform, and risk-based food safety legislation and commission the National Academy of Sciences or a blue ribbon panel to conduct a detailed analysis of alternative organizational food safety structures.[31] We also recommended that the executive branch reconvene the President's Council on Food Safety to facilitate interagency coordination on food safety regulation and programs.

These actions can begin to address the fragmentation in the federal oversight of food safety. Going forward, to build a sustained focus on the safety and the integrity of the nation's food supply, Congress and the executive branch can integrate various expectations for food safety with congressional oversight and through agencies' strategic planning processes. The development of a government-wide performance plan that is mission-based, is results-oriented, and provides a cross-agency perspective offers a framework to help ensure agencies' goals are complementary and mutually reinforcing. Further, this plan can help decision makers balance trade-offs and compare performance when resource allocation and restructuring decisions are made. . . .

HR 1148 and S 654: A bill to establish the Food Safety Administration to protect the public health by preventing food-borne illness, ensuring the safety of food, improving research on contaminants leading to food-borne illness, and improving security of food from intentional contamination, and for other purposes.

Findings: Congress finds that–

(1) the safety of the food supply of the United States is vital to the public health, to public confidence in the food supply, and to the success of the food sector of the Nation's economy;
(2) lapses in the protection of the food supply and loss of public confidence in food safety are damaging to consumers and the food industry, and place a burden on interstate commerce;
(3) the safety and security of the food supply requires an integrated, system-wide approach to preventing food-borne illness, a thorough and broad-based approach to basic and applied research, and intensive, effective, and efficient management of the Nation's food safety program;
(4) the task of preserving the safety of the food supply of the United States faces tremendous pressures with regard to–
    (A) emerging pathogens and other contaminants and the ability to detect all forms of contamination;
    (B) an aging and immune compromised population, with a growing number of people at high-risk for food-borne illnesses, including infants and children;
    (C) an increasing volume of imported food, without adequate monitoring and inspection; and
    (D) maintenance of rigorous inspection of the domestic food processing and food service industries;
(5) Federal food safety standard setting, inspection, enforcement, and research efforts should be based on the best available science and public health considerations and food safety resources should be systematically deployed in ways that most effectively prevent food-borne illness;
(6) the Federal food safety system is fragmented, with at least 12 Federal agencies sharing responsibility for food safety, and operates under laws that do not reflect

current conditions in the food system or current scientific knowledge about the cause and prevention of food-borne illness;

(7) the fragmented Federal food safety system and outdated laws preclude an integrated, system-wide approach to preventing food-borne illness, to the effective and efficient operation of the Nation's food safety program, and to the most beneficial deployment of food safety resources;

(8) the National Academy of Sciences recommended in the report 'Ensuring Safe Food from Production to Consumption' that Congress establish by statute a unified and central framework for managing Federal food safety programs, and recommended modifying Federal statutes so that inspection, enforcement, and research efforts are based on scientifically supportable assessments of risks to public health; and

(9) the lack of a single focal point for food safety leadership in the United States undercuts the ability of the United States to exert food safety leadership internationally, which is detrimental to the public health and the international trade interests of the United States.

(b) Purposes–The purposes of this Act are–

(1) to establish a single agency to be known as the "Food Safety Administration" to–
   (A) regulate food safety and labeling to strengthen the protection of the public health;
   (B) ensure that food establishments fulfill their responsibility to produce food in a manner that protects the public health of all people in the United States;
   (C) lead an integrated, system-wide approach to food safety and to make more effective and efficient use of resources to prevent food-borne illness;
   (D) provide a single focal point for food safety leadership, both nationally and internationally; and
   (E) provide an integrated food safety research capability, utilizing internally-generated, scientifically and statistically valid studies, in cooperation with academic institutions and other scientific entities of the Federal and State governments, to achieve the continuous improvement of research on food-borne illness and contaminants;

(2) to transfer to the Food Safety Administration the food safety, labeling, inspection, and enforcement functions that, as of the day before the effective date of this Act, are performed by other Federal agencies; and

(3) to modernize and strengthen the Federal food safety laws to achieve more effective application and efficient management of the laws for the protection and improvement of public health.

TITLE I—ESTABLISHMENT OF FOOD SAFETY ADMINISTRATION

Sec. 101. Establishment Of Food Safety Administration

(a) Establishment–

(1) IN GENERAL–There is established in the executive branch an agency to be known as the "Food Safety Administration".

(2) STATUS—The Administration shall be an independent establishment (as defined in section 104 of title 5, United States Code).
(3) HEAD OF ADMINISTRATION—The Administration shall be headed by the Administrator of Food Safety, who shall be appointed by the President, by and with the advice and consent of the Senate.

(b) Duties of Administrator—The Administrator shall—
(1) administer and enforce the food safety law;
(2) serve as a representative to international food safety bodies and discussions;
(3) promulgate regulations to ensure the security of the food supply from all forms of contamination, including intentional contamination; and
(4) oversee—
(A) implementation of Federal food safety inspection, enforcement, and research efforts, to protect the public health;
(B) development of consistent and science-based standards for safe food;
(C) coordination and prioritization of food safety research and education programs with other Federal agencies;
(D) prioritization of Federal food safety efforts and deployment of Federal food safety resources to achieve the greatest possible benefit in reducing food-borne illness;
(E) coordination of the Federal response to food-borne illness outbreaks with other Federal and State agencies; and
(F) integration of Federal food safety activities with State and local agencies.

SEC. 102. CONSOLIDATION OF SEPARATE FOOD SAFETY AND INSPECTION SERVICES AND AGENCIES

(a) Transfer of Functions—For each Federal agency specified in subsection (b), there are transferred to the Administration all functions that the head of the Federal agency exercised on the day before the effective date of this Act (including all related functions of any officer or employee of the Federal agency) that relate to administration or enforcement of the food safety law, as determined by the President.

(b) Transferred Agencies—The Federal agencies referred to in subsection (a) are—
(1) the Food Safety and Inspection Service of the Department of Agriculture;
(2) the Center for Food Safety and Applied Nutrition of the Food and Drug Administration;
(3) the part of the Agriculture Marketing Service that administers shell egg surveillance services established under the Egg Products Inspection Act (21 U.S.C. 1031 et seq.);
(4) the resources and facilities of the Office of Regulatory Affairs of the Food and Drug Administration that administer and conduct inspections of food establishments and imports;
(5) the resources and facilities of the Office of the Commissioner of the Food and Drug Administration that support—

(A) the Center for Food Safety and Applied Nutrition;
(B) the Center for Veterinary Medicine; and
(C) the Office of Regulatory Affairs facilities and resources described in paragraph (4);

(6) the Center for Veterinary Medicine of the Food and Drug Administration;
(7) the resources and facilities of the Environmental Protection Agency that control and regulate pesticide residues in food;
(8) the part of the Research, Education, and Economics mission area of the Department of Agriculture related to food safety and animal feed research;
(9) the part of the National Marine Fisheries Service of the National Oceanic and Atmospheric Administration of the Department of Commerce that administers the seafood inspection program;
(10) the Animal and Plant Inspection Health Service of the Department of Agriculture; and
(11) such other offices, services, or agencies as the President designates by Executive order to carry out this Act.

Michael R. Taylor, "Lead or React? A Game Plan for Modernizing the Food Safety System in the United States," *Food and Drug Law Journal*, Vol. 59, No. 3. (2004), pp. 399–403.

Fortunately for all Americans, the food safety system is not in crisis. If it were, the system's key stakeholders and politicians of all stripes would be clamoring for reform, as they did in response to the Alar pesticide scare of the 1980s and the *E.* coli-in-hamburger disease outbreaks of the 1990s. The lack of crisis is a good thing, but it means that much-needed modernization of the system runs squarely into the inherent inertia of the American system of government. And modernization is very much needed, despite diligent effort and some modest progress over the last decade. The U.S. food safety system has not solved the long-standing public health problem of food-borne illness—including an estimated 5,000 largely avoidable deaths every year—and it faces important new challenges posed by the globalizing food system, as illustrated by America's reliance on food imports, the emergence of mad cow disease, and the threat of bioterrorism. While the U.S. food safety system has many strengths, it is ill-equipped for these challenges. It has become, over the century of its existence, organizationally fragmented, bound by obsolete statutes, and unable to make the best use of its scarce resources to protect the safety and security of the American food supply. Serious modernization is needed, but, absent an action-forcing food safety crisis, meaningful reform depends on extraordinary effort and leadership from the top of the nation's government. This article sketches out a game plan for modernization of the food safety system that involves leading rather than reacting, and that calls specifically for a White House-led, bipartisan effort to design the food safety system of the future and to implement it in a way that builds on current strengths but prepares the system for future success. The reform should focus the system more effectively on prevention of food-borne illness; improve accountability across the system for meeting science-based food safety performance standards; establish an integrated food safety strategy and leadership structure; and emphasize risk-based resource allocation. It should be reform from which all food safety stakeholders can benefit. . . . Virtually universal agreement exists that if one were to start from scratch, the food safety system would not be designed the way it is today, with multiple agencies and with statutes that both lack a modern food safety mandate and contain old mandates that block effective prevention of food safety problems and risk-based allocation of resources. The principle opposition to change comes from those who argue that the current system is working well enough and that the costs and disruption of transitioning to a new system outweigh the benefits. This argument needs to be taken seriously in

Source: Excerpted with permission of the Food and Drug Law Institute, Washington, DC. From Food and Drug Law Journal, Volume 59, Number 3, 2004.

the formulation of the implementation and transition plan. It overlooks, however, the fact that the costs of reform are incurred in the relative near term, while the benefits will be enjoyed over the long term. If the functioning of the system over the near term were the only concern, we might just try to do the best we can with the tools we have and hope that a major food safety crisis does not occur in the next few years. But if the concern is for the future, we should be more willing to invest now in change that will return benefits for many years to come. This reality of the long-term nature of the benefits of food safety reform is why White House leadership is so important. In the past, some of the strongest resistance to change has come from the food safety agencies themselves, whose managers and leaders understandably are focused on the unrelenting stream of immediate problems that they are responsible for addressing today and every day. It is unrealistic and unfair to expect the agencies to lead the way on fundamental structural reform. It is rather for society, through its political leadership, to judge whether the current system is performing well enough and whether the country's long-term health and economic well-being will be served by sticking with the status quo on food safety. Among the U.S. political leaders, the president is best situated to make that judgment, to make the case publicly for change, and to lead the process. Without presidential leadership, change is unlikely to occur, at least until circumstances force change in an atmosphere of crisis.

Caroline Smith DeWaal and David W. Plunkett, *Building a Modern Food Safety System: For FDA Regulated Foods*, Center for Science in the Public Interest (2007).

The food safety system in America is broken. As a result hundreds of thousands of Americans may require hospitalization and as many as 5,000 may die this year from preventable food-borne illnesses.

Foods regulated by the Food and Drug Administration (FDA) have caused a number of recent national outbreaks and recalls:

- August and September 2006: *E. coli* in bagged spinach sickened 204 people in 26 states, killing three.
- September 2006: *Salmonella* found in tomatoes sickened 183 people in 21 states.
- December 2006: Iceberg lettuce contaminated with *E. coli* at Taco Bell and Taco John restaurants sickened 152 people.
- February 2007: Peter Pan peanut butter contaminated with *Salmonella* sickened 425 people in 44 states.
- February and March 2007: One hundred brands of pet food distributed nationwide were recalled after the FDA received thousands of complaints of illnesses and deaths among cats and dogs due to melamine contamination.
- June 2007: Veggie Booty snacks caused 65 illnesses in 20 states from *Salmonella.*
- July 2007: Canned chili and meats containing C*lostridium botulinum* were recalled after causing eight illnesses in three states.
- August 2007: Almost one year after the September *E. coli* outbreak a nationwide recall of fresh spinach followed discovery of *Salmonella* in a test batch.

Foods regulated by the U.S. Department of Agriculture (USDA) have also triggered many nationwide outbreaks and recalls:

- January to October 2007: Illnesses were reported in 31 states before Banquet Turkey and Chicken Pot Pies carrying *Salmonella* were recalled in October.
- September 2007: The second largest beef recall in U.S. history (21.7 million pounds) began after *E. coli* contamination was found in Topps Frozen Hamburgers and Patties.
- June 2007: Ground beef contaminated with *E. coli* caused 14 illnesses leading to a recall of ground beef that had been shipped to 11 western states.

These outbreaks have shaken consumer confidence in the safety of their food supply. Congress must act to create a strong food safety system that has adequate resources and authority to meet the demands of a modern, globalized food system and restore public confidence—before another crisis occurs.

This white paper addresses problems and solutions linked to FDA regulated foods.

Congress has an unprecedented opportunity to fix a broken food safety system. Recent nationwide outbreaks have exposed extensive gaps in protections of the food supply, prompting calls for reform from industry and consumers and hearings in Congress. This white paper examines the issue of food safety, reviews the status of current efforts to address problems in our food safety system, and recommends steps Congress should take to address those problems. Finally, it examines legislation currently pending in Congress covering FDA and discusses how those bills fit into a broader reform effort. . . .

The heart of a modern food safety system lies in preventing—not merely responding—to food safety problems. Mandatory process controls, coupled with government-enforced performance standards, should be the central features of a new system. These systems can be used from farm-to-table and with both domestic and imported foods.

Most food-borne illnesses are the result of contamination that occurs during production, processing, shipping, or handling. These lapses result in illness, recalls, and loss of public confidence in the safety of our food supply. While in-plant and border inspections form the core of the government's food safety program, inspection is often little more than a spot check on performance. The reality is that the industry holds the key to addressing and preventing food contamination.

The safety and security of the food supply requires an integrated, system-wide approach to preventing food-borne illness, with oversight by federal food safety agencies. . . .

INSPECTIONS

Inspection of commercial food processors is an integral part of the food safety system. It provides an audit of food safety programs managed by the establishments and ensures accountability for meeting food safety performance standards. The FDA is responsible for overseeing approximately 210,000 domestic food establishments. However, the number of field staff has dropped by 12 percent since 2003, which has resulted in significantly fewer inspections. In fact, between 2003 and 2006, FDA food safety inspections have dropped by 47 percent. . . .

FEDERAL AND STATE COOPERATION

State inspection programs are an important component of the nation's food-safety inspection system. The FDA has increasingly relied heavily on states to do inspections of FDA-regulated products because of budget and staff constraints. The agency needs a national food safety plan to assure that state food inspection programs are capable of and in fact provide a level of public health inspection that meets FDA standards. The FDA must have the resources to work with states to carry out food safety activities in a coordinated cost-effective manner. The agency must provide both technical and advisory assistance to the states, while also supporting work on the state level to strengthen inspection programs and recalls.

PUBLIC HEALTH ASSESSMENT

The current public health system in the U.S. has limited capacity to identify and track the causes of food-borne illness. FoodNET, an active public health surveillance system run by the CDC, is beginning to produce more information on illnesses associated with foods, but this information needs to be shared on a more timely basis with other governmental agencies as well as the public. More thorough outbreak investigations and analysis of available information is needed to identify the root causes of food safety problems and develop preventive interventions. Additionally, a sampling system is required to assess the nature and frequency of food-borne hazards in food. Such investigation and analysis would allow the public health agencies that regulate food to rank products based on risk to human health and help to identify appropriate industry and regulatory approaches to minimizing hazards in food.

RESEARCH

Research is a vital tool in the effort to reduce the incidence of food-borne illness and is integral to the programs of all public health agencies. Research is needed to evaluate the effectiveness of control and prevention strategies and to conduct risk assessments. It is also needed to improve sanitation and food safety practices during processing. The FDA and industry must improve techniques to monitor and inspect food and develop efficient and sensitive methods for detecting contaminants and reducing harmful pathogens.

PUBLIC EDUCATION AND ADVISORY SYSTEM

Public education is another essential component of improved food safety. Rates of illness could be reduced if food preparers and handlers were better informed of risks and related safe-handling practices. Educational programs that promote better understanding and practice of proper food-safety techniques, such as thoroughly washing hands and cooking foods to proper temperatures, could significantly reduce food-borne illness. Programs are also needed to help health professionals improve their diagnosis and treatment of food-related illness and to advise individuals at special risk. . . .

Today, the FDA's food safety program does not have the modern enforcement tools used by other agencies or even the authorities the agency has to regulate drugs and medical devices. The FDA can take a few limited actions, such as issuing warning letters, urging companies to voluntarily recall product, and getting court-ordered seizures, injunctions, and criminal penalties. These weak tools do not equip the FDA to protect consumers from the threat of food-borne illness. The following new authorities are essential to modernize FDA's food surveillance and enforcement:

Recalls. Today recalls of contaminated food are voluntary. The Federal Food, Drug, and Cosmetic Act does not give the FDA the power to order a producer to recall a food product, with the exception of infant formula. If a firm does not recall a product, the FDA can go to court to seek an injunction or seizure of the product. But these legal actions waste precious time, and if a food company or importer fails to recall a contaminated product, it can continue to reach consumers. Mandatory recall authority would ensure that recalled foods are removed from the market more quickly and effectively.

Traceback. The FDA needs the authority to identify the source of foods that pose health hazards to consumers. The ability to trace a contaminated product back to the source of production would allow the agency to conduct more rapid and thorough investigations. It would also allow producers to more precisely identify the source of a problem in order to improve production practices and could help narrow the scope of recalls by more quickly identifying the specific plant or country of origin.

Detention. If an FDA inspector has reason to believe that a domestic or imported food is unsafe, adulterated, or misbranded, the agency must have the authority to temporarily detain the food for a reasonable time. If it is determined that the detained food cannot be brought in compliance with food safety requirements, the FDA should be able to condemn the food.

Civil and Criminal Penalties. An essential element of any enforcement capability is the power to penalize manufacturers and producers for violating food safety laws as a deterrent to future violations by the guilty party and others. Food companies must be subject to civil and criminal penalties for violating food safety laws. A person that has been harmed as a result of a violation of food safety law should have the power to commence a civil action.

Whistleblower Protection. Federal employees must be protected from the threat of being fired, demoted, suspended, or harassed as result of providing information or assisting in the investigation of a violation of a food safety law. . . .

Key U.S. food safety laws are a century old and were not designed to deal with modern issues such as escalating imports, bioterrorism, or tainted produce. The last several years have demonstrated the need for enhanced national security, and the recent outbreaks serve as a reminder that much more must be done to protect the food supply. Comprehensive reform should draw from these recommendations.

Change is hard, but it has been done abroad. The United Kingdom reformed its food safety program to establish a single Food Standards Agency in 1999. That agency has proven effective in reducing the incidence of food-borne illness and building public confidence. Food-borne illnesses declined 18 percent within the first three years of the new agency, with a reduction from 37 percent to 6 percent in the occurrence of eggs and poultry infected with *Salmonella*. Public confidence in the safety of the food supply rose from 44 percent to 60 percent. The change came after food scares in the 1990's led all sides to recognize the need for change, and that realization built the momentum needed to reach a workable compromise. The U.S. is at the same nexus of crisis and consensus and the momentum for reform is building. We urge Congress to take action this year to modernize food safety laws and to fully fund federal food safety programs.

NOTES FOR CHAPTER 9

1. Jill Hollingsworth, FMI, personal communication to committee, April 1998; Appendix Dl.
2. Jackie Nowelly United Food and Commercial Workers Union, personal communication to committee, April 1998; Appendix D.
3. Food Safety: Federal Efforts to Ensure the Safety of Imported Foods Are Inconsistent and Unreliable, GAO/RCED-98-103, April 30, 1998.
4. Food Safety: Changes Needed to Minimize Unsafe Chemicals in Food, GAO/RCED-94-192, September 26, 1994.
5. EPA officials stated that further review of the 20 states using a methodology different than EPA's may reveal that some of them are actually using a methodology similar to EPA's.
6. Food Safety: Agencies' Handling of a Dioxin Incident Caused Hardships for Some Producers and Processors, GAO/RCED-98-104, April 10, 1998.
7. Food Safety and Quality: Uniform, Risk-Based Inspection System Needed to Ensure Safe Food Supply, GAO/RCED-92-152, June 26, 1992.
8. Food Safety: U.S. Lacks a Consistent Farm-to-Table Approach to Egg Safety, GAO/RCED-99-184, July 1, 1999.
9. On July 1, 1999, FDA announced proposed regulations for ensuring the safety of eggs that contained, among other things, refrigeration requirements for eggs at the retail level.
10. See *Nat'l Inst. of Medicine/Nat'l Research Council, Ensuring Safe Food From Production to Consumption*, National Academy Press, Washington, DC, 1998.
11. *Id.* at 79.
12. *Id.* at 87.
13. *See* Cornell University Cooperative Extension Service, November–December 1998, *Benecol, Margarine or Supplement, Food and Nutrition.*
14. This was well documented in a 1998 Government Accountability Office (GAO) report. *See* GAO, 1998, Food Safety: Federal Efforts to Ensure the Safety of Imported Foods Are Inconsistent and Unreliable, GAO/T-RCED-98-191, Available from http://www.gao.gov/archive/1998/rc98191t.pdf, Accessed September 9, 2004.
15. U.S. Department of Health and Human Services, 2001, *Food Code*, Available at http://vm.cfsan.fda.gov/~dms/fc01-toc.html, Accessed 19 August 2008.
16. Food Safety: Actions Needed by USDA and FDA to Ensure That Companies Promptly Carry Out Recalls, GAO/RCED-00-195, August 17, 2000.
17. Food Safety: Federal Oversight of Seafood Does Not Sufficiently Protect Consumers, GAO-01-204, January 31, 2001.
18. In January 2001, FDA finalized regulations requiring HACCP for fruit and vegetable juices.
19. Meat and Poultry: Improved Oversight and Training Will Strengthen New Food Safety System, GAO/RCED-00-16, December 8, 1999, and Food Safety: Federal Oversight of Seafood Does Not Sufficiently Protect Consumers, GAO-01-204, January 31, 2001.
20. Food Safety: Federal Efforts to Ensure the Safety of Imported Foods Are Inconsistent and Unreliable, GAO/RCED-98-103, April 30, 1998.
21. Food Safety: Improvements Needed in Overseeing the Safety of Dietary Supplements and "Functional Foods," GAO/RCED-00-156, July 11, 2000.
22. *Agricultural Exports: U.S. Needs a More Integrated Approach to Address Sanitary/Phytosanitary Issues*, GAO/NSIAD-98-32, December 11, 1997.
23. Food Safety: Agencies' Handling of a Dioxin Incident Caused Hardships for Some Producers and Processors, GAO/RCED-98-104, April 10, 1998.
24. Food Safety and Quality: Salmonella Control Efforts Show Need for More Coordination, GAO/RCED-92-69, April 21, 1992.

25. Food Safety: Controls Can Be Strengthened to Reduce the Risk of Disease Linked to Unsafe Animal Feed, GAO/RCED-00-255, September 22, 2000.
26. Food Safety: Experiences of Four Countries in Consolidating Their Food Safety Systems, GAO/RCED-99-80, April 20, 1999.
27. A number of federal, state, and local agencies have responsibility for responding to deliberate acts or threats of food contamination. Besides FDA and FSIS, other federal agencies include CDC, the Federal Bureau of Investigation, and USDA's Office of Inspector General.
28. Food Safety: Agencies Should Further Test Plans for Responding to Deliberate Contamination, GAO/RCED-00-3, October 27, 1999.
29. Under the act, the agencies would have to enter into a memorandum of understanding that would include provisions to ensure adequate training of USDA officials and to address reimbursement.
30. Government Accountability Office, February 2005, *21st Century Challenges: Reexamining the Base of the Federal Government,* GAO-05-325SP, Washington, DC.
31. Government Accountability Office, October 10, 2001, Food Safety and Security: Fundamental Changes Needed to Ensure Safe Food, GAO-02-47T, Washington, DC.

APPENDIX

A Checklist for a Reorganization Analysis

A major premise of this volume has been that federal government reorganizations take many different forms, serve a number of different purposes, and attempt to respond to a range of attributes of programs and policies. As such, it is extremely difficult (if not impossible) to define the components of a successful reorganization. Students of reorganization are likely to find it more useful to establish a checklist of questions that should be considered when either planning or evaluating a reorganization within the federal government rather than setting up an ideal situation.

The following questions may be helpful when attempting such an analysis.

1. What is the location of the reorganization?
2. Have there been previous reorganizations that may affect this situation?
3. What events, issues, and dynamics stimulated an interest in moving to a reorganization effort?
4. Are there developments within the environment or context of the agency that pushed a proposal?
5. What are the goals of the effort? Do they appear to be policy, political, or administrative issues?
6. Did the ideas behind the reorganization emerge from a commission, a study group, an interest group, or some other actor?
7. What was the legal framework and/or authority available to the relevant decision makers?
8. What process was used to develop the proposal? Who participated in such a development?
9. Who actually has the ability to decide on the reorganization? Who influenced those decision makers?
10. What influenced the proposal's scope or timing?
11. Did the development process and/or the decision-making process consider the following issues:
    - Resistance to the idea from staff
    - Resistance to the idea from members of Congress
    - Resistance to the idea from external interest groups
    - The aspects of the culture of the organization that supports or opposes the idea
    - Costs of disruption
    - Laws or regulation required to implement the decision
    - Impact on budget

- Impact on personnel
- Space or other resources required

12. Did the process include a discussion of criteria for evaluating the reorganization?
13. Was there any consideration of future changes that might be required?
14. Was it possible to develop a calculus that indicates supporters, opponents, and neutral players in the process?
15. Are there alternative approaches to structural change that might address the situation?

INDEX